5cc

P9-EMM-415

CIRCLE
IN THE
SAND

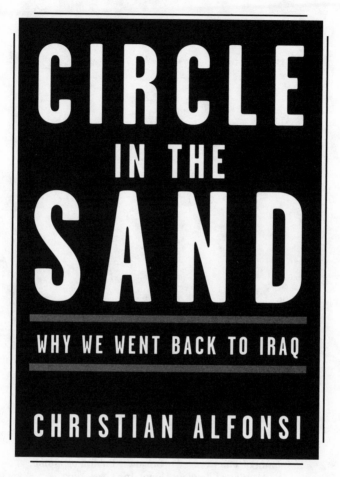

CIRCLE
IN THE
SAND

WHY WE WENT BACK TO IRAQ

CHRISTIAN ALFONSI

DOUBLEDAY

New York   London   Toronto

Sydney   Auckland

PUBLISHED BY DOUBLEDAY

Copyright © 2006 by Christian Alfonsi

All Rights Reserved

Published in the United States by Doubleday,
an imprint of The Doubleday Broadway Publishing Group,
a division of Random House, Inc., New York.
www.doubleday.com

DOUBLEDAY and the portrayal of an anchor with a dolphin are
registered trademarks of Random House, Inc.

Book design by Michael Collica

Library of Congress Cataloging-in-Publication Data
is on file with the Library of Congress.

ISBN-13: 978-0-385-51598-6
ISBN-10: 0-385-51598-7

PRINTED IN THE UNITED STATES OF AMERICA

3 5 7 9 10 8 6 4 2

TO MY BROTHER BENJAMIN

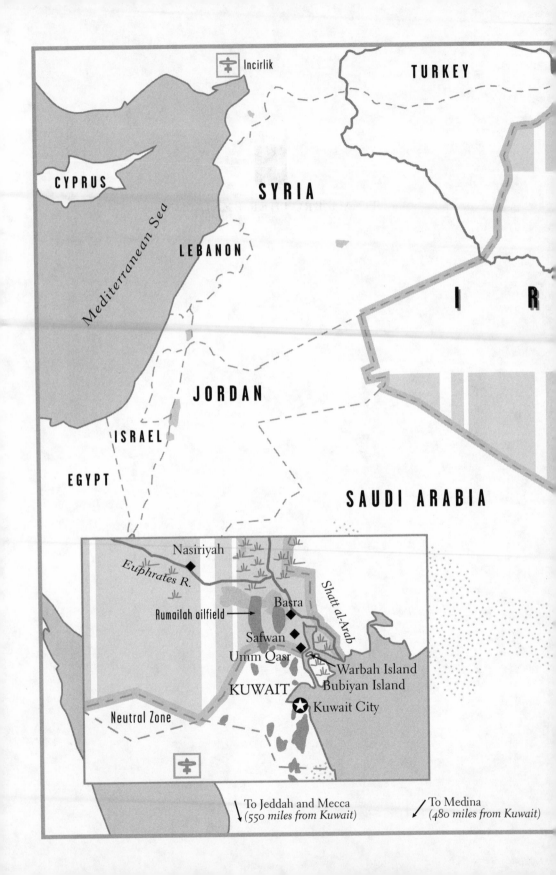

Incirlik

TURKEY

CYPRUS

SYRIA

Mediterranean Sea

LEBANON

I R

JORDAN

ISRAEL

EGYPT

SAUDI ARABIA

Nasiriyah

Euphrates R.

Basra

Shatt al-Arab

Rumailah oilfield

Safwan

Umm Qasr

Warbah Island

Bubiyan Island

KUWAIT

Kuwait City

Neutral Zone

To Jeddah and Mecca
(550 miles from Kuwait)

To Medina
(480 miles from Kuwait)

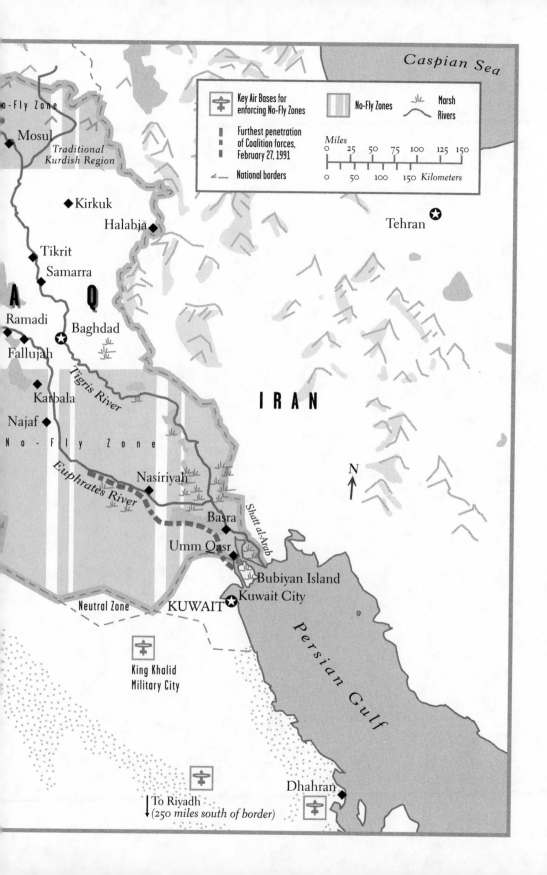

Caspian Sea

Key Air Bases for enforcing No-Fly Zones

Furthest penetration of Coalition forces, February 27, 1991

National borders

No-Fly Zones

Marsh

Rivers

Miles

0   25   50   75   100   125   150

0   50   100   150   Kilometers

No-Fly Zone

Mosul

Traditional Kurdish Region

Kirkuk

Halabja

Tehran

Tikrit

Samarra

A   **Q**

Ramadi

Baghdad

Fallujah

Karbala

Tigris River

I R A N

Najaf

No - Fly   Zone

Euphrates River

Nasiriyah

N

Basra

Shatt al-Arab

Umm Qasr

Bubiyan Island

Neutral Zone

KUWAIT   Kuwait City

King Khalid
Military City

Persian Gulf

Dhahran

To Riyadh
(250 miles south of border)

Once the present danger passes, however, we cannot let its lessons go unheeded. We have a responsibility to assure the American people that a decade from now their sons and daughters will not be put in jeopardy because we failed to work toward long-run solutions in the Gulf.

—Secretary of State James A. Baker III, 1990

Iraqi commander: "George Bush get rid Saddam NOW!"
Maj. Archie Gates: "Not exactly, no."
Iraqi commander: "Congratulations. Congratulations."

—from the film *Three Kings*

CONTENTS

INTRODUCTION

This is a book that will overturn much of what you may know, or think you may know, about the two Bush presidencies and their respective wars against Saddam Hussein.

Circle in the Sand is the first work to explore George W. Bush's decision to invade Iraq in March 2003, for the specific purpose of removing Saddam from power, from the perspective of his father's handling of Saddam Hussein and the first Iraq War twelve years earlier. The book uncovers the hidden reasons why many of the same senior officials, serving in two different Bush administrations, came to hold radically different views about Iraq and Saddam the second time around. *Circle in the Sand* traces the shifting foreign policy beliefs of the Bush inner circle over the course of those dozen years, revealing how the "lessons" of the first Bush administration directly impacted decisions on Iraq in the second. The overarching theme of the book is how the worldview of American leaders can undergo drastic changes in response to unexpected political setbacks—and the perceived mistakes of previous leaders.

In this book, I argue that understanding what really happened inside the first Bush White House after the 1991 Gulf War is vital for understanding the true motivations behind the current Bush administration's controversial decision to invade Iraq. The Iraq policy of George W. Bush and his advisers did not hatch fully formed on January 20, 2001; or even September 12, 2001. Rather, these beliefs were molded in great part by their interpretation of what had gone wrong in Iraq during the first Bush presidency. The unprecedented circumstance of father-and-son presidents confronting the same foreign enemy, both times against the backdrop of cataclysmic world events, is not merely a historical curiosity. It is the factor of central importance for understanding America's present entanglement in Iraq.

Had any U.S. president waged a costly and controversial war against a decade-long enemy, the actions of that president would rightly have become an all-consuming topic for an entire generation of historians. That the president who did so is the son of a former president who had waged war against the same enemy, served by largely the same cast of advisers, elevates the importance of the relationships between these two presidencies to almost Shakespearean proportions. Yet among the many books that have appeared about the two Bush presidencies, no work has appeared that systematically explores the inescapable impact of the first on the second. This book does.

Circle in the Sand will show how a series of catastrophic decisions made by the first Bush administration shattered the Pax Americana of 1991 and unintentionally helped create the dangerous world of the twenty-first century. The book focuses on two developments in particular: 1. how the twelve-year standoff with Saddam Hussein that followed the 1991 Gulf War damaged America's relations with the Arab world, radically transformed Republican foreign policy, and made a second war with Iraq almost inevitable; and 2. how the inconclusive aftermath of the 1991 Gulf War led to the emergence of a new generation of al-Qaeda terrorists committed to driving American forces out of Saudi Arabia and the Persian Gulf at almost any cost.

What *Circle in the Sand* argues is that neither of these developments was inevitable, and that both could have been avoided. The convoluted aftermath of the first Gulf War, Saddam Hussein's survival in power, and the terrorist war by al-Qaeda against the American people didn't just happen. They were the unintended consequences of some questionable foreign policy choices that the American people have never heard about. I believe this book offers a compelling and coherent explanation for why these choices were made. In doing so, it answers the question of *why* al-Qaeda suddenly became such a threat to the United States in the decade leading up to September 11; *why* Saddam Hussein remained the bogeyman of American foreign policy for a dozen years after the U.S. victory in Operation Desert Storm; and perhaps most important, *why* the very group of Republican policymakers who had maintained for over a decade that Saddam Hussein was safely contained in Iraq became such vehement advocates of a war to remove him.

• • •

For me, *Circle in the Sand* represents the culmination of over a decade spent researching and writing about the two Bush presidencies. And yet, I did not originally set out to write a book that would span two Bush administrations. Indeed, I began to write this book long before I knew that there would be two Bush administrations.

Circle in the Sand first took shape as a Harvard doctoral thesis about the first Bush White House. While I was at Harvard, the breaching of the Berlin Wall marked the end of the Cold War. A month later the Bush administration conducted its invasion of Panama to remove Panamanian dictator Manuel Noriega—at the time the largest American military intervention abroad since Vietnam. A decade of divisive national debate on Central America evaporated almost overnight with the defeat of the Sandinistas in Nicaragua, not at the hands of the *contras*, but at the ballot box. And the next summer brought with it the Iraqi invasion of Kuwait and the seven intense months of crisis diplomacy that culminated with Operation Desert Storm.

The seeming invincibility of the Bush foreign policy team at the time captured my imagination. We sometimes forget now that after its two-year run of unalloyed successes, the first Bush White House briefly enjoyed the same stature in national security affairs that a second Bush White House would briefly enjoy after *its* seemingly decisive victory in Iraq. George H. W. Bush and the national security team surrounding him believed that they possessed an intuitive knack for foreign policy, and reveled in the fact. Like the self-assured cadre of Democratic officials that had gravitated around President John F. Kennedy in an earlier era, the Bush national security team seemed to represent "the best and the brightest" of Republican foreign policy. I came to understand only later why David Halberstam did not intend his famous description of the foreign policy luminaries surrounding President Kennedy as a compliment.

But what cemented my interest in the Bush inner circle were the two years that followed. The convoluted aftermath of the first Gulf War — which marked the beginning of the first President Bush's decline — came as almost as rude a surprise to me as it must have been to the White House itself. I could not fathom at the time how the same group of policymakers, who over the course of the preceding seven months had choreographed the most successful collective security action of the century, could allow the postwar situation in Iraq to disintegrate in a matter of seven weeks. How the same president who had acted with almost Churchillian vigor in defense of beleaguered Kuwait could equivocate as a million Iraqi Kurds fled in terror from Saddam Hussein's reconstituted Republican Guard.

Then came 1992, the *annus horribilis* of the Bush dynasty, a year that I now know continues to haunt the councils of the Bush inner circle even to this day. The first Bush administration's foreign policy collapsed nearly everywhere, and with it George Bush's chances at reelection. Iraq's brazen defiance of UN weapons inspections was a constant mocking refrain throughout the year. The Bush administration's failure to act in response to the outbreak of genocide in the Balkans destroyed any residual claims to idealism it might have still possessed from the liberation of Kuwait. Far from being able to rest on the foreign policy laurels of its first two years in office, the Bush White House spent much of the 1992 presidential campaign defending virtually every foreign policy decision it had made since then.

George Bush had long dreamed of making a triumphal return to his hometown of Houston for the 1992 Republican National Convention as a liberator revered on three continents, and the architect of a New World Order. Instead, his administration found its triumphs in Eastern Europe and the Persian Gulf rendered hollow by more recent failures in both of those regions. Not even Bush's loss to Bill Clinton in the presidential election ended the ordeal of 1992. December of that year saw a lame-duck President Bush ordering Operation Restore Hope — a controversial military intervention in famine-ravaged Somalia — an operation that less than a year later would become in the streets of Mogadishu the very watchword for failed American attempts at nation building. And in perhaps the perfect metaphor for its reversal of fortune, a forlorn Bush White House spent its final night in power conducting a series of meaningless air strikes against its once-beaten adversary in Iraq.

It was against the backdrop of these events that I decided to explore the reasons behind the inconclusive aftermath of the 1991 Gulf War: to learn why the same group of senior officials that had appeared so masterful in managing the confrontation with Saddam Hussein had proven so ineffective in managing its aftermath. Fortunately, the first Bush administration offered a near-perfect opportunity for exploring this theme. George H. W. Bush and his advisers had come to power with a complex set of beliefs about foreign policy born from many years spent in the international arena. They had left behind a lengthy paper trail that revealed their thinking during every stage of the 1990–91 crisis in the Gulf.

During the late 1990s, I conducted an initial wave of on-the-record interviews with virtually all of the principal officials from the first Bush administration. All spoke freely about the motivations behind their most controversial decisions during and after Operation Desert Storm. I believe these figures were so forthcoming with me because, at the time, they saw the events I was inquiring about as finished business: matters of historical, but not political, interest. All evinced a desire to make sure that the historical record included their own explanations and justifications for the policies they had advocated. Looking back, I believe they would have been less candid, to say the least, had they anticipated a second Bush presidency, in which so many who had served the father would be called back to serve the son, and once again find themselves struggling to engender public support for an inconclusive war with Iraq.

As part of my research, I also made a number of research trips to the newly opened Bush Presidential Library in Texas, where I unearthed literally hundreds of key documents on the foreign policy struggles within this administration. Many of these documents had only recently been made available to scholars, but I had a special advantage in finding meaning in them, in that my interviews had illuminated the political context in which these documents were originally produced.

After the election of George W. Bush in 2000, what had been merely an intriguing idea for a book in the back of my mind took on a new urgency. The most salient fact about the new Bush administration was an obvious one: its extraordinarily deep ties to the people and ideas of an earlier Bush administration. This was especially true in foreign policy. I knew that the accession of a second George Bush to the White House would create a need for scholarship that could illuminate the thinking of the Bush inner circle for a larger American audience. There would never be a better time for a book on how the worldview of the first Bush presidency would influence the decisions of the second. With this in mind, I began writing this book during the spring of 2001.

I knew the sort of book I wanted to write. The story of the Bush dynasty's rise to prominence in world affairs was in many ways the story of Republican foreign policy in the twentieth century. George Herbert Walker Bush had been a living metaphor for his party's journey in world affairs: from the isolationism of the pre–World War II era to the internationalism of the postwar era; from Vietnam and Watergate to the Ford administration's attempts at renewal; from American retrenchment in the 1970s to American resurgence in the 1980s; from Cold War to Gulf War. The elder President Bush had been a firsthand participant in all of these transformations. Might his son become a metaphor for Republican foreign policy in the twenty-first century?

I can remember even now that flying home from one of my many research trips to the Bush Library, during the final week of August 2001, I was running late for my flight, but the gate agent let me bypass security and board the airplane directly.

How America, and the world, would soon change.

●   ●   ●

As I watched the horror of September 11 unfold outside the window of my home in Brooklyn Heights, I realized that the story I was telling had been radically transformed. I had always assumed that *Circle in the Sand* would be primarily a book about the first Bush administration, with a short epilogue speculating about its influence on George W. Bush and the foreign policy team he had assembled. This assumption had reflected two beliefs on my part. First, that President George W. Bush had come to the White House determined to focus on domestic issues, not foreign policy. And second, that no series of events could possibly occur on the younger Bush's watch that would rival in importance the watershed events that had taken place during his father's administration.

After September 11, the importance of policymakers whose actions I had already been researching and writing about for years would only be magnified. And George W. Bush's administration would become an extraordinary laboratory for observing just how the "lessons" American leaders learn from the past affect their decisions at moments of great national peril.

I never imagined that my task would also require me to examine the actions of a second president and a second administration also consumed by the question of military intervention in Iraq.

·　　·　　·

An admiring commentator once described Livy, the great historian of imperial Rome, as "an epic poet in prose." The comment paid tribute to Livy's gift for seeing the people and events of his time as subjects worthy of epic treatment. The more I delved into the history of the Bush era, the more I came to realize that it, too, was a tale of epic events, peopled by characters who in their tragic flaws would have fascinated Livy or any other epic writer of antiquity.

Consider the protagonists of this story:

George Herbert Walker Bush, patriarch of the most important political family in American history, who made decisions about war and peace that doomed his presidency, and perhaps even his son's, not out of ignorance or cowardice, but after tortuous reflection upon what he believed were the lessons from a lifetime of experience; George W. Bush, for much of his life a disappointment to his father and himself, like the scions of so many famous men throughout history, but destined to launch two fateful crusades—the first to avenge his country's worst defeat, the second to avenge his father's; Dick Cheney, trusted counselor to five U.S. presidents and architect of two Iraq wars that were each supposed to restore prestige to the presidency, but each of which went terribly wrong; Colin Powell, America's most respected general, regarded like an adopted son by the first President Bush and thus bound by his fierce sense of loyalty toward the Bush dynasty to advocate a war that violated almost every precept of war he held dear; James Baker, whose talent was outstripped only by his ambition; and Donald Rumsfeld, whose talent was outstripped only by his hubris; Brent Scowcroft, the gray eminence of Republican foreign policy for nearly three decades, who became increasingly disenchanted with the policies of a Republican president who happened to be his best friend's son; Condoleezza Rice, Scowcroft's prize protégée, a favorite of two presidents, whose role in helping create the post–Cold War world left her ill-equipped for the crises that would define that new world; and Paul Wolfowitz, the American Cato, whose personal obsession with Saddam Hussein became that of an entire nation (Livy would have seen in him shades of the original Cato).

•   •   •

I first began interviewing members of the Bush inner circle for this book in the 1990s, when they were out of power and eager to tell their story. Many of them did not know they would one day be back in power, and eager to tell a very different story. This irony, and the historical uniqueness of the Bush era, became most clear to me in 2005, when I conducted my final wave of interviews for the book. By then, many well-known officials who had loyally served the Bush dynasty during both the 1991 Gulf War and the 2003 Iraq war had left government service after George W. Bush's first term, dismayed by how the invasion of Iraq had turned out.

One conversation in particular still sticks out in my mind. In March 2005, I sat down with Richard Haass, president of the Council on Foreign Relations in New York. I had first met and interviewed Richard Haass nine years earlier, when he had been in residence at the Carnegie Endowment for International Peace in Washington. I had been struck at the time by both his loyalty to President George H. W. Bush, and his candor. A strong defender of former President Bush's handling of the

1991 Gulf War, Haass nonetheless had been open to questioning some of the decisions made in the conflict's aftermath. I thought that he reflected the best attributes of the Republican foreign policy establishment during the first Bush administration.

Haass had left a senior position in the Bush State Department for the Council shortly after the 2003 invasion of Iraq. Although he now occupied one of the most important platforms for discussing foreign policy in the United States, a role for which he was infinitely well suited, it was an open secret in Washington that Haass had left the government largely over his concern at the direction of George W. Bush's foreign policy.

The years since had been kind to Haass; he had changed remarkably little since we had last spoken face-to-face. But the context for our conversation had changed dramatically. I was mildly surprised by the vehemence of his critique of this Bush administration's preemptive war against Iraq; which, as one of Colin Powell's top deputies, he had helped to "sell" to the United Nations. More striking to me, however, was that Haass himself still had no idea why the United States had invaded Iraq. Candid as ever with his recollections of what had taken place during the run-up to war in 2003, the reason why the conflict had been fought eluded him. This troubled me greatly. As I well knew from my previous research, Haass had been one of the half dozen most important U.S. officials in managing the first Gulf War, a participant in nearly every important meeting during the crisis, and privy to some White House deliberations even many historians did not know had taken place. His loyalty to the first President Bush was unshakable. If he could not be entrusted with the real rationale for the 2003 invasion of Iraq, who could be?

Three years after the invasion of Iraq, I continue to be amazed that no other author has attempted to do what I am doing with this book. But I have since come to understand why. In writing this book, I was fortunate to possess the one advantage essential to telling this particular story: a head start on history. Long before anyone else knew there would be a second Bush administration, or a second Iraq war, I had already ventured down entire avenues of research that are forever closed to future authors. Policymakers' interpretations of the past can and do change with time and circumstances. The aftershocks of events like September 11, and the costly U.S. military occupation of Iraq, have so roiled the sands of history that the author of a book like *Circle in the Sand* would almost need to have completed much of the research for it before these events took place.

What follows is my own understanding of how the "line in the sand" against Iraq first drawn by President Bush in 1990 finally came full circle during his son's presidency.

1

THE WOOLLY MAMMOTH

The Americans were coming, and Saddam Hussein was on his best behavior.

He had good reason to be circumspect on this morning of April 12, 1990. The preceding two weeks had been bad ones for Iraq's relations with the United States, and Iraq faced the likely threat of U.S. sanctions. And better than anyone else within his narrow ruling circle, Saddam knew that sanctions were a prospect that Iraq's decimated economy and bankrupt treasury could ill afford.

The Iraqi ruler's longtime obsession with acquiring weapons of mass destruction had fueled this latest flare-up with Washington. On March 28, Britain had arrested five men accused of trying to smuggle U.S.-made kryton switches—sophisticated devices used only for detonating nuclear warheads—to Iraq. Three days later, the *Washington Post* reported that U.S. Customs had intercepted a similar shipment of nuclear detonators the previous year. On April 2, Saddam boasted in a televised speech to the Iraqi people that their country's arsenal of chemical weapons was on par with that of the United States and the Soviet Union. The Iraqi ruler promised his subjects, "By Allah, we will make the fire eat up half of Israel if it tries to do anything against Iraq." Saddam spoke cryptically in his speech of a special "double chemical" that Iraq possessed—to military and intelligence experts, an unmistakable reference to a binary chemical agent like the poison gas VX.

Tensions had escalated even further in the ten days since Saddam's speech had sparked widespread criticism of Iraq in the American media.

On April 5 the Bush administration had expelled an Iraqi diplomat for plotting to murder a number of Iraqi dissidents who had taken refuge in the United States. Iraq retaliated by expelling an American diplomat from Baghdad. Britain's ambassador to Baghdad had already been recalled a month earlier, in protest over the hanging of British journalist Farzad Bazoft, whom Iraq had accused of spying for Israel, after a one-day mockery of a trial. The case had enflamed British public opinion and convinced British prime minister Margaret Thatcher that the Iraqi dictator was an incorrigible menace. As if having the Iron Lady furious at him were not enough, on April 7 Saddam had responded to the Bush administration's expulsion of his diplomat with a speech sharply criticizing President George Bush.

But even Saddam Hussein finally seemed to have realized he had gone too far with his bombastic rhetoric threatening to burn half of Israel with chemical weapons. While he could not afford to be seen by the Iraqi people as backing down in the face of pressure from the West, Saddam recognized the need to adopt a more moderate posture in his backstage dealings with the United States. Fortunately, a group of distinguished Americans was visiting Iraq on this day, and Saddam planned to capitalize on the opportunity to repair the damage to his image in Washington.

Senator Bob Dole had long been planning to lead a delegation of senators from farming and ranching states to Iraq, a routine visit to discuss trade opportunities. Several months earlier the Bush administration had approved $1 billion in export credits for Iraq from the U.S. government's Commodity Credit Corporation (CCC), and the Kansas Republican wanted Iraq to spend most of the CCC money on American agricultural products, above all on Kansas wheat (for which Iraq was already one of the world's largest customers). However, the deterioration of U.S.-Iraqi relations in the weeks preceding the Dole team's visit had greatly increased the stakes for both countries. Before leaving Washington, Dole had been briefed by Secretary of State James Baker on the points that President Bush wanted conveyed to Saddam.

Accompanied by four other senators—fellow Republicans Alan Simpson of Wyoming, Frank Murkowski of Alaska, and James McClure of Idaho; and Ohio Democrat Howard Metzenbaum—Dole arrived at Saddam's residence in Mosul with a small coterie that included the U.S. ambassador to Iraq, April Glaspie. The decision to meet in Mosul, the old Ottoman capital of northern Iraq, rather than at Saddam's massive presidential palace complex in downtown Baghdad, had been made by the Iraqi leader himself—an effort to lend a more intimate atmosphere to the proceedings.

A twenty-year veteran of the Foreign Service who had spent most of her diplomatic career in the Middle East, Glaspie immediately realized that Saddam must have attached great importance to this meeting, because he was going out of his way to be as accommodating as possible. Grandly, he offered to provide the visiting senators with a helicopter tour of northern Iraq, lush and green at that time of year, after their meeting. Glaspie, who had met with Saddam on several occasions, was surprised by this uncharacteristic goodwill gesture from the normally imperious Iraqi leader. Fluent in Arabic, she also noticed that Saddam was using the formal, polite form of the language to address the senators rather than the more guttural Tikriti dialect in which he customarily spoke.

If Saddam's demeanor was out of character, the substance of his remarks was even more so. He had obviously reflected carefully on what he wanted to say, Glaspie would later report back to her superiors in Washington. Claiming that he only wanted good relations with the United States, Saddam scrolled through the litany of charges that the U.S. government had lodged against him in recent weeks. Denying that Iraq had tried to acquire kryton switches for nuclear weapons, Saddam produced a thick dossier of Iraqi government documents that he claimed proved Iraq's noninvolvement in the affair. Conveniently enough, all of the documents in the dossier had been translated into English for the senators to read on their trip home. Moving on to the matter of the diplomat accused of conspiring to assassinate Iraqi exiles on American soil, Saddam assured the senators that he, Saddam, had personally conducted an investigation and determined that the man was innocent of any wrongdoing. It was obvious, he concluded, that these charges were all part of a calculated campaign against Iraq by the United States in collusion with its ally Israel.

Dole interrupted, "If there is a campaign against Iraq, President Bush is not a part of it," he said. "He wants better relations, and the United States wants better relations with Iraq." Dole added for the benefit of the others in the room that he had conveyed the same message privately to Saddam earlier, when the two of them had spoken by phone. Saddam appeared momentarily taken aback, then pleased by the directness of Dole's statement. "That is good enough for me," he told the Americans.

As the atmosphere in the room grew noticeably more relaxed, the Iraqi leader even offered something akin to an apology for his own speech attacking President Bush five days earlier. Glaspie was surprised; this was uncharacteristic behavior indeed from Saddam. In the same spirit, Dole apologized for an editorial criticizing the Iraqi regime for human rights violations, which had been broadcast by the Voice of America several months earlier. The editorial had been unauthorized, Dole assured Saddam, and the offending VOA staffer had been fired. Saddam was even more pleased by this piece of news.

Dole's colleague Alan Simpson chimed in, "I believe your problem is with the Western media, not with the U.S. government, because you are isolated from the media and the press," he said. Simpson gamely tried to explain some of the facts of life about the American media, as he saw them, to Saddam. "The press is spoiled and conceited," the lanky Wyoming Republican drawled. "All the journalists consider themselves brilliant political scientists. They do not want to see anything succeeding or achieving its objectives. My advice to you is that you allow those bastards to come here and see things for themselves."

Saddam then launched into a rambling justification for his speech threatening Israel with chemical weapons. Reverting to a more typical tone of voice, Saddam said that he would not apologize for claiming a right to "self-defense" against the Israelis. If Israel attacks with nuclear weapons, he told the suddenly attentive American delegation, Iraq would respond with binary chemical weapons. "Even if Baghdad is pulverized, Iraqi field commanders have their orders" to launch chemical weapons, the Iraqi ruler declared somberly. Saddam shrugged. "What else is Iraq expected to do? Iraq must try to deter."

Coming from Saddam, this was no empty boast. As everyone in the room was aware, Iraq was believed to have used chemical weapons against Iranian troops on numerous occasions during the Iran-Iraq War of the 1980s. Of greater concern, Saddam had also used chemical weapons against his own people. Only two years earlier, during the winter of 1987–88, the Iraqi army had repeatedly used chemical weapons to suppress a rebellion by the Kurdish population of northern Iraq. The most notorious attack, outside the town of Halabja in March 1988, had claimed the lives of over five thousand civilians, many of them women and children. The visiting senators were all familiar with this recent history. Saddam's use of chemical weapons against the Iraqi Kurds had been the topic of extensive hearings on Capitol Hill and were documented in an investigative report prepared by the staff of the Senate Foreign Relations Committee.

Having rattled this saber, Saddam stopped speaking and invited the visitors to ask him their questions. Not surprisingly, the question that was top of mind for Dole's delegation was the obvious one: Did Iraq also have nuclear weapons?

In a conversation that lasted the better part of an hour, Saddam repeatedly denied that Iraq possessed a nuclear bomb, though he pointedly refused to deny that it was conducting research to acquire one. He also denied that Iraq had biological weapons, but again demurred on the question of whether Iraq was conducting research in this area. If Iraq did have a nuclear device or biological weapons, Saddam reasoned with the senators, the country would announce its capability to the world since that would maximize deterrence for Iraq. Falling back on a favorite hobbyhorse of the Iraqi regime, Saddam dramatically announced to his guests that Iraq was ready to give up all of its existing chemical weapons, sign a declaration making the Middle East a zone free of weapons of mass destruction, and even permit voluntary inspections of its weapons facilities—provided, of course, that Israel was willing to agree to the same conditions and give up its nuclear arsenal. Glaspie frowned in annoyance at this ploy. Anticipating that Saddam would broach this very topic, she had taken pains before the meeting to remind Tariq Aziz, Saddam's puckish foreign minister, that the United States was opposed as a matter of long-standing policy to any linkage of nuclear and chemical weapons issues.

Nevertheless, despite Saddam's unapologetic admission that Iraq possessed chemical weapons and was prepared to use them, the meeting ended on a cordial note. Saddam had achieved his objective: He had persuaded the visiting senators that the president of Iraq was a reasonable leader, and this was the message they would take back to Washington. Toward the end of the three-hour meeting, Dole voiced a promise to Saddam from President Bush that the senator had been given back in Washington, that the Bush administration would oppose any attempt by Congress to place economic sanctions on Iraq. The senators pledged their own opposition to sanctions. The lone Democrat in Dole's delegation, Howard Metzenbaum, said to Saddam, "After listening to you for about an hour, I realize that you are a strong and an intelligent man and that you want peace." Reminding Saddam that he was Jewish and a strong supporter of Israel, the Ohio senator continued: "If a certain shift in your thinking makes you concentrate on the peace we need in the Middle East, there will be no other leader in the Middle East who can be compared with you." A week later, back on the Senate floor, Dole echoed Metzenbaum's remarks: "We asked Hussein a number of difficult questions. I think we came away feeling that this is an intelligent man."

.   .   .

But if Saddam Hussein had succeeded in persuading some American officials that he was an intelligent man who wanted peace, his inflammatory rhetoric in the spring of 1990 had caused others to arrive at the opposite conclusion. At the State Department, Dennis Ross was one of several officials who were beginning to see a disturbing pattern emerge in Saddam's recent behavior.

Ross occupied one of the key foreign policy jobs in the U.S. government: director of the Policy Planning Staff, the secretary of state's personal think tank, which was responsible for identifying the long-term strategic challenges for American diplomacy. A youthful Californian whose owlish glasses and thoughtful cadences of speech gave him an almost scholarly air, Ross had a PhD in political science from UCLA, where he had written his doctoral thesis on Soviet politics. His real passion, however, was the history and politics of the Middle East, a subject to which he had devoted a lifetime of study. Ross enjoyed an unusual degree of influence within the councils of the Bush administration, owing to the fact that he had been George Bush's principal foreign policy adviser during the 1988 presidential campaign. At State, he was one of only a handful of aides who had direct access to Secretary Baker at all times.

Like virtually all of the Bush administration's top foreign policy figures, Ross worked almost exclusively on managing the end of the Cold War in Europe after the dramatic fall of the Berlin Wall in November 1989. This had left the State Department bureaucracy to oversee policy toward Iraq, which essentially meant a continuation of the policy that had been put in place after George Bush's accession to the White House in 1989. National Security Directive 26, the official distillation of U.S. policy toward countries in the Persian Gulf, had been drafted by the National Security Council and signed by the president on October 2, 1989. It called for closer U.S. ties to Iraq as a counterweight to Iran's influence in the region. NSD 26 expressly called for the United States to use economic aid, such as export credits, to nurture closer ties between the two countries. "Normal relations between the United States and Iraq would serve our longer-term interests and promote stability in both the Gulf and the Middle East," it asserted. "The United States Government should propose economic and political incentives for Iraq to moderate its behavior and to increase our influence with Iraq."

The directive acknowledged the WMD proliferation threat from Iraq. It warned that "the Iraqi leadership must recognize that any illegal use of chemical and/or biological weapons will lead to economic and political sanctions, for which we would seek the broadest possible support from our allies and friends." The same held true of Iraq's nuclear research programs: "Any breach by Iraq of IAEA [International Atomic Energy Agency] safeguards in its nuclear program will result in a similar response." Notably, however, NSD 26 mentioned only the United States responding with sanctions in the context of Iraq actually using weapons of mass destruction, primarily its chemical munitions. It did not address the issue of Iraq's existing stocks of such weapons, or identify their elimination as an objective of American policy.

Ross now began to believe that both the policy itself and the lack of attention paid to Iraq at the Cabinet level may have been a mistake. "When Saddam gave his speech where he talked about burning Israel, it made me wake up and say, 'Maybe there is a problem here,'" he would recall later.

From his earliest days in government service, Ross had been concerned about the threat Iraq posed to the larger Middle East. As a young Pentagon staffer in 1979, he had written a cautionary policy study with another rising colleague in the Pentagon at the time, the Bush administration's undersecretary of defense, Paul Wolfowitz. The study examined possible U.S. responses to a hypothetical Iraqi invasion of the Persian Gulf states. At the time, it had been a contingency about which few in the Pentagon were worrying. Most of official Washington had been preoccupied by the Cold War, and by the increasingly aggressive behavior of the Soviet Union, which was believed to have eclipsed the United States in both strategic and conventional arms. In the Persian Gulf, the main concern of U.S. foreign policy was the fall of the Shah in Iran, which had deprived the United States of its strongest ally in the region and threatened to unleash chaos in Iran itself. These fears were realized in November 1979, when supporters of the Ayatollah Khomeini in Iran stormed the U.S. embassy in Tehran and took fifty-three Americans hostage, a crisis that consumed the rest of Jimmy Carter's presidency.

But Ross and Wolfowitz had seen Iraq at the time as an equally dangerous long-term threat. The country was oil-rich and technologically advanced by the standards of the Arab world. It was also the most important client state for the Soviet Union in the Gulf. With the assistance of Soviet military advisers, Saddam Hussein had built one of the most powerful militaries in the region, armed with the latest-model Soviet tanks, aircraft, and short-range missiles. Saddam and the ruling Ba'ath Party in Iraq espoused a strongly nationalistic vision of the country's role in Arab and world affairs, one that rejected traditional Islamic values in favor of military and economic power. Iraq and its young leader had clearly been on the rise. Already, Iraq's armed forces dwarfed those of neighboring Kuwait and Saudi Arabia. Ross and Wolfowitz had warned in their report: "If Iraq precipitated a crisis with Kuwait or Saudi Arabia, it would be totally dominant until U.S. force arrived. Without forward deployments, the U.S. could not get significant ground forces to the region for 10–20 days at best. . . . In the absence of opposition, Iraq could conquer Kuwait, seize Saudi oil fields, and capture critical airfields and ports within a week or two."

The more he examined Saddam's record and recent speeches, the more it became apparent to Ross that Saddam was consciously trying to resurrect the unfulfilled vision of an earlier Arab leader, Gamal Nasser, president of Egypt during the 1950s and 1960s. Long after his death, Nasser remained an iconic figure for much of the Arab world. The Egyptian president had advocated a policy of pan-Arabism, which urged Arab nations to set aside their traditional differences and unite in pursuit of military and technological greatness. A central tenet of Nasser's policy was implacable hostility to Israel and the Western nations that supported it.

Two months earlier, in February 1990, Saddam had given a speech to an Arab summit in Jordan in which he claimed that Iraq's technological prowess and huge oil reserves now made it, not Egypt, the true leader of the Arab world. Claiming the mantle of Nasser, Saddam promised that Iraq would lead the Arab peoples in challenging the American military presence in the Gulf region and called for U.S. naval forces to be withdrawn from the Persian Gulf. Even his April 2 speech, which had threatened the use of chemical weapons against Israel, had given this warning in the context of boasting about Iraq's advanced technology compared to that of the other Arab states.

Here is a radical leader who rejects everything we want, Ross thought to himself. Just like Nasser.

But the most disturbing aspect of a Nasser-Saddam comparison was another salient fact about the Egyptian president. Nasser had been the instigator of two major wars during his years as Egypt's ruler.

In 1956, shortly after the United States and Great Britain withdrew offers to provide financial support for the construction of the Aswan Dam project, Egypt seized and attempted to nationalize the Anglo-French–owned Suez Canal. This would have left Nasser and Egypt the power to determine just whose ships would be allowed to pass through the canal. Israel understood that its commerce would surely be barred, and so in October 1956 it joined with Britain and France in the attack to retake the canal. The ensuing Suez War had led to a major falling-out between those three countries and the United States. The Eisenhower administration, having made recent pronouncements renouncing the use of military force as an instrument of foreign policy, refused to take part in what most of the world saw as a "neocolonialist" venture by the French and British. The episode led to the fall of Prime Minister

Anthony Eden's government in Britain. Though Egyptian forces did not acquit themselves particularly well in the war, Egypt did manage to sink forty ships in the canal, effectively closing it to commerce until the nationalization of the canal was accepted and terms of the buyout were worked out. Suez was widely seen throughout the Arab world as a huge symbolic victory for Nasser and pan-Arabism.

Then, in 1967, Nasser had been the architect of a complex plan for the Arab nations bordering Israel to launch a combined attack on the Israelis along three fronts. Seeing the Arab armies massing on its borders, Israel had attacked first and won a decisive victory in the Six-Day War. Even so, Nasser had briefly achieved his vision of Arab nations uniting to take military action against Israel.

Saddam Hussein had already started one war of his own, invading Iran in 1980 after the fall of the Shah. The ensuing Iran-Iraq War lasted eight long years and ended in a stalemate, after decimating an entire generation in both countries. Iraq was now burdened with over $40 billion in debt from that war, which seemed to rule out the possibility that Saddam would start another war anytime soon. However, Saddam's rhetoric about forcing the U.S. military out of the Gulf and attacking Israel seemed to indicate that he was at least thinking about taking military action again in the not-too-distant future. If he was, Ross thought, then this was not the kind of foreign leader the United States should be trying to cultivate.

Ross took his concerns to James Baker. The whole thing about giving this guy credits is just crazy, Ross argued to the secretary of state, referring to the decision to extend CCC credits to Iraq. Baker was surprised by Ross's sudden interest in the issue, but agreed to put the Bush administration's entire Iraq policy under review. Start talking to the other Arabs and see what they have to say, he ordered.

.   .   .

Dennis Ross was not the only one talking to the Arabs about Saddam Hussein's intentions. In May 1990 the White House dispatched a senior National Security Council official, Richard Haass, to the Gulf to make some discreet inquiries about another matter of concern: the growing tensions between Iraq and Kuwait over OPEC oil prices. Haass's job at the NSC was senior director for Near East and South Asian affairs—President Bush's principal adviser on the Middle East.

Arriving first in Kuwait, Haass met on May 15 with the country's oil minister, Sheikh Ali Khalifa al-Sabah. The U.S. ambassador to Kuwait, Nathaniel Howell, also sat in. The tensions between Iraq and Kuwait over oil prices were the first item on the agenda. The sheikh, a member of the ruling al-Sabah family of Kuwait, brought to the Americans' attention a recent announcement by Iraq that all OPEC members should abide by the cartel's recent decision to cut production by 1.5 million barrels a day, with each member making proportionate cuts depending on its production. It was a measure designed to boost prices, and thus revenue, for financially strapped members of the cartel like Iraq. Kuwait, one of the wealthiest members of the cartel, was less sensitive to a temporary downturn in prices and thus agreed to a cut of only 600,000 barrels a day. Saddam Hussein had declared that any OPEC member's failure to abide by the OPEC production quota would be considered "an act of aggression" against Iraq. "If the Gulf States do not give me money," he said ominously at the time, "I will know how to get it from them."

Nevertheless, the sheikh did not seem overly concerned with Saddam's veiled threats of dire consequences for Kuwait if it did not agree to the OPEC quota. Saddam's recent statements were the product of insecurity and desperation, he assured Haass. The Iraqi public was fed up with war. The sheikh observed with some satisfaction that more and more Iraqis were openly complaining about their declining standard of living, despite recent crackdowns by Iraq's internal security forces. He added his own view that the only reason that Saddam had not already reached a compromise with Kuwait over the quota issue was that Saddam was afraid to back down, because it would make him look weak to his internal opponents.

Several days later Haass traveled to Baghdad to hear the Iraqi side of the story. He met first with the Iraqi oil minister, Issam al-Chalabi,* who

---

* No relation to the prominent Iraqi opposition figure Ahmed Chalabi. Ironically, Issam al-Chalabi would resurface in the United States over a decade later, after the March 2003 invasion of Iraq that toppled Saddam Hussein. Speaking at an oil industry conference in Houston, Saddam's former oil minister would charge that the United States had failed to formulate a "well-defined oil policy" before the invasion began.

had just returned from conferring with his counterpart in Saudi Arabia. Iraq and Saudi Arabia would comply with the OPEC quota, al-Chalabi told Haass, as would Iran. Only Kuwait and the United Arab Emirates are obstacles to better coordination, he complained. OPEC did not want another 1970s-type oil shock, the minister maintained, only modest price increases that would keep pace with inflation. The Kuwaitis were liars, he added, who routinely violated the quota despite regular pronouncements from their emir that Kuwait supported the OPEC agreement.

Before leaving Baghdad, Haass called on an old acquaintance, Nizar Hamdun, whom Haass knew from Hamdun's years as Iraqi ambassador to the United States during the 1980s. A fastidiously well-groomed man who spoke excellent English, Hamdun was considered a relatively moderate, pro-Western figure by Washington. He now held a top position in the Iraqi Foreign Ministry and was said to be Saddam's principal adviser on the United States.

The two officials touched only briefly on the growing tensions between Iraq and Kuwait in their conversation. They spent most of their time together discussing the potential for war between India and Pakistan over the disputed Kashmir region.

●   ●   ●

Even before these conversations had taken place, however, one senior American official had already determined that Saddam Hussein was a threat to world peace, and had even gone so far as to predict that his next gambit would be a move against Kuwait.

Earlier that spring, the top U.S. diplomats posted to capitals in Europe and the Middle East had convened for one of their recurring Chiefs of Mission conferences—an opportunity for the most senior diplomats in each embassy to share gossip and tidbits of intelligence they had garnered from various host governments with a larger group of their peers. There would also be discussions with the State Department leadership about the foreign policy issues they were most likely to confront in the near future. That year, there had been little debate over where the conference would meet. There was a sense of euphoria in State Department ranks over the collapse of the Iron Curtain in Eastern Europe and the impending reunification of Germany. Everyone agreed it was only appropriate that the Chiefs of Mission conference meet for old times' sake in Bonn, the West German capital, which would soon lose its capital city status to Berlin in a unified Germany.

In the weeks leading up to the conference, attendees were encouraged to draft confidential policy papers that would be circulated to the entire group for comment and discussion. As one would expect, most of the papers that year were optimistic in tone, focusing on the dramatic developments taking place in Europe and the thaw in relations between the United States and the Soviet Union. Morale in the career Foreign Service was sky-high. The peaceful end to the Cold War in Europe was widely seen as a vindication of the Containment doctrine that had been framed by one of their own, the legendary American diplomat George Kennan. While posted to the U.S. embassy in Moscow in 1947, Kennan had written his famous "Long Telegram" to Washington, a diplomatic cable which argued that if the United States could contain Soviet communism long enough, the Soviet system would eventually collapse on its own. Kennan's ideas had defined U.S. foreign policy throughout the Cold War, and his predictions were coming true all around them.

However, one person at the conference took a far more pessimistic view of the future. Charles W. "Chas" Freeman, U.S. ambassador to Saudi Arabia, saw in the next several years a period of awakening dangers for the United States. One of the most accomplished career diplomats in the State Department (a highlight of his early career had been serving as President Richard Nixon's translator on Nixon's famous trip to China), Freeman gave voice to his concerns in a series of three diplomatic cables prepared for the Bonn conference. In State Department lore, they became known as the Woolly Mammoth cables.

Freeman's core argument was that the strategic landscape at the end of the Cold War was like the landscape at the end of an Ice Age. Dangerous animals everyone had imagined to be extinct during the Cold War—such as rulers who espoused extreme forms of ethnic nationalism; or rivalries between nations over territory and natural resources—had in fact only been hibernating, like woolly mammoths during an Ice Age. The logical corollary was that the thaw in the Cold War would allow these forces to awaken and reemerge. Thus, Freeman argued, the last decade of the twentieth century would be characterized by many of the same problems of the 1930s, the last decade before the Cold War had frozen international politics in stasis. It was a grim vision.

But by far the most controversial argument advanced in the Woolly Mammoth cables, and the one that prompted the most criticism from Freeman's colleagues, was his assertion that a major crisis between Iraq and Kuwait was coming. From his perch in nearby Saudi Arabia, Freeman saw in Saddam Hussein's Iraq a perfect example of the sort of Woolly Mammoth against which he was warning. The Gulf War (as the Iran-Iraq War was then known) had left Iraq militarily supreme in the Persian Gulf, but bankrupt. The combination of unchallenged military capability and severe economic distress made Iraq a uniquely dangerous animal, like a sharp-tusked woolly mammoth that was not only awake, but ravenous. And the closest nearby prey was Kuwait.

Freeman did not venture a specific guess about what Iraq would do next. But he believed it inevitable that Saddam would go after Kuwait, which was now in real jeopardy. However, this prediction was almost universally dismissed by the State Department officials and other chiefs of mission attending the conference, even openly derided by some. A few murmured under their breath that it was Freeman himself who was the real Woolly Mammoth.

The only person at the conference who said she agreed with Freeman's analysis was April Glaspie.

2

"SADDAM HAS BLINKED"

By a curious coincidence, both the United States and Iraq celebrated their national holidays in July. For the United States, it was Independence Day. For Saddam Hussein's Iraq, it was July 17, the anniversary of the 1968 revolution that had brought the ruling Ba'ath Party to power. Just as in the United States, it was a holiday of patriotic speeches, including the annual equivalent of Iraq's State of the Union address. Each year Iraqi state television would remind citizens for days in advance of their duty to turn on their televisions and hear President Saddam's speech—which would invariably be read by some other official.

However, on July 16, 1990, Iraq's Information Ministry began an unprecedented, around-the-clock public relations blitz to promote the importance of that year's speech in Iraq and the larger Arab-speaking world. The next day the information minister appeared on camera and somberly called on Iraqis and other Arabs to hear what the President Leader had to say. Unexpectedly, Saddam himself appeared on camera and began to speak.

For the first several minutes of the speech, Saddam accused "Western imperialists" of trying to deny Iraq and the Arab world the means to achieve "scientific and technical progress"—by which he meant, of course, weapons of mass destruction. He repeated the charge he had made in his April 2 speech, that Israel was on the verge of attacking Iraq. This time he did not explicitly threaten to retaliate with chemical weapons, but merely reminded his audience of the "well-known warning" he had given previously.

But the bulk of Saddam's speech was devoted to another topic: how the "imperialists" and the "Zionists" (Saddam's standard boilerplate for the United States and Israel), in collusion with "evildoers" in some Arab nations, were waging economic warfare against Iraq by driving down oil prices. Rather than trying to gain control of the Middle East directly, Saddam claimed, the United States had set out on a more devious plot to do so indirectly, by weakening Iraq's economy. He averred to his subjects his own belief that this "new method" of keeping Iraq weak was even more sinister than the "old method." "Now they want to cut off the livelihood of the Arabs," Saddam railed angrily, "while the old method merely cut off their necks."

According to Saddam, the way the United States would achieve its goal of weakening Iraq was to conspire with the rulers and oil ministers of the Persian Gulf states to reduce oil prices. Each drop of $1 in the price of a barrel of oil cost Iraq $14 billion in annual revenue, Saddam explained to his subjects, which was why the Iraqi people were now enduring such economic hardship. Any Arab state that helped the United States implement its plot was in fact "anti-Arab" and guilty of "stabbing Iraq in the back with a poisoned dagger." The speech concluded with an ominous threat to those Arab nations guilty of such "bad behavior": "If words fail to afford us protection, we will have no choice but to resort to effective action. I have conveyed the message."

The reaction to Saddam's July 17 speech among longtime Iraq watchers was one of amazement. Not only had Saddam delivered what amounted to an ultimatum in person; but for the first time, he had openly admitted to the world that Iraq was in desperate financial straits. Glaspie wrote in her summary for Washington: "Saddam's speech, as it dealt with the oil price issue, was crude and discourteous in the extreme. . . . Saddam himself was careful not to name names, although his audience knew he was attacking Kuwait and the United Arab Emirates. This speech was his first public threat to those states, though not, of course, a military threat. Clearly, the GOI [Government of Iraq] needs money, NOW, and is not above saying so publicly. Saddam's speech was an unusual public admission of just how strapped the GOI treasury is."

The Iraqi Foreign Ministry, driving home the message that the speech was intended as an ultimatum, at the same time it released the transcript of Saddam's speech also made public an angry letter that Foreign Minister Aziz had sent to the Arab League two days earlier. The letter described Kuwait's "theft" of oil revenue from Iraq as an act of "military aggression" against Iraq. It went on to list the specific concessions that Kuwait would need to make in order to satisfy Iraq.

. . .

Ironically, Iraq's letter to the Arab League, with its ultimatum for Kuwait, did more to attract Washington's attention than Saddam's inflammatory National Day speech. On July 18, Iraq's ambassador to the United States was called into the State Department to clarify the intent of the letter. That day the department also issued an unambiguous statement that declared that the United States remained "strongly committed to the individual and collective self-defense of our friends in the Gulf." Meanwhile, in Baghdad, Glaspie was instructed to meet with Nizar Hamdun at the Foreign Ministry and deliver a set of talking points that had been drafted for Iraq. She requested an appointment the following day, July 19.

Glaspie handed Hamdun a copy of the State Department statement from the previous day. "We have never taken a position on bilateral issues between Iraq and Kuwait, and we do not intend to begin now," she began, scrupulously following the talking points she had been given. When Hamdun made no reply, Glaspie continued: "We had thought, however, that Iraq shared our desire not to escalate regional tensions. The Aziz letter seemed to us not calm in tone, but angry." Hamdun again said nothing, only nodded.

Glaspie tried to improve the tenor of the conversation with a conciliatory gesture that had been suggested back in Washington. She recalled for Hamdun that in 1981 the U.S. government had condemned Israel for the preemptive attack that destroyed the Osirak nuclear reactor outside of Baghdad, the facility that was the center of Saddam Hussein's nuclear weapons program at the time. Hamdun still said nothing, which surprised her. Usually the mere mention of Osirak was enough to animate any government official in Iraq, since the attack was considered a national insult delivered by the hated Israelis. Trying to draw out Hamdun, the ambassador elaborated on the principle that had been involved in American condemnation of the attack: "We believe that disputes must be resolved by peaceful means, and at that time we pointed out our view that peaceful methods of settling the dispute had not been exhausted." Still no response.

Glaspie now realized that Hamdun must be under strict orders from Saddam himself to make no comment on the ultimatum sent to the Arab League. "What precisely was meant when Aziz wrote, 'We hope our brothers will raise their voices high'?" Glaspie pressed. "What could the Arab League do to ensure good behavior by Kuwait and the UAE which the other major OPEC exporters could not do more effectively?" She reminded Hamdun that "even President Saddam had recently remarked that OPEC, not the Arab League, was the appropriate venue for oil issues." In fact, the next OPEC meeting was scheduled to begin on July 25 in Geneva.

Hamdun finally spoke. "I can well understand that you would be surprised by the letter," he said. "I wish I could make some comment or clarification to you," he added, his voice trailing into a frightened whisper, "but I am not authorized to do so."

*　　　*　　　*

That same day in Washington, Colonel Walter "Pat" Lang of the army sent an urgent flash message to General Colin Powell, chairman of the Joint Chiefs of Staff. Lang was defense intelligence officer for the Middle East at the Defense Intelligence Agency (DIA), the Pentagon's in-house intelligence service. For nearly a week DIA had been monitoring a massive movement of Iraqi troops and military equipment to Iraq's southern border. The sheer number of troops and vehicles making their way south went far beyond what would be necessary for a training exercise, or even a small show of force along the border. Of even greater concern to DIA's analysts, at least three of Iraq's elite Republican Guard divisions, which rarely conducted exercises with regular Iraqi army troops, were part of the force assembling on the Kuwaiti border. The Iraqi military activity taking place along the Kuwaiti border, Lang's message to Powell warned, was "not a rehearsal."

The next morning, July 20, the DIA received a disturbing piece of new intelligence. U.S. spy satellites had detected tank transporters—large flatbed trucks used to ferry tanks over long distances—only thirty miles north of the Kuwaiti border. To the military intelligence experts of the DIA, many of them current or former army officers, it was a small detail that spoke volumes about Iraq's real intentions. In 1973, Iraq had tried to send a large armored force to fight alongside other Arab nations in the Yom Kippur War against Israel. Foolishly, Iraqi tank commanders tried to drive their vehicles directly from their bases in Iraq to the Israeli front—a distance of many hundreds of miles across the harsh desert. Tank engines clogged with sand and overheated, tank treads wore out on the rocky soil, and only a tiny fraction of the Iraqi force ever made it into battle. Iraq's generals learned their lesson and acquired a large fleet of tank transporter trucks. In 1980, at the start of the Iran-Iraq War, Iraq used tank transporters to ferry its heavy armored units directly to the front. The American intelligence community had not seen Iraq make use of tank transporters on this large a scale since 1980.

The U.S. defense attaché stationed in Baghdad was ordered to find out all that he could about Iraqi troop movements. Since there was no possible way for Iraq to hide the movement of several hundred thousand troops and their equipment from U.S. satellite reconnaissance, Iraq had announced that it was conducting a major military exercise in its southern desert. The attaché asked for an opportunity to observe the exercise—the typical function of a military attaché. It was a reasonable request that Iraq could hardly refuse under the circumstances. The enterprising American officer seized upon the opportunity to observe an Iraqi "field exercise" as an excuse to travel all the way down to the Kuwait border, take photographs of which units were deployed, and even interview some Iraqi officers. This intelligence made its way back to Washington within forty-eight hours, along with one other salient fact: On the trip down to the border region, there had been over three thousand Iraqi military vehicles on the road to Kuwait.

• • •

By now the Bush White House was also well aware of the potential for a major international crisis to erupt in the Persian Gulf.

Every morning from 8:00 to 9:30 A.M., except when the routine was interrupted by travel or emergencies, three men met in the White House for the most important meeting in Washington. Promptly at eight o'clock, President Bush would enter the Oval Office and sit down for coffee with his chief of staff, former New Hampshire governor John Sununu, and his national security adviser, General Brent Scowcroft. Waiting for the three men would be three copies of the President's Daily Brief—PDB for short—the U.S. intelligence community's summary of the most significant new pieces of intelligence from the previous day. The PDB was the single most highly classified document in the U.S. government, restricted to only the president and a handful of his closest aides.

A CIA briefing officer would also be waiting and quickly take the three men through the PDB, answering any questions. The CIA briefer would then be excused. For the remainder of their ninety minutes together, Bush, Sununu, and Scowcroft would discuss the president's priorities for the rest of the day, beginning with what they had just read in the PDB. No other staff members were present and no minutes were kept, allowing for an unusually candid exchange of views among the three men. The conversation would be wide-ranging, covering everything from consultations with other world leaders to more mundane matters like which members of Congress should be rewarded with tickets to the Presidential Box at Lincoln Center. Typically Scowcroft would raise foreign policy concerns and Sununu domestic political issues, but not always; both were free to express their opinions on any topic, and usually did. At 9:30, Sununu and Scowcroft would return to their own West Wing offices and begin firing off memoranda to their staffs on what they had talked about at the meeting.

By mid-July 1990, the morning conversations among Bush and his two top aides were increasingly dominated by Iraq. Traditionally, the President's Daily Brief lists items in order of urgency, with the five or six most pressing or important items being listed first. Sununu had long since learned that one of the best ways to gauge whether trouble was brewing with a foreign country was to track its position in the PDB over the course of several days. If intelligence reports about that country steadily progressed to the top of the PDB, it was a good indication that a crisis was imminent. Saddam Hussein's inflammatory July 17 speech threatening Kuwait and the United Arab Emirates had been reported in the next day's PDB, but as a lower-priority item. Each successive day, however, as more intelligence about Iraqi troop movements began filtering back to Washington, items about Iraq were more prominently featured in the PDB, until by the following week Iraq occupied the marquee position.

The three men discussed what to do about Iraq's threatening behavior. They agreed that the United States should do something to display its concern to its friends in the region. Unnerved by Saddam's July 17 speech, the UAE had already requested that an element of U.S. Air Force refueling aircraft be deployed to their country as a signal of American military commitment to the region. After a brief discussion, President Bush acceded to the request, and a symbolic flight of two aircraft arrived in the Emirates on July 24.

●   ●   ●

Reaction in Baghdad was impressively swift. At 12:30 A.M. on the morning of July 25—just hours after the announcement in Washington that U.S. military aircraft had been deployed to the Emirates—Nizar Hamdun summoned Ambassador Glaspie back to the Foreign Ministry. Glaspie was mildly surprised. While not unheard-of in the stifling July heat of Baghdad, the request for a middle-of-the-night meeting was hardly typical.

When she arrived at the Foreign Ministry, the atmosphere was almost electric. Whereas only a few days earlier Hamdun had been almost non-responsive, he was now almost frenetic with anxiety. Without preamble, Hamdun said that the Iraqi government wanted information on the purpose and timing of what he called the American military "maneuvers" with the UAE. Who was the target of these maneuvers, he asked angrily.

Glaspie calmly replied that if the United States were engaged in a military exercise with another country, it would be directed at no specific target. "We are still waiting for some clarification of our own from the government of Iraq," she countered. Thinking that Glaspie was alluding to their earlier conversation about Tariq Aziz's ultimatum letter to the Arab League, Hamdun replied that he could add nothing to what Aziz had written.

"You know full well we do not want clarification of Iraq's disputes with Kuwait," Glaspie retorted. "These are not our business. What we do want is to know Iraq's intentions. The government of Iraq has described Kuwait's actions as the equivalent of military aggression, and now thousands of the Republican Guard have gone south."

Temporizing, Hamdun seized on the last part of Glaspie's statement. "Who are these 'attachés' whom the Washington Post cited this morning on Iraqi troop movements?" he demanded to know accusingly. That morning's edition of the Post had carried a story about the U.S. defense attaché office at the embassy in Baghdad warning Washington about the recent Iraqi troop movements toward Kuwait.

"No one needs an attaché to see thousands of troops," Glaspie snapped back sarcastically, beginning to lose her temper. She told Hamdun that she herself had spoken to a Western businessman who had spent hours on the road that weekend threading his way through military convoys. Rising to leave, Glaspie reiterated, "Washington is waiting with some impatience for a response to a fair and important question: What are Iraq's intentions?"

As her official car pulled out of the Foreign Ministry compound, Glaspie saw that it was going to be a sleepless night for Hamdun; the UAE ambassador's car, recognizable by its distinctive flags, was just pulling in.

·　　·　　·

It would also turn out to be a sleepless night for Glaspie. She had barely arrived back at the embassy and begun composing a summary of her conversation with Hamdun for Washington when a message arrived from the Foreign Ministry: The U.S. ambassador had been summoned to a meeting with President Saddam at noon.

Glaspie was stunned. In the entire collective memory of the Western diplomatic corps in Baghdad, Saddam had never, not once, summoned an ambassador for a meeting. Sensitive about his image, the Iraqi ruler considered it beneath his dignity to be seen asking to meet with a foreign envoy. Instead, in the lexicon of the Iraqi Foreign Ministry, Saddam invariably "received" foreign ambassadors, which allowed him to adopt one of his favorite poses on Iraqi state television: that of the wise President Leader whose counsel was sought by dignitaries from around the globe.

Arriving alone at the presidential palace later that morning, Glaspie found Saddam waiting with Tariq Aziz and several members of his office staff. The Iraqi ruler was in an expansive mood. He wished the American ambassador to convey a message to President Bush, he told her.

Saddam embarked on a lengthy history of relations between the United States and Iraq. After diplomatic ties had been broken in 1967, when Iraq joined the Arab coalition during the Six-Day War with Israel, the two countries had not reestablished diplomatic relations for seventeen years, until 1984. The decision to reestablish relations had actually been made in 1980, Saddam claimed, but Iraq had not wanted to appear "weak" and "needy" while at war with Iran. He then spoke of the many "blows" that the relationship between the two nations had suffered since then: most notably the Iran-contra scandal (even Saddam referred to it colloquially as "Irangate"), during which the Reagan administration had secretly tried to sell advanced arms to Iran while that country was locked in its deadly struggle with Iraq, as a means of secretly financing the *contras* in Nicaragua.

Ever paranoid about threats to his rule, Saddam turned to more recent blows. "Some circles in the U.S. government, including in the intelligence community and the State Department, are not friendly toward Iraq," Saddam charged. "Some are even gathering information on who might be Saddam Hussein's successor," he accused in a hurt tone of voice. Saddam quickly added that he did not believe that President Bush or Secretary Baker was involved in these efforts to see him replaced. But others in the American government were working with the Gulf states to ensure that no help would come to Iraq.

Saddam repeated that Iraq had emerged from the Iran-Iraq War with $40 billion in debt. Iraq deserved something like a Marshall Plan for having saved the Arab world and the West from Iran, he said bitterly (neatly overlooking the fact that it was he who had attacked Iran first), but the United States only wanted lower oil prices. He renewed his usual complaint that the American news media was engaged in a calculated assault on Iraq and its president. Saddam had fresh reasons to worry on this score. In the preceding two months he had been the subject of both an unflattering television profile by Diane Sawyer of ABC News, and a *U.S. News & World Report* cover story entitled "The World's Most Dangerous Man." Both the Diane Sawyer profile and the magazine story highlighted Saddam's decade-long quest to build a nuclear bomb, and his use of chemical weapons against the Iraqi Kurds during the 1987–88 uprising.

With these preliminaries out of the way, Saddam changed the subject to the main purpose of the meeting as far as he was concerned: gauging the seriousness of Washington's commitment to Kuwait and the UAE.

"We hope that the United States will not misunderstand," he began, choosing his words carefully. "Of course, it is the right of every country to choose its friends. But it was Iraq, not the United States, which protected your 'friends' during the war with Iran," he reminded Glaspie. "Had the Iranians overrun the region, American troops could not have stopped them, except by the use of nuclear weapons." Explaining why only Iraq had been able to stop Iran, Saddam made a remark that would be repeated often in the months ahead: "Yours is not a society that can accept ten thousand dead in a single battle, as Iraq did."

Quoting the State Department's July 18 statement verbatim, Saddam asked rhetorically, "What does it mean for the United States to announce that it is committed to the defense of its friends, individually and collectively?"

He answered his own question: "It means flagrant bias against Iraq." The American "maneuvers" with the UAE had emboldened the Emirates and Kuwait to defy Iraq on the oil price issue, Saddam complained. "Iraq's rights will be restored one by one," he promised, "whether it takes a month or much more than a year. The United States wants to secure the flow of oil. That is understandable. But you must not use methods like arm-twisting, which you claim you do not like."

Saddam adopted a more somber tone. "You can send planes and missiles and hurt Iraq deeply," he mused, as if contemplating the prospect, "but do not force Iraq to the point of humiliation at which logic must be disregarded." A solution to the dispute with Kuwait and the UAE should come through Arab diplomacy, he insisted. Iraqis knew what war was and wanted no more of it, Saddam claimed. "Do not push us to it," he pleaded melodramatically. "Do not make it the only option left with which we can protect our dignity."

Glaspie reiterated President Bush's desire for a better relationship with Iraq. There were indeed "some circles" in the American government hostile to Iraq, she admitted, but it was the president who set policy for his administration. As for the media, Glaspie said, not even the president could control the American press. If he could, she reasoned, criticism of the president would not exist. Saddam interrupted to say that he understood this. "I saw the Diane Sawyer program," Glaspie added in an apologetic tone. "I thought it was cheap and unfair." The more important thing, the ambassador said, was that President Bush himself had demonstrated his desire for better relations by opposing trade sanctions against Iraq.

Saddam laughed. "There is nothing left for Iraq to buy in the United States except wheat," he replied, still chuckling to himself. "And no doubt even that will soon be declared a dual-use item."*

The tension in the room momentarily relieved by this attempt at gallows humor, Glaspie thought the time right to raise the main issue with Saddam and Tariq Aziz.

"Mr. President, we can see that you have deployed massive forces in the south," she began. Saddam nodded. "Normally that would not be any of our business. But when this happens in the context of what you said on your National Day, and we read the details in the letters of the foreign minister, is it not reasonable for us to be concerned?" Glaspie asked. "When both you and the foreign minister say that Kuwaiti actions are the equivalent of military aggression, and then we learn that many units of the Republican Guard have been sent to the border, is it not reasonable for us to ask—in a spirit of friendship, not confrontation—a simple question: What are your intentions?"

Saddam again nodded, agreeing that it was indeed a reasonable question. "But how can we make them understand," he lamented, referring

---

* Under the terms of previous U.S. trade sanctions against Iraq, so-called dual-use items (i.e., those that could be redirected to military purposes) were prohibited.

to the Kuwaitis, "how deeply we are suffering?" The financial situation was so dire, he said angrily, that even the pensions for war widows and orphans would need to be cut. Saddam gestured to his female interpreter and one of the stenographers in the room (both presumably war widows), who, on cue, burst into wails of inconsolable weeping at the prospect of having their pensions cut. Saddam nodded grimly at this evidence of Kuwaiti perfidy.

The Iraqi ruler elaborated on his theme. He had tried everything to bring the Gulf states around to his point of view: sent envoys, written letters, asked King Fahd of Saudi Arabia to mediate, even made a personal appeal to Sheikh Zayid of the UAE. Each time he thought that an agreement had been made, Kuwait and the UAE had violated it.

At that moment, word came of an urgent telephone call for Saddam from Egyptian president Hosni Mubarak. Saddam left the room to take the call in private. Upon his return, Glaspie asked hopefully if he had any news he could share with her. Saddam replied that through the mediation of his brother president, Mubarak, the Kuwaitis had just agreed to negotiate. A preliminary meeting would be held in Jeddah, summer capital of the Saudi monarchy on the western coast of Saudi Arabia, and then the crown prince of Kuwait would come to Baghdad for direct one-on-one negotiations with Saddam no later than Monday, July 30. "I told Mubarak that nothing will happen until the meeting, and nothing will happen after the meeting if the Kuwaitis will give us some hope," Saddam assured her, smiling.

All smiles herself, Glaspie congratulated Saddam on the good news. "I had been planning to go to the United States next Monday," she informed him, "but had thought to postpone my trip because of the difficulties we are facing. But now I will fly on Monday."

The next morning Glaspie sent a jubilant cable back to Washington: "Saddam has blinked. As far as Iraq's government-directed media on July 26 are concerned, the dispute with Kuwait was a 'summer cloud.' Gone are the headlines outlining Kuwaiti misbehavior; gone are the *ad hominem* attacks on Kuwaiti Foreign Minister al-Sabah; gone are the editorials outlining Iraq's case."

Her message noted one other curious fact: "July 26 is the first day for a week when we have not seen railway cars loaded with military equipment in the marshaling yards." Glaspie speculated on the significance of this piece of information. "This could either mean that all of the equipment the Iraqi forces on the border need is already in place," she wrote, "or that no new forces are being sent south."

●   ●   ●

If Saddam had blinked, no one had told the Republican Guard. At the bunkerlike DIA headquarters adjacent to the Pentagon, many were now so convinced that Iraq intended some form of military action against Kuwait that on July 25 the DIA had gone to WATCHCON II (Watch Condition II), its highest peacetime alert level. WATCHCON II was defined as a "significant threat to U.S. citizens, interests, or operating forces." In its entire history, the DIA had never gone to WATCHCON I, except during a shooting war. Also on July 25, Pat Lang and his staff in D-8, the Middle East section at DIA, prepared a Defense Special Assessment—a high-priority intelligence warning for the entire Department of Defense community—which cautioned: "With forces currently in place, Iraq would be able to overwhelm Kuwaiti forces and likely occupy its limited objectives within 48 hours, or all of Kuwait within five days." On Friday, July 27, even as intelligence reached Washington that Kuwaiti military units along the border were standing down as tensions between Iraq and Kuwait had seemingly abated, the DIA received the most ominous piece of intelligence yet about Iraqi intentions. Multiple sources confirmed that the logistics train for the Republican Guard divisions deployed along the Kuwaiti border had been sighted heading south toward Kuwait. Made up of the hundreds of supply trucks and maintenance vehicles necessary to support a modern mechanized army in the field, the logistics train would not have been needed for a temporary deployment of a few days. No army would load its cumbersome supply trucks with thousands of tons of water, fuel, and perishable food, then drive them across hundreds of miles of desert merely for show. To professional soldiers it was a dead giveaway that the Republican Guard units deployed along the Kuwaiti border intended to remain there for a very long time and might be intending to travel a considerable distance beyond the border.

That afternoon, in a secure conference room at the Pentagon, Lang and a team of briefing officers met with Sheikh Saud Nasir al-Sabah, the Kuwaiti ambassador to the United States, and told him point-blank that Iraq was going to invade his country.

* * *

That same Friday afternoon, another group of U.S. officials met to discuss the potential crisis between Iraq and Kuwait. Within the Bush administration, the highest-ranking group of officials that handled day-to-day national security policy was the Deputies Committee — the DC, in Executive Branch shorthand. As its name implied, the Deputies Committee consisted of the most senior sub-Cabinet-level officials from each of the five major stakeholders in defense and foreign policy: State Department, Defense Department, National Security Council, Joint Chiefs of Staff (JCS), and CIA. An innovation first proposed to improve policy coordination across government departments before the Bush administration's 1989 invasion of Panama, the DC had proved so effective that it had been retained on a permanent basis.

The deputies would meet daily (during crises even more frequently) to share information about key developments taking place within each of their respective organizations. They would also discuss any pressing national security matters and arrive at a "meeting of the minds" on a recommended policy response by the United States. Each member of the DC would in turn brief his or her immediate boss, the principal who headed each organization — at State and Defense, Secretaries Baker and Cheney; at the NSC, National Security Adviser Brent Scowcroft; at JCS, General Colin Powell; and at CIA, Director of Central Intelligence William Webster — on what had transpired at the meeting, and any outstanding issues that needed to be handled at the principals level.

The system worked smoothly because the deputies themselves were all seasoned Washington veterans with decades of experience in national security affairs. That afternoon the gathering included Undersecretary of State Robert Kimmitt, a West Point graduate and the third-ranking official in the State Department; Undersecretary of Defense Paul Wolfowitz; Admiral David Jeremiah, vice chairman of the Joint Chiefs of Staff; and

Deputy Director of Central Intelligence Richard Kerr, a career CIA officer. Ordinarily, the fifth person in attendance would have been Deputy National Security Adviser Robert Gates, but he was on vacation. NSC was represented instead by Sandra Charles, a Middle East expert from the NSC's Near East and South Asia directorate.

Iraq was the only item on the agenda for the deputies, and most of the meeting was devoted to parsing the latest intelligence. Besides the DIA's reports on Iraqi troop deployments, Richard Kerr shared the CIA's latest thinking on Saddam Hussein's intentions. After several hours of discussion, the deputies' consensus was that Saddam would likely seize the disputed Rumailah oilfield that straddled the Iraq-Kuwait border, and possibly the islands of Warbah and Bubiyan off the Kuwaiti coast, which had been disputed territory between Iraq and Kuwait for decades. "The agency was reporting that to get his message across to the Kuwaitis, he might temporarily invade and occupy the oilfield and the two islands," another person at the meeting recalls.

While bothersome, the prospect of an Iraqi border incursion in July 1990 was not perceived as a cataclysmic event, since military intimidation of Kuwait was a gambit that Iraq had tried on numerous previous occasions. Long before the Ba'ath Party or Saddam himself had assumed power in Iraq, annexation of Kuwait had been a rallying cry of the various nationalist political movements in Iraq, occasionally flaring into overt attempts to seize Kuwaiti territory. The independent emirate of Kuwait had been created in 1961 by the British (at the time the dominant military power in the Gulf region) by setting aside territory that had traditionally belonged to the Iraqi province of Basra. Britain's action was partly a response to its loss of influence over Iraq and its vast oil reserves several years earlier. In 1958 the so-called Free Officers' Coup, the seminal event in the twentieth-century history of Iraq, had toppled the British-imposed monarchy in Baghdad and replaced it with a military government. The new nation of Kuwait, geographically tiny but possessing oil reserves nearly as large as those in Iraq, was intended to become a British protectorate far more amenable to Western influence.

No sooner had Kuwaiti independence been declared than Iraq's new military ruler, General Abdelkarim Kessem, had threatened to annex the country outright. Kessem described Kuwait as "a long-lost but integral part of Iraq." The threat of an invasion, accompanied by a rapid deployment of Iraqi troops from Baghdad to the Kuwaiti border, had forced Britain to dispatch significant land and naval forces to protect Kuwait. British prime minister Harold Macmillan acidly commented on what he saw as the real reasons behind Iraq's action, making an observation that would remain valid three decades later: "Irredentism is always a popular battle cry for revolutionary leaders; but when the patriotic hook is baited by many millions of tons of oil and many millions of money it becomes almost irresistible."

The Iraqi threat became an even more pressing national security concern for the Kuwaitis after the United Kingdom announced that it would withdraw all of its forces from the Persian Gulf region by 1971. With the imminent departure of the Royal Navy from the Gulf, the ruling al-Sabah family in Kuwait sought a new protector to replace the British. Shortly after the 1968 presidential election in the United States, Emir Abdullah of Kuwait visited the United States and was one of a handful of foreign leaders to meet personally with president-elect Richard Nixon. Nixon's National Security Adviser-designate, Henry Kissinger, had mistakenly assumed that the emir would want to discuss Arab-Israeli relations after the previous year's Six-Day War, and had briefed Nixon accordingly. To both Nixon's and Kissinger's surprise, "the Emir wanted, above all, to learn what plans the Administration had for the Persian Gulf after the United Kingdom vacated the area" and especially wanted to learn "what were America's intentions if, for example, Iraq attacked Kuwait."

The emir's concern was not misplaced. In 1969 the newly installed Ba'ath regime in Iraq had "requested" that the Kuwaitis allow Iraqi troops to occupy positions on the Kuwaiti side of the border, ostensibly to protect the Iraqi coastline against an impending Iranian attack. Although permission was not forthcoming, Iraqi forces crossed the border anyway, the beginning of a decade-long Iraqi troop presence in the Contested Zone, the disputed border region between the countries. When Kuwait urgently pressed for a final resolution of border issues between the two countries—including drilling rights in the Rumailah oilfield that straddled the border—Baghdad demanded in return that Kuwait lease the islands of Warbah and Bubiyan to Iraq for use as offshore military bases. After rejecting this idea throughout the 1970s, Kuwait reluctantly did allow Iraqi forces to occupy the two islands at the height of the Iran-Iraq War of the 1980s, concerned by the prospect of an imminent Iranian victory in the conflict.

Charles was surprised by the apparent lack of concern among the deputies at the prospect of another Iraqi border incursion. A career official from the Pentagon's Office of International Security Affairs, she was coming to the end of a three-year assignment to the NSC staff at the White House. Charles was something of an expert on Kuwaiti issues. She had played a key role in planning Operation Earnest Will, the 1987 reflagging of Kuwaiti oil tankers by the U.S. Navy to protect them from attack during the final stages of the Iran-Iraq War. Even taking into account that it was a late Friday afternoon in July, the discussion in the DC had seemed overly casual, Charles thought, and had not resulted in the creation of a set of action items for preempting any further escalation of the crisis.

It was already early Friday evening when she arrived back at her office, but Charles did not want to leave before writing a quick summary of the DC meeting for her immediate bosses at the NSC, Brent Scowcroft and Richard Haass. "Analysts believe that a shallow incursion into the northern oilfield, Rumailah, cannot be ruled out," she wrote, "while drastic military action is also possible if less likely." Under the heading "Contingency Planning," Charles shared with Scowcroft and Haass her dissatisfaction with the DC meeting. "There was a disjointed discussion among the Deputies on this. We need to talk Monday about where we are heading."

•   •   •

That evening a minicrisis erupted between Baghdad and Washington over chemical weapons—Israel's chemical weapons.

In Tel Aviv, Israeli energy minister Yuval Ne'eman was asked by a reporter about Saddam Hussein's April statement threatening Israel with chemical weapons. "The answer," replied Ne'eman, "is to threaten him with the same goods. There is no doubt that there is no problem today preparing chemical weapons . . . and if there is such an enemy, he must be met with such a threat."

While Ne'eman did not explicitly say Israel possessed chemical weapons, and retracted his remarks the next day, the propaganda value of a statement like this from a member of the Israeli Cabinet was simply too good for Iraq to ignore. On the evening of July 28, Ambassador Glaspie was summoned to the Foreign Ministry by Hamdun to receive a demarche (an official note of protest) from the Iraqi government about Israel's likely possession of chemical weapons. Glaspie promised to raise the issue back in Washington, but pointed out that while Iraq and the United States were both signatories to the Chemical Weapons Convention, Israel was not and was therefore in a different position under international law.

The next day, July 29, Glaspie's deputy chief of mission, Joseph Wilson IV, was summoned back for another meeting with Hamdun, along with the Chiefs of Mission from Canada and the West European countries that had embassies in Iraq.

"The Government of Iraq does not approve of loose talk about weapons of mass destruction," Hamdun began primly. Wilson barely restrained himself from laughing at the chutzpah of this remark. Ne'eman's statement, Hamdun lectured, was the first confirmation by an Israeli official that Israel possessed weapons of mass destruction. It was this knowledge that had led President Saddam to announce in April that Iraq, too, possessed chemical weapons and would use them in retaliation against an Israeli attack.

Later that evening, Iraqi state television continued to reap the propaganda windfall from Ne'eman's remarks, devoting extensive coverage to the incident in prime time. American "silence" over the affair, an Iraqi government spokesman declared, was evidence of a "double standard" by the United States where chemical weapons were concerned. American policy, he editorialized, was to make Israel the dominant power in the region by "divesting the Arabs of the legitimate means of self-defense."

If there was a double standard in Washington where chemical weapons were concerned, however, Israel was not to be the beneficiary.

In contrast to the almost cavalier response that had greeted Saddam Hussein's frank admission to the visiting Senate delegation in April that Iraq had binary chemical weapons, the Bush administration's reaction to Ne'eman's far more ambiguous statement was prompt and unequivocal. Samuel Lewis, the U.S. ambassador to Israel, was instructed to request immediate clarification on the issue from Israeli defense minister Moshe Arens. The Bush administration had a powerful stick to hold over the Israelis, and now used it: continued Israeli participation (with nonvoting, "observer" status) in talks on the Chemical Weapons Convention (CWC). "When Israel expressed a desire to be an observer at the Geneva talks on the CWC, the United States expended a great deal of effort to enable Israel to be granted observer status," Lewis's talking points reminded Arens. If Israeli interest in participating in the CWC was genuine, the United States warned, Israel was encouraged "to declare whether you have chemical weapons and that you intend to destroy them."

"Your declaration will help us convince Arab states to sign the CWC," the talking points concluded.

•   •   •

For Saddam Hussein, the brief imbroglio over whether Israel had chemical weapons was an unexpected and welcome distraction, because by then he had already decided to invade Kuwait.

At the time his meeting with Ambassador Glaspie concluded on July 25, Saddam's brinksmanship with Kuwait had been hugely successful and appeared to have achieved all of his objectives. He had frightened the Kuwaitis back to the bargaining table. He had enlisted President Mubarak of Egypt and King Fahd of Saudi Arabia as advocates on his behalf. He had won prestige throughout the Arab world as a strong ruler who could not be intimidated by Israel or the United States, but could be dissuaded from waging war on brother Arabs. He had retained his WMD programs. He had convinced much of the political leadership in the United States that he was an intelligent man who wanted peace.

Most important, he had achieved the higher oil prices he wanted. The crisis that Saddam had instigated in the Gulf had led to a sharp rise in oil prices throughout the month of July. Then, at the OPEC meeting in Geneva on July 25, the cartel had acceded to Iraq's demands for a guaranteed minimum price per barrel.

But for Saddam, the decreased revenue flowing to Iraq's coffers as a result of low oil prices had been only part of the problem. The other part was a $40 billion debt from the Iran-Iraq War that was a threat not only to the pensions of Iraq's war widows, but to his very rule. Most of the debt was owed to Saudi Arabia and Kuwait, immensely wealthy Arab countries that Iraq had "protected" during the Iran-Iraq War. According to Saddam, Iraq had fought that costly war to protect the interests of these fellow Arabs against non-Arab Iran. Thus, the fair and proper solution to Iraq's economic difficulties lay in forgiveness of the debt—or its elimination through other means.

The Saudis could eventually be reasoned with, he believed. Awash in oil and desiring stability in the Gulf region above all else, liquidation of Iraq's debt on favorable terms would be a small price to pay for long-term peace. Besides which, the more conservative Saudis found this whole business of moneylending a bit distasteful, if for no other reason than charging interest to other Muslims is forbidden in the Holy Koran. Iraq's war debt was not even carried on Saudi Arabia's books.

The Kuwaitis were another matter. Of Iraq's $40 billion in war debt, $30 billion was owed to them, and they intended to collect every penny.

Shortly after her meeting with Saddam on July 25, Glaspie heard a disturbing rumor from a colleague in another Western embassy. Two separate, highly placed Saudi sources had told Glaspie's friend that the Kuwaiti government had recently tried to collect a $2 billion debt note from Iraq and had given Saddam Hussein a deadline of July 31 to remit payment. In the context of escalating tensions between the two countries, it was a foolish and dangerous act by the Kuwaiti government. "This surprising story, should it prove true, would shed considerable light on the Iraqi conclusion that Kuwait is not as sympathetic to Iraqi financial straits as it should be," Glaspie reported back to Washington.

On July 29 the ambassador sent one of her last cables from Baghdad. She offered two suggestions directly to James Baker and President Bush. The first was that the U.S. government should hold off on deciding to impose any new coercive sanctions against Iraq while the negotiations mediated by King Fahd of Saudi Arabia and President Mubarak of Egypt were taking place. "If those decisions were announced in the next few days," Glaspie wrote, "Iraqis would believe that they are politically inspired and will take them as part of President Bush's response to Saddam, a response equivalent to thumbing our nose at him and doing it in public. This would be likely to complicate the efforts of Fahd and Mubarak."

The second suggestion had to do with the long-running border dispute between Iraq and Kuwait.

"We have defined our national interest in these circumstances as the maintenance of stability," Glaspie advised Washington. "We want the oil to flow without hindrance, but we have never taken substantive positions on intra-OPEC or Arab border disputes. If we maintain our tactic of relying on Arab diplomacy, and I agree this is our best bet, we will have to swallow our distaste at the Iraqi protection racket." By this, Glaspie meant that the United States might need to be willing to accommodate an Iraqi seizure of the Rumailah oilfield or other disputed territory along the border.

"Saddam and the Iraqis, all of them, believe they have provided protection to the neighborhood," Glaspie explained. "If the Kuwaitis will not give Iraq the cash Saddam insists he needs (and he will accept indirect donations, e.g., through some fund device), Kuwait will be faced with consequences."

Just so there was no confusion in Washington over what "consequences" meant, Glaspie elaborated: "Even if we were to change radically our policy, for example, by adopting the Kuwaiti legal position on the border, Iraq could occupy the narrow strip which Iraqis insist is theirs, and on which there are new Kuwaiti wells and farms, within the space of an hour or so."

. . .

By Monday morning, July 30, many individuals throughout the U.S. government believed that some form of Iraqi military action against Kuwait was imminent. But the one person whose opinion mattered most remained unconvinced.

President Bush had been watching the escalation of tensions in the

Gulf with growing concern. He had been relieved by Glaspie's report on her July 25 meeting with Saddam Hussein, and even more so by the pricing concessions made to Iraq at the OPEC meeting in Geneva. Saddam himself had sent Bush a conciliatory message. On July 28 the president had responded with a personal letter to Saddam, suggesting that Iraq refrain from taking any provocative actions while Arab diplomacy was at such a critical phase.

But the military buildup on the Kuwait border continued inexorably. Each day Bush's morning intelligence briefing contained more and more details that seemed to point to an Iraqi attack on Kuwait.

If ever there was a president prepared to handle the intelligence-related responsibilities of his office, it was George Bush. The only member of the intelligence community ever elected to the White House, Bush had served as CIA director under President Gerald Ford. He could digest the material in the President's Daily Brief from the unique perspective of someone who had read hundreds of intelligence reports during his time at the Agency, and who had himself briefed a sitting president. Better than any other president, George Bush understood how the *business* of intelligence worked: how the raw material of information from human, satellite, and electronic sources needed to be parsed and analyzed before it could yield actionable estimates.

Precisely because of this background, though, Bush had become something of a skeptic about intelligence. In his experience, the U.S. intelligence community was superb at gathering information on what was happening, but less effective at providing American leaders with the type of intelligence they wanted most: accurate predictions of what a potential adversary would do next. Bush himself once reflected on the lessons he had taken away from his experience at the Agency: "At CIA, I learned firsthand what intelligence can and cannot do. Intelligence will always find it difficult to predict the 'intentions' of leaders, whereas intelligence can accurately show a POTUS [President of the United States] what forces are arrayed, show how and when they have moved." For that reason, he would later admit privately, "While some blame CIA for a failure of intelligence for failing to predict Iraq's invasion of Kuwait, I do not; not at all."

Because of his skepticism about the U.S. intelligence community's ability to divine Saddam Hussein's intentions, Bush turned instead to another source for insights during the final week of July 1990. He began to work the phones.

While George Bush may have had reservations about the value of intelligence in many areas, he had an almost unreserved confidence in the value of information provided by foreign leaders whom he trusted. The president cherished his friendships with his counterparts in other countries and thought of them in that way: as friendships. He invested an unusual amount of time on the telephone discussing foreign policy matters with other heads of state. It was one of Bush's favorite parts of his job, and he was extraordinarily good at it. All presidents spend hours speaking on the phone with foreign leaders; but few other presidents had already established so many personal relationships with so many world leaders before being elected to the White House as had George Bush. Many within the president's inner circle were frequently awestruck by his ability to resolve seemingly intractable issues through a few minutes of warm conversation with one of his old friends. He could tirelessly call leader after leader in succession, leaving each with the impression that their conversation had been the high point of the president's day.

Naturally, then, as tensions worsened between Iraq and Kuwait during the final two weeks of July, Bush was in frequent contact with the three most important pro-Western leaders in the Middle East: President Hosni Mubarak of Egypt, King Fahd of Saudi Arabia, and King Hussein of Jordan. Mubarak had been especially reassuring. The swaggering Egyptian president had taken an active role in mediating the dispute and was adamant on the need for an "Arab solution" to the crisis. He had put his own credibility on the line to arrange direct negotiations between Iraq and Kuwait in Jeddah, to be followed by a summit meeting between the Kuwaiti crown prince and Saddam Hussein himself in Baghdad.

But even as Iraqi and Kuwaiti envoys were meeting in Jeddah, intelligence reached the White House that the Republican Guard divisions on the Kuwaiti border were fanning out into attack formations and moving their field artillery into firing positions. Bush anxiously sent a message to his old friend King Hussein, asking him to call the White House with an update from Jeddah.

No other Arab leader inspired greater trust at the White House than

King Hussein. A perennial favorite of American presidents, on account of his generally moderate views and British-instilled courtesy, the king had known Bush for nearly twenty years. Off the world stage, the Jordanian monarch and his glamorous American-born wife Queen Noor were close socially with George and Barbara Bush. The king would be the last Arab head of state with whom Bush would speak before the Iraqi invasion.

The president took Hussein's call in the Oval Office at 9:47 A.M. on the morning of July 31. Bush admitted that he had been "very anxious to get this call" from the king and pressed him about Iraq's intentions.

"On the Iraqi side, they send their best regards and highest esteem to you, sir," Hussein replied unctuously. "They are a bit angry about the situation, but I believe that hopefully something will be worked out."

"Without any fighting?" Bush asked pointedly.

Hussein immediately sought to reassure the president on this score. "Oh yes, sir, that will be the case," he replied. The king then offered his own analysis of the situation.

"If you permit, sir, some thoughts on the future as they see it. They have been through a war of eight years, a terrible experience for the country. They need to repair, and for that, stable oil prices are necessary.

"Iraq feels the need for a broader plan for the area, in which a way can be found to help out those nations that are less fortunate." Hussein's enthusiasm about this idea was not feigned. As both men knew, wealth redistribution in the Middle East would also benefit Jordan, one of the poorer countries in the region.

Reassured by his conversation with the usually reliable Hussein, Bush asked the king's permission to issue a press release on the call, which was granted. The president was confident now that an Iraqi attack on Kuwait had been averted. So confident, in fact, that he instructed his NSC staff to begin preparing talking points for a telephone conversation with the next world leader on his call list: Saddam Hussein.

Sandra Charles, who had been the notetaker on the call with the king, quickly drafted a half page of bulleted points and forwarded them to Scowcroft and the president for review.

"I appreciate the recent exchange of messages we have had, and your comments to our ambassador that you intend to refrain from the use of military force to resolve your current dispute with Kuwait," Bush intended to tell Saddam. "King Fahd, President Mubarak, and King Hussein also have reported to me on the talks they have had with you, and I have been encouraged by what they have said." Ironically, the conversation was to have concluded with a suggestion from Bush to Saddam that "it would send a positive signal that Iraq intends to resolve this matter peacefully if you were to draw down some of your forces from the area."

The unused talking points were dated August 1, the day of the invasion.

3

"WE ARE DEALING WITH A MADMAN WHO HAS SHOWN HE WILL KILL"

Iraq invaded Kuwait in the predawn hours of August 1, 1990. Three of Saddam Hussein's elite Republican Guard divisions spearheaded the assault. The Republican Guard brushed aside the tiny Kuwaiti security force along the border and drove methodically down the modern four-lane highway that ran north-to-south in Kuwait. By midday there were over one hundred thousand Iraqi troops inside Kuwait.

One Republican Guard division entered the Kuwaiti capital, Kuwait City. American personnel stationed at the U.S. embassy in the capital took to the roof of the embassy building, where they were able to provide Washington with a running account of the invasion in progress. Simultaneous with the ground assault, Iraqi special forces troops staged daring commando raids by helicopter inside Kuwait City itself. Their first target, perhaps not surprisingly, was Kuwait's central bank and national mint. There, the Iraqis laid hands on the prize: $4 billion in gold and currency reserves. It was later learned that Saddam Hussein was disappointed at the news; he had been expecting much more. Other Iraqi commandos landed on the grounds of the emir's palace, where they encountered the only spirited Kuwaiti resistance. The Kuwaiti defenders were heavily outnumbered, however, and overwhelmed within a few hours. The emir himself, along with most of the royal family, fled the country within the first hour of the invasion.

The other two Republican Guard divisions bypassed the capital and continued advancing southward, toward the Saudi border seventy miles south of Kuwait City. The mission of these troops appears to have been twofold: to prevent Kuwaiti residents from escaping with their valuables by crossing the border into Saudi Arabia; and to deter any possible attempt, however unlikely, by Saudi Arabia and the other Gulf states to come to the aid of Kuwait. Such an attempt would have been unlikely in the extreme. The only Saudi troops anywhere near the theater of combat were a small border patrol force of the Saudi Arabian National Guard (SANG). Heavily outnumbered and equipped only with light armored vehicles, the approximately ten thousand SANG troops would have been no match for the Republican Guard divisions, powerful armored formations equipped with hundreds of late-model Soviet tanks.

By the time CNN began broadcasting the first live images of the invasion to the American public, Iraqi forces had achieved most of their objectives and were "mopping up" small pockets of resistance. Overall it had been a bold, efficient, and rapid operation by Iraq. "They have conducted a highly professional operation," Colin Powell would say at the first NSC meeting on the crisis on August 2, when the details had become clear. It was a soldier's compliment to the technical proficiency of the Iraqi army, if not to their motives.

The invasion's success was primarily due to the strategic surprise achieved by Iraq. Despite months of threatening rhetoric directed against Kuwait, and the fact that the deployment of two hundred thousand Iraqi troops along the Kuwaiti border had been taking place for weeks and had been impossible to hide from the rest of the world, Saddam Hussein had managed to achieve a fait accompli. His troops had faced only token resistance inside Kuwait. The Kuwaitis had no allies ready to spring to their defense. There was no force in the Persian Gulf capable of stopping, or even delaying, the Republican Guard.

· · · ·

It was a testimony to just how completely the Kuwaitis had been taken by surprise that no one could find the Kuwaiti ambassador to the United Nations.

In New York, Thomas Pickering, the U.S. permanent representative to the UN, had been notified personally about the invasion by President Bush late in the evening of August 1. Pickering's first thought was to notify the Kuwaiti ambassador. After calling the envoy's office and home numbers to no avail, he finally learned from a colleague that the Kuwaiti was having dinner with the UN ambassador from Bahrain. When Pickering dialed the Bahraini residence, the phone was answered by the Bahraini ambassador's precocious ten-year-old daughter.

"He is not available at the moment," she replied crisply when Pickering asked if he could speak to her father. Patiently, Pickering asked if she knew where her father was. The young woman reflected for a moment.

"You might try the Russian Tea Room," she suggested, a little less certainly. Though Pickering wanted to laugh at the absurdity of having to rely on help from a ten-year-old to find the Kuwaiti ambassador at this moment of crisis, he made sure to thank her with all due diplomatic courtesy.

At the Russian Tea Room, a famous Manhattan restaurant popular with well-heeled members of the UN diplomatic corps, Pickering finally tracked down the two ambassadors enjoying a late supper together. He was surprised that neither had heard about the invasion from their respective governments, and even more surprised that the Kuwaiti had not even considered invasion to be a possibility. "The Kuwaiti ambassador said that night was the shock of his life," Pickering recalled later.

Pickering knew that his night was only beginning. A tall, balding man with piercing blue eyes, he had already been ambassador to four different countries before being selected for the UN mission. Shortly after the 1988 election, President-elect Bush had tracked Pickering down while the diplomat and his wife were on a camping trip in a remote part of Egypt with another couple. Over a scratchy satellite phone connection, Bush had asked Pickering to take the UN job, but informed him that the UN ambassador would not have a seat in his Cabinet because Bush wanted a "real professional" in the post, not a political appointee. Pickering accepted the implied compliment without comment and took the job. He knew that having served as UN ambassador himself during the early 1970s, George Bush was deeply attached to the United Nations. Even without Cabinet rank, President Bush's UN envoy would be a major player in his administration, and the UN would figure prominently in Bush's handling of any major international crisis.

Like now, Pickering thought to himself. Here was an ideal moment to showcase the effectiveness of the United Nations, provided only that the world's sole surviving superpower made an early commitment to marry the moral authority of the UN to the military strength of the United States. Pickering intended to do his best to bring about such a marriage. The UN Security Council had been called into emergency session to draft a resolution condemning the invasion. All through the early morning hours of August 2, Pickering worked the phones and the corridors of the UN headquarters building in New York, pigeonholing as many delegates as he could find to get a sense of where UN opinion on the invasion was. He was mildly surprised by the broad-based anger against Iraq among the countries with whom he spoke. Ordinarily, Pickering could almost predict where a UN member state would vote on an issue just by knowing whether or not that state had good relations with the United States—but not this time. Even countries normally hostile to American interests in other areas were expressing outrage over the invasion.

Shortly after 6:00 A.M., a weary but triumphant Pickering called the White House. By a vote of 14-0 (Yemen abstaining), the Security Council had passed Resolution 660, calling for the immediate withdrawal of Iraqi troops from Kuwait and a peaceful settlement of the crisis. After he reported the good news to Brent Scowcroft—the two men had known each other for years, having both worked for Henry Kissinger at one time—Scowcroft asked if Pickering could attend the 8:00 A.M. meeting of the National Security Council in Washington. Pickering glanced at his watch and ran to make his flight.

•   •   •

Unfortunately, President Bush's first public comments on the invasion, as he conversed with reporters for a few minutes before the NSC meeting began, created the perception of a temporizing administration. In response to a pointed question from Helen Thomas of UPI, the doyenne of the White House press corps, Bush declared: "We're not discussing intervention. I would not discuss any military options even if we agreed upon them. One of the things I want to do at this meeting is hear from our Secretary of Defense, our Chairman, and others. But I'm not contemplating such action."

The meeting, which began once the reporters had been shooed out, was a disappointment to many in the room. Compared to the intense all-night session at the Security Council from which he had just come, Pickering found the discussion in the White House Cabinet Room oddly lacking in passion. Where was the outrage on behalf of Kuwait? "There was a tendency on the part of the military at that meeting, and a tendency on the part of the meeting itself, to take the view that our only requirement was to defend Saudi Arabia," he complained later. Brent Scowcroft would later give voice to similar complaints in his joint memoirs with President Bush: "I was frankly appalled at the undertone of the discussion, which suggested resignation to the invasion and even adaptation to a *fait accompli*. There was a huge gap between those who saw what was happening as the major crisis of our time, and those who treated it as the crisis *du jour*." Further hamstringing debate was the absence of Secretary of State Baker, who was on a visit to the Soviet Union and Mongolia.

Several participants tried to rally the room, to no avail. In characteristically blunt language, Deputy Secretary of State Lawrence Eagleburger, who was sitting in for Baker, urged the president, "You must kick Saddam out of Kuwait and wreck him in the process."

Toward the end of the meeting, Pickering also raised his concerns directly with Bush. "Mr. President, I don't think your policy is sustainable if you're willing to sit by and allow Kuwait to be gobbled up by Iraq without pushing back," he said. "I think that is a losing policy."

The meeting adjourned at 9:00 A.M. with no clear consensus on what U.S. policy would be. Bush, Scowcroft, and John Sununu departed the White House for Andrews Air Force Base, where Air Force One would fly them to an event at the Aspen Institute, a foreign policy think tank in Colorado. The president would have an opportunity to confer there with British prime minister Margaret Thatcher, who was also at Aspen.

Undersecretary of Defense Paul Wolfowitz stayed behind for a few minutes, literally stunned into silence by the lack of consensus he had just witnessed in the meeting. Years earlier, he and his then Pentagon colleague Dennis Ross had foreseen this very sort of crisis erupting with Iraq and had written a contingency plan on how the United States should respond. Now, it was not clear just what the U.S. response would be. "I was dismayed," Wolfowitz remembers. "I left that meeting deeply disturbed."

•   •   •

On one point, though, there was surprising and almost unanimous consensus among the Bush administration's top officials: Had Saddam Hussein limited his invasion of Kuwait to seizing only the Rumailah oilfield and other disputed territory from Kuwait, there would have been no American military response.

In the days leading up to the invasion, many within the American national security community had correctly warned that Iraq was going to attack Kuwait, but they got both the size and the goal of the attack wrong. The consensus was that the most likely scenario was Iraqi occupation of the Contested Zone, which extended approximately twenty miles into Kuwaiti territory and included the Rumailah oilfield, the islands of Warbah and Bubiyan offshore, and other land claimed by both countries.

There was much to support this conclusion. An Iraqi invasion limited only to the Contested Zone would have offered Saddam many advantages, at minimal risk to either Iraq or himself. It was by far his most rational strategy. Iraq would have gained exclusive possession of the Rumailah oilfield, the most productive in southern Iraq and one whose potential was still largely untapped. Iraq's oil reserves, and thus its influence within OPEC (and over future OPEC oil prices), would have been greatly enhanced. Likewise, Iraqi occupation of the two offshore islands would have improved access to Umm Qasr, landlocked Iraq's only deepwater port. Kuwait, conversely, would have seen its revenue and influence within OPEC weakened from the loss of the Rumailah production. Its already tiny land area further truncated by the loss of the islands and other territory in the Contested Zone, the country would have become a de facto satellite of Iraq.

Iraq's prestige in its immediate "neighborhood" would have soared to new heights. A successful military action, even on as grubby a scale as a land grab for a dozen miles of Kuwaiti territory, would have confirmed the country's status as the military superpower of the Persian Gulf region. Saddam's ability to cajole and intimidate the other Gulf nations into doing his bidding would have increased commensurately. Few in the region would have spared much sympathy for the Kuwaitis, who were widely perceived by other Arabs as crass and greedy, deserving of a comeuppance.

Most important to Saddam Hussein, a quick, successful action against Kuwait would have increased Saddam's stature in the eyes of his own people and his own military. It would have cemented his position as a strong, decisive leader who acted boldly against Iraq's external enemies. Ordinary Iraqis genuinely despised the Kuwaitis. April Glaspie, who had spent much of her life in the Arab world, including Kuwait, had been taken aback by the widespread resentment against Kuwaitis when she first arrived in Baghdad. "It is difficult to overstate the depth of anti-Kuwait sentiment in Iraq," she had written in one report back to Washington. "Even the most sophisticated Iraqis become Neanderthal on the issue of Kuwaitis." Finally, a quick, successful military operation would also have been a tonic for the morale of Iraq's army, which was still recovering from the Iran-Iraq War.

And though Saddam did not know it, all of this could have been achieved without a military response by the United States. Recalling his conversations with Bush and Scowcroft during the first hours after the invasion, White House chief of staff John Sununu maintains that it was Saddam Hussein's unexpected attempt to wipe an entire nation off the map rather than just seize some of its territory that elevated the perceived stakes of the crisis in the eyes of the president and his national security adviser. "He overreached," Sununu says of Saddam's action. "That was an overreach. I think if he had gone into the Contested Zone, and somehow said that he was willing to abide by a redrawing of the Contested Zone and stuff like that, he might have gotten away with it."

Robert Gates, George Bush's deputy national security adviser and later his CIA director, is even more categorical on the point: "Rewinding the clock on history, we all agreed that if he had simply occupied the Rumailah oilfields, we would have never moved. We would not have taken military action against Saddam if he had occupied just a piece of Kuwait. It was the occupation of the entire country that did it."

Gates's NSC colleague at the time, Sandra Charles, concurs with this view. "Nobody anticipated a wholesale invasion of Kuwait; maybe occupation of the oilfield or of the islands. If he had sent 5,000 troops to occupy something, it would have been a very heavy emphasis on just diplomacy alone."

Indeed, the conventional wisdom among many seasoned diplomatic hands in the hours immediately following the invasion was that Saddam had attacked Kuwait merely as a negotiating ploy, and would pull back after seizing Rumailah and the two islands as a trophy. Soviet foreign minister Eduard Shevardnadze's reaction to news of the invasion was representative of that among longtime Saddam-watchers. "I know he's a thug, but I never thought he was irrational," Shevardnadze told his American counterpart, James Baker. "It would be more like him to go in and then withdraw."

●   ●   ●

As compelling as the arguments for doing so may have been, Saddam Hussein could not afford to content himself with just a piece of Kuwait. The threat to him was the existence of any sovereign Kuwaiti government with a $30 billion debt claim on Iraq. Only elimination of the al-Sabah regime and annexation of Kuwait as Iraq's "nineteenth province" could remove the threat. Besides which, there was plunder on a fabulous scale to be had in Kuwait: billions of dollars in cash and gold bullion in the vaults of Kuwaiti banks; billions of dollars in gold jewelry and precious gems in the lavish souk of Kuwait City. It was more than enough to tempt the Thief of Baghdad.

Here, however, Saddam Hussein made a blunder that had a decisive impact on the Bush administration's subsequent handling of the Gulf Crisis. With his conquest of Kuwait complete, Saddam ordered the main body of his army in Kuwait to continue moving south, to seal the border between Kuwait and Saudi Arabia. They would also be perfectly positioned there to deter any possible counterattack by the Saudis or Kuwait's other friends in the region.

But the Bush administration interpreted the menacing southward advance of Iraq's elite shock troops as a direct threat to Saudi Arabia, and above all to the oilfields in Saudi Arabia's Eastern Province. The greatest oil production area on the planet was centered around the Eastern

Province city of Dhahran, just sixty miles south of the Kuwaiti border. For George Bush and his advisers, the consequences of Iraq gaining control over Saudi Arabia's oil reserves, whether by seizure or threat of seizure, were simply too horrible to contemplate. More was suddenly at stake than just a few dozen contested square miles.

After the Shah of Iran, America's closest ally in the Persian Gulf for decades, was deposed from power in 1979—putting an end to what Henry Kissinger had termed the "Twin Pillars" strategy—U.S. interests in the region had increasingly come to rest on a single, manifestly vulnerable pillar: the House of Saud.* That same year the Soviet Union invaded Afghanistan, a severe blow to American prestige in the Middle East and one that brought Soviet troops closer to the Persian Gulf than at any time in Russia's long history of attempting to acquire greater influence in the region. The two events in tandem led to an oil shock, which in turn triggered a painful three-year recession that became the worst economic downturn in the United States since the Great Depression.

In recognition of the growing threat posed to Saudi Arabia and the Gulf region by these developments, the Carter administration had announced a new regional security doctrine centered on upholding the security of the Gulf states and their irreplaceable oil reserves. In his January 1980 State of the Union address President Carter himself framed the core principle of the doctrine that would come to bear his name: "Any attempt by any outside force to gain control of the Persian Gulf region will be regarded as an assault on the vital interests of the United States of America and such an assault will be repelled by any means necessary, including military force."

The Carter Doctrine had represented a bold departure for U.S. foreign policy, which heretofore had defined only Europe and East Asia as regions where truly vital American national interests were at stake. However, it merely institutionalized an American commitment to the Persian Gulf that had already been developing over the course of decades. The

---

* Under the Twin Pillars strategy, the United States empowered two oil-rich, staunchly anticommunist allies—Iran and Saudi Arabia—to act as American proxies in the Persian Gulf. The strategy was intended to reduce the need for a major U.S. military commitment to defend the region's oil supplies.

Carter Doctrine was an explicit admission that Western dependence on Persian Gulf oil now made the region too important for the United States to ignore, or to fall into hostile hands.

With the Reagan administration's rise to power in 1981, the Carter Doctrine hardly fell by the wayside. Indeed, it was during the Reagan years that the United States developed the military "teeth" necessary to enforce the doctrine. The Carter-era idea of an American "Rapid Deployment Force" ready to deploy to the Persian Gulf at a moment's notice evolved into the U.S. Central Command, a full-fledged operational command with its own commander in chief and access to potentially vast reserves of troops and equipment. American power had been projected to the Gulf on a more routine basis through a standing U.S. naval force in the Gulf. These developments were accompanied, indeed mandated, by growing threats to the region's security throughout the 1980s: escalation of the Iran-Iraq War to include attacks on oil tankers in the Gulf's sea-lanes; a sharp rise in terrorist attacks sponsored by the revolutionary regime in Tehran; and alarming attempts by both Iran and Iraq to acquire weapons of mass destruction. The Reagan years also witnessed the first actual military action conducted by U.S. forces under the auspices of the doctrine, Operation Earnest Will, the 1987 reflagging of Kuwaiti tankers by U.S. naval forces.

Perhaps the single most important influence of the Reagan administration on the evolution of the Carter Doctrine, however, was a gradual blurring of the distinctions between the security of the Persian Gulf region and the security of Saudi Arabia proper. With Iran an antagonist, Iraq fighting for its very survival against the Khomeini regime, and the various emirates of the Persian Gulf far too small to matter, only Saudi Arabia—with its vast oil reserves, dominant position within OPEC, and moral authority as the home of Islam—appeared capable of preserving the existing Gulf order. Not insignificantly, the Saudis also had an indispensable role to play as the producer of last resort in moderating the price of oil on world markets, a function they had served on numerous occasions.

Consequently, the Reagan administration had pursued as a core principle of its Middle East foreign policy a significant increase in the degree of U.S. security cooperation with Saudi Arabia. The most tangible indication of the Reagan White House's commitment to closer security ties with the Saudis was its politically contentious sale of AWACS aircraft and other advanced weaponry to the kingdom, a radical departure from previous U.S. policy. For better or for worse, by the end of the Reagan years a Twin Pillars strategy had become a single pillar strategy, and the Carter Doctrine had evolved into a special relationship between the United States and the kingdom of Saudi Arabia.

If anything, George Bush, the former West Texas oilman, accepted the notion that maintaining access to Saudi oil reserves was a vital U.S. national interest even more intuitively than his two predecessors in the Oval Office had. During the Reagan years, Bush had functioned as the Reagan administration's de facto "oil minister," since Ronald Reagan possessed little background or interest in energy policy. In this capacity, Bush had actually visited Dhahran only four years earlier, in 1986, where he had toured the oil facilities located in the Eastern Province and been the guest of honor at a banquet hosted by King Fahd.

Virtually all of the Bush administration's leading figures—including Brent Scowcroft, Dick Cheney, James Baker, and the president himself—had occupied key positions in the Nixon, Ford, and Reagan administrations and had grappled firsthand with the painful aftereffects of the 1973 OPEC oil embargo and the 1979 oil shock. They had lived in an era when Richard Nixon and Henry Kissinger had spent hours at a time speculating on how an increase in the price of a barrel of oil might impact world events. All of them had sat through similar conversations. Needless to say, of course, the Bush principals were also aware that any reprise of the 1973 or 1979 recessions would be a political catastrophe for the president at home: reason enough for any White House to be concerned about the prospect of an Iraqi stranglehold over Persian Gulf oil reserves.

Besides the potential impact on the American and world economies, there was another consideration of unique importance to the Bush administration. At a moment when the United States had an indispensable role to play in bringing about a peaceful transformation in Eastern Europe after the collapse of communism, a 1970s-style oil shock could plunge the United States into a deep recession and rule out an activist

American role in managing the end of the Cold War. This prospect was anathema to the president and his inner circle, who attached supreme importance to the epochal events taking place in Eastern Europe. An Iraqi-instigated oil crisis raised the specter of a "Prague winter": a season of discontent in the disintegrating Soviet Union and nascent democracies of Eastern Europe, which would leave millions of cold, hungry, and desperate citizens with little incentive to undertake fundamental reform of their political and economic systems. This concern also applied to the oil-dependent nations of Western Europe and above all to West Germany, which would have a major part in underwriting the social and economic costs of peaceful reunification with the former East Germany.

·　　·　　·

Iraq's wholesale invasion of Kuwait, coupled with the ominous move south of the Republican Guard toward the Saudi border, greatly sharpened the perception of a threat to Saudi Arabia. By the morning of August 3, when the second NSC meeting on the invasion took place, President Bush's attitude toward Iraq had crystallized and hardened. In contrast to the previous day's meeting, when the president had sat back in his chair for much of the session and listened impassively to the discussion taking place around him, the George Bush of August 3 was hyperactive with intensity.

"It's been a remarkable twenty-four hours," the president declared. Recapping his previous day of consultations with Thatcher, Bush said, "It's fortunate Mrs. Thatcher is at Aspen. I am glad we're seeing eye-to-eye. Important that she plans. She shared her views 100 percent with me. Many governments are prepared to take political and economic action. I am pleased with the Soviet stand." The previous day in Moscow, Secretary of State Baker had read a historic joint declaration condemning the invasion with Soviet foreign minister Eduard Shevardnadze.

The president was less pleased by the initial reaction of the Middle Eastern leaders with whom he had spoken. "King Fahd, King Hussein, Mubarak, and [Yemeni president] Saleh and I talked at length. They expressed great concern and some other disquieting factors. Their reaction was hand-wringing," the president said dismissively. "King Fahd's reaction was the strongest, and he was the most concerned for obvious reasons."

For the first time since the crisis had begun, Bush explicitly raised the prospect that the United States might need to take military action to reverse the invasion. "Diplomatic efforts are under way to get Saddam to back off. He is ruthless and powerful," Bush warned. "Others' efforts might not succeed to get his troops out, and Kuwait's ruler back in. We need to weigh the implications of taking this on directly." The president added softly, "The status quo is intolerable."

Next came a briefing on the latest intelligence by Director of Central Intelligence (DCI) William Webster, a square-jawed man who looked every inch the former federal judge that he was. In vintage Langley fashion, the CIA—having failed to predict the full extent of the actual invasion—had produced a suitably dire assessment of the invasion's consequences. Focusing primarily on the likely political scenarios that would result if Iraq consolidated its conquest of Kuwait, the CIA analysis concluded that Iraq would come to dominate OPEC politics, gradually supplanting the Saudis, and would seek to take a much more activist role in promoting the Palestinian cause. Webster ended his briefing with the bleak appraisal that some sort of accommodation with Iraq might be necessary. Like the president himself, the CIA was pessimistic about the ability of the Arab states in the region to manage the crisis on their own. "We don't expect the Arabs to confront Iraq," Webster concluded, "but instead to buy their way out."

Seeing this second NSC meeting begin like the previous day's, with more talk of accommodating Iraq, Scowcroft took control of the discussion.

"It would be useful to take a minute to look at our objectives. I detected a note in the end there that we may have to acquiesce to an accommodation of the situation," Scowcroft complained. "My personal judgment is that the stakes in this for the United States are such that to accommodate Iraq should not be a policy option. There is too much at stake. It is broadly viewed in the United States that a commitment to Kuwait is de facto based on our actions in the Gulf before." The national security adviser was referring to Operation Earnest Will, the 1987 reflagging of Kuwaiti tankers in the Gulf by the U.S. Navy. Scowcroft believed that Earnest Will had established an implicit precedent that the United States would guarantee the flow of Kuwaiti oil. Any failure to act now, Scowcroft believed, would be greatly damaging to American credibility in the region.

"Beyond that, the consequences of a successful move by Iraq are what else [Webster] said: that they would dominate OPEC politics, Palestinian politics and the PLO, and lead the Arab world to the detriment of the United States and the great stakes we have in the Middle East and Israel." Scowcroft ended his remarks by warning his colleagues, "It seems that while the alternatives are not attractive, we have to seriously look at the possibility that we can't tolerate him succeeding."

As it happens, Scowcroft's eruption was a planned one. Not willing to run the risk that a second NSC meeting would end without the White House arriving at a consensus on a U.S. response, a few minutes before the August 3 meeting began, he and the president had quietly agreed that Scowcroft would breathe a little fire into the discussion immediately after Webster had finished his briefing. Cheney and Eagleburger (a close friend of Scowcroft's for two decades, including a stint together at Kissinger Associates, Henry Kissinger's foreign policy consulting firm) had also been informed of the plan and had agreed to support Scowcroft's case.

Taking care to remind his colleagues that he was speaking for himself and not for Baker (in little over a year of serving as his deputy, Eagleburger had already learned that the secretary of state was a stickler about even senior aides stealing any of his thunder), Eagleburger endorsed Scowcroft's position.

"This is the first test of the post–Cold War system," Eagleburger said. Couching his views in terms familiar to the veteran Cold Warriors in the room, Eagleburger argued that without the constraint of the U.S.-Soviet rivalry, other ambitious Third World rulers might follow Saddam's example were he not stopped. "As the bipolar contest [between the United States and the Soviet Union] is relaxed, it permits this sort of thing, giving people more flexibility because they are not worried about the involvement of the superpowers." The Soviets were only a shadow of the superpower they had once been, Eagleburger continued. "Saddam

Hussein now has greater flexibility because the Soviets are tangled up in domestic issues. If he succeeds, others may try the same thing. It would be a bad lesson.

"On the oil issue, he would dominate OPEC over time. As to his intentions, Saudi Arabia looks like the next target. Over time he would control OPEC and oil prices. If he succeeds, then he would target Israel. This is what we could face unless he leaves the scene. We need to think of this as a very, very critical time."

Defense Secretary Cheney concurred. "The last day or so I have thought about the stakes and consequences of Iraq taking Kuwait," he said. "Initially, we should sort this out from our strategic interests in Saudi Arabia and oil. He has clearly done what he has to do to dominate OPEC, the Gulf, and the Arab world. He is forty kilometers from Saudi Arabia, and its oil production is only a couple of hundred kilometers away."

Cheney believed that even without invading Saudi Arabia, Saddam would be able to intimidate the Saudis militarily. "If he doesn't take it physically, with his new wealth he will still have an impact and will be able to acquire new weapons, including nuclear weapons. The problem will get worse, not better." The secretary of defense concluded by cautioning, "We should not underestimate the U.S. military forces we would need to be prepared for a major conflict."

Recognizing that this topic was political dynamite, Scowcroft quickly interjected, "This should be kept in this room. The press has already indicated an interest in this."

Sununu was concerned that Saddam would not stop at just Saudi Arabia. "I agree with Larry and Dick on production control. If he moves into Saudi Arabia, he would control 70 percent of Gulf oil. If he moves into the UAE [United Arab Emirates], then he would have 90 to 95 percent of the oil in the Gulf, or 70 percent of all of OPEC. It would be very easy for him to control the world's oil. This would be heady for Saddam."

Richard Darman, director of the Office of Management and Budget, shared Cheney's belief that even without Saudi Arabia, Saddam would control the world's oil supply.

"Even without that, he would be in control of world oil prices with Kuwait plus Iraq," Darman argued. "Even without a physical takeover [of

Saudi Arabia], he will do this if he is not undone." With his height and aquiline profile, the elegantly tailored Darman cut an imposing figure in any meeting. A former investment banker whose pronouncements on economic matters were rarely challenged, the outspoken Darman was sometimes described by his admirers as "the smartest man in Washington" (a characterization he went to no great pains to dispute).

Famously impatient with the pace of the White House bureaucracy, Darman thought the time for presidential action had long since passed. "We should introduce a bold statement of concerns and it must be linked with options," he declared.

"There is no question the reason we are here is to review our options now, and then go into what we can and what we can't do," Scowcroft said coolly. Darman's domineering manner of speech always grated on him.

Discussion shifted to what those options should be. Eagleburger gave a positive report on developments at the UN.

"I am encouraged on the diplomatic front," Bush interrupted. "What about Iran?"

Eagleburger replied, "According to the Kuwaiti ambassador here, Iran said to them, 'You tell us what you want, and we will do it.' Kuwait said, 'We want you to persuade Iraq to leave.' After some delay, Iran is now saying it will be supportive."

"On the Iranian border Iraq still has troops," Bush said meditatively.

"They have forces astride the Shatt," Powell corrected.*

"Can Iraq sustain a two-front war?" Bush wanted to know.

"There is no war in the south," Powell reminded him. Webster added that Iraq appeared to have pulled some of its forces out from along the border with Iran.

"What about Iran's capability?" Eagleburger asked.

"There is not much to sustain a confrontation," answered Powell.

Bush was not persuaded that the Iranian army was as decimated as the Pentagon believed. "It's been enough to hold Iraq at bay for two years," he pointed out.

---

* The Shatt al-Arab is the small body of water where the two great rivers of Iraq, the Tigris and the Euphrates, both empty into the Persian Gulf. It marked the traditional border between Iraq and Iran along the Gulf.

"What about on the other side, with Syria?" Scowcroft queried, picking up the president's theme. Like Bush, he was concerned by the possibility that one or more of Iraq's neighbors might capitalize on the fact that most of the Iraqi army was committed in Kuwait in order to seize territory from Iraq.

"Syria asked us to push the Arab states in twenty-four hours," Eagleburger replied, not hiding his amusement at the reflexively anti-American Syrian government asking the United States to take a tougher line on other Arabs. "There will be an Arab [summit] in Cairo. There is clear evidence Assad is nervous," he revealed, referring to Syria's longtime ruler, Hafez al-Assad. "It may be fertile ground in that they're thinking of the damage of action on the Iraqi-Syrian border." Assad knew that Iraqi Scud missiles targeted at Israel were based in the western desert of Iraq. He further knew that if Saddam fired missiles at Israel, the Israeli air force would likely fly through Syrian airspace to retaliate against Iraq.

"What about the summit?" Bush asked.

"It's a mini-summit with some of the Arab states, including Syria," Eagleburger explained.

Scowcroft raised his eyebrows. "The Arab summit might buy off Saddam?" He was concerned that Saudi Arabia and the other Gulf oil states would pay Saddam a huge bribe to leave Kuwait (though they would, of course, call it an "aid package").

Eagleburger backed off putting too much faith in that possibility. "Kuwait is not very popular in the Arab world. So it might be difficult."

"They want an 'Arab solution' to the question," Bush said sarcastically, returning again to his earlier conversations with his friends in the region. "Mubarak wanted forty-eight hours after the summit with King Fahd. There was hand-wringing, wanting us not to do anything. There was even more distance from Yemen. We'll figure it out. King Fahd was the exception. He was very firm. He equated Saddam to the most evil person; he was very unflattering."

With diplomatic developments having been discussed, conversation now turned to military options. Somewhat ruefully, Cheney noted that the most powerful American asset in the region, a naval battle group centered around the aircraft carrier USS *Independence*, was currently in the

Indian Ocean. The battle group had encountered a storm and would not be within striking distance of Iraq for another two days.

"We are concerned about the aircraft on the carrier," Cheney said. "In reality, where they will be located, there is not a lot you can do with naval aircraft," he admitted. "They can reach some targets, but they won't alter the military situation. The options require access to ground facilities."

Colin Powell elaborated: "Looking at force packages for a contingency, there are two: The first, to deter further Iraqi action with Saudi Arabia would require U.S. forces on the ground. This is the more prudent option. Saddam Hussein looks south and sees a U.S. presence. This would include an air package or U.S. troops to exercise to deter Iraq.

"The second would be to deploy U.S. forces against Iraqi forces in Kuwait to defend Saudi Arabia, or possibly go after Iraq." Having broached the topic of an American force on the ground in Saudi Arabia, Powell warned his colleagues about the more serious prospect of going after Iraq.

"This would be the NFL, not a scrimmage. It would mean a major confrontation. Most U.S. forces would have to be committed to sustained [operations], not just for one or two days. He is a professional and megalomaniac. But the ratio is weighted in Saddam's favor. They also are experienced from eight years of war."

Bush was less impressed with the fighting qualities of Iraq's army. "But why weren't they able to kick Iran?" he demanded to know.

"They tried and over time adapted, and came out okay in the end," Powell replied.

The president was still not convinced. "I am not certain he is invincible. They tried for five years, and could not get across a small part of land," Bush argued, referring to Iraq's failed attempts to capture the Fao Peninsula, a small tongue of land along the border between the countries, during the Iran-Iraq War.

"But Iran paid in manpower," Powell shot back. "The real solution must be long-term. It is an international and regional problem, so the whole world must realize this has got to be dealt with internationally."

The JCS chairman then raised a topic that, though he could not know it at the time, would later come to haunt him and many others in the room: whether or not to remove Saddam Hussein himself from power.

"One question is how individualized is this aggression?" Powell asked rhetorically. "If he is gone, would he have a more reasonable replacement?"

At this question, Scowcroft exchanged a frown with his NSC colleague Richard Haass, who had been intently following the debate. Both men were traditionalists where the Middle East was concerned, and found any talk of toppling Saddam Hussein's regime unsettling. For them, the unwritten law of power politics in the Middle East was that however unsavory or undemocratic the authoritarian regimes that held sway in the region were, one never seriously considered the possibility of toppling them, because the alternatives were invariably worse. The prime illustration of this tenet was of course Iran, where the fall of the Shah had led to a civil war that unleashed the most radical elements in Iranian society, to the detriment of the United States and virtually every country in the Middle East. Whatever his other failings, Saddam had managed to keep Iraq firmly under control and on a reasonably secular course for nearly two decades, and neither Scowcroft nor Haass wanted to see him brought down precipitously.

"Iraq could fall apart," the national security adviser warned.

Haass promptly seconded his boss's observation. "It's unlikely anyone else would have the same cult of personality" needed to hold the country together, he pointed out.

With most of the viable military options dependent on whether Saudi Arabia would allow American forces into the kingdom, this left economic sanctions as the main option available for coercing the Iraqis. Debate swirled around the idea of cutting off Iraq's two main oil pipelines, which ran through Saudi Arabia and Turkey. Scowcroft and Eagleburger both raised the possibility that Saddam would likely respond to any cutoff of Iraq's only source of foreign exchange by seizing American hostages in Kuwait and Iraq.

U.S. citizens abroad were the State Department's responsibility. Eagleburger consulted his notes. "There are thirty-eight hundred U.S. citizens in Kuwait," he estimated. "Five hundred are in Iraq. There are fourteen or fifteen citizens reported in Iraqi custody. Reports are that others are being held in hotels in Kuwait. Planning has been done, but an evacuation needs to be in a permissive environment.

"I have sent Hamdun a telegram on this, saying very forcefully that U.S. citizens must be protected and those in Kuwait should be allowed to leave," Eagleburger informed Bush. "We have called in Mashat [the Iraqi ambassador in Washington]. He made no promises. Saddam is a tough son of a bitch. He recognizes this asset."

At the mere mention of hostages, Bush was apoplectic.

"This would change the ball game," the president said, his voice growing louder. "We should tell Saddam this would be a new ball game, and give him our bottom line. Whatever resolve it takes, with or without our friends, we will do it," Bush stated, committing his administration to the rescue of any hostages that were not released. "It would be a very different equation." Recognizing the difficulty of mounting a major hostage rescue operation without logistical support from countries in the region, Bush looked apologetically at Colin Powell. "For the CINC [the commander in chief of U.S. Central Command, Gen. Norman Schwarzkopf] and the Chairman, it would make life more complicated."

But for Bush, the prospect of another hostage crisis involving Americans taking place on his watch was unthinkable.

"We need a bottom line. This clearly changes everything. The change is that U.S. deaths and hostages will not be tolerated."

The others in the room could have almost predicted his reaction.

George Bush enjoyed a distinction shared by no other president. Literally every stage of his long political career, dating back to the late 1960s, had been punctuated by a major international crisis in which Western citizens had been taken hostage by rogue states or terrorist groups. Bush's career before reaching the Oval Office had been impacted by no fewer than *six* such crises.

His brief sojourn in Congress had witnessed the 1968 *Pueblo* incident, in which North Korea seized the crew of the naval vessel USS *Pueblo* and held the men prisoner for nine months, extracting humiliating diplomatic concessions from the United States. The Johnson administration's handling of the incident had been one of the signature issues during Bush's failed 1970 run for the U.S. Senate.

Bush's period of service as UN ambassador in the early 1970s had been marred by one of the most heinous acts of hostage-taking ever perpetrated: the 1972 massacre of Israeli athletes by Palestinian terrorists at the Munich Olympics. The future president had made a formal speech on the floor of the world body communicating American outrage at this atrocity. Munich developed into a major headache for Bush throughout the remainder of his tenure at the UN. The incident provoked angry protests from virtually every major American Jewish organization, many of which were headquartered in New York and saw nearby UN headquarters as a hotbed of anti-Israel sentiment sympathetic to the Palestinian cause (which, in that era, it was). Bush's voluminous "Jewish files" at the UN documented the hours he had to spend responding to angry letters and editorials from Jewish organizations and hundreds of concerned private citizens about Munich.

During his time as the lead U.S. envoy to China, Bush had played a rarely chronicled role in the Ford administration's handling of the 1975 *Mayaguez* crisis, in which Cambodian forces seized the crew of an American-flagged merchant vessel, the *Mayaguez*. President Ford ordered a costly but successful military operation to rescue the hostages. Since the United States did not have diplomatic relations with Cambodia, Secretary of State Henry Kissinger used Bush as the Ford administration's back channel to the Cambodian government, since both countries had diplomatic missions in Beijing. It was Bush who conveyed President Ford's ultimatum to the Cambodians demanding release of the ship.

Forty American military personnel were killed in the operation to rescue thirty-nine *Mayaguez* crewmen, an irony often cited by critics of Ford's action. But Brent Scowcroft would later say that he and Bush, like most of the Ford team, viewed the U.S. response to the *Mayaguez* seizure as "the prototype of a successful operation."* Indeed, when President Jimmy Carter had the temerity to criticize Ford's handling of *Mayaguez* during his 1980 reelection campaign, he drew a shrill counterattack from Scowcroft in the op-ed pages of the *Washington Post* for his "cheap shot at the *Mayaguez* incident." Scowcroft derided Carter's perceived weakness in foreign policy by explicitly comparing the outcome of the

---

* The team that advised Ford during the *Mayaguez* crisis reads like a *Who's Who* of Republican luminaries who later held senior positions during the two Bush presidencies. Besides George H. W. Bush and Scowcroft (national security adviser to President Ford as well as to the first President Bush), it included Dick Cheney (White House chief of staff to Ford) and Donald Rumsfeld (then also secretary of defense).

Mayaguez rescue with the failed mission to rescue the hostages in Iran: "I hope that President Carter's action in dealing with that crisis will be viewed with more charity than he has seen fit to grant to President Ford. I myself am quite sanguine about the eventual verdict of history over the comparative handling of these two crises where U.S sovereignty and the freedom and safety of its citizens were under attack."

Bush's private "China Diary" recorded for posterity how the rescue of the *Mayaguez* hostages influenced the future president's own views about the desirability of using military force to resolve hostage crises. "This will help," Bush confided to his diary only hours after learning that the ship had been released. "It shows our spine. It shows our unwillingness to be pushed around."

As director of central intelligence during Ford's final year in the White House, Bush had become aware, ex officio, of the constant intelligence "chatter" warning of hostage threats to American civilians during the 1970s, a period rife with anti-American sentiment around the globe. While Bush was at CIA, the Ford White House had quietly ordered the Agency to provide intelligence support to the Israelis during their famous 1976 rescue of a hijacked airliner at Entebbe in Uganda. A number of the Israeli hostages had had family in the United States.

The 1980 election that brought Ronald Reagan and George Bush to power was dominated by the most notorious hostage crisis of all: the Iranian embassy hostage crisis, in which radical followers of Iran's Ayatollah Khomeini stormed the U.S. embassy in Tehran and held the American embassy staff hostage for 444 days. If Reagan and Bush shared one foreign policy conviction, it was that the Carter administration's handling of the crisis had greatly damaged American credibility in the eyes of the world. They also recognized the resonance of the issue for ordinary voters. In his campaign to become Ronald Reagan's vice president, "Iran" and "Desert One" (a reference to the abortive mission launched by President Carter to rescue the hostages) became for George Bush shorthand expressions that captured all of Carter's perceived shortcomings as a world leader. "Though I supported Jimmy Carter's rescue mission after he undertook it," Bush would later say privately, "I felt he had waited too long, and of course, the mission's failure was a tremendous embarrassment to the U.S.A."

Then, during his eight years as vice president, Bush had witnessed firsthand the enervating effects that the seizure of American hostages in Lebanon had on the Reagan administration's entire foreign policy. Bush's tangential involvement in the Iran-contra affair (which began as an attempt to swap arms to Iran for the release of the hostages) nearly derailed his long-cherished presidential ambitions. Bush was also affected by the Lebanon hostages' ordeal on a more personal level; Marine lieutenant colonel Rich Higgins, one of the hostages murdered in Lebanon, had served as his military aide.

The coincidence of a future U.S. president having direct personal involvement in so many hostage crises was in and of itself remarkable. More remarkable, though, was the cumulative effect of these crises on Bush's worldview. By the time he became president, George Bush harbored a near obsession about the dangers of hostage crises for any White House. Those who worked with him were well aware of his fixation on the topic. For an entire generation of Republican foreign policy figures, hostage-taking had become the very symbol of American and presidential weakness. But George Bush not only subscribed to this shared Republican belief; he was in many respects the avatar of the belief within his own administration.

The belief translated into a deep, almost personal sense of responsibility for Americans at risk of being taken hostage abroad. This was especially true of military and diplomatic personnel. Giving voice to this feeling in his own words, Bush once confided his own belief that "a president must go the extra mile to protect his military forces and to protect his diplomats who are often at risk as they serve in foreign lands."

Bush had already gone the extra mile once during his first year as president. In December 1989 he had ordered twenty-five thousand U.S. troops into Panama to topple the regime of Gen. Manuel Noriega, after Noriega's thuggish paramilitaries had killed an off-duty U.S. Marine and abducted an American naval officer and his wife. At the time it had been the largest American military intervention since the Vietnam War.

After the brief pause in the discussion that followed Bush's harangue on hostages, Eagleburger resumed. "Ambassador Glaspie is in London," he reported to the president. "The issue is whether to send her back to Iraq. It could send the wrong signal, but we could send her back with a strong message from you. I prefer we do that."

"Why don't you talk to Brent about that?" Bush suggested.

"That is highly relevant," Darman commented. "We should also consider actions to protect Saudi Arabia and the oilfields in the short term."

"That brings up the question of what if Iraqi troops keep going south," Eagleburger added, looking up at Cheney and Powell. As it happened, Cheney had received a briefing from the Defense Intelligence Agency on the threat to Saudi Arabia.

"The estimate today is that in seventy-two hours they could take the Eastern Province," he said.

By the time the oft-photographed NSC meeting at Camp David on August 4 took place, Bush's views on an appropriate U.S. response to the crisis had essentially solidified, even as the president listened attentively but noncommittally to a presentation of various Gulf policy options by General Norman Schwarzkopf and other U.S. military leaders. Ironically, the presidential statement that would later come to epitomize Bush's resolute stance against Iraqi aggression—his famous declaration on August 5, as he stepped off his helicopter from Camp David, that "this will not stand"—came not as a formal attempt at public diplomacy, but as a candid vocalization of the president's own assessment of the ultimate stakes in the Gulf crisis. Paul Wolfowitz underscores the importance of the president's public declaration in channeling the internal administration debate on the crisis.

"I think to an extraordinary degree the decision-making process was shaped by a very gutsy decision," Wolfowitz would later recall. "This shall not stand. There was a sense that analysis wouldn't matter. The president had said what we were going to do, so it wasn't a matter of weighing all the costs and benefits. The president decided to do it, and so a whole lot of things became simple."

· · ·

After an all-day Saturday NSC session at Camp David on August 4, the NSC meeting late on the afternoon of Sunday, August 5, was intended to have been a small group session to discuss possible covert actions that could be taken against Iraq. Only a dozen officials gathered in the Cabinet Room at the White House, including James Baker, who was attending his first NSC meeting since making a triumphant return from Moscow, joint declaration in hand. Dick Cheney had departed for Saudi Arabia earlier that day with a mini Deputies Committee in tow: Robert Gates, Paul Wolfowitz, Assistant Secretary of State Richard Clarke, and Gen. Norman Schwarzkopf. Their mission was to secure King Fahd's permission for a cordon of U.S. troops and aircraft to be deployed on Saudi soil.

However, new intelligence reports from the Persian Gulf momentarily put the topic of covert action on the back burner. Shortly after the meeting began at 5:00 P.M. on Sunday afternoon, the president announced, "The original reason for this meeting was to discuss covert options, but there are some other things now."

He then turned the meeting over to CIA Director Webster, who announced tersely that an Iraqi invasion of Saudi Arabia was likely to occur at any moment.

Thus far, the CIA had been badly bruised by the Gulf crisis. The Agency had failed to predict the invasion of Kuwait, and the most accurate estimates of Iraqi intentions and troop movements had been produced by DIA. Besides being shown up by its smaller sister agency in the intelligence community pecking order, what made the intelligence failure even more galling to many at Langley was that they had let down George Bush, the first "Agency man" ever elected president, and one still remembered fondly by many there.

There had been additional troop movements by the Iraqis overnight, and having been fooled once previously by Saddam, CIA was now taking no chances. Written in the Agency's somber institutional tone, and delivered in Webster's somber judicial tone, the August 5 estimate highlighted those pieces of data that supported the CIA claim that an invasion of Saudi Arabia could happen at any moment.

But Colin Powell and James Baker flatly disputed the CIA assessment. Both men had access to their own sources of intelligence: Powell could leverage the resources of the DIA, the Pentagon intelligence branch; while Baker could call on the State Department's Bureau of Intelligence and Research (INR), its own small but highly professional intelligence service.

Having reviewed the same raw data that formed the basis of the CIA estimate, Powell observed, "There is not factual disagreement between CIA and DIA, but DIA leans less forward in its assessment."

The CIA prediction of an immediate move against Saudi Arabia by Iraqi forces was based on incomplete data, the JCS chairman criticized. There were key clues that would need to be seen before any conclusion could be drawn that Iraq was poised to strike over the border.

Baker quickly concurred. "INR agrees with DIA about the key missing pieces of intelligence," the secretary said.

Warming to his theme, Powell the professional soldier elaborated on the shortcomings of the CIA estimate from a field commander's perspective. "We would need to see more missiles, logistics, and tanks to conclude an invasion is imminent," he explained to the others in the room.

Powell and Baker were right to question the CIA view. The Iraqis were not intending to invade Saudi Arabia. The next day a chastened Webster would admit to his colleagues at the August 6 NSC meeting that there were no further indications of an invasion, and that in fact Iraq's forces in Kuwait appeared to be hunkering down for a long occupation.

But by then the die had already been cast. The ominous intelligence assessment had hardened the resolve of President Bush to respond to Iraq's invasion of Kuwait with military force.

"My sense is that Iraq does not believe we will act. Saddam is riding an emotional high," Bush theorized, attempting as he often did to look at the situation from a foreign leader's perspective. To Bush, the antidote for the Iraqi ruler's euphoria was obvious.

"Maybe if he sees it is not business as usual he will change," the president concluded.

"Why not get someone to talk to Saddam?" asked Treasury Secretary Nicholas Brady, suggesting French president François Mitterrand as a possible envoy.

"What would he say?" Bush asked dubiously.

Brady replied that it would at least buy some time, but the suggestion drew quick objections from the three most powerful men in the room.

"We don't want to appear to be negotiating," cautioned Scowcroft.

"We could lose momentum with the Arabs," added Baker.

"Our solidarity would crumble if we are seen talking to Saddam," concluded Bush.

But when Baker, still riding his own emotional high from his triumph in Moscow, asked, "Should we ask the Soviets to weigh in?" he drew an equally quick rejoinder from Scowcroft.

"We don't want to ask the Soviets," the national security adviser cautioned. "It would send a bad signal."

Scowcroft was thinking not just about Saddam Hussein, but about what the rest of the world would think. He wanted the United States to project an image of complete self-sufficiency in protecting the Gulf, especially to the Soviets.

"This could slow things down," objected Sununu. He thought that the Soviets might be helpful in defusing the crisis. It was well known that Saddam had close ties to a number of senior officials in the Soviet Foreign Ministry, and they might be able to reason with him.

"I am not sure we want to slow things down," Scowcroft replied.

"This is a Catch-22," admitted the president, genuinely torn between the symbolic appeal of another historic gesture of U.S.-Soviet cooperation and what Scowcroft was saying. "If he slows down, our side will slow down as well."

Baker gracefully conceded the point to Scowcroft. "The only thing that will influence Saddam is our deterrent," he agreed.

Powell was still considering the possibility that Saddam might invade Saudi Arabia. "Even after he is in Saudi Arabia we could kick him out," the JCS chairman mused. That kind of thinking alarmed Scowcroft.

"We want to deter him from invading and protect Saudi Arabia," he reminded Powell, "so when we begin to clamp down economically, Saddam has no military option."

"I am interested in the ability of our F-16s to destroy his tanks," Bush interrupted impatiently. "Knocking them out would send a strong signal. Why was it so easy for Israel to clear out Syrian SAMs [surface-to-air missiles] in Lebanon?"

"They used drones," Vice President Dan Quayle explained to him.

"Can we do this?" Bush asked, intrigued.

"Yes," Powell replied confidently, "they were using U.S.-made equipment, and we can do it, too."

Baker returned to the topic of diplomacy. "On another question, the British propose we send our ambassadors back to Baghdad." This reminded Bush of another issue important to him.

"Didn't I hear something that our people in our embassies are being threatened?" the president countered. "Should we maybe pull out of Iraq rather than sending back our ambassador? Saddam is irrational."

"We have talked about a drawdown in Kuwait," Baker agreed. "Maybe we ought to consider doing the same in Iraq."

"These questions need more study," Bush encouraged. "I am concerned that if we put forces in Saudi Arabia, Saddam might grab our people."

"The problem goes beyond the embassies," Powell reminded them. "We are talking about thousands of Americans."

"We are dealing with a madman who has shown he will kill," the president agreed gravely.

Sununu asked if there was any plan for protecting the embassy in Baghdad. Powell shook his head. "No. There is no 'Desert One' solution."

"If they move against our people," Bush observed, rising from his chair as the meeting adjourned, "it would be so overt that it would rally everyone."

·　　·　　·

Presidents are people, too. Like many people, George Bush had become lifelong best friends with two very different individuals, each of whom reflected very different aspects of his personality. Because for Bush the personal was inevitably political, these two friends now occupied senior positions in his inner circle and were each destined to play critical roles in shaping Bush's approach to the crisis in the Gulf. And in the NSC meeting that had just adjourned, each had foreshadowed the position he would take throughout the crisis.

There was George Bush the young striver. From his late teenage years, the future president had always been a worldly, gregarious, and ambitious man, comfortable among the Yankee aristocracy as only those born to it truly can be. This George Bush had a healthy ego—no one could survive nearly a quarter century at the highest levels of American politics without one. Bush's restless energy and innate competitiveness translated into a lifelong passion for competitive sports. The traveling White House press corps of the Bush years would learn to its dismay that the president's idea of a "vacation" was an almost frenzied dawn-to-dusk litany of outdoor activities: tennis, horseshoes, "polo golf" (the latest contribution to the game from a man whose family had helped create the Walker Cup), and hours spent racing his speedboat off the Maine coast. And while never the most talented or instinctive athlete on the team, Bush had nonetheless been elected captain of almost every team on which he had ever played.

Like many of his caste, George Bush harbored an unshakable belief in the Protestant ethic: the creed that success in business was a barometer of success in life. It was essential to his self-esteem that he succeed in business—and be seen by others to be succeeding. Bush was always eager to discuss and pursue new business ventures with longtime acquaintances, a theme that ran through his entire adult life, as much for the opportunity to cement friendships as to make money. For him as for his father, the late Senator Prescott Bush, there were few distinctions between business, political, and social connections. It was an outlook he also passed on to his four sons, with mixed results.

In this regard, Bush's career after leaving the Oval Office was instructive. Well into his late seventies, at a time of life when most former presidents limit themselves to writing their memoirs and making the occasional commencement speech, he would join the Carlyle Group, the secretive Washington merchant bank founded by former Reagan defense secretary Frank Carlucci. Not just to contribute his name to the letterhead, either: Soon after joining Carlyle, Bush would be jetting around the globe pitching the firm to potential clients, particularly in the Persian Gulf, where his name was still worth its weight in gold. Carlyle, whose letterhead constituted a veritable *Who's Who* of the Republican foreign policy establishment from the Reagan and Bush years, was a surprising choice of second career for a former president. Its reputation was one of inveterate cronyism, the sort of firm that shamelessly played on the insider connections of its principals to secure "sweetheart deals" with defense contractors and foreign governments.

But for Bush, the thought of working once again with longtime friends like Carlucci, former British prime minister John Major, and former Canadian prime minister Brian Mulroney would be irresistible; as would be the prospect of doing business with other old friends, like the Saudi royal family and the al-Sabahs of Kuwait. The frequent allegations of "crony capitalism" leveled as a result against the former president genuinely mystified him. What could be better than for a man to go into business with some of his good friends? And if many of his friends happened to be Middle East oil potentates or Washington insiders; if his sons happened to go into business with his former campaign contributors and soon found themselves millionaires? Then, as they say in the Texas oil business, the biggest rig wins.

James Baker had been the perfect boon companion for this half of Bush's life. The two men were outwardly so close in personality and interests that they themselves viewed each other more like brothers than mere friends. Each had succeeded in living up to, and then surpassing, the achievements of immensely successful fathers who had been pillars of their respective communities. The Baker family were every bit as much Houston society royalty as Prescott Bush and the Bush family had been Connecticut Yankee royalty.

Like Bush, Baker was a country club Republican in the most literal sense. The center of his personal and professional life was the exclusive River Oaks Country Club in Houston, long the retreat of choice for the city's business elite. George Bush was also a member. It was said that more oil deals were done in the men's locker room at River Oaks than in any of the skyscrapers that dotted the downtown Houston skyline. At any rate, it is doubtful that any other country club will ever figure as prominently in a secretary of state's memoirs as River Oaks figures in Baker's. Baker was entirely at home in this bastion of privilege and exertion. Like Bush, his longtime tennis partner at the club, Baker was a tireless sportsman, vain about his height, physical appearance, and athletic prowess. He, too, had a healthy ego.

Baker shared Bush's absorption with getting ahead in business and politics, though with a slightly different bent. By talent, training, and temperament he was the quintessential corporate attorney; the deal itself was everything to him. Thus, while George Bush had made his personal fortune by founding an oil company, James Baker had made his by fronting deals for oil companies. While Bush had built the Texas Republican Party almost single-handedly from scratch during the early 1960s before being elected to Congress in 1966, Baker disdained the sort of small-town "backyard barbecue politics" that built political careers and won elections in Texas. A brilliant campaign strategist at the national level—during his career he would manage five Republican presidential campaigns and win three of them—Baker was a signal failure as a candidate himself: far too patrician and glib to ever connect with ordinary voters. His run for Texas attorney general had ended in a crushing defeat. Baker possessed the same restless energy and political ambitions as Bush, but lacked his friend's easy personal touch.

Still, despite never having won election to any office in his native state, Baker was convinced that his smooth style, family history, and political instincts made him the outstanding Texas Republican of his generation. In private, he occasionally voiced disappointment that this mantle had fallen instead upon the shoulders of George Bush—a transplanted New Englander prone to frequent malapropisms. Baker could never quite grasp that the very shortcomings that exposed Bush to easy caricature—his habit of speaking in sentence fragments; his excitable, somewhat reedy voice; and his overeager embrace of all things Texan, which only did more to expose his Yankee roots—also served to humanize Bush with the electorate.

Yet the two friends needed each other. Baker owed his entrée into national Republican politics to George Bush, who had secured his first job in the Executive Branch as deputy commerce secretary during the Ford administration. Each subsequent step in Bush's inexorable march to the White House had brought Baker positions of increasing responsibility and visibility, beginning with his plum appointment as Ronald Reagan's chief of staff in 1981—a concession that Bush had demanded in return for throwing his support to Reagan.

In turn, George Bush needed a man of Baker's talents to be the expediter of his political career. For all of his experience at all levels of American politics, Bush lacked the organizational skills necessary to field a national campaign. In Baker, he had the political operative par excellence. And once Bush was in power, Baker demonstrated himself to be even more valuable as a Cabinet officer: a peerless negotiator, a decisive executive, and a master at manipulating (he would have said managing) the press. Baker's ability to bend the Washington bureaucracy to his will was best gauged by the detested nickname he first acquired in the Reagan White House: the Velvet Hammer.

Not surprisingly, then, at the moment when the Bush dynasty's political fortunes hung in the balance, during the 2000 Florida recount, Bush senior would insist that Baker be enlisted to oversee his son's legal and public relations strategy. It spoke volumes about the relationship between the two men that despite the elder George Bush's lingering resentment at Baker's performance as his campaign manager during the 1992 election, he would turn to Baker at this moment of crisis—and that Baker would immediately answer his old friend's call, despite having been frequently snubbed by the Bush family during the eight intervening years. As Bush might have described the situation, using one of his favorite stock phrases: "Where would we be without friends?"

But there was another side to George Bush as well, and thus another friendship came to define his life and his foreign policy.

Ambition and outgoing personality notwithstanding, Bush was fundamentally a sensitive and deeply reflective person. A born worrier, the future president thought constantly from a young age about the major issues of the day. He unburdened himself in his personal diary, and in long, rambling letters to family and friends in which Bush shared his views on important political questions. Bush's diary and many of his letters have been preserved, providing an extraordinary glimpse into his thinking and the issues that mattered to him most.

Significantly, the issues that concerned Bush most of all related to foreign policy and American credibility in world affairs. Like many members of the Greatest Generation, his view of America's place in the world was forever changed by the Second World War. Bush's lifelong obsession with extracting "the lessons of history" from past events was also born in that conflict. While serving in the Pacific theater, Bush became a voracious reader of history and would remain one for the rest of his life. In later years, during some of the most critical crises of his presidency, Bush would exhort his advisers and even foreign heads of state to "read their history" in order to make the right policy choices.

By any standard, Bush was also a thoughtful man, extraordinarily considerate of others' feelings. In this respect, the president showed himself to be every bit as much his mother's son as his father's. Dorothy Bush had constantly preached to her four sons that modesty and sharing credit for one's success were virtues, while boastfulness and self-aggrandizement were serious faults of character. George, the son with the most potential but also the healthiest ego, was her special project. These early lessons influenced the way Bush treated others and even perceived others throughout his political career.

In 1974, while serving as the U.S. envoy in Beijing, the future president had played host to Secretary of State Henry Kissinger on one of Kissinger's high-profile trips to China. Bush's personal "China Diary" captures his mixed impressions of Kissinger: admiration verging on awe at the secretary of state's diplomatic abilities; distaste verging on disgust at Kissinger's overbearing treatment of subordinates. Kissinger, the son of a schoolteacher who had arrived in the United States as a penniless refugee, seemed to take an almost perverse pleasure in treating his retinue like lackeys—and Bush, the son of a senator who had enjoyed a privileged childhood in a Greenwich mansion, scrupulously documented every offense. Kissinger spoke to even his most senior aides in an imperious tone that Dorothy Bush would have never allowed her sons to use with the Bush family servants; his treatment of the U.S. Liaison Office staff, Bush's people, was even worse. "More bad behavior by Kissinger today," the future president wrote gloomily after one especially trying afternoon. He spent weeks after Kissinger's departure soothing egos in his little diplomatic outpost.

A member of the Greatest Generation. A foreign policy wonk. A man obsessed with history and his place in it. A courtly man who cringed at Henry Kissinger's brusque, high-handed treatment of subordinates. All of these were aspects of George Bush's personality beyond Baker's ken.

For one thing, Baker was almost seven years younger than Bush and a generation apart in worldview. Pearl Harbor had been a transformative event for Bush, disrupting the comfortable, preordained pattern of his life and thrusting him into combat half a world away from Connecticut before his twentieth birthday. Baker had been in grammar school at the time. The American crusade against fascism had been something he learned about in school, not experienced firsthand.

Perhaps for this reason, Baker did not share Bush's deep intellectual interest in foreign policy—a somewhat surprising claim to make about a secretary of state, but something that even Baker himself admitted. In his memoirs, Baker revealed that he had accepted Bush's offer to serve as secretary of state not because he had a particular foreign policy agenda he wished to advance, but because State was the senior Cabinet post and thus represented a promotion from his previous job as secretary of the Treasury. Were the situation reversed (as it is, for example, in Britain, where the chancellor of the exchequer is senior to the foreign secretary), it would have been easy to imagine Baker declining the State portfolio.

And Baker would not have been especially bothered by how his predecessor Henry Kissinger treated his or anyone else's subordinates. He himself was not the sort of boss to engender affection among those who worked for him. Baker's arrival at any new Washington job inevitably took on the atmosphere of a palace coup, in which remnants of the old regime were swiftly and brutally purged, Baker's own loyal lieutenants installed, and the rank and file told to obey instructions or else. Even the secretary's protégés regarded him more with respect than affection. A decade after leaving his service they still referred to him in the third person as "Baker" or "the secretary"; never "Jim."

But George Bush did have a friend who mirrored the more sensitive, reflective side of his character: Brent Scowcroft. Ironically, although the two men had known each other well for almost twenty years and had worked together in the Nixon and Ford administrations, they had not been particularly close until Scowcroft became Bush's national security adviser. Afterward they were inseparable, with Scowcroft becoming what Bush would describe as his "closest friend in all things."

Like the president, Scowcroft's life and career had been shaped by the call to arms during the Second World War, but with a twist. The future éminence grise of Republican foreign policy had responded to Pearl Harbor by attending West Point, graduating just months after the war ended. Like Bush, Scowcroft had been an aviator, learning to fly the famous

P-51 Mustang fighter which won the air war in Europe before a training crash nearly crippled him and took him off flight status.

For a young Air Force officer this was a career-threatening mishap, but Scowcroft never looked back. He became a professor at West Point and later an expert on arms control before becoming Henry Kissinger's deputy national security adviser. The rest, as they say, is history.

Intellectually, he and George Bush were kindred spirits. Both were unapologetic devotees of foreign policy, consumed by the study of history, the subject Scowcroft had taught at West Point. For them statecraft was as much an avocation as a profession, and the two men could spend hours discussing it, lost to everything and everyone around them. Few were surprised when they wrote their memoirs together, or that the book in question dealt exclusively with foreign policy. Bush and Scowcroft also shared a keen fascination with China that went far beyond the requirements of conducting diplomacy: Bush's dating to his time as U.S. envoy there; and Scowcroft's to the Nixon administration's famous opening to China.

Temperamentally the two also had much in common. Like the president, Scowcroft had been a serious young man well before his time. He possessed Bush's melancholic personality, but without Bush's gregarious side and need to be liked. Scowcroft, too, worried constantly about American credibility in world affairs and would share his concerns with anyone who cared to listen.

Both men treated everyone they met, from stewards to kings, with the same Old World courtesy. Both were worshiped by their respective staffs; in turn, Bush and Scowcroft were fiercely loyal to staffers and went out of their way to advance the careers of those, like Richard Haass or Condoleezza Rice, who had won their favor. They showed the same loyalty to longtime political supporters, sometimes to a fault.

If James Baker had been the perfect companion for George Bush's life as a sportsman, businessman, and rising politician, Scowcroft was the perfect confidant for his life as a president. And as Bush grew older, and thus more philosophical; as he thought less in terms of his place on the tennis court and more in terms of his place in history; as the measures necessary to ensure American credibility became less obvious than they had been during the Cold War; the importance of Scowcroft's friendship and Scowcroft's advice only increased.

Never before in American history had the president's two top foreign policy advisers also been his two best friends. The potential benefits of such a situation were obvious. The potential pitfalls were less immediately apparent, but would steadily become more so. Especially when Bush's two friends disagreed on how to handle the most important foreign policy crisis of his presidency.

Both Baker and Scowcroft agreed that the outcome of the Gulf crisis would determine the shape of the post–Cold War world. They disagreed on what America's priorities in that world should be.

As his comments during the August 5 NSC meeting had hinted, Baker viewed the Gulf crisis primarily through the prism of how it would affect U.S.-Soviet relations. During the first forty-eight hours of the crisis, while the Bush White House was still trying to arrive at a consensus on how to respond to the invasion of Kuwait, Baker and his top aides had been crafting a joint response with their counterparts in Moscow, always several time zones ahead of Washington both literally and figuratively.

The joint declaration with Shevardnadze had not only been a feather in Baker's cap; it also reflected his policy priorities in the Gulf. To Baker, deepening the Bush administration's partnership with Gorbachev and Shevardnadze should be both the desired outcome from a successful resolution of the Gulf crisis, and the primary means for achieving such an outcome. Therefore, Baker wanted the Bush administration to take no actions that might imperil the hard-won cooperation with the Soviets, and also wanted the White House to showcase Soviet involvement at every turn.

For this reason, Baker favored giving sanctions as much time to work as possible in Iraq and reaching a negotiated settlement to the crisis if at all possible. If force did become necessary, the secretary of state believed strongly that every possible diplomatic measure should be taken to respect Soviet sensitivities about one of their longtime client states being attacked.

Brent Scowcroft wanted the Soviets kept as far away from the Gulf crisis—and the Gulf—as possible. A lifelong Cold Warrior, he still mistrusted Soviet motives in the Middle East. Like many career Sovietologists (academics who specialized in understanding Soviet behavior), Scowcroft viewed relations between the United States and the Soviet Union as fundamentally static, a bipolar rivalry between two superpowers. He and his NSC staff were less optimistic about the prospects for U.S.-Soviet cooperation than were Baker and his top aides at State. Even with the dramatic changes that had taken place in Eastern Europe, Scowcroft believed there were still critical differences remaining between the two countries, especially in the Middle East.

Scowcroft worried greatly about the future stability of the Gulf region and above all about projecting American credibility to the rest of the world during the current crisis. For James Baker, Saddam's invasion of Kuwait was one act in the larger drama of the Cold War coming to an end. For Scowcroft the invasion of Kuwait was "the central crisis of our time." It was a test case: not of U.S.-Soviet partnership after the Cold War, but of America's ability to lead a new international order that would replace the Cold War.

Scowcroft was convinced that military action in the Gulf would become inevitable, and not just because he doubted that sanctions and diplomacy alone would be enough to drive Saddam out of Kuwait. The United States needed to demonstrate a willingness to use force against Iraq, so that future challengers to American global leadership would think twice before acting. Richard Haass, who worked side by side with Scowcroft during the Gulf crisis and through all four years of the Bush presidency, distinctly remembers his thinking on this score: "Brent was a real traditionalist, worried about America's reliability, worried about credibility, comfortable with using military force, very much comfortable with the idea of America as a great power, totally comfortable with carrying it out. Brent was and is extremely comfortable with the idea of the United States as a world leader."

Because of their long-standing personal ties to Bush, Baker and Scowcroft each had one ear of the president, and each made a case that resonated strongly with him. But Scowcroft had one advantage over Baker. His role as national security adviser brought him into constant daily contact with the president. As Bush's nearly inseparable confidant during a major international crisis, he had far more of the president's ear and far more of the president's time than Baker. And as the crisis progressed, this advantage would become decisive in getting his point of view across.

·　　·　　·

Dick Cheney's delegation arrived in Saudi Arabia early in the afternoon of August 6 and spent the remainder of the day waiting for an audience with King Fahd. They had been joined at the last minute by Ambassador Chas Freeman, who had cut short his summer leave in the United States. Besides his familiarity with the Saudi royal family, Freeman would serve as unofficial translator for the American side, since none of the other members of Cheney's group spoke Arabic. Prince Bandar, the influential Saudi ambassador to the United States, had flown home just for this meeting and would translate for the king.

An audience was finally arranged for shortly past midnight on the morning of August 7 in Saudi Arabia—which in the desert climate of Jeddah, the summer retreat of the Saudi monarchy, was government meeting time. During the long flight to Saudi Arabia, Freeman had tried to give the visitors from Washington a crash course on the workings of Saudi government. Everything was done by consensus, he explained to them. King Fahd was not a king in the Western sense, but only first among equals. Real power resided collectively in the dozens of princes who were direct descendants of Ibn Saud, the founder of modern Saudi Arabia.

Much of this collective power was assembled in a single room when the American delegation arrived at the palace designated for the meeting. After some opening remarks on the long history of ties between the two countries, Cheney turned the floor over to General Schwarzkopf, who was to brief the king and the assembled princes on what U.S. intelligence was showing about Iraqi troop movements.

Though based on essentially the same raw intelligence, Schwarzkopf's briefing on the threat to Saudi Arabia was far less categorical than CIA Director Webster's briefing at the White House the previous day; it indicated only that there was a *potential* threat to the kingdom. Even so, it had succeeded in capturing Fahd's attention, Freeman realized. At one point the burly American general knelt beside the equally burly king to show him the latest U.S. satellite photographs of Iraqi troop positions along the Saudi border. Freeman thought this was an inspired gesture by Schwarzkopf—exactly the display of courtesy and deference that went far with the Saudis.

Cheney then made the Bush administration's closing arguments. His most important point was one that had been stressed repeatedly by the president and Scowcroft in their conversations with the defense secretary before the trip: that after the immediate threat to Saudi Arabia was removed, all American forces would be withdrawn and the United States would seek no permanent bases in the kingdom.

Fahd was clearly relieved by this pledge, Freeman saw. The ambassador knew better than anyone that merely to be having this meeting, the king had needed to overcome strong objections from some of the more conservative princes as well as from the powerful Islamic clerics who held sway over every aspect of life in the kingdom. Now Fahd was contemplating an even more controversial step: allowing the deployment of tens of thousands of U.S. military personnel in his religious, socially conservative country, which would entail among other things the presence of thousands of female GIs. King Fahd presided over a society in which women were required to wear veils and cover their bodies from head to toe outside the home. Saudi women were not permitted to serve in their country's armed forces, or even to drive a car. But female personnel made up nearly a fifth of the U.S. armed forces and were integral to its operations. There was no possible way Saudi citizens would be able to avoid seeing female GIs, none of whom would be veiled, and many of whom would work in shirtsleeves in the suffocating summer heat of Saudi Arabia. Women soldiers would not just be driving cars, but trucks and armored vehicles.

The king gave a short speech saying he was inclined to grant the American request. The United States had no ulterior motives, he declared, while Saddam Hussein had proven that he could no longer be trusted. Saddam had personally assured the king that he would not attack Kuwait, but had lied. It was impossible to know what his intentions were regarding Saudi Arabia, but the king intended to act before it was too late. His remarks concluded, Fahd then asked the princes for their thoughts.

As he listened to the ensuing debate in Arabic, Freeman could immediately tell that the king's position was deeply unpopular among his fellow royals. A few were genuinely unconvinced that the threat from Iraq was imminent. But most objected on principle to any presence of American soldiers on Saudi soil, regardless of what Iraq's intentions were. Crown Prince Abdullah, second in line to the Saudi throne, acted as the informal spokesman for the princes opposed to the American deployment. It was impossible to even contemplate such a step, the crown prince warned in strong language, without extensive consultations taking place with tribal elders and religious scholars.

Fahd cut him off. "There is no time. If we delay, we will end up like Kuwait. Today, there is no Kuwait."

"There is a Kuwait," Abdullah insisted.

"Yes," the king replied sarcastically, "and its territory consists of hotel rooms in London and Cairo."

The decision was made. Fahd would later reveal privately to Freeman that it was the only time during his entire reign that he made a decision that did not reflect the consensus.

*   *   *

The American delegation's reward for having convinced Fahd to accept the deployment of U.S. forces was another diplomatic mission. Cheney's official aircraft had barely cleared Saudi airspace when Scowcroft called his deputy, Robert Gates, aboard the plane.

"The president wants you to stop in Egypt and see Mubarak," the national security adviser told him. Ostensibly the purpose of the visit was to obtain Mubarak's permission for the aircraft carrier USS *Eisenhower* to traverse the Suez Canal. The real purpose of the trip, however, was to gauge the likelihood of Mubarak's support for U.S. military action against Iraq.

Exhausted by his last-ditch attempts to negotiate an Arab solution to the crisis, Mubarak was spending several days at his summer residence in Alexandria, the faded, elegant seacoast city founded by Alexander the

Great. Because the airport at Alexandria could not handle Cheney's plane, a large Boeing jetliner, arrangements were made to land in Cairo and take another aircraft to Alexandria.

At Cairo West, the military airfield outside the Egyptian capital, Cheney, Gates, and Schwarzkopf were met by Frank Wisner, the U.S. ambassador to Egypt, and two security officers. The six men boarded the U.S. military attaché's plane, a small twin-engine Cessna, for the cramped flight to Alexandria—a flight made even more cramped by the presence of the six-foot-four Schwarzkopf and his thick binders of briefing materials. Upon landing, the Cessna taxied to a stop beside a large, ostentatiously liveried Boeing 727 jet—the official aircraft of Iraq's vice president, also there to see Mubarak. Gates, who possessed the acerbic wit of many former CIA employees, wisecracked that it was not a good sign if Iraq already had air superiority.

The Americans met with Mubarak on the verandah of his marble villa, which enjoyed a spectacular view of the shimmering blue Mediterranean. But the beauty of his surroundings had not improved the Egyptian president's mood. A former combat pilot and general in the Egyptian air force, Mubarak still favored the blunt language of the pilot ready room. To the surprise of his visitors, the first target of his ire was the Kuwaitis.

"They're a bunch of sons of bitches who have never done anything for Egypt," he said contemptuously of the al-Sabah family that ruled Kuwait. Unlike the other wealthy oil nations of the Persian Gulf, which shared some of their largesse with poorer Arab nations like Egypt through foreign aid and philanthropic contributions, the Kuwaitis were notorious for their tightfistedness. The Egyptian president continued in the same vein for a few minutes on the theme of why the rest of the Arab world despised the Kuwaitis. Clearly he was annoyed at having been dragged into this crisis on Kuwait's behalf.

But Mubarak was even more furious at Saddam Hussein.

"Saddam broke his word to me," he railed, recalling the Iraqi ruler's pledge not to attack Kuwait when Mubarak had telephoned him on July 25. "He said he would not do this. And for that reason we will be on your side." The immediate outcome of the meeting was that the aircraft carrier *Eisenhower* and other U.S. Navy vessels could make use of the

Suez Canal in deploying to the Gulf—a shortcut that would eliminate many days on the journey from the eastern United States. But both Mubarak and the Americans understood that Egypt's cooperation would only begin there.

After another cramped flight back to Cairo, the Americans gratefully transferred back to Cheney's aircraft for the long trip back to Washington. The plane had barely cleared Egyptian airspace when the secure phone buzzed. It was Scowcroft again.

"The president thinks he may want you to go to Morocco and see King Hassan, but he hasn't reached the king yet," he informed Gates. "So just hang loose." While Morocco had little military significance, Hassan knew Bush well from his years as vice president and was friendly toward the United States. The president, he realized, was already thinking in terms of assembling the broadest possible diplomatic coalition against Iraq.

"Brent," Gates replied reasonably, "you can't just hang loose in the Mediterranean."

"Find out how much time you have before you have to turn around," Scowcroft instructed. Gates checked with the pilots and told Scowcroft that the aircraft had only enough fuel to loiter off the coast of Morocco for forty-five minutes before it needed to turn west and head for home. Scowcroft promised that the president would try to telephone Hassan immediately.

Fortunately, Bush was able to reach the king a few minutes later and the American delegation made one more stop, where the king agreed to support the U.S. position on the crisis. Gates was impressed. "It showed how the president was really working it in real time."

* * *

Several hours after Dick Cheney informed the White House that King Fahd had agreed to accept U.S. forces, President Bush and a small group of officials gathered in the Cabinet Room for a restricted NSC session. The purpose of the meeting was to assess the economic fallout from the invasion for the U.S. economy as well as to discuss ways to pressure Iraq economically. But while no one in the room at the time knew it, this meeting would determine the fate of the Iraqi people for the next twelve years.

"What I wanted to do was get a quick update and then talk about economic implications," the president began. But Brent Scowcroft wanted to talk first about an even more pressing issue.

"Before we begin, I want everyone to look at today's headline in the *Washington Post*," Scowcroft instructed. The headline related to covert actions against Iraq that were allegedly under consideration by the Bush administration. "If leaking continues, it will force us to limit the decision circle," Scowcroft threatened.

"What this does is risk something very serious and undermines our efforts," said Bush, echoing the warning.

Webster then reported that rather than moving against Saudi Arabia, as CIA had predicted the previous afternoon, Iraq appeared to be consolidating its conquest of Kuwait. "In the last twenty-four hours the situation has stabilized," he concluded. "There is no real increase in preparations at the Saudi border. Iraq still has not withdrawn any significant forces from Kuwait, and may be augmenting them with units from its border with Iran.

"There are some worrisome developments that suggest Saddam may be preparing for a major war: reserve call-ups, base preparations. But we have not yet seen their Republican Guard units re-forming for attack."

"Between now and yesterday, what are the developments?" Bush pressed. The potential threat to Saudi Arabia was still his foremost concern.

"There are no significant developments," the DCI replied.

Conversation then turned to the main agenda item, the invasion's impact on the U.S. economy. Deputy Secretary of Energy Henson Moore had been invited to the meeting to deliver the Department of Energy's assessment of what the loss of oil supplies from Iraq and Kuwait would mean. DOE was estimating a price increase of between $10 and $30 a barrel—effectively a doubling of energy prices. Moore suggested that the president authorize releasing oil from the Strategic Petroleum Reserve (SPR) as a temporary measure to stabilize prices.

"The Federal Reserve has a similar study," Scowcroft concurred. "The price of oil could go up to $36 a barrel." It had been at only $18 a barrel the day before the invasion, even after all of the tensions between Iraq and Kuwait during the month of July.

"The financial markets are down badly," Treasury Secretary Brady added gloomily. "The price of oil is rising. This would bring our growth down to zero." Zero growth meant a recession.

"How long can Iraq withstand the pain of this economic isolation?" the president demanded in frustration. "All this military preparation must be expensive for them. This is a question for the intelligence community," he said pointedly, glancing at Webster.

"Do we have a prediction of how much of Iraq's oil will get out?" Attorney General Dick Thornburgh asked.

"Iraqi oil will only get to market if they are physically able to do so," Scowcroft reminded the room. Everyone at the table knew that the national security adviser was talking about a military blockade of all Iraqi oil shipments, besides the closing of Iraq's two main pipelines that had already taken place.

"That is correct," agreed Moore. "We need to distinguish between an embargo and a blockade." An embargo meant only that Iraq could not legally sell its oil to foreign buyers. A blockade would require the U.S. Navy to intercept any Iraqi oil tankers caught trying to transport oil from Iraqi ports.

"We also need to discuss cheating," Baker said. "The Central Bank of Jordan is allowing Iraq to use Jordanian accounts. We called in the Jordanian ambassador and warned him. Also, Mark Rich* is offering storage for Iraqi crude through Swiss banks." If foreign banks were permitted to purchase oil delivery contracts from Iraq, it would be an easy matter for Saddam Hussein to circumvent the embargo.

"Now, with international law on our side, we should lean on them," ordered the president. Bush was furious at King Hussein and the Jordanians for their tacit support of Iraq.

Richard Darman had not said anything up to this point. But he was

---

* Rich, one of the FBI's most wanted fugitives, was living in exile in Switzerland because of an earlier U.S. indictment for illegal oil trading with Iran. The husband of Hollywood songwriter Denise Rich, a prominent Democratic Party supporter, he later received a controversial presidential pardon from President Bill Clinton.

troubled by the direction the conversation was taking. As far as Darman was concerned, the Bush White House had not even begun to think through the long-term implications of a confrontation with Saddam Hussein. Only a few days into the crisis, the president was already asking about Iraq's ability to withstand economic pain. But as Bush's OMB director, Darman knew better than anyone that the United States was about to experience economic pain of its own, a recession that the crisis in the Gulf would accelerate and deepen. A prolonged military deployment in the Gulf would also increase the size of the U.S. budget deficit, which meant that an unpopular tax increase would almost certainly become necessary soon.

Darman believed that the Bush administration was in fact far more vulnerable to a long-term embargo of Iraqi crude than Saddam Hussein. Ordinary Americans would respond to a recession and higher gas prices by voting against the incumbent party in the White House, while Saddam could ride out an oil embargo by cracking down even more harshly on any dissent by ordinary Iraqis. Cheating on the embargo would help Saddam, and over time the amount of cheating would inevitably increase; it was a matter of basic economic laws of supply and demand. He now tried to convey some of these points to the others.

"With time, cheating will go up," Darman warned. "If things work, the value of cheating will go up. Unless the Saudis increase production, the effect on us will be a recession." Use of the SPR to stabilize energy prices would be only a stopgap measure. "The SPR is not a perfect substitute, as it is a depletable resource."

Darman tried to impress on the others some of the advantages that Saddam Hussein would bring to an economic battle of wills against the United States. "Democracies and market-oriented economies are less prepared to wage this kind of battle than nonmarket economies," he said, "especially given that modern communications will affect us more than them." For economic warfare to work against Saddam, Darman argued, it was not enough for the Bush administration merely to slap an oil embargo on Iraq. The real vulnerability of Iraq was not oil, but food. A densely populated, urbanized nation, Iraq imported millions of tons of grain each year (including, of course, American wheat) to feed its people.

"We need to assess what it takes to starve them," Darman said soberly. "We will be more responsive to ordinary pain than they will. The key will be giving them *extraordinary* pain. We will therefore need to target their key vulnerabilities."

"But food will be exempt," protested James Baker.

"No," Richard Haass of the NSC amended. "Under the Security Council resolution, we can block food shipments except those that can be shown to be for humanitarian purposes."

This was a sobering thought for everyone in the room. They knew that the sight of hungry Iraqi children on CNN (which had already become the key media outlet in this crisis) would instantly erode any consensus for taking strong action against Iraq, especially among America's allies in the Arab world.

"Part of what is driving up the price of gas is uncertainty," Scowcroft reasoned. "If following the UN resolution we can get increased production and some oil from the SPR, we can minimize the advantage of cheating," he concluded optimistically.

"I am not arguing against tough action," Darman assured him. "A blockade makes sense. My personal opinion is that it won't be enough, without using the SPR, increased production from Saudi Arabia, and," he emphasized, wagging a finger, "a willingness to tolerate recession given the current weakness of the economy."

Darman sighed heavily. "Either way, you have to get this guy out of there."

"Yes," agreed the president, "that is the bottom line."

"The bottom line," Darman corrected, in the tone that only he felt comfortable using with Republican presidents, "is that Saddam with Kuwait is a long-term problem."

After a moment's uncomfortable silence, both at Darman's tone and the policy implications of what he was saying, Scowcroft quietly rebuked, "That is the reason for the president's policy."

"Darman is making a point I agree with," interposed Bush. "All will not be tranquil until Saddam Hussein is history."

4

THE FIFTH OBJECTIVE

The first wave of American troops in the Gulf was soon joined by contingents from other nations as a large, diverse, and—at times—wildly implausible Coalition evolved in response to the invasion. Ultimately, over thirty nations would contribute air, naval, or ground forces to Operation Desert Shield. Armored units from traditional NATO allies such as France and the United Kingdom would find themselves bivouacked alongside infantry units from places as varied as Bangladesh, El Salvador, and Niger in one of the most unusual manifestations of alliance bandwagoning ever seen. More ominously for the Iraqis, virtually every Arab government with the exception of King Hussein's Jordan expressed its solidarity with the aims of the UN Security Council. Arab leaders, most notably Egyptian president Hosni Mubarak, lent their personal prestige to the diplomatic campaign against Iraq. Even Syria, long considered a pariah by the United States because of its support for international terrorism, would eventually join the Coalition. Both Egypt and Syria would later commit tens of thousands of troops to the Gulf. Never in its history had the United Nations confronted an aggressor state so unequivocally, or with such broad support from the international community, as it did Iraq.

That such unprecedented diplomatic and military cooperation took place was largely due to the efforts of President George Bush. In a sense, this was the crisis Bush had spent all of his life preparing to manage. Calling upon his diplomatic experience in China and at the UN as well as his seemingly innumerable friendships with other world leaders, Bush choreographed the most successful collective security action of the century. Within a week of invading Kuwait, Baghdad was diplomatically isolated.

Shortly after 9:00 A.M. on the morning of August 8, the president went before the American people in a nationally televised speech to announce the deployment of U.S. forces in Saudi Arabia. "In the life of a nation," Bush declared, "we're called upon to define who we are and what we believe. Sometimes these choices are not easy. But today as president, I ask for your support in a decision I've made to stand up for what's right and condemn what's wrong, all in the cause of peace."

Bush enunciated the "four simple principles" that he said would define his approach to the Gulf crisis: "First, we seek the immediate, unconditional, and complete withdrawal of all Iraqi forces from Kuwait. Second, Kuwait's legitimate government must be restored to replace the puppet regime. Third, my administration, as has been the case with every president from President Roosevelt to President Reagan, is committed to the security and stability of the Persian Gulf. And fourth, I am determined to protect the lives of American citizens abroad."

Later that afternoon the president held his first televised news conference on the crisis. Bush was asked, "Was there any one single thing that tipped your hand into deciding to send U.S. troops and aircraft into Saudi Arabia?" The president's response drew an explicit connection between the Iraqi army's advance to the Saudi border and his administration's decision to intervene. A small Freudian slip revealed just how heavily the danger to Saudi Arabia had been weighing on his mind.

"I can't think of an individual, specific thing," the president declared. "If there was one, it would perhaps be the Saudis moving south when they said they were withdrawing."

"You mean the Iraqis, sir?" the reporter corrected.

"I mean the Iraqis," Bush corrected himself. "Thank you very much. It's been a long night. The Iraqis moving down to the Kuwait-Saudi border when, indeed, they had given their word that they were withdrawing. That heightened our concern."

The president was also asked: Did our intelligence let us down? When did you get an indication Iraq would be moving into Kuwait?

Bush credited the U.S. intelligence community for observing the Iraqi troop buildup, but implied that Iraq's attack was planned and executed at the last moment, so that even with this information in hand, "interested parties" in the U.S. government had not had adequate time to deter the invasion.

"No, I don't feel let down by the intelligence at all," the president said. "When you plan a blitzkrieg-like attack that is launched at two o'clock in the morning, it's pretty hard to stop, particularly when you have just been given the word of the people involved that there wouldn't be any such attack.

"I think the intelligence community deserves certain credit for picking up what was a substantial buildup and then reporting it to us," Bush continued. "This information was relayed properly to interested parties, but the move was so swift that it was pretty hard for them to stop it." This formulation neglected to mention that intelligence warnings that Iraq intended to invade at least part of Kuwait had been blinking red for nearly a week before the invasion took place.

The president was also asked whether the invasion's effects on oil prices would lead to a recession.

"I have not been advised of that," Bush replied quickly, despite the fact that both his treasury secretary and his budget director had explicitly warned him about the likelihood of a recession less than forty-eight hours earlier. "I hope that is not the case." The president repeated almost verbatim Scowcroft's optimistic view about the ability of the Strategic Petroleum Reserve to cushion oil prices.

Toward the end of the press conference, Bush was asked about the long-term threat from Saddam Hussein and Iraq, even if the withdrawal of Iraqi forces from Kuwait was achieved.

"Mr. President, assuming that you achieve your withdrawal of Iraqi forces out of Kuwait, Saddam Hussein is still going to be sitting there on top of a million-man army that he's shown an inclination to use. What happens in the long run after that? And can you contain that, short of removing Saddam Hussein from power?"

Unlike difficult questions about the economy and recession, this was the kind of foreign policy question that George Bush relished.

"I would think that if this international lesson is taught well that Saddam Hussein would behave differently in the future," the president replied confidently. "And that's what has been so very important about this concerted United Nations effort—unprecedented, you might say.

"A line has been drawn in the sand. The United States has taken a firm position. And I might say we're getting strong support from around the world for what we've done. I've been very, very pleased about that. Large countries and small countries—the world reaction has been excellent. And I would hope that all of this would result in Saddam Hussein or some calmer heads in Iraq understanding that this kind of international behavior is simply unacceptable. We see where we go."

A week later, at the Pentagon, the president repeated his four simple principles for ending the Gulf Crisis. Addressing a cheering crowd of military personnel and civilian employees on August 15, George Bush the World War II veteran drew an implicit analogy between Saddam Hussein's invasion of Kuwait and Adolf Hitler's inexorable march across Europe during the 1930s. "A half century ago our nation and the world paid dearly for appeasing an aggressor who should and could have been stopped," Bush reminded his audience. "We're not about to make that same mistake twice. Today Saddam Hussein's Iraq has been cut off by the Arab and Islamic nations that surround it. The Arab League itself has condemned Iraq's aggression. We stand with them, and we are not alone."

Speaking directly to the military personnel in attendance, the president concluded his remarks by stressing the importance of their role in enforcing the UN sanctions that had been imposed on Iraq. "Sanctions are working," Bush claimed. "The armies and air forces of Egypt, Morocco, the United Kingdom, and the Gulf Cooperation Council* states are shoulder to shoulder with us in Saudi Arabia's defense. Ships of numerous countries are sailing with ours to see that the United Nations sanctions, approved without dissent, are enforced. Together we must ensure that no goods get in and that not one drop of oil gets out."

●   ●   ●

* The Gulf Cooperation Council was a mutual defense alliance consisting of Saudi Arabia and the smaller oil monarchies of the Gulf, which had been formed during the Iran-Iraq War. Kuwait had been a member before the Iraqi invasion.

The Bush administration was soon presented with an opportunity to do just that. Three days later, on August 18, five oil tankers laden with Iraqi crude were sighted by a U.S. Navy vessel in the Persian Gulf and refused to turn back. From his headquarters in Saudi Arabia, General Norman Schwarzkopf contacted the Pentagon for authorization to attack the Iraqi vessels.

It immediately became clear that the Bush national security team had not thought through some of the practical questions associated with ensuring that "not one drop of oil gets out." What ensued was a heated debate among President Bush's advisers on what to do about the tankers, a debate complicated by the fact that Bush and Brent Scowcroft were not in Washington but at the president's vacation home in Maine. Scowcroft's initial instinct, strongly supported by Dick Cheney, was to authorize an attack on the Iraqi ships. James Baker was adamantly opposed. Without an additional Security Council resolution explicitly authorizing the use of force to enforce the embargo, Baker warned, they would risk losing the invaluable support they had received from the Soviet Union thus far during the Gulf crisis.

Meanwhile, back at the Pentagon, the Joint Staff ordered Schwarzkopf not to attack the Iraqi vessels. This order was subsequently countermanded several times, leading the outspoken Schwarzkopf to complain bitterly that his orders about the tankers were changed four times over the course of twenty-four hours. The tankers were ultimately allowed to slip away.

Further complicating matters, the Bush administration had consulted its two most important European allies, each of which had come down on opposite sides of the issue. The French government supported the view that additional authorization from the Security Council was necessary.

By contrast, British prime minister Margaret Thatcher had wanted the Iraqi ships to be intercepted and, predictably, wanted it to happen immediately. Bush's handling of the standoff furnished the occasion for one of Mrs. Thatcher's famous aphorisms: "Now George, this is no time to go wobbly."

•   •   •

UN ambassador Tom Pickering learned about the flap over the Iraqi tankers while in Colorado, where he was attending a conference at the Aspen Institute. The president had come down on Secretary of State Baker's side in the tanker debate, and Pickering was needed back at the UN to shepherd a new resolution authorizing enforcement of the embargo through the Security Council. Pickering canceled the remainder of his sessions at Aspen and rushed to New York. On August 24 the Security Council passed Resolution 665 by a 15-0 vote, authorizing "all appropriate measures" to support the naval blockade of Iraq—the Security Council's euphemism for "military action if necessary."

Nevertheless, the entire episode had raised Pickering's concern. The internal administration debate over the tankers had exposed sharp divisions within George Bush's war Cabinet over what the UN's role in the Gulf crisis should be. It had become apparent to Pickering that Dick Cheney and the Pentagon "really didn't want to stay with the UN activity. They basically wanted to free themselves from the need to consult with anyone." Conversely, Pickering knew that President Bush was committed to making the UN Security Council the main vehicle for resolving the crisis. Partly this was a product of Bush's own personal attachment to the United Nations, as an ideal and as an institution. The main reason, though, was that Bush intuitively sensed the widespread suspicion of American motives in the Islamic world and wanted to build a broad international coalition against Iraq that included significant participation by other Arab and Islamic states. For this, the legitimacy conferred by the UN was essential.

The problem, as Pickering saw it, was the lack of a plan for integrating the Bush administration's diplomatic strategy at the UN with its military actions in the Gulf—in the parlance of the State Department, a "politico-military strategy." President Bush's four principles for resolving the Gulf crisis worked fine as a set of general guidelines, but were far too broad to work as a guide for day-to-day decision-making. The confusion over what to do about the tankers had just illustrated this. Without a politico-military strategy in place, the urgent exigencies of military action would always trump all other considerations. Military requirements in the Gulf region would come to dictate U.S. policy rather than the other way around.

There was another, even more important argument for framing such a strategy. America's involvement in the security of the Persian Gulf would not end the day after the last Iraqi soldier left Kuwait, and the four principles declared by President Bush had been met. For reasons of oil security, global stability, and credibility with allies, the United States had a permanent stake in the future of the Gulf. Therefore, besides defining the goals that would govern its approach to the current crisis in the Gulf, the administration needed to be thinking about America's long-term goals in the region, and managing the crisis with these long-term objectives in mind.

Above all, there needed to be a plan for dealing with Iraq *after* the Gulf crisis. Regardless of how or when Saddam Hussein was forced to abandon his conquest of Kuwait, the threat posed by Iraq would not end there. Iraq's size, highly educated population, and huge oil reserves would always make it one of the most powerful countries in the Gulf region, and thus always a potential threat to the region. An effective politico-military strategy would therefore need to define the set of conditions that would prevent another crisis with Iraq from taking place in the future. It would also have to provide a detailed road map for how these conditions could be achieved.

Since no one else in the Bush administration had framed such a strategy, Pickering decided that he would do it himself.

Drawing on the talents of his large staff at the U.S. Mission in New York, Pickering worked feverishly to outline such a broad strategy in draft form. Six days later, on August 30, he forwarded his ideas to President Bush and Secretary of State Baker in two NODIS cables (restricted, "NO DIStribution" messages reserved only for sensitive communications among the most senior U.S. officials). "Our stated goals in the Iraq-Kuwait crisis and the UN resolutions, which we have fully supported, provide a firm structure for our objectives," Pickering wrote. "However, we need now to begin to think about amplifying these as they relate to a solution." The ambassador continued:

We need to begin to find a way to reassure our friends and allies, or UN supporters, and the American public, that we are proceeding in a way which is sensitive to the need to assure that,

if we can roll back Saddam with our present strategy, that strategy
also has within it the basis for providing reasonable assurances
that we do not intend to let it happen again.

Pickering's proposed strategy was based on two central ideas. The first
was that the vast desert border region shared by Iraq, Saudi Arabia, and
Kuwait would remain a constant potential flash point in the Middle East
as long as any Iraqi government was free to mobilize large numbers of
troops along the border anytime it wanted, threatening Saudi Arabia, or
Kuwait, or both. The only real solution, Pickering believed, was the creation of an "exclusionary zone": a large region of southern Iraq that
would be declared off-limits to Iraqi troops and monitored by a UN
peacekeeping force.

It was not a new idea. As a rising young Foreign Service officer in
1973, Pickering had been offered the prestigious assignment of executive
secretary at the State Department—the official who manages the flow of
communications to and from the secretary of state. He assumed the job
just in time for the October 1973 Yom Kippur War and had witnessed
firsthand the famous "shuttle diplomacy" by Secretary of State Henry
Kissinger in the Middle East that had brought about a cease-fire in that
war. Pickering had been struck at the time by Kissinger's insistence on
the need for a permanent separation of Egyptian and Israeli forces on the
Sinai Peninsula in order to achieve a lasting cease-fire between the two
countries. This had led to the creation of a narrow UN exclusionary zone
in the Sinai desert, patrolled by a small UN observer force. The zone had
prevented border incidents between the two countries for years, even after the voluntary return of the Sinai to Egypt by Israel following the 1978
Camp David peace accords.

There was no reason why a similar idea could not work with Iraq,
Pickering believed. Indeed, the geography of Iraq made it perfect for
such a zone. Virtually all of the country's population lived either in towns
along the Tigris and Euphrates or in the northern, mountainous part of
the country, which possessed a temperate climate and Iraq's most fertile
farmlands. Iraq's vast southern desert, where the border with Saudi Arabia and Kuwait extended for hundreds of miles, was barren and nearly
uninhabited.

Pickering's plan called for an exclusionary zone extending 100 kilometers (approximately 60 miles) into Iraqi territory along Iraq's southern border. This would be enough of a buffer to guarantee the security of Saudi Arabia and Kuwait from any foreseeable Iraqi threat. Monitoring Iraqi compliance within the exclusionary zone would be child's play: In the featureless moonscape of Iraq's southern desert, a single squadron of UN aircraft equipped with light observation planes would be more than enough to spot any unauthorized Iraqi troop presence. Pickering recognized that Iraq had legitimate national security needs in its southern port of Umm Qasr and along its southern border with Iran, both of which lay inside the 100-kilometer exclusionary zone. His plan designated these areas a "limited force zone," where Iraq would be allowed to deploy some troops, but where "offensive weapons" like tanks, artillery, and helicopters would be restricted.

Enforcing the exclusionary zone would be two small, permanent UN peacekeeping forces (PKF Iraq and PKF Saudi Arabia) that would patrol the Iraqi and Saudi sides of the zone, similar to the UN observer force that had successfully kept the peace in the Sinai. Pickering had strong opinions on where the troops for these forces should come from. As a concession to Iraqi national pride, he believed that PKF Iraq should be "drawn from Arab states acceptable to Iraq." Owing to the religious sensibilities of the Saudi people, PKF Saudi Arabia would similarly be drawn only from "Arab and Moslem states acceptable to Saudi Arabia." There would be minimal involvement by the U.S. military.

The second key idea in Pickering's plan was the need for a reduction in Iraq's overall military capability, even after Iraq had been compelled to withdraw from Kuwait and an exclusionary zone had been put in place. This was a controversial and potentially explosive idea. Thus far the Bush White House had framed its objectives in the Gulf entirely in terms of reversing Iraq's occupation of Kuwait and guaranteeing the safety of American citizens in the crisis zone. It had said nothing publicly—and very little privately—about reducing Iraq's military capability. President Bush himself had defined the criteria for success in the Gulf as Iraqi compliance with the UN resolutions calling for an Iraqi withdrawal and the restoration of the al-Sabah regime in Kuwait. The assumption was that if Saddam voluntarily withdrew his forces from Kuwait, he would have learned his lesson from the international community. Therefore, his army would not be attacked, UN sanctions against Iraq would be lifted, and things could return to the way they had been before.

But Pickering felt strongly that this was a formula for disaster. Iraq's invasion of Kuwait was not a random, one-off event. It was a symptom of a larger problem: the imbalance between Iraq's huge military establishment and those of its neighbors in the Gulf. His message to Washington argued that an effective politico-military strategy would need to address this issue:

> Our ideas . . . are based on the need to find a broader basis to ensure that Iraq does not return to the *status quo ante* in a position where its considerable military muscle can be a source of intimidation and threat to Kuwait, Saudi Arabia, Jordan, or other states in the region. Therefore, any withdrawal of [UN Coalition] forces from Saudi Arabia should be complemented by a significant reduction in the size and capability of Iraqi military forces.

This view had been the subject of much heated discussion among Pickering and his staff in New York. The idea of capitalizing on the crisis as an opportunity to weaken Iraq militarily was bold, but also highly unconventional, especially coming from a senior U.S. diplomat. But Pickering and his colleagues ultimately came to agree that Saddam's naked aggression against Kuwait, and his elaborate campaign of deception beforehand, merited an unconventional response.

"We were in a position to err on the side of extreme prudence towards Saddam Hussein," Pickering says, remembering the deliberations. "He'd already shocked us by going into Kuwait, so he had shown a propensity to misjudge colossally in throwing his weight around. We looked at the current situation as one in which we could take a challenge and perhaps turn it into an opportunity. The opportunity, obviously, was at the end of this particular event to see if we could reduce the potential of Iraq to cause trouble in a significant way."

Pickering envisioned that immediately after Iraqi troops had withdrawn from Kuwait and UN peacekeeping forces were in place, Iraq would be required to participate in "regional negotiations on security and high-tech weapons" as a condition for having the UN embargo lifted. Like Germany at the end of the First World War, or Germany and Japan at the end of the Second World War, Iraq would need to accept limits on both the size and offensive capability of its conventional armed forces. Saddam Hussein could no longer be permitted to retain a million-man army and three thousand tanks after having invaded two of his neighbors in the space of a decade. Pickering proposed limiting the size of the Iraqi army to two hundred thousand men—enough to guard the country's borders and maintain civil order, but not enough to launch an invasion. In addition, he urged "clear limits on armor, aircraft, artillery, and missiles, to be verified by the UN." Just as important as restrictions on Iraq's conventional arms would be regional negotiations aimed at eliminating Iraq's weapons of mass destruction, which at that point consisted primarily of Iraq's chemical arsenal and short-range missiles.

Once these measures to reduce Iraq's military capability had been implemented, Pickering was convinced that Saddam's own survival would pose little future threat to American interests in the Gulf. In the most controversial part of his paper for Washington, the UN ambassador argued:

> The principal problem has been and is whether we can seek and accept any solution in which Saddam Hussein remains in power, Iraq is heavily armed and developing sophisticated weapons, and is able as a result to bully and threaten its neighbors. In our view, the answer is obviously no, and we need to relate this response to our objectives.
>
> However, the continuation of Saddam as president should not be a major issue for us. . . . While Saddam is a dangerous catalyst in an Iraq which is malevolent, it is his military strength, power, and his economic potential that are concerning, not his personality (others might be worse).

.   .   .

Pickering's ideas drew a mixed reaction from the White House. The fundamental shortcoming of his plan, of course, was its assumption that Saddam Hussein could be compelled to withdraw voluntarily from Kuwait in the first place, and then would accept the highly intrusive security arrangements being proposed. Richard Haass, President Bush's senior Middle East security adviser and one of only a handful of administration officials who were privy to Pickering's thinking, was skeptical. On his personal copy of the Pickering document, Haass had highlighted the phrase *"any withdrawal of [UN Coalition] forces from Saudi Arabia should be complemented by a significant reduction in the size and capability of Iraqi military forces"* with a gigantic question mark and scrawled his own comment in the margin: "I think this is impossible."

Pickering himself was not naïve about the prospects of UN sanctions alone bringing Saddam Hussein to the negotiating table. "This is a tall order," he had admitted in his policy paper for Washington. "There is no certainty that sanctions will work, although Iraq seems uniquely suited to be the country in which to test the possibility." To the extent sanctions did work, Pickering believed "they should be encouraged to work in the direction of a full settlement, rather than merely returning Saddam to within Iraq's borders with his very considerable potential intact with which to threaten the peace and stability of the Gulf region any time he might wish to do so in the future."

However, while the overall plan may have been perceived as unrealistic, one of the main insights contained within it struck a deep chord at the White House and the State Department. For the first time, the Bush administration's senior figures began to think seriously about the long-term implications of an Iraq that escaped the Gulf crisis with its formidable military intact. This consideration would take on ever greater importance in their deliberations during the months ahead.

Pickering's work also highlighted the need to curtail Iraq's WMD programs as part of a larger settlement in the Gulf. The Bush administration, which had rarely mentioned Iraq's weapons of mass destruction in its public (or private) comments during the first month of the Gulf crisis, would now increasingly use Saddam Hussein's attempts to acquire these weapons as justification for taking decisive action against Iraq.

•   •   •

Another senior official besides Thomas Pickering had also arrived at the conclusion that the president's four principles were not enough to define America's objectives in the Gulf crisis.

In the Bush White House, as in every White House, presidential speechwriting was a collective endeavor. The speechwriters would produce an initial draft of most remarks made by the president. Then, depending on the topic and importance of the speech, subsequent drafts would be circulated to various senior staff members for review and comment before a final draft was given to the president to glance at. Chief of Staff John Sununu's office was the central clearinghouse in the process, and Sununu saw multiple drafts of virtually every speech the president made. His would also be the final word on most speeches about domestic policy.

For speeches about foreign policy, the final vetting would be done by the NSC staff at the White House. That meant they had to pass the Scowcroft test.

The national security adviser was a famously tough critic of draft policy documents. A former professor accustomed to reading (and grading) the papers of West Point cadets, Scowcroft was not bashful about correcting documents submitted to him, whether on minor points of grammar or major policy shortcomings. He would read every word and catch every misplaced comma with unforgiving gimlet eyes, and send shoddy documents back to their perpetrators riddled with changes.

And the same week that Pickering forwarded his ideas to Washington, the White House staff was working feverishly on the most important speech of George Bush's presidency. On September 11, 1990, the president would address a joint session of Congress, in a speech that would be nationally televised in prime time. The stakes could not be higher. The speech would be President Bush's first formal address to the Congress on the Gulf crisis, and his best opportunity—maybe his only opportunity—to explain to the American people why American troops were in the Gulf. It would be an essential speech for building public and congressional support for the difficult decisions that lay ahead. Scowcroft and the president had begun discussing major themes for the speech weeks earlier while vacationing together at the president's summer home in Maine, and the joint session speech had never been far from their thoughts in the eventful weeks since.

On the morning of September 11, Scowcroft sat in his spacious "power" office in the West Wing, reviewing the final draft of the speech. Something was missing.

The speech began in the same way as nearly every other public statement President Bush had made on the crisis since announcing the deployment of U.S. troops to Saudi Arabia: by repeating the president's "four objectives" in the Gulf. "Our objectives in the Persian Gulf are clear," read Scowcroft softly to himself, "our goals defined and familiar: Iraq must withdraw from Kuwait completely, immediately, and without condition. Kuwait's legitimate government must be restored. The security and stability of the Persian Gulf must be assured. And American citizens abroad must be protected."

That was all true; but something important was still missing.

Scowcroft realized that while the president's "four objectives" were an excellent set of criteria for defining a successful outcome to the Gulf crisis, they did little to define the stakes for the United States in the crisis: to explain *why* the United States should be in the Gulf at all.

And yet the stakes could not be clearer to Scowcroft and the president. Iraq's invasion of Kuwait was the first major challenge to international security after the Cold War. How the United States and the rest of the international community responded would determine what the post–Cold War world would look like. Scowcroft could not imagine bigger stakes. Indeed, this very point was made later in the speech.

Scowcroft turned his attention to the heart of the speech, which talked about the historic cooperation thus far between the United States and the Soviet Union. "Clearly, no longer can a dictator count on East-West confrontation to stymie concerted action against aggression," he read. Scowcroft changed this to "concerted *United Nations* action against aggression." This was the key point. In the post–Cold War world, the UN Security Council was to be the main instrument for confronting Iraq's aggression, and all future acts of aggression. The next paragraph read:

No longer will the machinery of the United Nations be sabotaged by the Cold War. When the Soviet Union joined with us in the United Nations to condemn the aggression of a former ally, then I knew at long last, we could put forty-five years of history behind us. At long last: the Cold War is over.

Scowcroft thought for a moment, then discarded the entire paragraph with three merciless strokes of his pen. As far as he was concerned, this speech—and this crisis—were about the future, not about the Cold War. Besides which, Scowcroft was not entirely convinced that the Cold War was over. And the less anyone was reminded that the Soviet Union had been an ally of Iraq for decades, the better.

He came now to the most important section of the speech:

We stand today at a unique and extraordinary moment. The crisis in the Persian Gulf, as grave as it is, also offers a rare opportunity to establish an historic precedent of cooperation. Out of these troubled times, a new world order can emerge, making the post–Cold War era freer from the threat of terror, stronger in the pursuit of justice, and more secure in the quest for peace.

Suddenly Scowcroft realized what was missing. In the draft he had just read, the president would first lay out his four objectives in the Gulf, and then later speak in sweeping historical language about the emergence of a new world order—as if these were separate things. But for Bush, the emergence of a new world order *was* an objective of U.S. policy in the Gulf. Not only an objective, but *the* objective. The national security adviser wrote the phrase *our fifth objective* above the phrase *a new world order*, and made a few other changes. The paragraph now read:

We stand today at a unique and extraordinary moment. The crisis in the Persian Gulf, as grave as it is, also offers a rare opportunity to *move toward* an historic *period* of cooperation. Out of these troubled times, *our fifth objective*—a new world order—can emerge: *a new era*—freer from the threat of terror, stronger in the pursuit of justice, and more secure in the quest for peace.

Scowcroft believed this language needed to go into the joint session speech as written, because it now perfectly captured what he and Bush had been talking about for the better part of a month. He gave a few instructions to the NSC Executive Secretariat on what the White House routing memo attached to the edited speech should say.

Attached is the edited version of the speech, the memo proclaimed. *General Scowcroft feels very strongly about his changes. Any questions please call his office—extension 2255.*

The president delivered the speech with Scowcroft's changes intact.

.   .   .

In Baghdad the next day, the staff of the U.S. embassy pored over a transcript of the president's speech. Joseph Wilson, the chargé d'affaires (the formal term for a senior diplomat acting in place of an ambassador) at the embassy, was especially pleased to see that the president had criticized Saddam Hussein's holding of foreign nationals as hostages in his speech. Because after completing the task he had just been ordered to perform by Washington, Wilson thought, he might become one.

On September 11, the day of the president's address to Congress, the White House received credible intelligence that terrorist groups based in Iraq were preparing to attack American interests in the Middle East. After an impromptu conversation among Bush, Scowcroft, and Haass, the president ordered that a warning be issued to Saddam Hussein.

While the rest of the White House staff was absorbed with preparations for that night's speech, Haass quickly banged out the text of an emergency "flash" telegram for the embassy in Baghdad and showed it to Scowcroft. At four o'clock the text was forwarded to the State Department for transmission to Baghdad.

Wilson reread the message flimsy in his hand:

NODIS

IMMEDIATE BAGHDAD

EYES ONLY FOR CHARGE WILSON

1. Secret {Entire Text}

2. Charge is to seek earliest possible appointment with Hamdun to deliver the following message.

— *I have been instructed to pass the following message to the government of Iraq and to request that it be relayed to President Saddam Hussein as soon as possible.*

— *The United States is aware that terrorist groups based in Iraq and supported by Iraq are making preparations at Iraqi behest for attacks against targets associated with the United States and its friends.*

— *Should any of these attacks take place, President Saddam Hussein should know that the United States will hold him personally accountable.*

3. Charge should not respond to any questions about the nature and source of any information in our possession or to how we would respond to any such attacks.

The first six weeks of the Gulf crisis had already been eventful enough for Wilson. The deputy chief of mission (DCM) in Baghdad, he had been April Glaspie's second-in-command at the embassy throughout the summer of 1990 as tensions rose between the United States and Iraq. The two diplomats were a study in contrasts: Glaspie, an intense, tough-talking workaholic; Wilson, possessing a laid-back demeanor and a flow-ing mane of brown hair that betrayed an adolescence spent as a California surfer (a hobby in which he occasionally still indulged while on his annual home leave in the United States). Glaspie harbored a deep fascination with Arab culture and had spent most of her Foreign Service career in the Middle East. Wilson was an Africa expert and had held more varied postings. Because of the sensitive relations between the United States and Iraq, the posting to Baghdad as DCM was considered a high-profile, career-building assignment for him, and Wilson had been looking forward to an ambassadorship of his own for his next job.

Everything changed when Iraq invaded Kuwait. Glaspie, who had left Baghdad several days before the invasion on a routine visit to Washington, had been formally recalled by President Bush in protest. Wilson suddenly found himself the senior American diplomat at a besieged embassy in a hostile country that might soon be attacked by the United States. He had already had one extremely unpleasant face-to-face meeting with Saddam himself. On August 6 the Iraqi ruler had summoned Wilson to his presidential palace to relay a message to President Bush.

"Convey to President Bush that he should regard the Kuwaiti emir and crown prince as history," a relaxed and confident Saddam had boasted. Echoing his remarks to Glaspie from several weeks previously, that the United States could "send planes and missiles and hurt Iraq deeply," Saddam continued: "I will tell you how you will be defeated. You are a superpower and I know you can hurt us, but you will lose the whole area. . . . You can destroy some of our economic and industrial base, but the greater the damage you cause, the greater the burden to you."

The situation in Baghdad had grown even more uncomfortable on August 22, when the Iraqi government had announced that all Western embassies in Baghdad would be closed and had given the diplomatic corps a deadline of forty-eight hours to leave the country or face arrest. That same day Wilson had been instructed by Washington to arrange an appointment with Iraqi foreign minister Aziz on a related matter: Iraq's announcement that it intended to detain citizens of the United States and other Western nations as "guests" of the Iraqi regime.

Concerned at the potential for another Iranian-style hostage crisis, the State Department evacuated most of the embassy staff in Baghdad. Wilson was left with a small skeleton staff of volunteers and temporary employees in an embassy suddenly surrounded by armed Iraqi troops. Then the Iraqis shut off the water and power. For weeks Wilson and his people had been subsisting on canned goods and brackish water.

Even so, morale was high. They were doing important work, and they knew it. Moreover, they had not abandoned hope in reaching a negotiated settlement to the crisis. The UN response to Iraq's aggression had been unprecedented. Economic sanctions might eventually start to bite in Iraq. Wilson and the other members of the embassy staff were determined to stick it out as long as possible.

* * *

But as the autumn of 1990 arrived, it appeared that Iraq's chances of retaining its Kuwaiti conquest appeared quite good. Even with Saudi Arabia now firmly garrisoned against invasion, Saddam Hussein occupied a very strong position in the Gulf. The U.S.-led Coalition forces arrayed against him were not sufficient to eject the Iraqi army from Kuwait. Although the UN economic sanctions imposed on Iraq were beginning to be felt, Richard Darman's prophecy two months earlier had been bitterly and entirely vindicated: The United States was proving less prepared to wage a prolonged sanctions battle than the authoritarian regime in Iraq.

The Bush administration's domestic political situation was beginning to unravel on all fronts. Iraq was not the only country that now had an empty treasury and a massive debt problem. By October 1, the beginning of the U.S. government's fiscal year, the Executive Branch had technically run out of money and Congress had not yet approved a new budget. During the first week of October the federal government had been kept running by temporary spending bills, but the White House faced the prospect of a government shutdown for the Columbus Day holiday, October 8.

Moreover, as Darman had also predicted, the cost of the American deployment in the Gulf had also widened the U.S. budget deficit. Secret negotiations were already under way between the White House and the congressional leadership on a budget that would include a significant new tax increase: a violation of the famous "Read my lips—no new taxes" pledge George Bush had made during the 1988 presidential campaign. Bush and the political side of the White House were already bracing for the certain fury of fiscal conservatives in the Republican caucus when the tax increase was announced.

There was also trouble in Congress from the left. With the safety of Saudi Arabia's oilfields no longer in jeopardy, consensus was growing among the Democrats who controlled both houses of Congress that the White House should allow plenty of time for sanctions to work. There was increasing pushback against the idea of any more U.S. troops being deployed to the Gulf without congressional authorization.

And even if Congress had been willing to support military action to force the Iraqis out of Kuwait, there was no workable plan to do so. On October 11 a team from U.S. Central Command headquarters in Riyadh had briefed the president and the principals of his national security team on CENTCOM's working plan for launching a military offensive to liberate Kuwait. The CENTCOM plan featured an unimaginative frontal assault directly into the teeth of Iraq's defensive positions in Kuwait. The president and his advisers were shocked at the rudimentary nature of the plan. Scowcroft in particular was incensed, commenting tartly that it was a plan designed to show why the United States shouldn't take military action.

Finally, 1990 was a midterm election year, and both the president and members of Congress had been distracted throughout the month of October by campaigning. Privately, Republican Party officials were already warning George Bush that there would be a significant number of Republican seats lost, as was usually the case for the party that held the White House during a midterm election. Whatever the president decided to do about Iraq, he would soon have to do it with less support on Capitol Hill than he had now.

The Bush administration was losing momentum and running out of time. And nowhere was this more apparent than in Saudi Arabia.

●   ●   ●

It was the B-52s that did it.

If Ambassador Chas Freeman could point to a single moment that crystallized for him Washington's inability to comprehend the larger strategic realities of the Gulf crisis, it had been the Bush administration's attempt to base B-52 bombers forty miles from Mecca.

Back in early August, when the deployment of U.S. ground forces to Saudi Arabia was just getting under way, the kingdom had still been largely defenseless against a possible Iraqi invasion from Kuwait. Washington had been desperate to get a military deterrent of any kind in place. One option had been to deploy B-52s to the region—large, lumbering

Air Force bombers that were synonymous with the "carpet bombing" of North Vietnam and Cambodia during the Vietnam War. The thinking was that if Iraq's forces poured across the Saudi border, the B-52s would rain tons of bombs down upon them from thirty thousand feet.

Gen. Norman Schwarzkopf had barely settled in at his headquarters in Riyadh when he received a "frag order" about the B-52s—a preliminary message alerting a field commander that a major deployment order was about to be issued. The frag order informed Schwarzkopf that a large contingent of B-52s was to be deployed at the Saudi forces base in Jeddah, on the Red Sea coast of Saudi Arabia. At the same time the Pentagon issued its order to Schwarzkopf, the State Department instructed Freeman to inform King Fahd about the deployment.

Freeman was horrified. The Saudi forces base at Jeddah was adjacent to the city's international airport, which just happened to be the airport through which millions of devout Muslims passed each year on their way to visit the Holy Mosque at Mecca: the most sacred shrine in Islam. Millions of Muslim pilgrims making the hajj (the religious pilgrimage to Mecca that all Muslims are required to make at least once in their lives) would arrive at the terminal in Jeddah and see the huge, ugly American bombers parked on the tarmac just beyond the airport perimeter. The faithful *in Mecca itself* might even be able to see the unmistakable silhouettes of the bombers as they took off and landed at Jeddah, less than forty miles away.

Freeman immediately sent a reply back to John Kelly, the assistant secretary of state for Near Eastern affairs, who oversaw U.S. embassies in the Middle East: No way. If Washington puts a single B-52 in the hajj terminal, he argued furiously, we're dead in the Arab world. This one picture will kill us. You will cause all of the instabilities that you managed to keep under control to break out.

This was not hyperbole on Freeman's part. Because Mecca has a large population of Islamic clerics, the region surrounding the city is the most culturally conservative in all of Saudi Arabia. The city of Mecca itself is closed to non-Muslims. When word got out that foreign infidels were basing planes near Mecca that would be used to kill other Muslims, there would be an uproar.

Freeman disputed the necessity of actually basing the B-52s in Jeddah.

That was asinine, he argued. B-52s could conduct bombing missions from bases thousands of miles away. Why not just put maintenance crews and equipment in Jeddah, so that the B-52s could attack from somewhere else and recover in Jeddah if necessary? If Saudi Arabia were actually defending its territory from an Iraqi attack, it would be a different story. Then it would be the Iraqis who would be committing a crime against Islam, and no one would care about the planes. But Saudi Arabia was not yet at war with Iraq. And the last time he looked, Freeman commented sarcastically, B-52s were not a defensive weapon.

Freeman did not hear back from Kelly. Instead, he received a cable from Kelly's superior, Robert Kimmitt, the undersecretary of state for political affairs and the third-ranking official in the State Department. The cable again instructed him to inform the king about the B-52 deployment.

You don't appear to have read my previous response, because you haven't addressed any of the arguments in it, Freeman shot back to Kimmitt. I'd like to be sure you've read and considered the previous response before I do this. I'm not going to do this on the basis of your instruction. Technically, this last line made Freeman guilty of insubordination, but that was the least of his worries.

The next order to see the king about the B-52s was much shorter, and was signed by Secretary of State Baker and General Scowcroft. Wearily, Freeman made the same reply. You don't seem to be listening to or paying attention to any of my arguments, he told Baker and Scowcroft. Recognizing that his days in Riyadh might now be numbered, the ambassador added: If you want to pull me out of here, make my day. I'm here to do a job, and I'll do it the best that I can, but it doesn't include executing stupid orders.

Throughout these back-and-forth exchanges, Freeman had been consulting with Norman Schwarzkopf about the B-52 deployment. Since Schwarzkopf's appointment as commander in chief of Central Command, he and Freeman had become fast friends. The blunt-spoken general and the equally direct ambassador appreciated each other's style, and each viewed the other as an ally in the inevitable bureaucratic battles with Washington. Schwarzkopf had a deep intellectual curiosity about the Islamic world, dating from his boyhood years when his father (also a

West Point graduate and army general) had served as a U.S. military adviser in Iran. A twelve-year-old Schwarzkopf had accompanied his father to Tehran and been enthralled by the region. Schwarzkopf was only too happy to pick Freeman's brain on the subject of diplomatic protocol in the Middle East. He had also discovered that Freeman had the ear of King Fahd and could discreetly run interference for him on sensitive matters related to the U.S. deployment.

"Do you want these things?" Freeman asked Schwarzkopf on the phone one day. "Do you need them? Because if you do, of course I'll support it."

"No, I don't know where this order came from," Schwarzkopf replied. "I don't want the damn things," he added, laughing heartily. Like many Vietnam-era infantrymen, Schwarzkopf had an ingrained skepticism about B-52 bombers. "I agree with you, it would be a big problem."

Freeman's next communication from Washington was a private message from President Bush. As a former ambassador himself, Bush's sympathies were always with the man on the spot. The president was far too tactful to upbraid one of his diplomats publicly; hence the private message. Why won't you do this? he pleaded with Freeman.

"Mr. President, I don't think your staff has familiarized you with the issues," Freeman replied. "Of course I'll do it, once I'm sure you've considered these arguments, and have rejected them."

By then, the pace of the U.S. deployment in Saudi Arabia had exceeded early expectations, and it had become clear that Iraqi forces were digging in defensively in Kuwait rather than preparing for an offensive against Saudi Arabia. Bush graciously let the B-52 matter drop. The president went out of his way to thank his ambassador for standing on principle when he visited Saudi Arabia later that year.

But the entire episode had filled Freeman with a sense of foreboding about the Bush administration's larger strategy in the Gulf. Worse, he now realized that the administration had not understood what King Fahd thought he had been agreeing to when Fahd accepted the deployment of American forces in his country.

For the president and his advisers, there had been one issue of overriding strategic importance after the invasion of Kuwait: countering the Iraqi threat to the oilfields in Saudi Arabia's Eastern Province. The key had been getting American boots on the ground in Saudi Arabia as quickly as possible, and the key to that had been getting the king to say yes to a deployment. The White House had pulled out all the stops to persuade Fahd to say yes: daily phone calls from President Bush to the king, Dick Cheney's high-profile diplomatic mission to Jeddah, even sharing sensitive U.S. satellite reconnaissance photos with the king and his counselors. It was a selling job of which Dale Carnegie would have been proud.

Once Fahd had accepted the deployment of American forces and the initial Iraqi bullet had been dodged, the Bush administration could take a breath and consider its next moves. With a "Desert Shield" in place to protect the Saudi oilfields indefinitely, the administration could allow time for sanctions and diplomacy to work against Iraq before it needed to reach a final decision on whether to force the Iraqis out of Kuwait through military action. In the meantime, the Saudis would accept any military deployments that American commanders deemed necessary for the defense of Saudi Arabia—even B-52 bombers near Mecca. This is what Washington thought King Fahd had agreed to.

The Bush national security team saw an obvious military threat to Saudi Arabia and reasoned that the Saudis could see the same threat. The only nation with the capability to protect Saudi Arabia in the near term was the United States. Therefore, while it was a bit uncomfortable for both sides, the only practical solution was the deployment of an American expeditionary force on Saudi soil. Saudi religious sensitivities were a challenge, but a practical challenge that could be surmounted through practical measures, like cultural sensitivity training for U.S. troops and placing strict restrictions on their behavior while in-country. At the end of the day, the White House reasoned, the Saudis would see this good-faith effort by the United States to respect Islam and recognize the need for the American forces to be there. After all, the king himself had invited them.

But most Saudis did not see the situation the same way. Their objection to the presence of American forces on Saudi soil was not based on practical considerations, but theological ones. They objected not to the behavior of the American troops, which was amazingly disciplined, or to their motives for being there, but to the very idea of their presence on

Saudi soil. Saudi Arabia was not just another Muslim country. It was *the* Muslim country: the birthplace of the Prophet Muhammad; the country where the two Holy Mosques of Mecca and Medina were located; the country from which the Prophet had launched the first jihad to bring Islam to the infidels. In this society, non-Muslims were considered infidels; non-Muslim troops were considered armed infidels, which was even worse.

The flap over the B-52 deployment had perfectly illustrated the chasm between these two worldviews. From Washington's perspective, the B-52s were a pragmatic solution to a daunting tactical problem. Confronted with the prospect of an Iraqi ground invasion in the weeks before there were enough troops on the ground to defend against one, the Pentagon had wanted to move one of its most powerful deterrent assets into the region. It was a sensible step, dictated by prudence. The Saudi air base at Jeddah was the most practical place to put the aircraft: easy to resupply, close to their area of operations, but out of range of Iraqi attack. That Jeddah was the port of entry to Mecca and that the B-52s themselves were fraught with negative connotations from the Vietnam era were considerations of secondary importance to the Pentagon.

The president and his advisers thought that they understood the issue of Saudi sensitivities about foreign troops, Freeman knew, and were sincere in trying to accommodate those sensitivities. But they had grossly underestimated the domestic pressures on Fahd over the issue. By early October, less than two months after the deployment of U.S. forces had even begun, the king was already under enormous pressure from religious conservatives in his country to bring matters to a head with Iraq and get the infidel soldiers out of Saudi Arabia.

The Saudi government had assumed that the next step after the deployment of U.S. troops would be an ultimatum to Iraq, and a deadline for Saddam to begin withdrawing from Kuwait. If that failed, they wanted immediate military action. The Saudis had not realized that there would be a long period of delay while the Bush administration waited for sanctions to work. Nor had they ever imagined that the initial American deployment—the nearly two hundred thousand U.S. servicemen (and worse, servicewomen) now in their country, and against whom Saudi clerics railed in their Friday sermons—might not be enough to drive Saddam Hussein away from the Saudi border.

The overriding strategic issue for the Saudi leadership was not just to remove the Iraqi threat to their Eastern Province, but to do so quickly, so that the non-Muslim troops could leave Saudi Arabia as fast as possible. King Fahd talked about little else in his meetings with Freeman.

President Bush and Secretary Baker were aware of the strains Fahd was under, because throughout the months of September and October, Freeman had been peppering them with telegrams on this very subject. But the secretary of state remained strongly committed to using sanctions to coerce Iraq out of Kuwait. Testifying to the House Foreign Affairs Committee on October 18, Baker declared: "We must exercise patience as the grip of sanctions tightens with increasing severity. Some may urge action for action's sake. But the only truly effective action we can take now is to continue to heighten Iraq's political, economic, and military isolation. Every day—in Washington, in New York, in the region—we continue our search for a peaceful solution."

On October 22, Baker sent a special "Eyes Only" cable to Freeman in Riyadh. The secretary reiterated his own commitment to UN diplomacy and sanctions as the keys to resolving the crisis. "A key element of our successful Coalition strategy is to keep the pressure on Iraq," he reminded Freeman. "The UNSC Resolution currently under discussion in New York is an example of the diplomatic efforts we will continue to promote along with the tightening pressure of economic sanctions." Baker remained sanguine about the efficacy of sanctions in Iraq: "Reports of gasoline rationing suggest sanctions are beginning to have the desired effect."

Responding to Freeman's warnings about the Saudis' impatience for a quick military resolution to the crisis, the secretary wrote:

> Until the necessary forces are in place, it is premature to speak too openly of deadlines or recourses to military measures. To reiterate, our policy at this point is to deter, defend, build force, and enforce sanctions. The steady buildup of Arab, Muslim, U.S. and allied military forces is narrowing Saddam Hussein's options in the manner most desirable to us.

Should it become clear that sanctions are not working, or should Saddam further provoke us, we would of course review all of the alternatives, including issuing deadlines and using military force.

We share the feelings of impatience which are so natural for Iraq's neighbors. And we understand the sense of urgency which you have expressed. But time is working against Iraq in many ways. We should let the pressure build on Saddam Hussein. Such time is necessary to allow sanctions to work and, if they do not, to demonstrate that we explored all peaceful options before resorting to military force.

But Freeman was convinced that Baker was wrong: Time was actually working against the United States and Saudi Arabia. He thought that the secretary of state's willingness to wait for sanctions to work in the Gulf was not only misguided, but dangerous. Sanctions in this case were a waste of time in the most literal sense: Not only were they not likely to work (and here Freeman was skeptical); they were also reducing the limited window of opportunity in which the United States *could* take military action.

Freeman expressed these views in one of the most remarkable strategy documents produced during the first Iraq War. On October 29, after consulting extensively with Schwarzkopf (who was also coming under pressure from his Saudi interlocutors to do something soon), the ambassador sent a NODIS cable to Bush and Baker. The cable's anodyne title— "Examining Our Military Options"—masked its explosive core premise: the Bush administration was running out of time to take military action against Saddam Hussein.

"Due largely to the weather," Freeman wrote, "there could be a shift in military advantage more toward the defense by the beginning of February. As we continue to tear pages out of the calendar, seasonal religious fervor, the return of summer heat, and the overall strain of maintaining an unwieldy international coalition may operate to make a large deployment of U.S. troops in Saudi Arabia increasingly untenable, especially if that deployment looks open-ended."

In particular, Freeman believed that the preparation period for the holy month of Ramadan and the subsequent hajj season (beginning in March 1991, barely four months away) was an absolute final deadline for American-led military action. During Ramadan and the hajj, any military activity in Saudi Arabia would be all but impossible:

> Initiation of offensive operations from Saudi territory during that period of religious affirmation and sacred peace will be in Saudi eyes virtually unthinkable. . . . Saddam Husayn [sic] will benefit from a much more receptive audience for his propaganda about desecration of the holy places by infidel troops. . . . He will likely find the Saudi government more on the defensive and more anxious to find a compromise solution.

Indeed, even the mere presence of non-Muslim troops in Saudi Arabia past March 1991 would be destabilizing, Freeman warned:

> Continued deployment of foreign troops during that period will bring into sharp focus underlying conservative Islamic opposition here and abroad. The strains on the Saudi government, as it confronts and addresses this opposition, will be prodigious and perhaps more than it can bear.

Thus, any American military operation against Iraq actually needed to be *completed* by the first week of March, Freeman argued, and preferably much sooner, so as to allow a full withdrawal of U.S. and other non-Muslim troops before the religious season in Saudi Arabia began.

It wasn't just the weather and the religious season in Saudi Arabia that Freeman was concerned about. He reminded Bush and Baker that Saddam's own strategy in the Gulf was served by a political war of attrition:

> Both we and Saddam are waiting for something to happen. We hope he will be overthrown or pressed by his followers to cut his losses by withdrawing from Kuwait. He no doubt sees a broader range of possibilities that events may serve to undercut us, and he retains the options of actions—like a partial withdrawal—to divide the coalition now arrayed against him.

Freeman ticked off some of the many possibilities that could benefit the Iraqi dictator:

- Incidents between Israelis and Palestinians that divide Arabs and Muslims from us and our European allies.

- Incidents between religious activists in Saudi Arabia and the non-Muslim forces deployed here, which could make our presence untenable for the Saudi monarchy.

- The crumbling of the Coalition at the UN as a consequence of one or more major actors going their own way, e.g., the French or the Soviets.

- A collapse of public support for the U.S. forces' presence in the Gulf, or more likely, a rise in domestic opposition to offensive action to liberate Kuwait and punish Iraq.

Looking at the calendar, and the likely need for a long air campaign to soften up Iraq's army, it was obvious to Freeman that preparations for a military offensive against Iraq needed to get under way immediately:

Given the lead times involved in additional U.S. and Arab deployments, judgments must be made NOW on whether we need to have an offensive option in order to resolve this crisis, because the favorable window for utilizing such an option begins to close just three months from now, by end of January.

As noted, the conditions for exercising an offensive option, if we then have one, will not be favorable between February and September. Holding the Coalition together over that period, given the amount of sand that could be thrown in its face, would be a major challenge.

In the meantime, the Saudis will face rising pressure from Islamic conservatives at home and abroad. We repeat our judgment, expressed in earlier messages, that a deployment of U.S. forces in Saudi Arabia which appears to be semi-permanent or of indefinite duration is not politically sustainable by the Kingdom.

For this reason, Freeman felt that the Bush administration had no choice but to take military action during the next four months. The alternative—leaving a large U.S. military presence in Saudi Arabia indefinitely to deter Saddam—was insupportable, in his view. "If we decide against developing an option to attack," he argued, "the decision should be based on a sober assessment of the prospects for non-violent means of achieving our objectives in a timeframe consistent with the limited half-life of our deployment."

Freeman highlighted the next-to-last sentence in the document, because he wanted to stress again that Saudi tolerance for the presence of American forces in their country *was* limited: "*It remains our judgment that Saudi and Arab political realities preclude a U.S. military presence in the Islamic holy land which appears to be open-ended or semi-permanent.*"

He ended his long telegram to Washington with a somber warning: "Not to decide soon, in this case, is also to decide."

.   .   .

Freeman need not have worried. However strong James Baker's preference for a diplomatic resolution of the Gulf crisis may have been, this preference was about to be trumped by a more decisive set of beliefs being awakened in the president. Even as his secretary of state was counseling the virtues of waiting for sanctions to work, Bush was beginning to think in terms of quite a different resolution to the Gulf crisis. Intriguingly, though, his reasons had little to do with Freeman's arguments, or with the other vital American interests at stake in the Gulf.

A first glimmer of Bush's change in attitude became visible during the final days of September 1990, which happened to coincide with a visit to the White House by the exiled emir of Kuwait. In his memoirs, Bush describes the sea change in his perceptions wrought by the emir's visit:

When he came to the White House on September 28, the Emir told me firsthand of the extent of the atrocities Iraqi troops were inflicting on his people, and this had a deep effect on me. It was during this period that I began to move from viewing Saddam's invasion as a dangerous strategic threat and an injustice to its reversal being a moral crusade. . . . His disdain for international law, his misrepresentation of what had happened, his lies to his neighbors all contributed; but perhaps it was hearing of the destruction of life in Kuwait which sealed the matter.

Many of the president's closest advisers also noticed a palpable change in his outlook during this period. Brent Scowcroft would later write: "It was my impression that somewhere in early to mid-October, President Bush came to the conclusion, consciously or unconsciously, that he had to do whatever was necessary to liberate Kuwait, and the reality was that that meant using force."

Bush's new hawkishness was becoming apparent to many in the press. In an exchange with reporters on October 9, the president expressed particular concern about Iraqi atrocities in Kuwait and the systematic looting of Kuwait's infrastructure, and hinted that this concern might prompt him to escalate the U.S. response to the Gulf crisis. Asked whether the systematic dismantling of Kuwait would affect his timetable for permitting sanctions to work in Iraq, Bush replied, "I am very much concerned, not just by the physical dismantling but the brutality that has now been written on by Amnesty International, confirming some of the tales told us by the emir about brutality.

"And so if your question is how long, I couldn't give you an answer in days or months. But it is a new equation in the last three weeks," the president said seriously. "The systematic dismantling of Kuwait concerns us enormously."

The ruling al-Sabah family of Kuwait was doing everything possible to reinforce this view. For a country whose territory consisted of "hotel rooms in London and Cairo," Kuwait was conducting an ambitious foreign policy, at least inside the Beltway. The al-Sabahs had access to nearly $120 billion in financial reserves invested outside of the Persian Gulf and were willing to part with at least some of it to get their country back. Shortly after the invasion of Kuwait, the exiled emir of Kuwait signed a $12 million contract with the blue-chip public relations firm

Hill & Knowlton to drum up support within the United States for military action to liberate Kuwait. At the time it was the largest PR campaign ever funded by a foreign government on American soil. The choice of Hill & Knowlton, over the many other public relations and lobbying firms in Washington, had been no accident: A senior executive in the firm's Washington office was Craig Fuller, a longtime Republican political operative and personal friend of the president, who had been Bush's chief of staff during his eight years as vice president, and had co-chaired Bush's presidential transition team after the 1988 election. Fuller took an active role in managing the Kuwaiti account for Hill & Knowlton.

The centerpiece of the firm's PR plan was a concerted campaign to call attention to the atrocities being committed by Saddam Hussein's regime. Hill & Knowlton had commissioned several million dollars' worth of polling and opinion research to frame its media approach. The research revealed that while many Americans were reluctant to see U.S. lives lost for oil, or to restore rich Arab sheikhs like the al-Sabahs to power, they were willing to support military action in the Persian Gulf to stop a power-mad dictator who was guilty of committing atrocities. "The theme that struck the deepest emotional chord," the head of the polling effort later said, "was the fact that Saddam Hussein was a madman who had committed atrocities even against his own people, and had tremendous power to do further damage, and that he needed to be stopped."

The PR campaign went into overdrive on October 10, 1990. That day on Capitol Hill the Congressional Human Rights Caucus held nationally televised hearings of testimony about alleged Iraqi atrocities in occupied Kuwait. While this was an entirely appropriate issue for Congress to take up, the choice of the Human Rights Caucus to convene the hearings was an odd one. Ordinarily, hearings about a major human rights crisis overseas would have been the province of one of the standing committees in Congress, like the Senate Foreign Relations Committee (which, of course, had conducted a major inquiry into Saddam Hussein's atrocities against the Kurds only a few years earlier). These committees had the subpoena power to require witnesses to testify under oath and possessed experienced professional staffs capable of conducting large-scale investigations. By contrast, the Congressional Human Rights Caucus was not even a real congressional committee. It was an informal group of congressmen interested in raising awareness about human rights issues. The group's leading figure was Democratic congressman Tom Lantos of California. The only Holocaust survivor ever to serve in Congress, Lantos commanded respect on human rights issues. The Human Rights Caucus was closely affiliated with the eponymous Congressional Human Rights Foundation, which occupied free office space at Hill & Knowlton's Washington headquarters. The cochairs of both the Human Rights Caucus and the Foundation—Lantos and Illinois Republican John Porter—chaired the hearings on Iraqi atrocities in occupied Kuwait.

Witness after witness came forward to provide graphic details on "the rape of Kuwait" by Saddam's forces. Unquestionably, however, the most riveting moment of the day was the testimony of a serious, dark-haired fifteen-year-old girl who was said to have been lucky to escape from occupied Kuwait. She was identified only by her first name of Nayirah. Her family name was being withheld, Lantos told the hushed audience in the hearing room, to protect her family from Iraqi reprisals. Tearfully, the girl testified that she had been a volunteer in one of the hospitals in Kuwait City on the day of the Iraqi invasion. "I volunteered at the al-Addan Hospital. While I was there, I saw the Iraqi soldiers come into the hospital with guns, and go into the room where babies were in incubators. They took the babies out of the incubators, took the incubators, and left the babies on the cold floor to die."

The story about the incubators created a national outcry among the American people. It was the lead story on every national newscast that evening, all of which replayed clips of Nayirah's testimony. No fewer than seven U.S. senators would later cite the incubator testimony in the floor speeches they gave in support of their votes to authorize military action against Iraq.

What the American public would learn only a year later was that Nayirah was not who she claimed to be. She was in fact the daughter of Sheikh Saud Nasir al-Sabah, Kuwait's ambassador to the United States and a member of the Kuwaiti royal family. The ambassador had been present at the hearings on Iraqi atrocities, but apparently had not felt compelled to fill in some of the gaps in his daughter's testimony—especially when she had already been coached for hours on what to say by a

Hill & Knowlton staffer. Perhaps more disturbing, Lantos had known the girl's actual identity but had kept the information to himself rather than impugn the star witness at his own hearings.

Not only had Nayirah misled the world about her family background, but the incubator incident she had described in such searing terms almost certainly never took place. Indeed, it was doubtful that she even had been in Kuwait at the time of the invasion. Amnesty International later conducted its own extensive investigation of the charge and determined "that the story about babies dying in this way did not happen on the scale that was initially reported, if, indeed, it happened at all." The testimony did resolve one unanswered question, however: why the Congressional Human Rights Caucus had been chosen to conduct the hearings rather than an actual congressional committee. As one observer later commented: "Lying under oath in front of a congressional committee is a crime. Lying from under the cover of anonymity to a caucus is merely public relations."

Perhaps the greatest irony of the entire episode was that there was no need to manufacture Iraqi atrocities in Kuwait, since there were plenty of real atrocities taking place. Iraqi troops may not have seized incubators with their babies still in them; but on Saddam Hussein's orders, they had laid hands on practically everything else of value in Kuwait, stripping homes and offices down to their plumbing fixtures. So many cars alone were expropriated and sent north to Iraq that automobile prices in Baghdad remained depressed for years afterward. The Iraqi security forces dispatched to quell any internal resistance to the occupation dealt with the captive population of Kuwait City much as they dealt with ordinary Iraqis back home: like thugs. There were dozens of killings and hundreds of rapes, many directed not against Kuwaiti citizens (who were a minority population within their own country), but against the large population of Palestinian expatriates in Kuwait who provided the bulk of the country's workers.

Nevertheless, the incubator story triggered a strong emotional response from President Bush. Speaking with reporters the day of the incubator testimony, the president declared how much the story had affected him. "It's just unbelievable," he said, shaking his head. "I mean, people on a dialysis machine cut off, the machine sent to Baghdad; babies in incubators heaved out of the incubators and the incubators themselves sent to Baghdad. It's just sickening."

What was most significant about Bush's outrage over the atrocities being committed in Kuwait was the direct impact these atrocities had on his stated preferences for handling the Gulf crisis. Bush later admitted that the atrocities made him "very emotional" and "really gave urgency to my desire to do something active in response. . . . I am sure the change strengthened my decision not to let the invasion stand, and encouraged me to contemplate the use of force to reverse it."

It was also during this period that Bush began drawing the direct comparisons of the Iraqi regime to Nazi Germany, and Saddam Hussein to Hitler, that would become the rhetorical signature of the Gulf crisis. In a speech on October 15, the president made his famous characterization of Saddam as "Hitler revisited." Bush completed the image by offering his opinion on what the Iraqi dictator's fate should be: "But remember, when Hitler's war ended, there were the Nuremberg trials."

Bush's increasing tendency to personalize the Gulf crisis as a conflict between Saddam Hussein and the rest of the world troubled many of his closest advisers. "He clearly personalized it," Richard Haass remembers, "at times to a degree that I was a little bit uncomfortable with because sometimes he departed from some of the things we'd written for him and personalized it." Haass was less concerned about the president straying off message than by the possibility that the president's strident rhetoric would create unrealistic expectations about the outcome of the Gulf crisis.

"It worried me that there was a gap between the stated war aims and the aims he was starting to suggest," Haass later admitted. "If you so demonized Saddam, I was worried that even if you liberated Kuwait, you would leave a sense of frustration or dissatisfaction. On the other hand, if you weren't prepared to do all of the things you needed to do to oust the regime, again you were setting yourselves up. I was uneasy about that, just because it seemed to get the United States leaning in the direction of outcomes that it couldn't guarantee unless it was prepared to occupy the whole country and essentially oust the regime. But to simply say those things and try to stimulate support (to the extent the president was doing that), it seemed to me it raised expectations beyond policy at that point."

Brent Scowcroft was so alarmed by the change in Bush's tone during this period that he quietly took steps to ensure that either he or Haass accompanied the president to all of his speaking engagements, to monitor any inflammatory remarks he made about Saddam.

The president himself identified the main source for his equation of Saddam Hussein to Hitler. In numerous public appearances throughout the month of October, the president alluded to the book he had been reading that autumn—Martin Gilbert's history, *The Second World War*—and admitted that he saw similarities between Gilbert's graphic accounts of Nazi atrocities in Poland and Iraq's occupation of Kuwait. Speaking at a Republican fundraising breakfast in Vermont on October 23, Bush revealed to his audience, "I'm reading a book, and it's a book of history—a big, thick history of World War II. And there's a parallel between what Hitler did to Poland and what Saddam Hussein has done to Kuwait."

If Saddam Hussein was Hitler revisited, that made Saddam's Republican Guard the modern-day equivalent of the SS. "Hitler rolled his tanks and troops into Poland," the president explained to the rapt Republican crowd in Vermont. "And do you know what followed the troops? It was the Death's Head regiment. Do you know what the Death's Head regiment of the SS was? They were the ones who went in and lined up the kids that were passing out leaflets. Do you know what happened in Kuwait the other day? Two young kids, mid-teens, passing out leaflets—Iraqi soldiers came, got their parents out, and [made them] watch as they killed them."

However facile the comparison of Iraq's heavy-handed ministrations in Kuwait to the Nazi overlordship of Europe may have been, Bush was quite sincere in accepting the validity of the comparison. Of particular resonance to the president was one of the central morals of Gilbert's history: that European appeasement and American isolationism had created the climate for Nazi aggression. Bush's statements at the time reflected an easy conversance with one of the main "lessons" of the 1930s: that failure to respond early and decisively to acts of aggression by atavistic regimes can lead to larger conflicts later. This lesson provided the cognitive prism through which the president began to interpret the nature and stakes of the Gulf crisis.

Bush's belief in the power of history to guide critical decisions about war and peace was not a recent development. In his mid-thirties, while still living in Midland, the future president had read *The Longest Day*, Cornelius Ryan's classic account of the D-Day landings, and was so moved that he felt compelled to write Ryan a letter.

"I think in this day and age many of us are inclined to view all of our international problems without due consideration to the human aspects of a total war," Bush wrote to the author. "We have short memories in this connection. Your forthright and sensitive treatment of D-Day is going to be crammed down the throats of each of our four boys as soon as they are old enough to digest the importance of this fine book." Bush saw this passing on of historical wisdom as one of his primary parental responsibilities.

Yet Bush's beliefs about confronting aggression were not only a product of his reading. These beliefs also dated back to his teenage years, when the future president had actually lived through many of the events chronicled by Martin Gilbert and Cornelius Ryan. Just as some would later describe George Bush's successor in the Oval Office, Bill Clinton, as a living metaphor for the conflicted 1960s generation from whence he came, Bush, too, was in many respects at the vanguard of his own generation. The youngest U.S. Navy pilot during the Second World War, George Bush was a charter member of the Greatest Generation that had defeated fascist aggression in Europe and the Pacific. He thought like one, and now he was beginning to act like one.

President Bush's insistence that Saddam Hussein and his "henchmen" be punished for their atrocities in Kuwait was not new. It was an attitude almost identical to the one expressed by the young Lieutenant Bush serving in the Pacific, forty-six years earlier. In a wartime letter to his parents, Bush shared his views on what the fate of those who started the war should be:

> I hope the guilty receive the treatment they deserve. I feel so
> strongly that the Nazis, fascist, or whatever moniker they use,

should all be dealt with severely. The leaders—those responsible for murder, famine, treachery, etc. must be *killed*. I hope our government and our allies act boldly and powerfully and mete out severe but just penalties.

If this is not done with all leaders who have collaborated with the Nazis, whether they be recognized heads of government or quislings ruling in conquered countries, I fear these 4 years of bloodshed will have been for naught.

The injection of these personal beliefs radically transformed Bush's views on what the ultimate disposition of the Gulf crisis should be. Before, Bush would have been content merely to see Saddam Hussein slink back to Iraq with his tail between his legs, having been taught a salutary lesson by the international community. Now, after the hostage-taking and other atrocities that Saddam had committed, the president wanted to see him punished personally.

But it was also true that in casting Saddam Hussein as an evil dictator in the mold of Hitler, and the Gulf crisis as a replay of the 1930s, Bush had—like Hill & Knowlton—finally discovered a rationale for American military intervention in the Gulf that resonated strongly with the American public, especially the patriotic, Greatest Generation voters who were the core of the Republican base. Hitler and atrocities were far more tangible to these Americans than any "new world order."

The discovery came not a moment too soon. On November 8, two days after the midterm congressional elections in which the Republican Party, as predicted, lost seats in both houses of Congress, the White House announced a major new deployment of U.S. troops to the Gulf, including an unprecedented call-up of reserves. This deployment would effectively double the number of American military personnel in the Gulf theater, from 250,000 to over 500,000. Shortly after President and Mrs. Bush returned from a Thanksgiving visit to U.S. personnel stationed in the Gulf, the UN Security Council took up debate on a resolution authorizing the use of force in the Gulf. On November 29, by a vote of 12-2 with China abstaining, the Security Council passed Resolution 678, which authorized members of the UN Coalition "to use all necessary means" to restore "international peace and security in the area." The resolution set a deadline of January 15, 1991, for Iraq to comply; only six weeks away.

•   •   •

During the months following the invasion of Kuwait, President Bush and the other senior figures of his administration had embarked upon an intense campaign of diplomacy to win support for the U.S. stand in the Persian Gulf. The primary targets of this diplomatic charm offensive were the major Middle East powers. The leaders of countries like Saudi Arabia, Egypt, and Turkey had been lavished with frequent telephone consultations from Bush himself, and with visits by James Baker, Dick Cheney, and other top U.S. officials. Even Syrian president Hafez al-Assad, long a bête noire of American foreign policy owing to his country's support for international terrorism, had been graced by a visit from Baker. Virtually every nation in the region could boast of having received similar high-level attention from the Bush administration.

Except one. During the first four months of the Gulf crisis, no Cabinet-level official from the administration had visited Israel, despite the fact that Saddam Hussein had repeatedly announced his plan to attack Israel in the event that any military action was taken against Iraq. The traditional U.S. alliance with Israel was under great strain.

In August 1990, three weeks after the Iraqi invasion of Kuwait, the United States learned that the Israeli air force planned to fly aerial reconnaissance missions over western Iraq, where Israeli military intelligence had long known that Scud missiles targeted against Israel were based. The Bush White House went ballistic over the news. Bush and his advisers were bending over backward at the time to soothe Saudi sensibilities about the deployment of U.S. forces to the region. They were also still hoping to lure King Hussein of Jordan into the anti-Saddam Coalition. For Israeli aircraft to fly reconnaissance over western Iraq, the planes would need to violate the airspace of Saudi Arabia, or Jordan, or both— an action that might instantly wreck Arab cooperation against Saddam.

On August 23, Ambassador Samuel Lewis was instructed to deliver a harsh warning to the government of Prime Minister Yitzhak Shamir in Israel. "We have heard disturbing reports to the effect that Israel might fly reconnaissance missions over Jordan and/or Western Iraq," the warning stated. In unusually strong diplomatic language for a communication to a friendly foreign government, it continued: "Israel needs to understand the enormity of the stakes involved for the U.S. and the reality that actions of the sort being threatened, which could easily create an incident that could jeopardize U.S. interests, would simply not be understood or found acceptable in Washington." The planned flights were postponed.

More tension was soon introduced. On October 8, Israeli troops fired on Palestinian protesters in Jerusalem, killing twenty of the protesters in what came to be known as the Temple Mount incident. Israel was immediately denounced in the UN Security Council. This the Israelis expected. What they did not expect was that the United States, Israel's traditional diplomatic ally at the UN, would cosponsor a resolution condemning the Israeli action and calling for an investigation into how the international community could better protect the Palestinians. Coupled with the harsh warning in August, the American response to the Temple Mount incident contributed to a strong sense within the Israeli Cabinet that the Bush administration was tilting unapologetically "Arabist" in its foreign policy orientation.

Further contributing to the perception of pro-Arab tilt within the Bush White House were memories of the actions taken by President Bush and Secretary of State Baker during an earlier crisis involving the United States, Israel, and Iraq. In 1981 the Begin government of Israel had launched a preemptive air strike that destroyed the Osirak nuclear reactor outside Baghdad—the centerpiece of Saddam Hussein's long-cherished dream of building an "Arab bomb." Far from supporting Israel's action on nonproliferation grounds, the Reagan administration had roundly condemned it. Two of the most ardent critics of the attack had been Ronald Reagan's vice president, George Bush, and his chief of staff, James Baker. At the time, the United States had been trying to forge closer ties with Iraq as a substitute for the relationship with Iran lost with the fall of the Shah in 1979, and Israel's action was criticized by Bush and Baker as damaging to this effort.

The contrast between President Bush's warm embrace of Arab leaders like Hosni Mubarak and King Fahd, and the cold shoulder directed toward Israel, filled the Shamir government with foreboding. That an American secretary of state had visited Syria but not Israel during a major crisis in the Middle East had not gone unnoticed by the Israelis.

It had also not gone unnoticed by Israel's many friends in Washington. The relationship between the Bush White House and the powerful Israel lobby on Capitol Hill had been strained since George Bush's earliest months in office. The strain, ironically, had begun with Bush's first meeting with Yitzhak Shamir. In March 1989, only weeks after Bush's inauguration, Shamir had visited Washington for a get-to-know-you meeting with the new U.S. president. Bush seized upon the opportunity to inform Shamir that his administration would be taking a more "balanced" approach on the Palestinian question, particularly on the contentious issue of new Israeli settlements in the West Bank.

"Your settlement policy is a real problem," Bush told Shamir privately.

"It won't be a problem," Shamir assured the president. Bush assumed this to mean that Shamir would do what the Bush administration wanted him to do, which was impose a freeze on new settlement activity. What Shamir meant was that Israeli settlement policy should not be a concern for the United States.

Shortly after Shamir left Washington, the White House received a report that the government of Israel was building a major new settlement in the West Bank.

"He lied to me!" the president fumed to his staff. Bush thought that Shamir had given his word that there would be no new settlements; and in George Bush's personal code of behavior, going back on one's word to another head of state was a major offense. From that point on, recalls one associate of the president, "there was no love lost between Bush and Shamir."

Two months later the Bush administration had also become embroiled in a dispute with one of the most important pro-Israeli organizations in the United States. In May 1989, Secretary of State Baker was scheduled to deliver a major speech to the American Israel Public Affairs Committee (AIPAC), one of the most powerful lobbying groups in all of Washington. Baker asked Dennis Ross and the Policy Planning Staff at the State Department to draft the speech. It was a difficult assignment.

Baker wanted to use the speech to stake out the Bush administration's tough new position on the settlement issue, which was sure to be a hard sell to an AIPAC audience.

Ross assigned the task of writing the speech to his deputy, Harvey Sicherman, but because the subject matter was so sensitive, he took an active role in the process as well. You can say the hard things, Baker was advised by Ross. I'm okay with you saying the hard things, added Ross, who was Jewish and considered himself a strong supporter of Israel. But you've got to have grace notes. Together, he and Sicherman produced a page and a half of "grace notes"—conciliatory statements about the importance of the American-Israeli special relationship in the eyes of the Bush administration.

On May 22, Baker delivered his speech at AIPAC's annual convention. "For Israel, now is the time to lay aside the unrealistic vision of a Greater Israel," the secretary of state declared, which entailed "a ban on new settlements." Ross listened to the rest of the speech with mounting concern. There was something crucial missing.

He took out all the grace notes, Ross thought glumly to himself.

Baker's hard line did not stem from any personal animus against Israel. He simply believed that a more "evenhanded" approach toward Israel was a key to improving America's relations with the Arab world. Having been involved with the Houston oil industry for most of his professional life as both a lawyer and an investor, Baker believed that cultivating stronger ties with the Arab oil states was essential for U.S. economic and national security interests.

Nevertheless, reaction to Baker's speech from AIPAC and other American Jewish organizations was predictably furious. The Bush White House went into full damage control mode. Richard Haass was enlisted to meet with representatives of several prominent organizations and hear their concerns about Baker's speech. Meanwhile, Bobbie Kilberg, the staffer in the White House Communications Office assigned to liaison with Jewish organizations, summarized the fallout from the speech in a May 24 memo to John Sununu.

"Secretary Baker's speech has generated widespread domestic political concern for us within the Jewish community," she wrote, "and we do not believe it is a one or two day story. While the controversy over the specifics of the speech may die down, the general anxiety within the Jewish community will persist." Baker's use of the loaded term "Greater Israel" (which was associated only with the most radical wing of the Zionist movement) had been perceived as especially antagonistic. "Several people noted that if Secretary Shultz [George Shultz, Baker's predecessor as secretary of state] had made the same speech he would have gotten away with it, because the Jewish community trusted him and felt warmly about him. They have not developed the same feeling about Secretary Baker," Kilberg observed drily.

Besides the domestic political damage, Kilberg worried about the repercussions on the administration's already strained relationship with the Shamir government: "This public strategy has undermined rather than strengthened Shamir's position in Israel, and will have the ultimate effect of solidifying the far right led by Sharon." Israeli general Ariel Sharon had been anathema in Republican foreign policy circles since 1982, when as Israel's defense minister he ordered a controversial Israeli invasion of Lebanon that inflamed Arab-Israeli tensions and indirectly led to the deaths of 241 U.S. Marine peacekeepers in Beirut.

The Gulf crisis had done nothing to repair the damaged relations between the White House and the American Jewish community. If anything, some decisions related to the crisis had only worsened matters.

On September 16, 1990, the *New York Times* reported that the Bush administration was postponing a long-planned UN debate on Resolution 3379, the infamous UN resolution from the 1970s equating Zionism with racism. The administration's thinking was clear: At a time when it needed as much UN support as possible from within the Arab bloc in order to maintain an international Coalition against Iraq, opening a debate on Zionism would only spark outrage in the Arab world. But the Zionism resolution was an issue of huge symbolic importance to many American Jews—as George Bush well knew from his days as UN ambassador. Even inside the White House, some were dismayed by what they saw as the president's betrayal on the issue. The day after the postponement was reported in the *Times*, William Kristol, chief of staff to Vice President Quayle, called a meeting of his small staff to confront the issue. "I'll get us together to discuss how to ensure that this 'postponement' isn't a retreat. . . . It seems to me the president should still mention this in his UNGA [United Nations General Assembly] speech," Kristol opined.*

Then in October 1990, the White House proposed to Congress a $15 billion arms sale to Saudi Arabia—at the time the largest foreign arms sale in American history. Again, the administration's rationale for the policy was the Gulf crisis. But the sale, which would include sophisticated weapons like F-15 fighter jets, would reverse a long-standing U.S. policy of maintaining Israel's qualitative edge in military technology over the Arab states. The proposed deal drew sharp criticism from members of Congress on both sides of the aisle.

On November 14, AIPAC got its revenge for Baker's speech the previous year. Speaking to the CJF General Assembly, a national gathering of Jewish community leaders in San Francisco, AIPAC executive director Tom Dine summarized his own views about President Bush's policies toward Israel.

"The administration seems to have lost its compass where it comes to the U.S.-Israel relationship," Dine said to loud applause. "Repeatedly, it has made the error of attempting to curry favor with Arab coalition partners by distancing the United States from its one permanent ally in the region." Dine went on to cite a litany of issues on which the White House was seen as having taken sides against Israel.

When Haass got wind of Dine's speech, he alerted Sununu and Scowcroft about this latest criticism of the president. Forwarding a copy of the speech to Sununu, he wrote his own assessment on the first page:

> John,
>
> Here's the speech I mentioned. As you'll see, Dine misses an opportunity to say something constructive re: the Gulf situation & avoids saying anything positive about the President at all. Then he draws battle lines against the arms sale going forward in late January.
>
> *Not helpful!*
>
> Richard H.

---

* The Zionism resolution was in fact revoked three months later by passage of Resolution 4686 on December 16, 1991.

But in early December 1990, with the January 15 deadline for the use of force against Iraq barely a month away, the White House began to think seriously about the possibility of a military campaign in the Gulf. Securing an Israeli pledge not to intervene in a possible war against Iraq suddenly became a top priority for the Bush administration. The threat that Saddam Hussein might respond to any U.S.-led military action by attacking Israel was very real. Another face-to-face meeting between President Bush and Prime Minister Shamir was hastily arranged for December 11.

One week before the meeting, on December 4, the Shamir government made known to Washington its price for keeping a "low profile" in any war against Iraq. Israeli foreign minister David Levy sent a private message to Secretary of State Baker which hinted that Israel might be willing to forgo unilateral military action against Iraq—provided that the White House expanded its five objectives in the Gulf to include also the elimination of Iraq's weapons of mass destruction.

The political section of the U.S. embassy in Israel was instructed to prepare an assessment of the thinking behind Levy's offer. The assessment, dated December 7, pulled no punches: The overriding concern of Shamir and his Cabinet was that Saddam and his huge military establishment might escape the Gulf crisis scot-free, to threaten Israel and the Middle East another day. "Concerned about Iraqi military capabilities for years, the GOI [government of Israel] has watched the Gulf crisis largely with a view to its eventual impact on Baghdad's strategic position," the assessment began. "In the GOI view, even a complete withdrawal would be problematic if it left Iraq's conventional and especially nuclear arsenal intact."

The analysis explained in detail the reasons for this position: "An Iraqi withdrawal that merely returned to the *status quo ante* would be unpalatable here. The GOI would consider such an outcome to be no real return to the status quo. . . . According to the GOI, Saddam would be able to portray this 'face down' of the U.S. and the West as a victory. Most important, from Israel's point of view, would be Saddam's retention and continued development of his formidable conventional and especially unconventional arsenal."

The Israelis need not have worried. The Bush administration was thinking along the same lines.

At ten o'clock on the morning of December 11, Bush met privately in the Oval Office with Yitzhak Shamir. Brent Scowcroft and the newly appointed Israeli ambassador to Washington, Zalman Shoval, were the only other officials present. Ostensibly the meeting was an opportunity for Shoval to present his diplomatic credentials to Bush. In reality the meeting was a belated attempt by the White House to reassure a skeptical Shamir and gain Israeli acquiescence to the Bush administration's strategy in the Gulf.

After a few stilted pleasantries, Bush got down to the matter at hand.

"We understand the fears in Israel based on the current situation," the president said. "I'm glad we have these private moments, because I have some sensitive comments to make.

"If Saddam Hussein does not get out, we will take him out—with overwhelming force. He may not realize it yet. Cheney can give you the details. I will use overwhelming force if required to force compliance with the UN Resolutions. In the talks with the Iraqis, we are not going to negotiate, we will just be informing them.

"I must ask for complete privacy for these comments," Bush added seriously. The president had good reason for this last request. He had neither informed the American people about his decision to use force nor obtained congressional authorization for doing so.

"First, we will respond," Bush assured the prime minister. "The Congress may be ambivalent, but I am not. I am still thinking about how to handle them.

"Second," the president continued, "there is no tradeoff against Israel. Nothing will be done at Israel's expense. No one has suggested such, but there won't be one at all.

"Third, I do understand the threat you face from Iraq. I thank you for your low profile. I know that it isn't easy and that he threatens you all the time."

Then came the clincher. Bush addressed the concern of Shamir's government that Saddam would survive the Gulf crisis with his formidable arsenal still intact.

"We have the capability to obliterate his military structure," the president boasted. "We have a beautifully planned operation, calculated to . . ."—Bush fumbled momentarily for the right word—"*demoralize* him forever."

The president's choice of verbs was not lost on the prime minister.

5

VICTORY FATIGUE

By this time the top echelon of Bush administration officials was talking openly among themselves about the need to "reduce" Iraq's military strength as an indispensable part of any resolution to the Gulf crisis. On December 18, during a major address to the Foreign Policy Research Institute in Philadelphia, Vice President Dan Quayle let slip remarks that hinted at war aims far beyond just ending the Iraqi occupation of Kuwait. "Once Iraqi forces have left and the legitimate Kuwaiti government has been restored, our job will still not be over," Quayle warned. "We cannot allow a situation in which an aggressive dictator has a million-man army, thousands of tanks, hundreds of jets, and access to billions of petrodollars."

Quayle's remarks caused a brief flutter of panic back at the White House. While his words reflected behind-the-scenes thinking that had been taking place within the Bush administration since Tom Pickering had advanced a similar idea back in August, no senior official had publicly described the systematic destruction of Iraq's military capability as one of the main reasons U.S. service personnel were soon to be put at risk in the Gulf.

Behind the scenes it was a different story. The Deputies Committee had been tasked by the administration with generating a formal list of war aims for a possible conflict with Iraq. Deputy National Security Adviser Robert Gates acted as the White House's eyes and ears during discussions on this topic. "The idea of a significant reduction of Iraqi military power, on a permanent basis, was a significant element of the whole discussion of what our war aims were," Gates recalls. "It was one of the principal aims that we put in the paper that the president signed."

The deputies ultimately agreed on three possible war aims and ended up endorsing two of them to the president. The first, obviously, was forcing Saddam Hussein out of Kuwait. This the deputies agreed on literally within five minutes. The second proposed war aim, a permanent reduction of Iraqi military power, sparked a little more debate. Not on the need for it to happen—on this point there was near unanimity—but on how much the Iraqi military should be reduced. Significantly, at this point in time, the deputies worried most about Saddam's massive conventional army and above all about his elite Republican Guard, the most powerful force of mechanized troops in the Arab world, which they saw as a constant overhanging threat to the Gulf region.

"We debated a while," Gates remembers, "but ultimately reached agreement on the elimination of the Republican Guard as a military force, period." Richard Haass, who also participated in the conversations, explains the reasoning behind this aim: "The war itself was something of an effort to ensure that Iraq itself did not emerge as the principal power of the Gulf. One of the reasons we did what we did was not simply for reasons of the rule of law, although that was important in the post–Cold War era, the precedent; it wasn't simply for reasons of energy; it was also to make sure that Iraq did not become the dominant power of the Gulf."

According to Haass, the imperative of reducing Saddam's army determined not only one of the main goals of U.S. military action against Iraq, but also the way the conflict would be fought. "There was a rationale for not simply fighting the war narrowly in Kuwait, but for taking the war to Iraq and to Saddam, because you could argue it tactically: that it was necessary so he couldn't bring them to bear in Kuwait. So it was a totally legitimate tactical argument. But I'm not going to sit here and say it didn't occur to some of us that there was also a strategic rationale for it, because it was a way of to some extent cutting Saddam down to size, so he couldn't do it again quite as easily."

Where weapons of mass destruction were concerned, the deputies were willing to accept a "significant degrading" of Iraqi capabilities as a realistic goal. Iraq's large stocks of chemical munitions and their associated delivery systems, like Scud missiles, would be a top-priority target of the Coalition air campaign because these could potentially be used on the battlefield against Coalition forces. Iraq's nuclear and biological weapons capability was believed to be at a more nascent stage of development. Bombing of the suspected nuclear and bioweapons sites would be enough, it was thought, to set these programs back for years, perhaps forever.

A third potential war aim was hotly debated by the deputies for weeks: replacing the regime in Baghdad. "Ultimately, we unanimously recommended to the president and to our bosses that that not be a war aim," Gates remembers. "Because we couldn't figure out how to guarantee that we could achieve it. That was for us the Vietnam scenario."

To a great extent the deputies' recommendation not to make the toppling of Saddam Hussein an explicit U.S. war aim was informed by lessons they had taken away from an earlier military intervention by the Bush administration, the 1989 invasion of Panama to remove the regime of Panamanian strongman Manuel Noriega. After U.S. troops had secured Panama within a matter of days, Noriega himself remained at large for several weeks before unexpectedly reappearing at the Vatican embassy in Panama City, where he tried to claim asylum. The embarrassing incident had made a deep impression on the Bush national security team.

"Saddam wasn't just going to wait on his verandah for the 24th Mechanized Infantry Division to arrest him," Gates observed. "And what it would require would be the occupation of most of Iraq, and probably a difficult time finding him, which sounds interesting in retrospect, given what subsequently happened in Iraq. Our view on that was shaped in some measure by the difficulty we had finding Noriega in Panama."

Gates also maintains that the budget-strapped Bush White House did not want to be left "holding the bag" in Iraq, forcing U.S. taxpayers to bear the cost of rebuilding Iraq after a major conflict to remove the Ba'ath regime. "Our concern was that if we had been in occupation, having bombed bridges and everything else, we would be expected to fix it all, and we didn't want any part of that."

•   •   •

Given the importance that the Bush administration's prewar planning attached to reducing the Iraqi military, the possibility that Saddam might pull out of Kuwait as abruptly as he had invaded—with his army unscathed—was a nightmare scenario for the White House. If Saddam were somehow to obtain international support for a deal that would end his occupation of Kuwait in exchange for assurances that no attack would be launched against him, the administration would need to find some pretext for refusing to accept the deal.

There were growing indications that Saddam himself was pushing hard for just such an eleventh-hour negotiated pullout. On December 21, Joseph Wilson in Baghdad reported to Washington that "Iraq is still actively looking for a way out of this mess." Apparently unaware of the administration's new set of war aims, he offered a tantalizing detail to demonstrate just how serious Baghdad was in exploring a negotiated settlement: "Saddam is clearly concerned about guarantees that his army will not be attacked during a withdrawal period." Wilson advised that the Bush administration should immediately issue a statement ("hopefully at the Secretary or Presidential level") announcing that "if Saddam withdraws, he leaves with his army intact."

Such a statement, he suggested, might "provide to the Iraqis the fig leaf that Saddam needs to get out of this peacefully." Once this statement was made, Wilson further recommended, "we should go home for Christmas and not say anything more. . . . I believe that our silence will terrify the Iraqis much more than our bluster."

Nor was Wilson the only channel through which Iraq was trying to secure such a promise. Several weeks earlier, on November 28, Margaret Thatcher had resigned as prime minister of Great Britain after losing an internal ballot for leadership of the ruling Conservative Party. Her replacement as prime minister was John Major. Apparently hoping that the new British government would be more amenable to compromise than the Iron Lady, Iraq communicated a similar suggestion to the British through diplomatic channels. British foreign secretary Douglas Hurd suggested to Major that a note be sent to Saddam assuring him that "if he withdrew from Kuwait, he would not be thumped."

Of course, the White House had no intention of providing any sort of "fig leaf" that might allow Saddam to leave Kuwait with both his army and his dignity intact. The plan firmly in place by late December 1990 was for Coalition forces to permanently weaken Iraq's ability to project military power outside its own borders, and "degrade" the country's WMD programs for years to come, while avoiding the risky steps of over-throwing the Ba'ath regime or occupying Iraq itself.

Nowhere was the divergence between the Bush administration's pub-licly stated objectives in the Gulf—the "four principles" Bush had de-clared during the first week of the Gulf crisis—and the more expansive set of goals it had framed in private more apparent than in another NODIS cable from Chas Freeman in Riyadh to the president and Sec-retary Baker. Freeman's December 30 message to Washington bore an evocative title that reflected the chasm between the administration's closely held war aims and what it was telling even many Coalition allies—"U.S. and Coalition War Aims: Sacked Out on the Same Sand Dunes, Dreaming Different Dreams."

Freeman's cable accepted as a given that the impending military ac-tion in the Gulf was as much about "reducing" Iraq as liberating Kuwait. The ambassador warned that camouflaging the disparity between Bush's publicly stated objectives for taking military action and Washington's ac-tual military objectives in the Gulf was becoming increasingly difficult.

"The greatest point of vulnerability," he wrote, "lies in war aims pur-sued by U.S. forces but which have neither been endorsed by the Secu-rity Council nor thoroughly discussed and agreed among the Coalition's members." His concern, he wanted understood, was not with the war aims themselves; only with the possibility that countries might abandon the Coalition if they realized that Washington was pursuing its own set of military objectives unrelated to enforcing UN resolutions.

"The Coalition could well fall apart during conflict over what military actions are and are not appropriate to achieve strategic objectives that seem to some to go beyond those explicitly endorsed to date by the [Se-curity Council]," Freeman warned. "These objectives—which focus on reducing Iraq rather than on liberating Kuwait—lie at the heart of our fundamental long-term interest in restored security and stability in the Gulf. They must be the center of our war planning against Iraq."

The key to maintaining the pretense that the United States had no agenda of its own in attacking Iraq, Freeman urged, would be to justify "attacks on military infrastructure units and lines of communication inside Iraq as paving the way for the liberation of Kuwait by Arab forces in the Coalition, rather than as ends in themselves." Freeman suggested that the same held true for the elimination of Iraq's chemical and biological warfare (CBW) programs: "The destruction of Iraq's CBW capabilities and missile forces should likewise be justified in terms of the need to protect Saudi Arabia from the immediate threat of Iraqi attack on their population centers, rather than as serving a long-term U.S. interest."

·　　·　　·

As the deadline for U.S. military action in the Gulf approached, President Bush's interpretation of the Gulf crisis in sweeping historical terms became an ever more prominent feature in his public and private statements. Only in a moral crusade against a "Hitler revisited" could Bush find a mission worthy of risking the lives of young Americans, as he had been required to risk his own a half century earlier.

In a deeply personal New Year's Eve letter to his five children, released only years after he left the White House, the president cast the coming Gulf War in terms of its relation to the Second World War. "My mind goes back to history," Bush wrote. "How many lives might have been saved if appeasement had given way to force earlier on in the late 30s or earliest 40s? How many Jews might have been spared the gas chambers, or how many Polish patriots might be alive today?"

Foreshadowing the sort of Manichaean language that one of his children would use twelve years later as the rationale for a second Gulf War, the president revealed the ultimate stakes of the Gulf crisis in his mind. "I look at today's crisis as 'good' vs. 'evil'," he wrote. "Yes, it's that clear."

·　　·　　·

Shortly after the invasion of Kuwait in August 1990, the White House had assigned the critical task of contingency planning for the aftermath of the Gulf crisis to the Deputies Committee. As military action in the Gulf became almost inevitable during the first weeks of January 1991, this subject increasingly dominated discussion in the deputies' meetings.

Besides the five permanent DC members—Deputy National Security Adviser (and later CIA director) Bob Gates; Undersecretary of State Robert Kimmitt; Undersecretary of Defense Paul Wolfowitz; Deputy CIA Director Richard Kerr; and Adm. David Jeremiah—the working group assembled for the Gulf crisis also included Richard Haass from the NSC staff.

The deputies' paper on "post-crisis Gulf security structures" was drafted by then Assistant Secretary of State Richard Clarke and his staff in the Politico-Military Affairs Bureau at the State Department. Clarke was an occasional participant in meetings of the Gulf working group. His paper reflected months of deliberations among the deputies on this subject. On January 11, only four days before the January 15 deadline for Saddam Hussein to withdraw from Kuwait before facing military action, Clarke circulated a draft of the paper to his peers for their review and comments. Clarke's draft dismissed Saddam's own personality and ambitions as the primary factor behind his invasion of Kuwait. Instead, it advanced the prevailing view among the deputies that a breakdown in the Gulf balance of power had been at fault. "Regardless of Saddam Hussein's motivations," Clarke wrote, "the Iraqi invasion of Kuwait was only possible because of a collapse of the regional balance of power. Iraqi military strength increased in the 1980s, while that of Iran diminished significantly." To Clarke and his colleagues, the deputies, the logical corollary was that "a key security objective is to help reestablish a balance so that future aggression against the [Gulf] states by either Iraq or Iran will be deterred." Here, Clarke alluded to President Bush's oft-stated promise that American troops would not remain in the Gulf "one day more than necessary" to force an Iraqi retreat from Kuwait. "In developing policy," he wrote, "we will have to take into account our extensive reliance on the UN in the current crisis and the President's statements on U.S. intentions toward a permanent presence of U.S. ground forces in the region."

Clarke's paper considered two possible "endgame cases" in the Gulf. The worst-case scenario, labeled "Case 1: Unchanged Capabilities," foresaw a situation "in which the continued viability of Iraq's military will enable it to launch a massive attack against Kuwait and Saudi Arabia on very short warning." Of even greater concern under this scenario were the limited options available for controlling Iraq's development of weapons of mass destruction—essentially, either a postwar continuation of the UN embargo against Iraq that had been established after the occupation of Kuwait; or opening negotiations with Iraq on the issue. Clarke and the other deputies were not sanguine about the latter alternative, noting tersely that "our leverage would be based upon the continuation of sanctions."

By contrast, "if Iraq is deprived of its conventional military capabilities and weapons of mass destruction" under "Case 2: Combat Destruction," Clarke saw a number of advantages for the United States:

- U.S. peacetime presence of ground troops would not be necessary.

- Need for staging/basing of U.S. aircraft in the region would be reduced.

- The requirement for prepositioning of U.S. material would be lessened, but not eliminated.

- The size of the multinational peacekeeping force and the extent of non-Arab participation would probably be reduced.

The advantages of the "Combat Destruction" scenario were even more pronounced where weapons of mass destruction were concerned. Clarke saw the ideal solution to the problem of Saddam's proliferation efforts as one "in which Iraq's WMDs and its production capability have been severely attrited by combat. The goal in Case 2 would be to prevent or limit rebuilding, and possibly to dismantle some capability that survived. The terms we sought to impose could be part of an armistice agreement and there might be a different leadership in Iraq."

.   .   .   .

There was now only one remaining obstacle to U.S. military action in the Gulf: Congress. Since the November midterm elections, and the

White House's surprise announcement on November 8 that it was doubling the number of American troops in the Gulf, opposition to the use of force had been steadily mounting among the Democrats in Congress. In perhaps the surest indication of the importance that legislators attached to the question, Congress had cut short its sacrosanct winter recess and had agreed to begin debating the use of force in the Gulf during the first week of January.

For months, advice had been flowing into the Oval Office from many quarters on how the president should "handle" Congress. The congressional Democrats, of course, with solid majorities in both chambers, wanted the final decision on whether to go to war to rest with them. On October 30, House Speaker Tom Foley had met with Bush and handed him a "letter of concern" signed by eighty-one Democratic members. The letter stated: "We are emphatically opposed to any offensive military action. We believe that the UN-sponsored embargo must be given every opportunity to work and that all multinational, non-military means of resolving the situation must be pursued." If these did not succeed, then the signatories wanted to seek a formal declaration of war from Congress as described in Article I of the U.S. Constitution. Even many of the Republicans in Congress, while supporting the White House's handling of the crisis on both political and policy grounds, also wanted Bush to obtain some sort of congressional authorization for the use of force.

Conversely, several members of Bush's war cabinet were adamantly opposed to involving Congress in the decision at all. Brent Scowcroft, for one, had long harbored a deep philosophical aversion to what he thought of as congressional "meddling" in the foreign policy prerogatives of the Executive Branch. The national security adviser's 1967 PhD thesis at Columbia had been a four-hundred-page jeremiad on this very theme. Scowcroft was invariably a pessimist about congressional performance in foreign policy. In his view, the membership of Congress was at best uneven in terms of foreign policy interest and ability; and at worst, even those members considered to be reliable voices in foreign policy were capable of breaking ranks with the White House without warning on issues of fundamental importance to the national interest. Scowcroft had drawn a cautionary conclusion in his thesis: "How easy it is to negate much of the good will patiently built up through years of skillful diplomacy in a relatively few moments of irresponsible action." A more quintessentially Scowcroftian comment would be difficult to imagine.

The Bush administration had already experienced one major congressional "defection" during the Gulf crisis, in the person of Democratic senator Sam Nunn. The Georgia lawmaker, long considered by Republicans the leading "national security Democrat" on Capitol Hill for his hawkish views and knowledge of defense matters, had stunned the White House by adamantly opposing U.S. military action in the Gulf. In his capacity as chairman of the Senate Armed Services Committee, Nunn had subsequently convened a panel of retired generals and admirals, including former JCS chairman Admiral William Crowe, to testify against taking offensive action to expel Iraqi troops from Kuwait. Most of the Bush national security team considered Nunn's stance to be nearly a betrayal, but to Scowcroft it was yet another illustration of why Congress could not be entrusted with important foreign policy decisions.

The other figure in the president's inner circle arguing against seeking congressional authorization for the use of force was more of a surprise: Dick Cheney. Cheney's opposition was surprising because, like Bush, he himself had served in the Congress, occupying Wyoming's lone seat in the House of Representatives for ten years. Cheney had even served in the House leadership as minority whip before being selected as Bush's secretary of defense. Naturally then, Bush sought his advice on how to deal with the current congressional leadership, one former member to another.

"It's such a vital problem that we have no choice but to move in and liberate Kuwait," Cheney privately counseled the president. "Even if the Congress votes no, we'd still have to do it." Cheney suggested that even asking for congressional authorization would be a mistake. "Asking for their approval and being turned down would create a major confrontation with the Congress of having asked for their authority and having it denied," he reasoned with Bush. "We would then have to say, 'Well, we didn't need that anyway, we've got the authority to proceed.'" Cheney thought this last outcome would be the riskiest course of all. For good measure, the former House Republican whip added a withering assessment of his "friends on the Hill."

"In the end," Cheney told the president, "they don't accept responsibility for tough decisions up there."

But Bush himself was committed to obtaining congressional authorization, for a very different reason. Having served in Congress from 1967 to 1971, at the height of the Vietnam conflict, Bush remembered the acrimony that waging an "undeclared war" had caused for both Lyndon Johnson and Richard Nixon. He was determined not to share their fate. One of his private hopes in the current crisis, shared only with Scowcroft and his immediate family, was that a decisive military outcome in the Gulf would go far toward "licking the Vietnam syndrome" that had plagued American foreign policy since the 1960s. For this to happen, however, Bush believed that it was essential that he act with congressional approval.

On January 12, just seventy-two hours before the UN-mandated deadline for the use of force against Iraq, Congress voted on the issue. After a nationally televised three-day debate marked by emotional speeches on both sides, both chambers of Congress provided the president with authorization to use force. In the Senate the vote was an agonizingly close 52-47. A shift of only three senators' votes would have caused the Gulf resolution to be defeated.

⋅ ⋅ ⋅

The night of January 15 came and went peacefully in the Gulf. During the predawn hours of January 17 (January 16 in Washington), Operation Desert Shield became Operation Desert Storm. The crusade to liberate Kuwait began with the most ambitious air bombing campaign in history. Within the first twenty-four hours of Desert Storm, Coalition aircraft flew over 850 sorties. It was a performance they would repeat night after night after night for the next six weeks. Among the Iraqi casualties the first night of the war was Saddam Hussein's presidential palace complex in Baghdad, which was razed to the ground along with several of his government's ministries. Saddam himself confronted the beginning of the Gulf War with customary bravado. "The great duel, the mother of all battles has begun," he intoned over Iraq's state radio network just hours after the first attacks. "The dawn of victory nears as this great showdown begins."

Although the initial wave of Coalition air attacks met with considerable success and few casualties, Saddam had made preparations for attacks of his own. In a long-anticipated ploy to erode the cohesion of the UN Coalition arrayed against him, he ordered that Iraqi Scud missiles be launched against Israel, a nonbelligerent in the conflict over Kuwait. On the evening of January 18, the unmistakable high-pitched warbling of air raid sirens began in Jerusalem, in Tel Aviv, and in dozens of smaller Israeli towns. Yet as the world watched in helpless empathy as Israeli families donned gas masks against the possible threat of poison gas, the White House achieved the impossible. In a private telephone conversation, President Bush persuaded a distraught Israeli prime minister Shamir to forgo making a retaliatory strike against Iraq—a reversal of Israel's long-standing policy of responding militarily to every attack on its soil. Thus, while Palestinians in Jordan and the West Bank took to the streets to celebrate the attacks and chant Saddam's name, no Arab government withdrew from the UN Coalition against Iraq. It was, perhaps, the ultimate tribute to Bush's immense credibility at that moment as leader of the international community.

·   ·   ·

"You know, the president usually likes what you write. He didn't like this."

These were not the words Richard Haass had been hoping to hear from his immediate boss, Brent Scowcroft. Several days earlier Scowcroft had quietly asked Haass to draft a new paper for President Bush on war termination. "The president and I had this conversation, and he asked that you do a piece for him on how all of this is going to end," Scowcroft said. The massive Coalition air campaign had begun only two days earlier, and the launch of the Desert Storm ground offensive was still more than a month off, but Bush was already having second thoughts about his administration's existing strategy for bringing the Gulf conflict to an end.

Haass had worked feverishly to produce the required document, and now the president's judgment was in, conveyed by Scowcroft.

"That memo you sent went over like a bomb," the national security adviser informed Haass, allowing himself a rare chuckle. Both men were under tremendous stress. "You want to try your hand at it again?"

"I can try my hand at it again, but I don't think you're going to get a different memo," Haass replied calmly.

"Why don't you try," urged Scowcroft. Haass trudged back to his office, clutching the rejected memo in hand like an errant schoolboy with a poor test paper.

There had not been many poor test papers in his past. Haass was a former Rhodes Scholar, with a doctorate from Oxford. Smooth and self-assured, with a sardonic sense of humor and occasional nasal twang that revealed his Brooklyn roots, he had taught briefly at Harvard's Kennedy School of Government before entering government service during the Reagan administration. Like many of the senior national security officials in the Bush White House, Haass had experience across a broad range of federal agencies. He had worked at both the State Department and the Pentagon during the Reagan years before accepting Scowcroft's offer to join George Bush's NSC staff. Naturally, Haass's role as Bush's main adviser on the Middle East had taken on even greater significance after the invasion of Kuwait.

Haass did not look forward to rewriting this particular paper. The difficulty, he anticipated, would be in finding language that could win the president's approval. Even before submitting his first draft, he had expected that its major conclusion would not be likely to please the president. In his view of what this war should achieve, George Bush was out of step with most of those advising him.

Just days before the start of the Desert Storm air campaign, the Defense Intelligence Agency had circulated its secret assessment of likely political conditions in a postwar Iraq. Back in July 1990 the DIA had been the only U.S. intelligence agency to correctly predict the Iraqi invasion of Kuwait, a circumstance that lent this DIA report great credibility. Titled "Iraq's Armed Forces After the Gulf Crisis: Implications of a Major Conflict," the report predicted confidently that "if military action is necessary to force Iraq out of Kuwait, it will require a major military effort and lead to the fall of Saddam Hussein." It further predicted that "a military resolution would largely eliminate the Iraqi non-conventional weapons threat." That was the good news.

The bad news lay in the memo's warning that Saddam's ouster could not be expected to alleviate all the problems associated with Iraq's aggressive foreign policy. "A successor government would display hostility towards the U.S., Israel, Egypt, and the Gulf Cooperation Council states, and also continue to promote Iraq's role in the Arab world," DIA warned. It added that a successor regime "would resume pursuit of weapons of mass destruction to support its ambitions."

The DIA report went on to suggest that "the successor to Saddam would most likely be a Ba'ath party official, probably from Saddam's Tikriti clan, who would govern with heavy military involvement; or a military officer who would probably also be a Ba'ath party official." Within the U.S. intelligence community, the odds-on favorite to replace Saddam was Izzat Ibrahim al-Douri, vice chairman of Iraq's Revolutionary Command Council and a longtime Saddam crony. (Ironically, the prediction that Saddam would be succeeded by Izzat Ibrahim turned out to be correct, but only twelve years later and under very different circumstances. Izzat, labeled the "king of clubs" on the United States' list of fifty-five most wanted Iraqi officials, assumed control of the remnants of the Ba'ath Party when Saddam himself went into hiding after the U.S. occupation of Baghdad in 2003. Loyal to the Iraqi dictator to the end, Izzat would become the principal architect and financier of the guerrilla campaign in Iraq that claimed thousands of American lives.)

Under the heading "Threat to Iraq," the DIA report also discussed the potential danger posed to a post-Saddam Iraq by two neighboring countries: Turkey, a NATO ally of the United States and a vital member of the Gulf War Coalition; and Iran, certainly no ally of the United States. "The most significant Iranian threat would be Tehran's potential support to Iraqi Shia and Kurdish separatists," it warned. "Iran could be expected to support Kurdish separatists, who would likely resume an insurgency aimed at independence or autonomy from Baghdad." DIA estimated that "dealing with Kurdish separatists and other internal security problems in the vulnerable post-crisis period would tie up many of Iraq's weakened forces," leaving Iraq's borders with Iran virtually undefended. Just as Saddam himself had attempted to capitalize on the fall of the Shah by invading Iran in 1980, setting off the eight-year Iran-Iraq War, Tehran might now be willing to return the favor. Should such an outcome occur, the United States would not be able to influence events in the Persian Gulf easily, if at all, with turmoil likely to descend upon the region.

Many of the conclusions in the DIA assessment turned out to have been seriously flawed. But flawed or not, the DIA report reflected the prevailing view of the intelligence available at the time. The dangers it pointed out appeared to be consistent with assessments from other intelligence sources, including one December report that warned: "The whole fertile crescent—Iraq, Syria, Lebanon, Jordan—is in question. The leaders of all of these states are standing on the edge of precipices. It is possible that a situation could develop in which U.S. troops circle the wagons around the oil fields of the Gulf as the region descends into primordial chaos."

One existing war-termination paper that Haass consulted, based on secret planning done by the Kuwaiti Task Force/U.S. Army Civil Affairs Reconstruction Group, painted a daunting picture of the conditions that U.S. forces would confront in the event of a regime collapse inside Iraq:

> If Iraq sustains massive damage to its civilian and economic
> centers *or* central government authority collapses, it will require
> significant foreign assistance, including emergency relief and
> possibly civil administration. The resulting chaos and civil unrest,
> however, could severely limit the scope of such assistance.
>
> The death of Saddam could cause a leadership crisis of
> indeterminate length. . . . The Iraqis' ability to restore civil order
> quickly would depend on whether the Ba'ath regime (with or
> without Saddam) survives. A political collapse, for example, could
> set off a struggle among competing Iraqi factions.

The paper went on to echo the warning that "political and military collapse could make Iraq vulnerable to the predatory ambitions of its immediate neighbors."

Predictions like these had helped Haass define the key question driving any war-termination strategy in the Gulf: What would the fall of Saddam Hussein mean to U.S. interests? It was Haass's answer to this most important question that had displeased the president. If the Bush administration wished to avoid a worst-case outcome, Haass concluded, then as much as everyone might detest Saddam Hussein, the United States should not make regime change a condition for terminating the war.

Haass knew beforehand that this was not a recommendation likely to find favor with George Bush. The president had not concealed from those close to him his desire to see the Iraqi dictator removed from power. Since the previous September, when the first reports of Iraqi atrocities began emerging from occupied Kuwait, Bush had been confiding to his staff that his preferred outcome to the crisis was "some kind of Ceauşescu scenario"—a reference to the Stalinist dictator of Romania, Nicolae Ceauşescu, who in December 1989 had been deposed and killed by an angry mob after the collapse of Soviet support for communist dictatorships in Eastern Europe.

The president's desire to see Saddam brought down had only intensified when the Ba'ath regime began detaining American and other Western civilians as hostages during the run-up to the Gulf War. Nothing could do more to convince this particular president that a foreign adversary was beyond rehabilitation than the act of taking Americans hostage. That Saddam's Western "guests" were eventually released had not diminished Bush's anger, or his conviction that the Iraqi leader and his "henchmen" should be removed from power and made to pay for their crimes.

And therein lay the problem Haass faced. While fully aware of the president's almost Manichaean views about Saddam, Haass also knew that his boss Brent Scowcroft did not share the president's position.

To galvanize public support for the battle to come, the president had been focused on persuading Americans that the brutal invasion and occupation of little Kuwait was an immoral act that could not be allowed to stand. But Haass knew that Scowcroft's war aims were more pragmatic than moral: 1. demonstrate American resolve to the rest of the world; 2. get Iraqi troops out of Kuwait and away from the Saudi oilfields as quickly as possible; and 3. reshape the balance of power in the Persian Gulf so that another invasion could not happen—in that order. Like many of the Republican foreign policy luminaries who had first risen to prominence in the 1970s as disciples of Henry Kissinger, Brent Scowcroft was a self-professed Realist, which to people with doctorates in international relations meant more than just having a commonsense outlook on life.

Realists subscribe to a theory of world politics predicated on the notion that it is a balance of power among nations that keeps the peace.

Conversely, the most dangerous situation is one in which the balance in a particular region is upset by a local power suddenly becoming disproportionately stronger or weaker. Realist theory predicts that if an aggressor state challenges the underlying stability of a region by trying to increase its relative power, other nations will create an alliance to stop the aggressor. Likewise, if a major regional power suddenly becomes much weaker because of a crushing military defeat or internal strife, Realism asserts that this invites aggression by neighboring countries.

Scowcroft often claimed to have "cut his foreign policy teeth" on Realist theory while studying for his doctorate at Columbia during the 1960s, when debate in academic circles raged between proponents and critics of what was then called *Realpolitik*.* He had recruited an NSC staff dominated by fellow Realists. Haass was one such person; another was Condoleezza Rice, the NSC's Soviet expert and Scowcroft's prize protégée, who would often tell journalists with a disarming smile that *Realpolitik* was one of her favorite words.

Iraq's attempt to dominate the Persian Gulf and the world's oil supply by seizing Kuwait had been a textbook example of a nation exploiting an imbalance in the regional balance of power. The Bush administration's creation of a Coalition to counter Iraq and restore stability to the Gulf had thus far been a textbook Realist response. And Realists within the Bush administration like Scowcroft and Haass wanted to make sure that once a balance of power had been restored to the Gulf region, it would not be upset again—as might occur should the overthrow of Saddam lead to turmoil and civil war inside Iraq. The United States was not about to fight Iraq in order to hand Iran an opportunity to exploit instability in the region and increase its own influence in the Gulf.

"The concern was more that a dramatically weakened Iraq would be in no way able to stand up to Iran," recalls Haass, "which would then free up Iran to do whatever it wanted in the region: whether it was incursions in Iraq, or problems for Bahrain, or problems for anybody else, or set the terms for OPEC decision-making. The concern was essentially that if Iraq were that weak, Iran would essentially have too much of a free hand."

---

* From the German for "realistic politics."

Now, in his second attempt at a paper outlining a war-termination strategy in Iraq, Haass had to try once again to move the president away from his own position and over to Scowcroft's.

•   •   •

The second draft of the war-termination paper was ready on January 20, 1991—the second anniversary of George Bush's inauguration.

Bush's reaction was not long in coming: Again no dice. Typically, the president had annotated the draft with margin comments written in his large, distinctive handwriting. His main comment (at least judging by the number of times Bush had written it on the document) appeared to be *Why Not?*

As he ruefully contemplated the task of writing yet another draft, Haass reflected on the oddity that as close as Scowcroft and the president were as friends, their views on how the war in the Persian Gulf should end seemed irreconcilable. After some reflection, the reason became clearer to Haass. Because the worldviews of the two men had been molded by very different formative personal experiences, they came to the question of just what the ultimate outcome of the Gulf War should be with very different starting assumptions.

Like most people who had spent any amount of time with George Bush, Haass knew that the Second World War was the frame of reference for much of what the president believed about the use of force as a tool of American foreign policy. Bush approached the Gulf crisis presuming that Desert Storm should end the way World War II had ended, with a surrender ceremony at which victorious American generals would dictate terms to a vanquished enemy, much as General Douglas MacArthur had done with the Japanese aboard the USS *Missouri* in Tokyo Bay. Bush's desire for an unambiguous end to the conflict was of a piece with his vilification of Saddam as "Hitler revisited" and his promise of war crimes trials for the Iraqi dictator and his "henchmen." In Bush's own experience, moral wars ended with the unconditional surrender of the aggressors into the custody of the victors, where they would be punished by the international community for starting the war in the first place.

By contrast, Scowcroft's formative experience had been working with

Henry Kissinger on the kinds of issues that would appeal to a lifelong disciple of *Realpolitik*: sweeping initiatives to reshape the global balance of power, such as President Nixon's opening to China, or Soviet-American détente. Scowcroft saw Iraq's invasion not primarily as an issue of justice or injustice, but as one of bolstering American credibility and restoring the balance of power in the Gulf. Scowcroft left it to Haass to tick off for the president the major reasons "a battleship *Missouri* ending" (which was how Haass had begun to describe the president's desire for a clean end to the conflict) was impossible in the Gulf: "It goes beyond our domestic writ; it goes beyond our international writ; it goes beyond what the Coalition would sustain; and most important of all, it would require an indefinite occupation of Iraq by U.S. forces."

Based on the realities of the situation, Haass argued that the best that could be hoped for was a conflict lasting long enough to allow the U.S. to degrade much of Iraq's WMD capability and destroy some of the Iraqi army, but not so much that Iraq could no longer maintain order within its own borders or defend itself against hostile neighbors like Iran.

"There was some concern that 'too successful' a war against Iraq, one that so decimated Iraq's military capabilities, would lead to a Persian Gulf imbalance, a balance of power rather, in Iran's favor. And there was some concern about that. One wanted a significantly weakened Iraq, but not necessarily a decimated Iraq. If I had to summarize it, that's where we came out."

And even if Saddam himself were toppled by an internal coup—not an outcome that should be an explicit objective of Desert Storm, Haass emphasized—his likely successor would be a Ba'ath Party general who would pursue the same confrontational policies against the West, including the development of weapons of mass destruction.

*   *   *

The third and final version of Haass's war-termination paper was ready on January 23. It ran nine pages. This time, he and Scowcroft went to discuss its conclusions with the president personally.

Usually gracious with his staff, almost courtly, the president was in a testy mood that day. Haass knew Bush well enough to recognize that he was anxious and frustrated. The Desert Storm air campaign was now a week old, and the United States was beginning to absorb casualties—and the first casualties had all been aviators, like George Bush had once been. Beginning on the second night of the war, Iraq had fired Scud missiles against Israel; not an unexpected development, but a huge military, diplomatic, and public relations headache nonetheless. Now, two of his most trusted advisers were telling him that the best outcome to an Iraq war that was already costing American lives was one that might leave Saddam Hussein in power.

Bush and Scowcroft listened impassively as Haass briefed them on the thinking behind the war-termination paper.

"Mr. President, I know what you want, I just don't see how it's going to happen," Haass admitted. "I don't think we're going to get our battleship *Missouri* here."

Haass argued that the United States would likely not be in a position to insist on the kind of clear, formal surrender that the president wanted. Rather, the Bush administration would have to accept a de facto end to the war, when the conditions of the UN resolutions that provided the legal basis for the conflict had been fulfilled. The UN resolutions did not deal with Iraqi armaments, or with the nature of the Iraqi regime; they simply dealt with the Iraqi presence in Kuwait. To demand more than that as a precondition for stopping military operations, Haass warned, would risk both domestic problems and international problems. It would mean going beyond UN resolutions that not only provided the legal basis for military action in the Gulf, but that also defined the global consensus for going to war. Haass believed that there was no domestic or international consensus to pursue the war until the ouster of Saddam's regime. The rest of the world was going to be satisfied with the liberation of Kuwait. And to insist on more than that would not be sustainable.

The conversation among the three men then drifted onto the question of limiting the scope of any ground advance deep into Iraq, lest they inadvertently bring down the entire Iraqi government. Haass knew the president did not want to see Saddam escape unpunished. Yet once Bush had committed himself to striking at Iraq, his options were limited. The collapse of the Ba'ath regime could leave the American military in charge of civil order in Iraq, where U.S. troops might suddenly find themselves bogged down in a multisided Iraqi civil war, in which all sides would see the Americans as occupiers.

The stress was obvious on the president's face and in his body language.

"Maybe we should just call it a day," Scowcroft tactfully suggested after a while, as much to spare Bush's nerves as to spare his staffer the ordeal of writing a fourth draft of the war-termination paper. As Haass rose to leave the Oval Office, he sensed that the president remained deeply troubled. Haass tried to cheer him by putting a positive spin on the situation.

"Mr. President, we may get lucky," he said in as upbeat a tone as he could muster. "This limited war in Kuwait, some of it fought in Iraq, may trigger events within Iraq that will allow us to get a new leadership in Iraq. But we can't guarantee that." Bush nodded his gratitude.

"It was one of those awkward moments," Haass recalled years later. "Clearly, the president had a hope for a clean demarcation that I just thought was unlikely. What you had from the president at that point was sort of a hope rather than a systematic policy."

●   ●   ●

Since the beginning of the Desert Storm air campaign, the relationship between the White House and King Hussein of Jordan had gone from bad to worse. For months, George Bush had been dismayed that his old friend, considered a strong ally of the United States since the 1970s, had refused to join the UN Coalition against Iraq. During an August 1990 visit by the king to Bush's summer residence at Kennebunkport, the president had entreated Hussein to change his position, but to no avail. Instead, echoing the same words he had used in his telephone conversation with Bush the day before the Iraqi invasion, Hussein had reiterated his theme that the root cause of the crisis was not Saddam Hussein's ambition to dominate the Gulf, but rather the economic disparity between the wealthy Gulf oil states and "less fortunate" Arab countries like Jordan. To Bush, the king's words had been like a personal betrayal.

The Gulf Arabs themselves, even the Kuwaitis, were far more forgiving of the king's stance. Kuwait's exiled finance minister, Sheikh Ali Khalifa al-Sabah, had tried to explain the facts of life in the Arab world to Washington. "The king had little choice in this situation," Sheikh Ali said tolerantly, "just as he had little choice in 1967. The king will not face the lion of discontent by condemning Saddam. Likewise, in 1967 [when Jordan joined the Six-Day War against Israel and lost the West Bank as a result], if he had not sided with Nasser, he would have been overthrown." In the world-weary way of the Middle East, the sheikh sighed. "Every twenty years, he commits a biggie."

The practical consequences of King Hussein's "biggie" this time were serious. From the earliest weeks of the crisis, Iraq had been using Jordanian banks and oil trading companies to sell oil outside the UN embargo. Iraq was also importing food, spare parts, and other essential supplies by truck along the Amman-to-Baghdad highway. As a result, the cordon of sanctions that the UN Security Council had erected to squeeze Iraq had a gaping hole along Iraq's western frontier.

Nevertheless, President Bush still held out hope that his old friend would come around. Several weeks after the start of the Desert Storm air campaign, Bush sent a private emissary to meet with the king. The man he chose for the mission was Richard Armitage, a former assistant secretary of defense during the Reagan years. Armitage was a respected member of the Republican national security establishment and a close friend of Colin Powell—the two men had both been favorites of former defense secretary Caspar Weinberger.

On February 2 the king sent Bush a letter thanking him for sending Armitage to visit.

Dear Mr. President,

I am indeed gratified that you were considerate enough to have chosen an old friend, a man of great integrity and moral courage, Rich Armitage, to talk to me.

Believe me, my friend, that it was my concern for you and the United States of America which caused me to seek to meet you at the outbreak of the crisis and later in Paris, which was not to happen.

Mine is, and possibly has been a lonely voice, different to many in this region. But before God, I am satisfied that it was and will be the voice of friendship, peace, and honor.

. . . Discussions must continue between us, Sir, whatever the venue. I fully agree we should continue this process.

Sincerely,
Hussein I.

Like many visitors exposed to the king's charm and hospitality, even Armitage—a husky, no-nonsense Navy SEAL who had served four combat tours in Vietnam—emerged starry-eyed from his meeting with Hussein. Several years later he would write an op-ed piece in the *Christian Science Monitor* making the bizarre suggestion that the United States should help topple the Ba'athist regime of Saddam Hussein and replace it with a monarchy presided over by King Hussein.*

Toppling Saddam Hussein was the last thought on King Hussein's mind, however. On February 6, only days after Armitage had left Jordan, the king made an inflammatory speech in which he accused the American-led air campaign of targeting innocent Iraqi civilians and "holy places" in Iraq. Since Iraq was the home of the two most sacred shrines in Shia Islam—the mosques of Najaf and Karbala—it was a serious and potentially explosive charge and one that played directly into Saddam Hussein's propaganda.

Bush had finally had enough. On February 9 he sent a curt letter to the king:

Your Majesty:

I am not going to hide my deep disappointment with your speech of February 6. I had not expected, so soon after I sent a personal envoy to you and immediately following your friendly letter urging further dialogue, to read such a vitriolic attack on the intentions and actions of the multinational coalition that is liberating Kuwait . . .

---

* Among the many ironies of Armitage's suggestion was the fact that the Iraqis had once had a king from the same Hashemite dynasty as King Hussein, and had deposed him in the 1958 Free Officers' Coup.

We are not targeting innocent people or holy places and we are not trying to destroy Iraq. Perhaps what was not in your speech was more telling: there is no mention of Kuwait. Instead, your words exculpate Saddam Hussein for the most brazen crime against the Arab nation by another Arab in modern times . . .

If we do not agree on these matters, so be it. But we must understand that a public, political posture that takes Jordan so far from the international and Arab consensus has damaged very seriously the prospects for eliciting international help for Jordan. If I am circumspect in my own public views on your accusations, it is only because I continue to place value, however unrequited, in your nation's well-being and stability. . . .

Under the circumstances, I reluctantly have concluded that Rich Armitage's trip did not help, so I intend to hold off sending anyone to Jordan.

Sincerely,
George Bush

Four days later, in an ill-timed stroke of bad luck for the Coalition, U.S. aircraft bombed the Amiriyah communications bunker in Baghdad, which local residents had been using as an air raid shelter. Over eighty Iraqi civilians were killed. Although the bunker had been a legitimate military target, the loss of innocent life created an uproar throughout the Arab world. King Hussein renewed his criticism that the United States was targeting innocent Arab civilians.

• • •

The outcry over the Amiriyah incident was a blunt reminder that the Coalition air campaign could not go on forever. For the preceding four weeks Iraq had experienced the most intense aerial bombardment in military history; but most of its forces in the Kuwaiti theater, including Saddam's vaunted Republican Guard, remained dug in, frightened but largely intact. The U.S.-led Coalition was reaching the limits of what airpower alone could achieve against the Iraqi military. And Saddam Hussein showed no sign of withdrawing his forces from Kuwait.

More important, strains were beginning to develop in the Desert Storm Coalition. Given the sheer number of targets struck by Coalition aircraft—many in Baghdad itself, a densely populated city of 6 million— it was astounding, and a testimony to the skill of Coalition pilots, that more accidents like Amiriyah had not taken place. Even so, the Arab street was starting to grow restive. For nearly a month, every night had brought the same grainy CNN images of explosions in the skies over Baghdad. The Arab countries of the Coalition were privately warning Washington that their citizens would not tolerate much more. Meanwhile, Israel's commitment not to retaliate against Iraq for Scud missile attacks was wavering. Although the number of attacks on Israel had decreased, they were still occurring on occasion without warning. Unaccustomed to assuming such a passive posture against its enemies, the Israeli public was exerting enormous pressure on the Shamir government to respond with force. Shamir, in turn, was venting his frustrations on the White House.

The only way that the U.S.-led Coalition could achieve the overriding objective of liberating Kuwait was by proceeding with the potentially costly ground phase of Desert Storm.

President Bush saw the liberation of Kuwait as only half the battle ahead. On February 20, only four days before the planned start date of the ground offensive, the president revealed his understanding that besides liberating Kuwait, the war could not end before the Iraqi army had been further reduced. "The truth of the matter is that we're going to have to capture his army, we're going to have to get rid of a lot of that armor," the president wrote in his diary. "Otherwise, we will have diminished his military, but we will not have accomplished our real goals."

Bush's support for the possibility of leaving Saddam's government in power was less than wholehearted.

"I don't quite see how Iraq with Saddam Hussein at the helm will be able to live peacefully in this family of nations," he agonized in the same diary entry, somewhat unsure he had made the right decision. Hamletlike, the president asked himself: "What is victory—what is a complete victory? Our goal is not the elimination of Saddam Hussein, yet in many ways it's the only answer in order to get a new start for Iraq in the family of nations."

●   ●   ●

That same week, another White House official was also thinking about what would happen in the Middle East after Desert Storm had ended.

On the morning of February 22, William Kristol sat in his power office, reading the editorial pages of the *Wall Street Journal* with unusual care. One of Kristol's primary jobs as Vice President Dan Quayle's chief of staff was to stay abreast of editorial opinion on important issues and keep Quayle briefed. Kristol would do this by selecting articles or op-ed pieces he thought the vice president should see and forwarding them to Quayle, often with the key passages highlighted. His position as gatekeeper allowed Kristol to choose much of what Quayle read on a day-to-day basis.

Reflecting his own background and views, Kristol tended to favor articles from think tanks or publications populated by neoconservative intellectuals: the American Enterprise Institute, the Heritage Foundation, the *Washington Times*, and of course the *Wall Street Journal*, whose editorial pages were the bellwether of conservative thought in America. It helped matters that Quayle himself was a deeply conservative Republican—far more so than George Bush—and agreed with the views expressed in virtually everything that Kristol sent him.

The particular opinion piece Kristol was reading in the *Journal* that morning had two things to recommend it: its subject was U.S. policy in the Middle East after the Gulf War, and it had been written by his father.

Irving Kristol was widely regarded as the founder of neoconservative thought in America—which made his son Bill neoconservative royalty, of a sort. During the glory years of the neoconservative movement in the early 1980s, both Kristols had enjoyed the run of the Reagan White House along with their fellow neocons. The ideas of prominent neoconservatives like Richard Perle and Jeane Kirkpatrick had provided the intellectual underpinnings for Ronald Reagan's muscular foreign policy, especially its emphasis on challenging Soviet expansionism in every corner of the globe from Central America to Afghanistan. Think tanks like Heritage and the American Enterprise Institute (where Irving Kristol was now comfortably ensconced as a senior fellow) had defined the national debate on foreign and defense policy.

Things had changed greatly since the election of George Bush as president. Bush had surrounded himself with a national security team composed largely of veteran officials from the Nixon and Ford years. Henry

Kissinger, a figure despised by neoconservatives, had dominated foreign policy during both of those administrations and had greatly influenced the worldview of all those around him. Their claim to fame in foreign policy had been supporting Kissinger-inspired initiatives, such as the opening to communist China and détente with the Soviets, both of which were considered catastrophic moral and geopolitical blunders by most neoconservatives.

Foreign policy in the Bush administration was conducted by the president, Brent Scowcroft, James Baker, and a small clique of like-minded, deeply loyal aides. And despite his exalted title, Bill Kristol was decidedly not a member of the clique.

Kristol had been hiding his disappointment at Bush's handling of the Gulf crisis for many months. An ardent supporter of Israel, he had been quietly incensed by the Bush administration's neglect of its traditional ally in the Middle East, and by George Bush's flirtation with Arab nations like Saudi Arabia and Syria, which were implacable enemies of Israel. Kristol knew, of course, that the ground phase of the Desert Storm campaign was set to begin in less than forty-eight hours. Vice President Quayle was entitled to a daily national security briefing, and his chief of staff had religiously sat in on nearly every one since the beginning of the Gulf crisis. Kristol was glad that the United States was finally taking the fight to Iraq's army. It was Bush's fawning behavior toward the Arabs and naïve vision of a New World Order that troubled him. He was not surprised that his father felt the same way.

"It is all a fantasy," the elder Kristol ridiculed in a piece captioned "After the War, What?" "There is not going to be a New World Order, just the old world disorder in new configurations." Taking a dig at President Bush's enshrinement of the United Nations as the principal vehicle for ensuring global security, Kristol asked mockingly: "Who but a dreamer could take seriously the notion that some 150 nations—ranging from the primitive to the civilized, the anarchic to the authoritarian, the stable to the chronically unstable—could collectively bring order and tranquility to the world?"

Kristol *père* believed that the eagerness of the White House and the State Department to form closer ties with the Arab world was wrong on a deep, fundamental level. The president and his advisers simply did not understand the psychology of the Arabs. Kristol denounced the preceding five hundred years of Arab history as a period of "relative stagnation and political impotence." Irving Kristol had his own theory on the root of the problem: "The answer unquestionably has much to do with Islam, and the Arab connection with Islam."

Because he viewed Islam itself as being at the root of much of what was wrong in the Middle East, Kristol dismissed the Bush administration's frequently expressed hope that Desert Storm would usher in a new era of cooperation between the United States and its "friends" in the Arab world. The antipathy between the Islamic world and the West was permanent and irreconcilable, Kristol believed. To believe differently was unrealistic.

Thus, only days before a Republican White House was about to launch the largest American military operation since D-Day, one of the Republican Party's most prominent intellectuals had just prophesied that whatever the military outcome in the Gulf, Desert Storm was doomed to become a political failure. It was a surprising view coming from a man whose own son stood high in the councils of the very White House whose policy he was lambasting.

But if Bill Kristol was troubled by the irony, he gave no indication. Carefully, he placed a copy of his father's article in the tray of materials to be forwarded to the vice president.

●   ●   ●

The Desert Storm ground offensive began in the early morning hours of Sunday, February 24. Two divisions of U.S. Marines supported by Arab troops from Egypt, Syria, and Saudi Arabia attacked into the teeth of the Iraqi army units dug in along the Kuwaiti border. Meanwhile, the two heavy armored divisions of the U.S. Army's 7th Corps, supported by a British armored division (the famed "Desert Rats" of World War II) conducted a flanking attack on the Iraqi forces in Kuwait from the left. Trained and equipped to counter a massive Soviet invasion on the plains of Central Europe, the heavy M-1 Abrams tanks and Apache attack helicopters of 7th Corps cut through Iraq's overmatched tank divisions like a scythe. But the boldest assaults of all took place far to the west of Kuwait.

Deep in the desert, the U.S. Army's 101st Airborne Division staged the largest helicopter assault in history, moving an entire division of eighteen thousand troops—with all of its weapons, vehicles, and supplies—in one fell swoop to a position eighty miles inside Iraq itself. Finally, the American 24th Mechanized Infantry Division roared into Iraq's Western Desert. Its mission was to outflank the entire Iraqi army and advance to the Euphrates River, which would prevent Iraqi troops in the Kuwaiti theater of operations from escaping northward.

The performance of U.S. troops exceeded even the wildest prewar expectations. On February 26, troops from the Arab nations in the Coalition entered Kuwait City itself, where they were greeted as liberators by cheering residents strewing flowers in their path. Just as their forefathers from the Greatest Generation had paused outside of Paris to allow Free French troops the privilege of liberating the city from the Nazis, so too had this generation of American soldiers and Marines paused their advance so that the Kuwaitis could be liberated by brother Arabs.

That same day an American armored division and an Iraqi armored division engaged in one of the largest tank battles in history. It was also the most lopsided tank battle in history. Eight hundred Iraqi vehicles were destroyed without the loss of a single American tank. Elsewhere on the battle front, thousands of Iraqi troops trying to escape from Kuwait along Highway 6, the main north-south artery into Iraq, were subjected to merciless attack by Coalition air forces. Highway 6 was now a graveyard of flaming hulks and destroyed vehicles; it had already been dubbed the "Highway of Death" by the Western media.

By the afternoon of February 27 the Iraqi army was in full retreat and appeared to be on the verge of collapse. Tens of thousands of Iraqi conscripts had walked across the lines with their hands above their heads to escape the carnage—so many prisoners, in fact, that they were clogging the advance of Coalition troops north. Most of Iraq's remaining troops were pinned against the banks of the Euphrates River. Coalition bombers had long since destroyed the bridges across the Euphrates. Iraqi army engineers were erecting pontoon bridges in the hope that Iraqi troops could evacuate to the relative safety of central Iraq, but if Coalition forces continued their advance, there was no possible way most of Iraq's army could escape in time.

Coalition troops now occupied a vast region of southern Iraq. The 101st Airborne was encamped at a forward operating base far up the Euphrates Valley, just south of the river town of al-Nasariyah. From there, its dozens of Apache helicopters could attack any Iraqi vehicles that tried to cross the river. The 24th Mechanized Infantry, under the command of Maj. Gen. Barry McCaffrey, had advanced so aggressively that it had swung all the way from a position at the extreme *west* of the Coalition front all the way to the outskirts of Basra, Iraq's second-largest city and the major metropolis of southern Iraq, which was due *north* of Kuwait. It had been a march so dramatic that McCaffrey's fellow officers were already expecting it to be talked about in military staff colleges for decades to come. If Coalition troops entered Basra, Iraq would literally be cut in two, and the hundreds of thousands of Iraqi troops still in the southern part of the country would have no means of escape.

The question of the hour in Washington and in the Gulf was now when to end the war.

Shortly after 2:30 P.M. in Washington (10:30 P.M. in the Gulf), President Bush met in the Oval Office with his war cabinet: Baker, Cheney, Powell, Scowcroft. Norman Schwarzkopf called in by secure telephone. It was a meeting enshrined years later in the thirty-foot oil painting by the artist Mark Balma that would greet generations of visitors at the entry to the George Bush Presidential Library in Texas. The painting was titled simply *Revolution*.

Balma's tableau captured many subtle details of the meeting that afternoon: the pinstripe of the president's suit; the fact that the tall Colin Powell needed to stoop low to reach the secure telephone unit in the bottom drawer of the president's desk in order to speak with Schwarzkopf; most of all, the sober yet confident faces of the five men in the room. What the painting could not capture was something that was not there: a formal plan for how to end the war.

During the seven months leading up to this moment, the civilian and military leaders of the Bush administration had invested thousands of hours in planning for every possible contingency. Before Desert Storm there had been plans about what to do if Iraq suddenly withdrew from Kuwait — with separate plans for Iraq withdrawing from some of Kuwait, most of Kuwait, or all of Kuwait. There had been plans about what to do if Iraq killed Western hostages. There had been plans about what to do if Iraq instigated terrorist attacks against Western troops in the Gulf. There had been plans about what to do if Iraq attacked Israel without warning.

After the war began, there had been more plans: plans about what to do if Iraq used chemical weapons against Coalition troops, and plans about what to do if one or more Arab nations suddenly defected from the Coalition. Operation Desert Storm itself was the result of the most intense planning process in the history of the U.S. military. The final war plan had been the third or fourth iteration of CENTCOM's original plan, and had been tweaked and refined countless times since.

But somehow, in the midst of all this planning, no one had ever produced a plan about what to do if the war ended in a decisive victory.

And so, in the absence of a formal plan, each of the five men in the Oval Office viewed the question of how to end the war through the prism of his own past experiences and expectations for the future.

James Baker had always been the most amenable of Bush's counselors to a negotiated solution, but he had nonetheless worked tirelessly to assemble the Gulf War Coalition and help hold it together. But now, with the crisis in the Gulf taken care of, the secretary of state wanted to return the focus of Bush administration foreign policy to major diplomatic initiatives. First, he wanted to kick-start negotiations with Gorbachev and the Soviets on a wide array of issues. But the immense goodwill that the United States had earned in the Arab world by defending Saudi Arabia and liberating an Arab country had opened up an even more exciting prospect. For months Baker had been discussing the idea of the Bush administration negotiating a comprehensive peace settlement between Israel and the Palestinians. Now, there was a good chance that America's Arab allies in the Gulf Coalition could be brought on board for such a conference: the Egyptians, the Saudis, even the Syrians. The Bush administration thus had nothing to gain and potentially much to lose by further humiliating another Arab country.

For Dick Cheney, the primary consideration was getting U.S. troops out of the Gulf as soon as possible. Coalition forces had liberated Kuwait and suffered fewer than one hundred casualties in doing so. The U.S. military, his direct area of responsibility, had performed magnificently. However, Cheney had been troubled by the televised images from the

"Highway of Death" the previous day and by stirrings of criticism among the American public that U.S. troops were now "piling on." Having served as Gerald Ford's chief of staff during the final stages of the Vietnam War, Cheney still remembered the hostility toward U.S. troops exhibited by some of the public during that era. U.S. forces had won enormous goodwill at home and abroad by their actions in the Gulf. Cheney was determined to retain this. Finally, Cheney and the Pentagon leadership were already drafting plans for a major reduction in U.S. conventional forces after the war (though for obvious reasons, the Bush administration had not announced this during the crisis in the Gulf). The sooner American forces returned home, the sooner the Bush administration could begin deactivating some units and benefiting from the "peace dividend."

Colin Powell had already been quietly thinking about a war-termination scenario that corresponded with his own beliefs concerning the appropriate uses of U.S. military power. A member of his staff at the Pentagon had given Powell a slim volume to read on the subject. Entitled *Every War Must End*, it had been written by Fred Iklé, a respected Republican defense intellectual associated with the party's neoconservative wing. Iklé had been head of the Arms Control and Disarmament Agency during the Ford years, where his staff had included such budding Republican foreign policy stars as Paul Wolfowitz and Scooter Libby, and he later served in the Reagan administration.

The central premise of Iklé's book was that war-termination strategy is rarely determined in advance, and that the crush of events surrounding a major conflict leaves policymakers with little opportunity to improvise an effective strategy "on the fly." As a result, vital national interests might be overlooked in the final resolution of a conflict, because these interests had no "caretaker" within the national security bureaucracy. Perhaps the most controversial argument advanced by Iklé was his warning against "treason of the hawks": namely, that in their eagerness to achieve victory and demonstrate loyalty to the government in which they served, stakeholders in the war-termination decision might let a conflict drag on for too long. Therefore, Iklé suggested, one of the prime responsibilities incumbent upon senior military officers was to "take the initiative" in pursuing an end to hostilities during the final stages of a conflict. Powell was impressed by this argument; it resonated so strongly with him that he had had excerpts from Iklé's book photocopied for his senior military aides as well as for Cheney and Scowcroft.

Brent Scowcroft, of course, had been having conversations about war termination with the president and Richard Haass for many weeks. Although the series of position papers on war termination that Haass had drafted back in January had not resulted in an actual war-termination plan, Scowcroft believed that the exercise had been a valuable one for clarifying the issues at stake. Like Haass, the national security adviser saw the war with Iraq against the grand chessboard of international power politics. Not only had the United States firmly established itself as the sole military and diplomatic superpower of the world, but the effectiveness of the United Nations in standing up for the sovereignty of one of its weakest members had set a valuable precedent for the post–Cold War New World Order. Now was the time to think about the future of the Gulf region. To everyone's relief, Iran had stayed out of the Gulf crisis, but it remained a long-term threat. The decimation of Iraq's armed forces and industrial infrastructure during Desert Storm had essentially restored the balance of power to the Gulf. The power and prestige of Saudi Arabia, America's most important partner in the Gulf and the pillar of the region's future security, had been greatly enhanced by its role in Desert Storm. Scowcroft could see no further advantage to killing more Iraqi troops. On the contrary, doing so might embolden Iran to engage in adventurism along its long border with Iraq, and especially among the Shia minority of southern Iraq, who were thought to be favorably disposed toward their coreligionists in Iran.

Finally, the president himself was thinking not about the future, but rather about burying the past. That morning Bush had written in his diary: "It's surprising how much I dwell on the end of the Vietnam syndrome. I felt the division in the country in the 60's and the 70's—I was in Congress. I remember speaking at Adelphi, and Yale was turning its back. I remember the agony and the ugliness, and now it's together."*

---

* The reference to Yale, the president's alma mater, alludes to an incident where members of one graduating class turned their backs on the commencement dais as a protest against American involvement in Vietnam.

Bush believed that his decisive use of U.S. military power in the Gulf had once and for all "licked the Vietnam syndrome."

At 9:00 P.M. on the evening of February 27, President Bush went before the American people from the Oval Office to announce the end of Operation Desert Storm: "Kuwait is liberated. Iraq's army is defeated. Our military objectives are met."

Still, Bush had mixed feelings about the war's ending. The next morning, February 28, he wrote in his diary: "It hasn't been a clean end—there is no battleship *Missouri* surrender. This is what's missing to make this akin to WWII, to separate Kuwait from Korea and Vietnam."

Still, the president believed that his willingness to use force during the Gulf crisis, in the face of what he felt was a daunting foreign adversary and tremendous political opposition at home, had permanently restored the credibility the United States had lost after its retreat from Vietnam. In future crises, no one would ever doubt again America's willingness to use force.

Not that Bush expected there to be many crises in the future. At a televised press conference on March 1, the president was asked about the larger meaning of the Desert Storm victory for American foreign policy.

"Mr. President, today you declared an end to the Vietnam syndrome and we've heard you talk a lot about the New World Order. Can you tell us, do you envision a new era of now using U.S. forces around the world for different conflicts that arise?" Bush reflected on the question for a moment.

"No, I think because of what has happened, we won't have to use U.S. forces around the world," he responded thoughtfully. "I think when we say something is objectively correct, like don't take over a neighbor or you're going to bear some responsibility, people are going to listen because I think out of all of this will be a newfound—put it this way, a reestablished credibility for the United States of America. So I look at the opposite. I say that what our troops have done over there will not only enhance the peace, but reduce the risk that their successors have to go into battle someplace."

.　　.　　.　　.

If the end of the Gulf War had left George Bush in a somber, reflective mood, it had left many other members of his party almost giddy with exultation.

In Washington, House minority whip Newt Gingrich was savoring the victory with a personal friend of his, best-selling author Tom Clancy. Clancy's novels, which celebrate the technological superiority of the U.S. military, had become almost required reading at the Pentagon during the military buildup of the Reagan years and had made the author a popular figure in Republican defense policy circles. But the virtuosity just displayed by the real-life U.S. military in the Gulf exceeded anything even he could have imagined.

The two men tried to place the Desert Storm victory in historical context. Both considered themselves serious students of history. Gingrich had a PhD in history from Tulane University and had taught the subject at the college level before entering politics. Clancy was proud of his classical education by the Jesuits. They both gravitated to Julius Caesar's famous Latin maxim *Veni, Vidi, Vici* ("I came, I saw, I conquered"), but both agreed that it was somehow not enough to capture the full extent of American military superiority during Operation Desert Storm.

Laughing, they settled on how Caesar's words could be amended to fit the situation in the Gulf. Somewhat sheepishly, Clancy realized that he did not know how to translate their modified statement into Latin. But he knew just the person to ask.

On March 1, Clancy sent Gingrich a fax at his Capitol Hill office. He had consulted with the Rev. Joseph Sellinger, the Jesuit priest who was president of Loyola College in Baltimore, Clancy's alma mater. Caesar's statement now read:

VENIMUS	we came
VIDIMUS	we saw
ICIMOS GLUTEOS	we kicked ass

While the correct translation of the Latin word *gluteos* was "asses," Clancy noted for Gingrich's benefit, "since English uses this term in the collective sense, I believe this rendition is linguistically correct."

But while not above engaging in some hijinks with a longtime supporter of Republican Party causes, Gingrich was also thinking more seriously about the long-term consequences of the Bush administration's triumph in the Gulf.

Almost immediately following President Bush's Oval Office address declaring that Iraq was defeated, planning had begun on the president's next major address, a speech on Desert Storm to a joint session of Congress, scheduled for March 6. It was the sort of opportunity every president dreams of having, but few are lucky enough to get. George Bush stood at the zenith of presidential power, in an America at the zenith of its military, diplomatic, and moral prestige. His approval ratings among the American people hovered in the 90th percentile. How to spend this political capital was the question of the hour at the White House.

For days John Sununu had been busy canvassing senior Executive Branch officials and Republican leaders in Congress for ideas on what the president should say in his joint session speech.

Dick Cheney's contribution was the shortest and focused on a single point: He wanted the president to announce that U.S. forces in the Gulf would be leaving the region immediately.

Clayton Yeutter, the Republican Party chairman, believed that the triumph in the Gulf had once and for all "licked the Vietnam syndrome" and wanted Bush to say so in his speech. "John, it seems to me that the President's message to the joint session of Congress should include a reference to Viet Nam veterans and their families," Yeutter wrote in his memo to Sununu. "They have had a tremendous load lifted from their shoulders by the events of recent weeks." Yeutter suggested the sort of language he wanted to see in the speech: "Our recent experience in the Persian Gulf clearly demonstrates that American fighting forces are the best in the world when they are unleashed in full force and supported vigorously at home and in the field. May that now be a comfort to (May that serve to uplift) every veteran of Viet Nam and their families." Because of objections from the Pentagon, all references to Vietnam were later removed from the final version of the joint session speech.

Craig Fuller, Bush's former chief of staff who had orchestrated Hill & Knowlton's successful campaign to publicize atrocities in Kuwait, captured the sentiments of most. "I think the Nation wants to celebrate with George Bush," he suggested. "I think they want to know that he feels the excitement and patriotism that is sweeping America. I know he feels there are many difficult issues ahead in the region, but I hope he can encourage a celebration for freedom!"

But Gingrich took a contrarian view. The Georgia Republican was a rarity in the House of Representatives: a genuine strategic thinker who tended to think about broad, national themes rather than the more parochial matters that dominate the concerns of most House members. Gingrich did not share the prevailing assumption that President Bush had been rendered invincible by dint of the U.S. triumph in the Gulf. Instead, he saw this moment as a crossroads for the Republican Party.

On the one hand, the success of Operation Desert Storm—in the teeth of opposition from the Democratic leadership in Congress—had put a long-cherished GOP goal within reach for the first time in a generation: regaining Republican control of Congress, and especially the House of Representatives, which had been under Democratic control for forty years. If the president played his cards right, 1992 could be a banner year for the Republican Party, with George Bush winning reelection in a landslide and his coattails sweeping a new Republican majority into Congress.

On the other hand, the president had an exceedingly narrow window of opportunity in which to act. The White House was expecting that because of the Desert Storm triumph, the president would enjoy a long "honeymoon" period with Congress and the American people. Gingrich believed this was almost certainly wrong. Accustomed to gauging sentiment among his fellow Republicans as minority whip, Gingrich knew that support for the president even within his own party was tenuous at best. The right wing of the GOP was still furious at Bush for raising taxes in October 1990 and had been only temporarily mollified by the need to maintain a united front against the Democrats during the Gulf crisis. Any "honeymoon" Bush enjoyed would be a short one—measured in weeks, not months.

Gingrich had already expounded his views within the House Republican Caucus. When Sununu asked for his input on the president's joint session speech, he jumped at the opportunity to share his thinking with the White House as well. He wrote in a March 4 memo to Bush's chief of staff:

Six weeks from now the American public will believe one of three things:

1) The President does not have a domestic agenda (and fortunately the Democrats at least have *some* agenda to modify the welfare state and make things marginally better); or

2) The President has a reform domestic agenda as useful and as innovative as what we did in Desert Storm, and the Democrats are deliberately blocking and smothering that agenda because it terrifies them; or (however unlikely)

3) The President has a reform agenda and the Democrats are cooperating in passing it

It is essential that, beginning Wednesday evening, the President begin to make the case for a reform agenda both innovative and useful (as defined by real people), and that we carry the fight for this agenda through 1992.

The key, Gingrich argued, was to couch the domestic policy agenda favored by conservatives in the language and imagery of Desert Storm, however tenuous the connection might be. In a section with the heading "Proposed Rhetorical Centerpiece of the President's Address," the congressman tried to illustrate how this could be done:

Ten years ago we rejected irrational defense policies and committed ourselves to finding methods and policies calculated to get the results we wanted. We saw the proof of that success in the triumph of Desert Storm. Now is the time to reject the irrational domestic bureaucratic policies that spend a fortune and deliver tragedy in the inner cities, the hospitals, the schools, and the streets of America.

War is always a tragedy. . . . But sometimes, the shock of war can get a nation's attention.

Now is such a time. We can see what works, we can see the price of failure. Those miserable Iraqi soldiers crawling out of their holes to surrender were there because of a terribly failed policy and judgment in Baghdad. How much wiser are our domestic policies? . . . It is time, and past time, to demand that our domestic policy be as competent, realistic, and performance-based as our defense policy.

Like many Republicans who had risen to power during the Reagan years, Gingrich believed that Republican preeminence on national security issues had been the key to Ronald Reagan achieving many cherished ideological goals domestically. But George Bush now had an opportunity to advance the conservative cause of which even Reagan could have never dreamed.

•   •   •

In fact, the White House already was preparing for the next phase of combat—against the Democrats. The political side of the White House smelled blood. Most of the Democrats in Congress, including the entire Democratic leadership in both chambers, had voted against the congressional resolution authorizing the use of force in the Gulf. Even more discomfiting, a number of leading Democrats had taken prominent roles in opposing the president's Gulf policy throughout the crisis and had used inflammatory language (including references to "thousands of body bags") to do so. The White House was determined to hang these words around their necks like millstones.

A dossier of embarrassing statements made by key Democrats during the Gulf crisis was circulating among senior staff at the White House. Georgia senator Sam Nunn, whose "betrayal" still rankled, was a target of special attention; two pages of the dossier were devoted just to him. There were also compromising statements on the Gulf from Senator Ted Kennedy, House Speaker Tom Foley, and virtually every Democrat of national stature, including prominent state governors who were thought to have presidential ambitions, such as New York's Mario Cuomo. The Bush White House was already assuming that the Democrats would offer only a sacrificial candidate in the 1992 election, but it was taking no chances.

Perhaps the most bewildering set of views contained in the dossier were those of Massachusetts senator John Kerry, who was quoted making three different statements before Desert Storm:

- A response to a letter from a constituent, saying Kerry voted "against giving the President immediate authority to go to war against Iraq to force it out of Kuwait, warning that a decision to go to war was rolling the dice with our future";

- A response to a second constituent letter the same week, saying Kerry "strongly and unequivocally supported President Bush's response to the crisis and the policy goals he has established with our military deployment in the Gulf";

- And third, a terse statement from Kerry blaming a computer in his office for the inconsistency.

• • •

Congratulations were pouring into the White House from all over the world. Even King Hussein sent the president an effusive letter praising him for his victory in the Gulf.

"Well done, my friend!" the Jordanian monarch had written, leading one State Department official to comment drily: "Hussein is trying to cast his vote with us though the polls may be closed."

President Bush himself was writing letters to thank the many world leaders who had supported his stand during the crisis. At the bottom of his letter to King Hassan of Morocco, the president used a thick black marker to jot a short personal message to Hassan.

I am glad the shooting has ceased. I hope Iraq will now comply with UN resolutions.

• • •

There was only one problem. The shooting in Iraq had not yet ceased.

The decision to call for a cease-fire on the evening of February 27 had been a unilateral one by the White House. No American official had been in touch with the government of Saddam Hussein, and it was unclear that Iraq had even accepted the fact that the Gulf War was over.

This became abundantly clear on March 2, nearly four days after the cease-fire announcement, when elements of the 24th Mechanized Infantry Division, the Coalition unit that had made the deepest penetration into Iraqi territory, suddenly found themselves in a pitched battle with one of Saddam Hussein's Republican Guard divisions. Apparently the Iraqi division had neither heard about the cease-fire nor been "reduced" significantly and was withdrawing in good order across the Euphrates. Though American reinforcements and airpower quickly turned the battle into a lopsided rout, it was evident that the situation on the ground in southern Iraq remained chaotic and unresolved.

Ironically, it was a situation that a number of senior U.S. officials had tried to warn against. In the "Sacked Out on the Same Sand Dunes" cable he had written back on December 30, nearly three weeks before the Desert Storm air campaign began, Ambassador Chas Freeman in Saudi Arabia had strongly advised the Bush administration to produce a formal plan on how to accept Iraq's surrender before the fighting actually began. As part of this process, Freeman advised, the administration should also draft a statement of the actual surrender terms Iraq would need to accept, so that U.S. officials would not be forced to draft these terms hurriedly, amidst the confusion that attends the end of any major conflict.

"I continue to believe that the crafting of a diplomatic mechanism to accept Iraqi capitulation to the terms set by the UNSC and to arrange a cease-fire must be accomplished *before* an offensive is begun," Freeman had written on December 30. "Knowing how we will end the conflict is as important as defining how we will conduct it."

The importance of doing so could not have been greater. It was the terms Iraq accepted to end the Gulf War, rather than the war itself, that would determine the long-term outcome in the Gulf. A carefully crafted set of cease-fire conditions would translate the inevitable military victory against Iraq by Coalition forces into a political victory as well.

"Achieving the earliest possible surrender of Iraqi forces is vital to preserving Iraq's role in the post-crisis regional balance," Freeman wrote in the same cable to Washington. "This cannot be achieved without a clear statement of the terms we are asking Iraq to accept, and an efficient and cohesive mechanism for negotiating their acceptance by Iraq."

Nor was this the only occasion on which Freeman made this argument to the Bush administration's top officials. The issue was so important to him that he had previously sent no fewer than three other cables on the same subject, including one NODIS cable to Bush and Baker titled simply "Defining Victory."

Immediately following President Bush's announcement of the cease-fire, UN ambassador Tom Pickering had begun advising his staff in New York to get ready for some frenetic diplomatic activity. Operation Desert Storm had been a resounding triumph: not only for the U.S. military and its Coalition allies, but for the entire United Nations system. Simply put, the UN had worked in this crisis, and Pickering was certain that President Bush was going to capitalize on the opportunity to make the UN Security Council the principal instrument for adjudicating future peace and stability in the Gulf.

The first priority would be establishing the conditions for a secure cease-fire. Pickering knew that the president wanted to get U.S. troops out of the Islamic Middle East as quickly as possible, so there would need to be some form of UN peacekeeping force ready to step in and replace the departing American forces. Once the combat zone was secure, the Security Council could take up other important issues related to Iraq at its leisure: the long-standing border dispute between Iraq and Kuwait; Iraqi reparations for the ravages its troops had committed in occupied Kuwait; and a regional arrangement for eliminating Iraq's weapons of mass destruction.

All of this would require a lot of intense, high-profile work by Pickering and his staff at the U.S. Mission in New York; but it was the kind of work they relished. While he had not yet heard any specifics from Washington, Pickering was in an ebullient mood. The United States and its Coalition allies held all of the cards in the Gulf. As Pickering had long been advocating, Iraq's military capability had been significantly reduced by Desert Storm, creating one of the necessary conditions for a more stable Gulf region. The forces of three permanent members of the Security Council—the United States, France, and Britain—occupied a huge swath of Iraq's southern desert, which would make the establishment of a UN buffer zone between Iraq and its neighbors a simple matter. However, Pickering had already been hearing reports that the long-oppressed Shia population of southern Iraq was beginning to rise up against the Iraqi government, so the time for UN action was now, before the situation inside Iraq destabilized any further.

So Pickering decided to take the initiative. He telephoned Robert Kimmitt, the undersecretary of state for political affairs, who was his contact in Washington for day-to-day matters. Kimmit was a savvy Washington insider and a member of Secretary Baker's tight-knit inner circle. He would already know what the Bush administration's next steps were, even if they had not been announced.

"Bob, what is it that we're doing, and what's our input?" Pickering asked, meaning his staff in New York. "And who's the political adviser going to be?"

The State Department political adviser would be the key figure in the process. Every war that the United States had fought in the twentieth century (except for Vietnam, which was not, technically speaking, considered a war by the State Department) had ended the same way: with an armistice negotiated by a joint team of military and civilian personnel. The senior military representative was usually a commanding general from the combat theater. General Norman Schwarzkopf was a logical choice to be the military representative in this case. The senior civilian was the political adviser, a veteran U.S. diplomat with the stature to negotiate face-to-face with foreign officials. Because of the stakes in the Gulf, the political adviser would likely be a senior State Department official or retired Republican foreign policy grandee, although Secretary Baker himself might want to play a hands-on role, given his strong negotiating skills and personal familiarity with the likely Iraqi interlocutor, Foreign Minister Tariq Aziz. Were he not needed for what was likely to be a busy week at the UN, Pickering himself might have been asked to be the political adviser. There was still a chance he might be asked.

The reason for the joint military/State Department delegation was obvious. The military representative would handle the technical details of an armistice: separation of forces, arrangements for the return of POWs, disposal of explosive ordnance from the battlefield, and so forth. The political adviser would handle the legal and political questions. However, because State Department officials have a professional background in negotiating treaties with foreign countries (something few military officers are trained to do), the political adviser generally becomes the key figure in the entire process.

"There's not going to be any of that," Kimmitt replied laconically.

Pickering was flabbergasted. Kimmitt explained that a decision had been made to allow Dick Cheney and the Pentagon to manage war termination. General Schwarzkopf would represent the UN Coalition at the armistice talks with the Iraqis. There would be no political consultation.

When Pickering shared the news with his staff in New York, they too were aghast. The issue was not that Schwarzkopf would be leading the U.S. delegation: The CENTCOM commander in chief was senior enough to convey the seriousness of the situation to the Iraqis and had more than earned the right to preside over Iraq's surrender. The real issue was that the failure to appoint a political adviser of equivalent stature revealed that the Bush administration had no real war-termination strategy, and no politico-military strategy for securing Iraq and the Gulf region after Desert Storm.

Pickering thought that the plan he and his staff had produced back in August 1990 would, with minor modifications, work beautifully. The two most difficult conditions necessary for that plan to work—reducing Iraq's military potential, and occupying an exclusionary zone in southern Iraq—had already been achieved by Coalition forces. If the Bush administration did not want to make an ambassador's recycled plan the centerpiece of its post–Desert Storm war-termination strategy, it was their prerogative not to do so. But Pickering had always assumed that either the White House or the State Department would then come up with a plan of its own.

"We bobbled it badly," Pickering said more than a decade later, "because we allowed two things to happen. We allowed the military to become consumed only by the minutiae on the spot, which was important to them but irrelevant in terms of the long term: the separation of forces, the return of prisoners, the cessation of further hostilities—the logistics of a cease-fire, but not the strategy of a cease-fire. And then we failed to pick up on all of the things we could have done with respect just to the piece about putting UN forces in.

"We lost sight, in our infinite capacity for super crisis management, of any distant view. In New York, we were aghast."

•   •   •

Had Pickering known that Schwarzkopf had received no instructions from Washington on what to say in the armistice talks with the Iraqis, he might have been even more aghast.

At CENTCOM headquarters in Riyadh, Schwarzkopf had been growing increasingly frustrated ever since he had given what some at the Pentagon had dubbed "the mother of all briefings" announcing a general Iraqi retreat on February 27. Nothing had gone right since then. First, a division of the Republican Guard had tried to ambush one of his units days after the cease-fire had been announced. Then, Schwarzkopf had learned that the location chosen for the armistice talks with the Iraqis, the remote airfield at Safwan along the Kuwaiti border, was still occupied by Iraqi troops. This latter piece of news had been enough to ignite Schwarzkopf's famously combustible temper.

But his biggest headache was working with his staff to draft the actual armistice terms for Iraq. Running a war with half a million troops from 25 different nations was in and of itself a 25-hour-a-day job. Having to produce the armistice document on top of that was just too much. Schwarzkopf had beseeched Washington for a State Department adviser to assist with the process, to no avail. In frustration, he turned to the next best thing: Ambassador Freeman in Riyadh.

Freeman empathized with his colleague's predicament. He too was astonished that the Bush administration had not assigned a political adviser to the talks. For Freeman, it confirmed his worst suspicions about the absence of a larger strategic framework for managing the post–Desert Storm period. Worse, the administration was about to make a blunder so stupendous that it boggled the mind: no senior Iraqi official would be required to attend the armistice talks, and there would be no surrender document for the Iraqi regime to sign.

This oversight represented in Freeman's view an almost "total failure of integration between military and political strategy"—exactly what having a political adviser on the scene was supposed to avoid. The first thing Iraq's generals would be expecting Norman Schwarzkopf to say in the meeting tent at Safwan was something along the lines of: "We're here today to talk about some military matters, technical issues. But Tariq Aziz will report to Geneva tomorrow to meet with Secretary Baker." Because Saddam Hussein had personally been the aggressor in this war, it was essential that he personally be required to sign a document of capitulation, either directly or (more likely) through Tariq Aziz. Freeman, a Harvard Law School graduate, thought of the legal equivalent: having a criminal who pleads guilty to a crime make an elocution of wrongdoing in open court as a condition of having his guilty plea accepted.

Without such an admission from Saddam, it would be next to impossible to force the Iraqi dictator's cooperation with the measures that the UN Coalition would need to impose on Iraq: measures covering important issues like war reparations for Kuwait and eliminating Iraq's weapons of mass destruction. Peering into the future, Freeman could almost see the history of the next decade in Iraq, and it was not a pretty picture: Saddam would fight tooth and nail to defy the UN on every issue; Iraq would not accept culpability for invading Kuwait and might even threaten the country again; and UN sanctions on Iraq would eventually become self-defeating. Just as in the months leading up to Desert Storm, time would once again be working on Iraq's side, and against the United States.

Worst of all, by allowing Saddam to insulate himself from the humiliation of Iraq's surrender and war guilt, the Bush administration was in essence ensuring his survival. For it was Freeman's contention, then and for a decade afterward, that had Saddam been required to sign a surrender document, he would have fallen from power. "But he didn't. He wasn't asked, and so he didn't."

Years later Freeman shared his own assessment of the Safwan talks:

"I thought when the Iraqi generals came out of that tent, they probably were hard-pressed not to do cartwheels."

How could such a catastrophic omission have taken place?

Virtually all of the civilian defense and foreign policy luminaries of the Bush years would come to recognize that the cease-fire at the end of the Gulf War had been a disaster for the United States. But they placed the blame squarely on what they perceived as Gen. Norman Schwarz-kopf's "freelancing" at the Safwan talks. The views of Robert Zoellick, Secretary of State Baker's top aide at the time, are typical in this regard.

"There were some anxieties right away in the State Department, but one of the lessons here should be, frankly, that it is very hard to challenge or reverse victorious generals in the aftermath. And I don't know if Bush wanted to or not, but all I'm saying is, in the world of what I'll loosely call bureaucratic politics, taking on a general who had just won a major war and saying 'You're not doing this right' is not easy.

"It could have been done," Zoellick adds, "but particularly given the way policy is made, it often requires civilian officials to get up to the president and others, and at each step along the way the uniformed military were going to be supporting the victorious general and are likely to not make it easy."

One senior Pentagon official with firsthand knowledge of the Safwan negotiations blames Colin Powell and the Joint Chiefs: "I think the cease-fire came too early. Safwan should have been less dignified. The military got preoccupied with their forces still in the Gulf theater, and these were the people who were part of the reason Bush was so cautious at the end."

Still, most members of the Bush administration genuinely believed that the situation in Iraq would more or less sort itself out to the benefit of the United States. Coloring all perceptions was a near-universal expec-tation that Saddam Hussein's days in power were numbered. Adm. David Jeremiah, vice chairman of the Joint Chiefs of Staff and a member of the Deputies Committee, recalls the tenor of discussions among the deputies during the confused aftermath of Desert Storm.

"I think we were surprised that the regime persisted. That wasn't the expectation. I think the expectation was that there would be a falling apart of Iraq of some form. Some were more hopeful about how that would play out than others, that there actually would be a coherent government. But I think there was a pretty strong feeling, much as there was later on, that the regime wouldn't survive. It might be a Ba'athist or some other kind of structure that would be a different way of governing Iraq."

Robert Kimmitt later coined his own phrase to describe the prevailing mood of the period: victory fatigue.

6

"WHY WON'T HE HELP US?"

The first casualty from victory fatigue was President Bush's oft-stated desire to bring Saddam Hussein and his "henchmen" to justice for the
atrocities that Iraq had committed. At his March 1 press conference announcing the end of hostilities in the Gulf, Bush had again reiterated
his pledge to hold the Iraqi regime accountable for its "war crimes" in
Kuwait and mistreatment of captured Coalition military personnel.
Three days later, Republican senator Thad Cochran sent a letter to the
president with a helpful suggestion on this score.

"In your press conference Friday, you said, 'Nobody can be absolved
from the responsibilities under international law on war crimes,'" the
Mississippi lawmaker wrote on March 4. "In that connection, I wanted
you to know that I introduced on January 30 a resolution urging the establishment of an international tribunal with jurisdiction to try Saddam
Hussein. I enclose a copy of the resolution in the belief that it may offer
an appropriate way to proceed."

Cochran's letter to the president went unanswered for six weeks. Unwittingly, he had touched a sensitive nerve inside the Bush White House.
While the president himself may have been open to the idea of a
Nuremberg-style tribunal for Saddam and his generals, Brent Scowcroft
and much of the NSC staff were leery of the idea. Their preferred war-
termination strategy in the Gulf—indeed, their only war-termination
strategy—was for a disillusioned Iraqi general to topple Saddam in a coup
and impose a new and hopefully more circumspect military dictatorship.

They had a precedent in mind. In 1958 a group of disaffected Iraqi army generals had toppled King Faisal, the country's British-imposed monarch, in the so-called Free Officers' Coup and created a modern secular state. During the first week of March 1991 the White House was expecting a similar coup to take place at any moment. Robert Gates recalls the NSC staff's expectations about how the post–Desert Storm scenario would play out. "A huge assumption and hope on our part was that after the end of the war we wanted to create circumstances that would encourage the Iraqi military to take Saddam out. And so there was some conversation about how do you structure any sort of postconflict scenario with respect to what happens to the Iraq forces, what happens to Iraqi generals, that builds up for them the desirability of taking out Saddam." Sandra Charles elaborates on the qualities the NSC staff was looking for in a putative successor to Saddam: "Somebody pragmatic, not necessarily pro-America. Probably a general, a military figure. To hold that country together, you would have needed somebody who was strong."

Nor was this sort of thinking limited to the White House alone. The Bush administration had left the details of war termination to the Office of the Secretary of Defense (OSD), the civilian side of the Pentagon. Secretary of Defense Cheney's two principal advisers on Gulf policy were his undersecretary of defense for policy, Paul Wolfowitz; and Zalmay Khalilzad, a young defense intellectual whom Wolfowitz had taught while Khalilzad had been a doctoral student at the University of Chicago and subsequently brought into government service during the Reagan years. Both men were familiar with the modern history of Iraq and shared the prevailing view that after two disastrous wars instigated by Saddam, one or more generals in Iraq's army would step forward to "restore the honor" of the Iraqi military.

Khalilzad had captured these views in a secret planning document written before the onset of hostilities in the Gulf. Entitled "Winning the War—and the Peace: Adaptive Strategies in Case of War with Iraq," it foresaw the likelihood that "Iraqi nationalists in the armed forces might see the fate of their country at risk because of his reckless ambition, and move against Saddam to save their country."

In fact, no such generals existed in the Iraqi armed forces. During the Iran-Iraq War of the 1980s, Saddam had quietly purged dozens of the most capable battlefield commanders in the Iraqi army: not because they had been caught plotting against his rule, but because their very competence was a potential threat to him. Invariably the murdered generals were said to have perished in "helicopter accidents." What remained in the general ranks of the Iraqi army were the dregs of the Iraqi officer corps, many of them members of Saddam's Tikriti clan who were fanatically loyal to him and complicit in the crimes of his regime. Norman Schwarzkopf had not been far off the mark when asked for his assessment of Iraq's generals at his first press conference following the invasion of Kuwait. "I think they're a bunch of thugs," Schwarzkopf had replied. Like every successful tyrant, Saddam had been careful to ensure that no one rose to a position of trust in his army without having first compromised himself.

But the perceived need to "build up the desirability of taking out Saddam" within the senior ranks of the Iraqi army had direct implications for how the U.S.-led Coalition dealt with the war crimes issue. Given the nature of Saddam's regime, any Iraqi general with the access and resources needed to mount a successful coup against Saddam would have necessarily been a longtime Ba'athist with a significant amount of blood on his own hands—in President Bush's words, a henchman. The White House could hardly announce the creation of a tribunal to prosecute Saddam and his henchmen for war crimes when it was doing everything possible to encourage one of these very henchmen to seize power in Iraq.

On April 12, Brent Scowcroft would finally reply to Senator Cochran. "As you know, violation of the laws of war [is] a matter of grave concern to the Administration," the national security adviser wrote. "We continue to gather evidence of war crimes. We also are currently conducting a review of possible action with our UN and Coalition partners."

No war crimes were ever prosecuted by the administration.

•   •   •

In the weeks preceding the Desert Storm ground offensive, the Bush administration had undertaken an intensive propaganda campaign inside Iraq intended to create unrest against Saddam Hussein's regime. Given the hatred of Saddam among many factions within Iraqi society, such a campaign offered an excellent opportunity to weaken his government

and bring about the military coup that Washington wanted, thus eliminating the need for a costly ground war by Coalition forces. Typical of
these subversive efforts was a statement made by President Bush on February 15, 1991, when he urged the Iraqi people "to take matters into their
own hands, to force Saddam Hussein the dictator to step aside." The
White House viewed this and a number of similar statements made by
President Bush at the time as part of its larger strategy to see Saddam
Hussein replaced by a military figure less inclined to adventurism in the
Persian Gulf.

. . .

But the frequent calls for the Iraqi people to rebel against Saddam had
unintended consequences. "I think that what we didn't appreciate was
the degree to which when the president would allude to this by saying
that the Iraqis had to take care of this problem themselves, the problem
of Saddam, those words would not only be read by the Iraqi military, but
by the Shia and the Kurds," Robert Gates recollects. Richard Haass
maintains that Bush's rhetoric was intended as a purely symbolic gesture;
the White House never expected Iraq's oppressed minorities to take the
president at his word. "We didn't want to get into a situation, we didn't
anticipate a situation, which was a version of Hungary in 1956. Those
people weren't just responding to a radio broadcast. They had other issues after two decades of living under Saddam."

Whether intended to be or not, the president's words were interpreted
by Iraq's long-suffering minorities as a pledge of American support in the
event of a revolt against the Ba'ath regime. Almost as soon as word of the
scope of Iraq's defeat in Kuwait reached Shia-dominated southern Iraq,
spontaneous armed uprisings began erupting among Iraqi Shi'ites in
Basra and other southern Iraqi cities. Several days later, on March 4, with
southern Iraq already in full revolt against the Iraqi regime and the Iraqi
army seemingly in disarray, the long-oppressed Kurdish minority of
northern Iraq also rebelled.

By the time General Schwarzkopf entered the meeting tent at Safwan
on March 6 to discuss cease-fire terms for the Gulf War, Iraq was already
a country being convulsed by two separate insurrections.

By mid-March the Kurds had seized control of almost their entire ancestral homeland in northern Iraq, including the key petroleum city of
Kirkuk. "We don't want to be like the Palestinians and ask for the impossible," Kurdish leader Jalal Talabani said. "If there were a democratic
government in Iraq, we would be happy to be Iraqis."

Negotiations with other dissident groups inside Iraq lent credibility to
these claims. The Kurds were well represented on the Free Iraqi Council, a Beirut-based confederation of opponents to the Ba'athist regime in
Baghdad, and Talabani had indicated to his Turkish contacts that his goal
for Iraq was a federal union encompassing all of the country's ethnic and
religious groups. For Talabani and the Kurds, "the most significant result
was Turkey's lifting its objection to the establishment of direct relations
between the Kurdish front in Iraq and the United States."

Talabani, who had returned home from exile in Syria to a hero's welcome in northern Iraq, declared that the Kurds would "continue the struggle until we defeat the regime of oppression in Baghdad and liberate the
whole of Iraq." These halcyon sentiments would prove to be short-lived.

Rather than creating the conditions for a military coup against Saddam Hussein, the Shia and Kurdish rebellions saved Saddam's regime.
Iraq's senior officer ranks were drawn almost exclusively from the country's Sunni minority, which comprised only 20 percent of the population.
Long accustomed to holding a privileged place in every aspect of Iraqi
life under Saddam, the Sunnis regarded the Shia and the Kurds with a
curious admixture of fear and contempt. Despite countless prewar intelligence briefings that had harped on the enmity between the Sunni elite
and Iraq's two historically oppressed populations, the Bush national security team had never seriously considered the possibility that even Iraqi
army generals who felt the humiliation of two disastrous wars begun by
Saddam might prefer the continuation of his rule to an Iraq ruled even
in part by the other two groups.

"The Kurdish and Shia uprisings in the immediate aftermath of the
war gave Saddam the opportunity to go and confront those generals
and say, 'Without me, you haven't got a country,' " recalls Robert Gates
ruefully. "Had those uprisings not taken place, would the military have

taken over? Nobody can ever know. But I think those uprisings gave him the opportunity to basically argue that they had to hang together, or the country was going to fall apart." Of course, Saddam was not content merely to rally support for his rule among his Sunni base. Intelligence soon reached Washington that the Iraqi dictator had capitalized on the chaos created by the internal strife inside Iraq to launch yet another purge of his army's Sunni-dominated senior ranks. "During putting down the uprisings," Gates observes, "he eliminated hundreds of officers."

Correctly assessing the Kurds as the far more dangerous adversary, Saddam chose to deal with the Shia revolt in southern Iraq first. Even as Saddam's government was preparing to negotiate armistice terms with the Coalition forces that still occupied a vast region of southern Iraq, Saddam boldly redeployed much of what was left of his Republican Guard—his best-armed and most loyal troops—to the Shia regions in the south. He also ordered his military representatives at the Safwan armistice talks to secure permission from the Coalition for the Iraqi army to operate helicopters inside Iraq's borders for "humanitarian purposes." General Schwarzkopf, attempting to be magnanimous in victory, agreed to what he saw as a reasonable request. Immediately, almost every Iraqi army helicopter that had survived the Gulf War was headed to southern Iraq to fly attack missions against Shia strongholds.

Suffice it to say that the helicopters used against the Iraqi Shia were far more capably piloted than those used to ferry Iraqi generals. Barely a week after the cease-fire at Safwan, the Shia revolt had been effectively crushed and tens of thousands of Shi'ites killed by Saddam's forces.

The speed and ruthlessness with which Saddam put down the Shia rebellion stunned Washington. After witnessing the massive destruction visited on Iraq's military by Coalition forces during the Gulf War, even some of the most experienced national security officials were amazed by how quickly Iraq's army had been able to regroup after the conflict. Admiral David Jeremiah expresses the sense of shock among members of the Deputies Committee. "We were surprised that they were able to reconstitute to the degree necessary to suppress the south. I don't think we appreciated what was going to happen in the south. We thought the south was much stronger, more capable of literally taking over and preventing [Saddam] from coming in."

"I think probably all of us had probably underestimated to some degree exactly how things would play out at the end of the war: with the Shi'ites, with the Kurds, with Saddam himself," concurs Robert Kimmitt, one of Jeremiah's fellow deputies. "So although I think for several months we had been quite proactive, both in our diplomatic and in our military engagement, all of a sudden we found ourselves in the uncomfortable position of being a bit reactive with the situation on the ground. A lot of people said we didn't react well: that we should have come to the aid of the Shi'ites, we should have come to the aid of the Kurds, earlier."

*   *   *

The Bush administration had reserved the week of March 11 for a post–Desert Storm victory lap with its Coalition allies. Secretary of State Baker was embarked on a whirlwind tour of the Middle East that would culminate with a visit to the Soviet Union. Meanwhile, President Bush was visiting Ottawa to thank Canadian prime minister Brian Mulroney for Canada's unflinching support during the recently concluded Gulf crisis. From there he would travel to Bermuda to meet with another Coalition ally, British prime minister John Major.

The president had been looking forward to his Canada trip. Within the large coterie of world leaders that Bush considered personal friends, Mulroney was one of his favorites. Like Bush himself, the Canadian leader was a moderate center-right politician with a keen interest in world affairs. More important, Mulroney had a personality similar to Bush's own and to which the president naturally gravitated: all business when discussing political matters, but gregarious and possessing a ribald sense of humor in private. A native of New Brunswick, the Canadian province just across the border from Maine, Mulroney and his wife Mila were frequent houseguests of George and Barbara Bush at the president's summer home in Kennebunkport.

Bush had expected to be showered with glowing testimonials to his leadership in the Gulf while in Ottawa. Instead, at a joint press conference with Mulroney on March 13, the president found himself being peppered with questions from both the American and Canadian press about Saddam's brutal suppression of the Shia revolt in Iraq, in particular

Iraq's use of helicopter gunships against civilians. A flustered Bush stammered that the helicopter attacks were a violation of the cease-fire terms that had ended the Gulf War, and he called on Saddam to desist.

Sitting just off camera, Brent Scowcroft and Richard Haass winced. While Saddam's use of helicopters to slaughter his own citizens was unconscionable, and bad from a public relations standpoint, it was not technically a violation of the cease-fire terms to which Iraq and the Coalition had agreed. As soon as the press conference with Mulroney was over, Scowcroft and Haass pulled Bush aside and reminded him of that fact in a hastily whispered conversation.

Three days later, in Bermuda, the president got more of the same. At a joint press conference with John Major (himself under fire from Fleet Street on the same issue) on March 16, the president categorically ruled out a military response by Coalition forces to the growing carnage in Iraq. Asked whether he saw the possibility of American or British intervention to stop the slaughter, Bush replied, "I do not. We are not—that would be going beyond our mandate. None of us want to move forces into Baghdad or to . . ." The president stopped himself. "Frankly, we don't want to have any more fighting."

Just before leaving for Bermuda, Major had deflected a battery of similar questions with a classic piece of British understatement. Standing in front of his official residence at 10 Downing Street in London, he had appeared to blame the Shia rebels rather than Saddam Hussein for the escalating violence inside Iraq.

"I do not recall asking them to mount this particular insurrection," the prime minister sniffed.

·   ·   ·

James Baker, meanwhile, was trying to bring an end to an insurrection in another country.

The secretary of state had arrived in Moscow on March 14 for talks with Mikhail Gorbachev and Soviet foreign minister Aleksandr Bessmyrtnykh. Baker found the Soviets relieved that the Desert Storm campaign was finally over, but ambivalent about the future. It was evident they had been more than a little unnerved by the recent demonstration of American military might in the Gulf, especially since the demonstration had come at the expense of a longtime Soviet client state armed largely with Soviet-made weapons.

Baker's top priority was to reassure his Soviet interlocutors that the Bush administration still valued its partnership with Gorbachev and welcomed Soviet participation in shaping the future of the Middle East. As far as the secretary of state was concerned, although the two countries had shared a few tense moments, the Soviets had for the most part "played ball" with the United States during the Gulf crisis, and Baker felt that the time was now right to reciprocate.

"The Middle East right now requires avoiding symbols, terms with a lot of baggage, and ideological rather than practical steps," he said soothingly to Bessmyrtnykh. Baker mentioned the idea that he had long been discussing with President Bush: capitalizing on the goodwill that the United States had won from Saudi Arabia and other Arab nations in the Gulf to convene a major conference on the Israeli-Palestinian peace process; a conference that would include all of the major powers of the Middle East. He invited the Soviets to participate.

Bessmyrtnykh leapt at the suggestion with almost pathetic eagerness. "Clearly, the possibility of being cut into the main diplomatic game in the Middle East has real attraction to the Soviets now," Baker gloated in a private message to the president and Scowcroft later that evening. The proposed Middle East peace conference was his baby. "We should use that to get them to support our concept, to commit to helping more where their help may be useful (Syrians and Palestinians), and to restore diplomatic ties with Israel."

There were only two issues where Baker sensed continuing hostility from the Soviets. The first was the size of the U.S. military presence in the Gulf. Bessmyrtnykh argued strongly for an immediate withdrawal of all American troops from the Gulf. He advanced the case that any increase in the American military presence from precrisis levels in the region would be seized upon by Soviet hard-liners who were already criticizing Gorbachev's accommodating policy toward the United States for paving the way for a Pax Americana.

The second point of contention for the Soviets was an announcement by the Bush administration that it planned to maintain the oil embargo against Iraq indefinitely, until Saddam Hussein was deposed, even though Operation Desert Storm was over and Kuwait had been liberated. The United States would only be seen as punishing the Iraqi people, Bessmyrtnykh asserted, and that would trigger a strong counterreaction from the Arab street. The Soviet foreign minister did not mention another consideration of which Baker was already well aware: that Soviet firms were major players in the Iraqi oil industry, and the Soviet Union stood to lose billions of dollars in oil exploration and construction contracts if the embargo continued—precious hard currency that Mikhail Gorbachev's cash-strapped government could scarcely afford to lose.

"That was the same argument we encountered throughout the crisis," Baker replied dismissively to Bessmyrtnykh's warnings about the dangers of the Arab street. "The Arab street is explosive, it will tear apart your Coalition, it will prevent your Arab partners from fighting with you, it will destroy you in the Arab world for years to come," Baker recited in a lightly mocking tone. "That reality was wrong before, during, and after the crisis and the war—witness how we are being welcomed now." Far from hurting America's standing in the world, he claimed to his Soviet counterpart, all of the Arab members in the Coalition actually favored the maintenance of the embargo as long as Saddam Hussein remained in power. While this may have been true in the weeks immediately following Desert Storm, few of these countries would have held to this view had they known that the sanctions would persist for another twelve years.

Toward the end of the conversation, Baker broached an issue that had long been of personal interest to him. He told Bessmyrtnykh that the Saudi government wished the U.S. State Department to convey an offer to the Soviets about Afghanistan. "If the Soviets would end lethal aid to Kabul, the Saudis would consider terminating lethal aid to the mujahideen, but at a later date," Baker relayed.

Bessmyrtnykh's eyes widened; he was obviously impressed. "This is a very important development," he admitted to Baker. "We would need to know more about what the Saudis mean by 'at a later date,' but this is clearly a potentially big step."

The secretary of state was not surprised by Bessmyrtnykh's reaction. Baker knew that Mikhail Gorbachev and his entire government were desperate to extricate themselves from Afghanistan for good. Ever since the Soviets had invaded Afghanistan in 1979 to install a puppet government, the country had been a running sore for the Soviet Union. During the 1980s, Moscow had pumped billions of rubles into a hopeless guerrilla war against the mujahideen: Afghan tribal insurgents who had been joined by Islamic fighters from around the world who saw the struggle against the "godless" Soviets as a jihad—a holy war. Wealthy Islamic countries, especially Saudi Arabia, had quietly funneled billions of dollars in aid to the mujahideen and sent some of their more idealistic sons to fight alongside them.

Having finally withdrawn its troops in frustration after suffering thousands of casualties, Moscow was now subsidizing an inept pro-Soviet regime in Kabul. The Saudis and other Islamic states continued to support the mujahideen. Afghanistan had strained the already tottering Soviet economy and had sapped the morale of the Soviet army. It was as unpopular among the Soviet public as Vietnam had been in the United States.

Baker had been deeply involved in U.S. policy toward Afghanistan almost from the beginning of the conflict, though on behalf of the other team. As White House chief of staff during the first five years of Ronald Reagan's presidency, he had played a key role in helping arrange covert U.S. support for the mujahideen. President Reagan and his entire national security team had believed, correctly, that creating a quagmire for Soviet troops in Afghanistan was an ideal means of weakening the Soviet Union in its Cold War struggle against the United States. They had made support for the Afghan freedom fighters one of the central thrusts of Reagan administration foreign policy. Reagan himself had a soft spot for the brave Islamic mujahideen who were fighting to rid Afghanistan of communism.

One of the initiatives organized by Baker at the time had been "Afghanistan Day" at the White House, a March 1982 meeting and photo op that brought President Reagan face-to-face with some of the very mujahideen on whom he doted. In a real sense Baker was more personally invested in the future of Afghanistan than any senior official still serving in the U.S. government.

Bessmyrtnykh told Baker that the Soviet government could not commit to signing a joint statement on Afghanistan during his visit, but talked animatedly about the possibility of making a joint approach to the Saudis and the Afghans about the Saudi offer. Baker was content. "I think the Saudi move puts us close to being able to end U.S. and Soviet involvement in the Afghan War," he wrote in his evening dispatch back to Bush and Scowcroft.

In the fall of 1989, Baker and his Bush administration colleagues had witnessed the defeat of the Sandinistas in Nicaragua in that country's first fair election, not only liberating the people of Nicaragua from an odious Marxist regime, but all of Central America from the debilitating ideological struggles of the 1980s. Later that year they had skillfully managed the collapse of communism in Eastern Europe. During the spring of 1990 the Bush foreign policy team had been the catalysts for the peaceful reunification of Germany and the end of the Cold War in Europe.

Now, in pursuing an end to foreign interference in the affairs of Afghanistan, Baker and the Bush administration sought to bring the same sort of closure to the people of that tormented nation. It was a magnanimous gesture by the world's sole remaining superpower, toward a benighted country that had once been its ally in the long twilight struggle against Soviet communism.

Never would a nation be repaid so poorly for a gesture so generous.

•   •   •

The worsening situation in Iraq had raised the concern of at least one Bush administration official, however. On March 15, Robert Gates received a confidential memo from a member of the NSC staff. "At the next small group or Deputies meeting," it warned, "Paul Wolfowitz may raise humanitarian assistance to the Iraqi people. He has forwarded a memo to Secretary Cheney, who evidently said that the subject should be considered by the Deputies Committee."

A colleague of Gates and Wolfowitz on the Deputies Committee distinctly remembers Wolfowitz's passionate insistence at that next meeting on the need for the United States to come to the aid of the beleaguered Iraqi Shia. "That was Wolfowitz predominantly driving that particular train," the official remembers. "It was the fallout from the helicopters and what was going on in the south. It was the way that Saddam Hussein used the helicopters to support what was going on down there."

But neither of the two Pentagon chieftains with whom Wolfowitz worked, Dick Cheney and Colin Powell, shared his view. Nor did the White House. Indeed, President Bush was still basking in accolades for his handling of the Gulf crisis. On March 18, perhaps the high-water mark of his presidency, George Bush received the Elie Wiesel Foundation's annual humanitarian award at a glittering ceremony where Wiesel himself handed the president his award. It was a high honor for any president, but a particularly rich one for a president whose political party had only a half dozen years previously been identified with Bitburg, the Nazi-filled cemetery that Ronald Reagan had visited with Chancellor Helmut Kohl and other German government officials, sparking worldwide outrage among Holocaust survivors.

Five days later the president attended the Gridiron Club dinner, an annual black-tie rite in the capital where senior government officials and the Washington press corps poke fun at each other with politically themed humor. A jocund George Bush brought down the house by joking that his only opponent in the 1992 presidential election would be George McGovern.

⚫   ⚫   ⚫

On March 28, having brought southern Iraq to heel, a regrouped Iraqi army began its campaign to recapture territory lost to the Kurds. This new offensive was spearheaded by Republican Guard units that had been spared during the Gulf War. More important, the same helicopter gunships that had proven so devastatingly effective against the Shia were now committed to support the attack in the north. In the face of a full-scale assault by Iraq's still formidable army, even the most spirited Kurdish resistance was doomed to failure. Within five days Saddam's forces had retaken virtually all of the Kurdish-occupied regions of northern Iraq, including the city of Kirkuk. The Kurds' pleas for military help from the Coalition during this period fell on deaf ears.

Saddam now felt confident enough to extract the full measure of his revenge on the Kurds. With their *pesh mergas* (armed militias) effectively eliminated as a fighting force, the Kurds had no defense against the Republican Guard. For the next two weeks, over a million Kurdish refugees fleeing Iraq in panic, along with their unlucky kinsmen remaining in northern Iraqi towns, would be subjected to almost incessant bombardment from artillery and helicopters. Over a thousand civilians would be killed in the barrage each day, with many more dying from exposure in the harsh mountain climate along Iraq's northern frontier.

·   ·   ·

The same day that Saddam Hussein launched his offensive to suppress the Kurdish revolt in northern Iraq, an unexpected and potentially dangerous public relations debacle erupted for the Bush administration. On March 28 the *New York Times* and *Washington Post* published excerpts from an interview conducted the previous evening with Gen. Norman Schwarzkopf by the veteran British journalist David Frost. The interview had been broadcast on public television stations around the country.

At the time Schwarzkopf had agreed to do the interview, he had been covered in glory from Operation Desert Storm. Only weeks later, however, the situation in Iraq had badly deteriorated. Media coverage of the Gulf War was now focused less on the resounding U.S. military triumph than on the inconclusive ending of the conflict and the growing refugee crisis inside Iraq's borders. Live images of Iraqi civilians being slaughtered by Saddam's once-defeated Republican Guard were becoming a staple on CNN.

Accustomed to fawning treatment from the global press corps in the immediate aftermath of the Gulf War, Schwarzkopf now increasingly found his conduct of the war being second-guessed at every turn. The victor of Desert Storm had become the scapegoat for the hasty termination of the conflict and the bungled armistice negotiations at Safwan. Even David Frost, a diffident interviewer who was a favorite of the Bush White House, could not avoid asking the obvious question: Why hadn't the American-led Coalition destroyed Saddam's Republican Guard when it had the chance?

"Obviously, we didn't destroy them to the very last tank," Schwarzkopf was quoted saying. Clumsily, he tried to make the point that the White House decision to stop the war had been an act of humanity by President Bush toward a vanquished enemy. Unfortunately, extemporaneous speaking was not Schwarzkopf's strong suit.

"That was a very courageous decision on the part of the president to also stop the offensive," he went on to say. "Frankly, my recommendation had been, you know, continue the march—I mean, we had them in a rout, and we could have continued to, you know, wreak great destruction upon them. We could have completely closed the door and made it in fact a battle of annihilation."

Having left the impression that there had been a difference of opinion between the president and his commander in chief in the Gulf over *when* to stop the war, Schwarzkopf implied with his next comment that it was Bush who had determined *where* the Coalition advance into Iraq should halt.

"And the president, you know, made the decision that . . . we should stop at a given time, at a given place, that did leave some escape routes open for them to get back out. And I think it was a very humane decision, and a very courageous decision on his part, also. Because you know it's one of those ones that historians are going to second-guess forever. Why, you know, didn't we go for one more day versus why we did stop when we did, when we had them completely routed?"

Schwarzkopf's remarks ignited a firestorm at the highest levels of the Bush administration. In the context of Saddam Hussein's unexpected survival and the growing strife inside Iraq, the last thing the White House could afford was a charge that President Bush had ended the Gulf War too soon. The administration immediately went into full damage control mode. There were furious back-and-forth conversations between the White House and the Pentagon. Within hours of Schwarzkopf's remarks becoming public, Secretary of Defense Cheney took the rare step of issuing an official statement refuting what Schwarzkopf had said:

> The decision the president made to stop military action was
> correct and courageous, and it was based on the recommendations
> of his senior military advisers. . . . The decision was coordinated
> with and concurred in by the commander in the field, Gen. [H.

Norman] Schwarzkopf. Gen. Schwarzkopf and Gen. [Colin L.]
Powell were consulted and made the recommendation to me and
to the President that we had achieved our military objectives and
agreed that it was time to end the campaign.

The next day, reporters accosted President Bush about the issue outside Bethesda Naval Hospital, where he had just received a medical
checkup. "Did General Schwarzkopf suggest that you keep the war going longer?" Bush was asked.

"No," he responded quickly. Looking noticeably ill at ease, the president tried to direct the reporters to Cheney's statement, but nervously
garbled his words.

"I understand that—that General—General Cheney—Dick Cheney,
Secretary Cheney put out a statement, having talked to Schwarzkopf,
and I don't think there's any difference between any of us—me, Cheney,
Powell, or Schwarzkopf.

"I have full confidence in General Schwarzkopf. But all I know is that
there was total agreement concerning when this war should end. And it's
total, and there's—not even questionable—and I think Schwarzkopf will
be the first . . ."

"Well, why did he say that, then?" a reporter interrupted.

Bush looked annoyed at the question. "I'd go ask him," he replied
curtly.

"He said he recommended going longer," the reporter persisted.

"Go ask him, go ask him," Bush repeated. "He didn't say that . . .
Look, there's no—I have such a high regard for General Schwarzkopf
that I'll let him explain what he said. All I'm talking about is the facts and
General—Secretary Cheney put the facts out very clearly. I just read the
statement. I would refer you to that. It is totally accurate and there's no—
no—I don't think you'll find anybody that disagrees with it."

But Cheney's somewhat legalistic statement distracted from the real
issue at stake. The issue was not whether the Bush war Cabinet had consulted with Schwarzkopf before announcing the end of hostilities in the
Gulf (they had); or even whether the president and his advisers had erred
in ending the war when they did. Rather, the real issue was the overall
strategy that had informed the Bush White House's decision on when to

end the war. That decision had been made as part of a complex calculation of America's long-term interests in the Gulf, one that still remained largely unknown and undebated by the American public.

And if the Bush national security team was unwilling to reexamine even a tactical question like whether Desert Storm had ended a day too soon, how much less willing might they be to allow for the possibility that their entire strategy for managing the aftermath of Desert Storm had been fundamentally flawed?

●   ●   ●   ●

While George Bush may have felt hurt and disappointed by Schwarzkopf's remarks, Dick Cheney had been positively enraged by what the CENTCOM commander had said. Cheney had already reprimanded Schwarzkopf privately. He had also ordered Colin Powell, who was still Schwarzkopf's superior officer, to have a bracing conversation with the war hero who had suddenly become a loose cannon. Despite his years in desk jobs, Powell had lost none of his parade ground voice, and his conversation with Schwarzkopf was not a pleasant one.

Cheney had zero tolerance for generals who spoke out publicly against White House or OSD policy. In barely two years as defense secretary, he had already relieved three different four-star generals of their commands, which was surely a record.

Within weeks of arriving at the Pentagon in 1989, he had fired Air Force Chief of Staff Larry Welch for airing his dissatisfaction with the air force's budget allocation a little too publicly. The entire Pentagon had been shocked at Welch's dismissal. Traditionally, service chiefs were accorded wide latitude to speak their minds during budget season, as part of the normal jockeying for position among the services. Welch had said nothing that could have been interpreted as insubordinate, but Cheney—who had never served in the military—had wanted to make a point about civilian control of the military in *his* Pentagon. The other service chiefs had received the message loud and clear.

Later that summer Cheney had dismissed Gen. Fred Woerner, commander in chief of U.S. Southern Command in Panama, for questioning the Bush administration's decision to pursue a more confrontational policy with Panamanian strongman Manuel Noriega. Woerner "had been able to find fourteen reasons not to do anything, I guess would be the way I'd describe it," Cheney would tersely say later. "He'd spoken out publicly against administration policy, so it was really necessary to remove him."

Most recently, in the fall of 1990, Cheney had relieved Welch's replacement as air force chief of staff, Gen. Michael Dugan, for having made bombastic claims to the press about the air force's ability to defeat Iraq with airpower alone, without the need for a costly ground invasion.

Cheney would have liked nothing more than to have made Schwarzkopf his fourth four-star victim, but his hands were tied. Schwarzkopf was politically untouchable. The quotable, larger-than-life general had captured the imagination of the American public like no other military figure since Eisenhower. As the face and the symbol of the U.S. military triumph in the Gulf, Schwarzkopf had already become a media superstar. Some had even begun talking about him as a future Republican presidential candidate. Publicly stripping Schwarzkopf of his command would have created a national outcry against the Bush administration, and of course against Cheney himself.

And there was a consideration of even greater importance to Cheney and the other senior figures of the administration. Alarmed by a situation in Iraq that was spinning out of control, the last thing they wanted to do was call more attention to the failure of war termination in the Gulf. Sacking General Schwarzkopf for raising concerns about the inconclusive ending of Desert Storm would have sparked a national debate over exactly what the Bush administration's war-termination strategy in the Gulf was. There might be discomfiting questions about the flawed policy assumptions that had led to this strategy. None of which could they afford.

Already Cheney and the rest of the Bush inner circle were regarding Operation Desert Storm in proprietary terms, as *their* victory. For better or for worse, President Bush had staked his political future—and by extension, all of their political futures—on his defeat of Saddam Hussein. Nothing could be allowed to foster the impression that the Gulf War had ended any way other than exactly how the Bush administration had wanted it to end.

Throughout much of this period, the Democratic majority in Congress had been lying low, waiting for some of the victory aura surrounding the White House to dissipate before planning its next moves. The stunning success of Operation Desert Storm had left the Democrats in some disarray. Most of the party's traditional titans in Congress had vehemently opposed President Bush's policy during the months leading up to Desert Storm and had voted against the congressional resolution authorizing the use of force in the Gulf.

In the Senate there was a generational power shift under way toward younger, more conservative Southern Democrats like Charles Robb of Virginia and Al Gore of Tennessee, both of whom had supported the Gulf War. In the House of Representatives the future was more uncertain. The linchpin of Democratic control in the House, in terms of both numbers and ideological fervor, was the post-Watergate class of 1974. This group of members had been elected near the end of the Vietnam War and had inherited from the Nixon years a deep distrust of Republican prerogatives in foreign policy. During the months leading up to Desert Storm, this shared sentiment had expressed itself as a strident determination to prevent the Bush administration from embroiling American troops in yet another "quagmire" in the Persian Gulf. The dazzling virtuosity of Desert Storm and the wave of support for the White House it had unleashed left many House Democrats off balance and worried about their political survival.

Nevertheless, the Democrats in Congress had been quicker than the White House to recognize that the tepid American response to Saddam's vicious suppression of the Shia and the Kurds—in an Iraq still completely at the mercy of American and Coalition military power—was beginning to tarnish President Bush's Gulf War laurels.

Already, the White House's handling of Iraq in the weeks leading up to the August 1990 invasion was coming under attack on Capitol Hill. On March 20, Ambassador April Glaspie testified before the Senate Foreign Relations Committee. At issue was the question of whether the Bush administration had given a green light to Saddam Hussein to invade Kuwait. The previous Sunday, reporter Don Oberdorfer of the

Washington Post had published a lengthy account of Glaspie's July 25, 1990, meeting with Saddam, the week before the invasion. Oberdorfer's article was based on the so-called official transcript of the meeting provided by the Iraqi regime, which it claimed demonstrated Washington's acquiescence to the invasion. In one sense, this was old news: the Iraqi Foreign Ministry had released the transcript six months earlier, and it had been published in the *New York Times* in September 1990. In the immediate aftermath of the U.S. victory in Desert Storm, however, the story had receded from the headlines. Now, though, with Saddam Hussein's apparent survival and the worsening violence inside Iraq, new questions were being raised about the Bush administration's larger strategy for Iraq.

Nevertheless, except for Senate confirmation hearings, it was almost unheard of for a U.S. ambassador to be asked to testify on Capitol Hill. Because they are supposed to implement policies made in Washington, not make policy themselves, it is considered unfair to subject ambassadors to questioning about policies they may or may not agree with. Glaspie's scheduled appearance was so unusual, in fact, that the State Department press corps bombarded Spokesman Richard Boucher with questions about Glaspie at the Department's daily noon press briefing.

"There is a general policy that we have that Ambassadors don't testify," Boucher clarified. "Given the interest in this case, we offered her testimony to the House and to the Senate as a one-time deal basically. She's appearing before the Senate Foreign Relations Committee this afternoon. She'll be in front of the House Foreign Affairs Committee tomorrow. We've made clear that policy. But the testimony was offered, and the dates and times were arranged."

"Richard, one more question," a reporter asked. "Did she discuss her testimony with any other senior U.S. official besides the Secretary in advance of today's appearance?"

The normally unflappable Boucher seemed momentarily taken aback by the question. "I know that we—you know, the appearance was discussed with her in terms of logistics, and that people have discussed with her the current policies, and we've given her copies of other testimony, and things like that. So I'm sure she's up to speed."

"So the answer is yes," commented the reporter drily.

Another member of the press corps raised the topic of Glaspie's July 1990 meeting with Saddam Hussein. "Richard, in Don Oberdorfer's article Sunday in the *Washington Post*, it says that 80 percent of what the Iraqis published from the transcript of the interview or the talk with Saddam Hussein—the meeting with Saddam Hussein—was true or accurate, or something. Is the State Department going to be putting this special document out in the open and according to the recollection of the embassy and Ms. Glaspie in the open?"

"We don't have any plans to do so," Boucher replied, "but I'm sure if April is asked questions like that this afternoon, she'll be in a position to explain things."

Far from resolving matters, however, Glaspie's four hours of grilling by the Senate Foreign Relations Committee only raised new questions. Her claim that the Iraqi transcript of the meeting had been "edited to the point of inaccuracy" was greeted with skepticism by the senators, as was her claim that Saddam Hussein had been "too stupid" to realize that the United States would respond to the invasion of Kuwait with military force.

Not surprisingly, Boucher's press briefing the next day, March 21, was dominated by questions about Glaspie's testimony.

One reporter asked why President Bush and Secretary Baker had not come to the defense of their beleaguered diplomat. "If, indeed, the Iraqis put out a doctored or inaccurate version of what she had said—that she had warned Saddam Hussein not to invade Kuwait—why did the president and the secretary of state not correct the record?" the reporter asked. "Why was she left sort of in the position of having been accused by a government you don't like of doing something that evidently she didn't do? Why did they leave her twisting in the wind?"

"Well, I'd have to disagree strongly with your characterization of what the president and the secretary of state did," Boucher disputed.

"Hanging out to dry," muttered a voice from the press gallery.

"I'll disagree with that too." Boucher frowned. "Have we got any other phrases you want me to disagree with? They both addressed the issue several times. We addressed the issue here many times. I think we reminded you that it was an Iraqi transcript that we could not, would not vouch for. We reminded you of its origins. We reminded you that we gave you on

July 26 a readout of the meeting where we described both what Ambassador Glaspie had said to Saddam Hussein and what Saddam Hussein had said to Ambassador Glaspie, and we've said repeatedly that we stood by our readout of that meeting."

"That's not entirely correct, Richard," a reporter shot back. "I mean, Secretary Baker, when he was on *Meet the Press*, was specifically asked whether Ambassador Glaspie's performance in the meeting was on his instructions. His answer was that '312,000 cables go out from the State Department every day,' and the clear implication was that it was not on his instruction. So he did not clarify the record. The fact is he muddied the record by making it appear that she was not acting on his behalf. And the question is why, as you said, we could not vouch for the transcript, but Ambassador Glaspie wasn't telling you that. She clearly was saying that she can vouch for the transcript. It's false."

Later in the same briefing, another journalist pointed out: "What started the whole story was the fact that a transcript was out there which suggested that April Glaspie appeased Saddam Hussein. April Glaspie has testified yesterday that that transcript was a fabrication. Had anyone during the last seven months, from this podium or any other government official, simply said, 'That transcript is a fabrication,' there would have been no story here. Why did no one say that?"

"During the period in question, forming the Coalition, prosecuting the war, we said repeatedly we weren't interested in starting a sideshow, starting a side debate, on who took better notes of the meeting," Boucher responded.

Toward the end of the briefing, a reporter commented: "The impression is there, right or wrong, that Baker has deliberately put some distance between himself and what she said. Were those instructions ones that he approved, that he was aware of, that he authorized?"

Boucher shrugged. "I frankly don't know what cables he authorized at the time."

·   ·   ·

Sensing the White House's newfound vulnerability on Iraq, the Democrats probed it in the most direct manner imaginable: by demanding some form of U.S. military intervention on behalf of the Shi'ites and the Kurds. Many members were apparently untroubled by the seeming contradiction with their nay votes in the Gulf resolution debate only a few months earlier. Here, it is no exaggeration to state that the Bush administration's victory fatigue throughout the entire month of March 1991 provided a badly needed tonic for the Democrats' political fortunes.

The most forceful voice calling for action in post–Desert Storm Iraq, and the one the White House feared most, was the Democrat who George Bush and his advisers already assumed would be their opponent in the 1992 election: Senator Al Gore. The Tennessee lawmaker had already made his first presidential run in 1988 and was considered one of the rising stars of the Democratic Party. On paper, Gore was a formidable candidate. Only forty-three years old, he was, like George Bush, the scion of a famous political family. His namesake father had been a Senate titan and a contemporary of Prescott Bush. The Harvard-educated Gore had an attractive family and an unsullied Vietnam draft history, having enlisted and served in Saigon as an army journalist.

Gore had made his reputation in the Senate working on the sorts of issues usually associated with Republicans: arms control and Middle East policy. He had been quick to recognize that his unequivocal support for the Gulf War had made him for the time being the leading Democratic voice on foreign policy issues in Congress. Already with one eye on 1992, Gore capitalized quickly on his newfound prominence. On April 3 he sent a long letter to President Bush containing his ideas about the worsening crisis inside Iraq.

"I want to urge you to change the course of American policy for dealing with the insurrection and its aftermath in Iraq," the senator wrote. "Our policy in the Gulf should not be mortgaged to the success of tyranny in Iraq, but we are coming painfully close to that position."

Gore wanted to make clear to Bush that he was not merely lodging a symbolic protest of the administration's failure to act in Iraq, but had several concrete steps in mind. "Of course, if I thought there were no alternative but to become deeply engaged in Iraq's internal struggle and to protract our military stay in the region, I would support your approach," the letter continued. "In my opinion, however, there are certain things we should do not only because they are right, but because they are *feasible*." Gore offered three specific suggestions on what to do next:

1. We should support the cease-fire strictly. Permission to fly Iraqi helicopters was not granted for the purpose of suppressing a rebellion: it was granted explicitly for administrative necessity. Now that we understand Iraq's real intent, we should stop this abuse. Many lives can still be saved if Iraq is forbidden to use these powerful weapons against people completely unable to defend themselves.

2. We should support the . . . effort to focus the Security Council on the plight of Iraq's Kurdish and Shi'ite population, and we should also mobilize support to provide aid to the refugees.

3. In the longer term, we should be using such leverage as we have to advance the day not just when Saddam Hussein is out of power, but when there exists in Iraq a government that grants reasonable consideration to all its peoples and which no longer rules by terror. Until that time, I would hope that the U.S. will be adamant about imposing sanctions in a very severe manner.

"I believe that the approach outlined above would not impede our planned drawdown of forces in the region," the senator concluded. "On the contrary, it might be part of the insurance that we want against ever having to bring them back again."

Gore ended his missive by reminding the president of his frequent comparisons of Saddam Hussein's Iraq to Hitler's Germany during the months preceding the Gulf War. "Saddam Hussein's external behavior is of a piece with the internal character of his regime," he pointed out. "As you would not have the world repeat the mistake that was made at Munich, I ask you to change your policy so that we do not replicate other situations in which Great Powers ignored the fate of peoples who rose up for their freedom, especially at a juncture when we have immense leverage to influence the outcome."

George Bush was initially determined to do no such thing. His administration's entire strategy for managing the aftermath of the Gulf War was predicated on leaving the regime in Baghdad—whether presided over by Saddam or one of his generals—with enough of an army intact to suppress internal strife and quickly restore order in a defeated Iraq. There was deep suspicion within the Bush administration about Kurdish aspirations for autonomy. Not only was it thought that a successful revolt against the regime in Baghdad could lead to the collapse of central government in Iraq and plunge the entire region into "primordial chaos"; but virtually every prewar intelligence analysis had warned that a successful Kurdish revolt would tempt Iran into increasing its influence in the Gulf by intervening in Iraq.

Visibly bothered by the criticism he was receiving over his administration's refusal to aid the insurgents, Bush asserted to a group of reporters on April 4: "I made it clear from the very beginning that it was not an objective of the Coalition or the United States to overthrow Saddam Hussein. So I don't think the Shi'ites in the south, those who are unhappy with Saddam in Baghdad, or the Kurds in the north, ever felt the United States would come to their assistance to overthrow this man."

But as the graphic images of "Saddam's slaughter" appeared on their newsstands and in their living rooms, the American public began demanding some sort of response to this new crisis in Iraq. Caren Firouz's poignant photograph of a napalm-scarred Kurdish toddler on the April 15, 1991, cover of *Newsweek* bore a reproachful caption: "Why won't he help us?"

The crescendo of criticism directed at the administration was steadily eroding the president's resolve to do nothing. "No one was happy with how things were going in March and early April," Richard Haass recalls. "No one liked the images on the television at all, and we were obviously frustrated and getting criticism congressionally. So through March and early April, we were essentially hoping that normal humanitarian efforts would be enough to handle the situation, but increasingly it became clear it was not." Robert Kimmitt also stresses the importance of the televised images of Kurdish refugees in escalating the stakes of the crisis in the eyes of the administration. "From a humanitarian perspective those images of March and early April were devastating, and obviously there were some things we would have done on a humanitarian basis even if we had not had the political and military interests that we had."

On April 5 the UN Security Council passed Resolution 688, which condemned "the oppression of the Iraqi civilian population . . . in Kurdish populated areas" and demanded that Iraq "immediately end this repression." Saddam, no stranger to either repression or UN resolutions, continued his terror unabated. Already a public outcry in Britain had prompted Prime Minister John Major to call for military action under UN auspices to protect the Kurds—a stunning reversal of the view he had stated only weeks earlier. Along with Turkish president Turgut Ozal, Major proposed the creation of "safe enclaves" in northern Iraq where Kurdish refugees would be protected by UN Coalition forces.

"The president didn't want to go that far," Haass remembers, "so the intermediate step was the idea of dropping food, and that was done on April 5 or 6. The U.S. military was dropping MREs [Meals Ready to Eat] and so forth, but the idea was still to keep ourselves at arm's length, to not have ground forces and all that."

On April 6, Bush publicly stated for the first time that he was inclined to support some form of U.S. intervention on behalf of the Kurds. At a joint press appearance in Houston with James Baker, who would be departing the next day to view Kurdish refugee camps in southern Turkey, Bush declared: "Well, it is possible that the United States will have a contribution, but that has not been finalized. It is essential that there be a force in there. But we're not talking about a lot of troops or anything of that nature."

•   •   •

Brent Scowcroft was appalled. The very last thing he had wanted to see after the Gulf War was an ongoing U.S. military commitment inside Iraq. As far as Scowcroft was concerned, the war had turned out exactly the way it was supposed to; in fact, better than anyone had a right to expect. Operation Desert Storm had wrecked Iraq's army and much of its infrastructure, rendering Saddam Hussein no threat to his neighbors. Coalition bombing was assumed to have destroyed most of Iraq's WMD facilities, and as one of the conditions for a cease-fire, the United States had secured an intrusive UN weapons inspection regime that would take care of the rest. Iran was staying out of the conflict. The balance of power in the Persian Gulf had been restored. At the same time, the U.S.-led Coalition had not destroyed Iraq's army to the last man during the Gulf War because it did not want to see the central government in Baghdad lose control over the rest of Iraq and cause the country to fall apart.

Scowcroft took an unsentimental view of the Kurdish uprising. In his earlier incarnation as Gerald Ford's national security adviser, he himself had played a major part in an earlier U.S. "abandonment" of the Iraqi Kurds back in 1975. At the behest of the strongly anticommunist Shah of Iran, the United States had encouraged the Kurds to rebel against the pre-Saddam Ba'ath regime in Iraq, at the time an important client state of the Soviet Union. The architect of this policy was Scowcroft's colleague and longtime mentor Henry Kissinger, then at the height of his influence in both Washington and Tehran.

In his memoirs, Kissinger would later explain that "our purpose was to raise the cost to the Iraqis of imposing their regime, and thereby to induce Baghdad to conduct a policy more respectful of the security concerns of Iraq's neighbors." But once the plan was deemed to have succeeded and the Kurds had served their purpose, covert American aid was unceremoniously withdrawn, allowing the Kurdish rebels to be slaughtered. Kissinger had justified abandoning the Kurds with one of his trademark aphorisms: "Covert action should not be confused with missionary work."

But now, as memoranda from his staff discussing the relative merits of "safe havens" and "no-fly zones" inside Iraq began landing on his desk, Scowcroft realized that the United States would not be able to extricate itself so easily this time. With a frown, he reached for the memo on the top of the pile. From a junior member of the NSC staff, it was a list of next steps to prepare for humanitarian operations in northern Iraq. Scowcroft did not like what he read. In his small, clerkish handwriting, he wrote in the margin of the document words that could have been a prophecy of America's future destiny in Iraq:

"Is this a one-time thing, or should we foreshadow more to come?"

●   ●   ●

Scowcroft was not alone in opposing further action. At the Pentagon, Dick Cheney and the Joint Chiefs also remained adamantly opposed to involving U.S. military forces in the internal affairs of Iraq.

On Sunday morning, April 7, Cheney appeared on the ABC News program *This Week with David Brinkley*. In his characteristic blunt-spoken style, Brinkley asked the secretary of defense, "Why didn't we go to Baghdad and clean it up when we had the chance?"

"Well, just as it's important, I think, for a president to know when to commit U.S. forces to combat, it's also important to know when not to commit U.S. forces to combat," Cheney replied. "I think for us to get American military personnel involved in a civil war inside Iraq would literally be a quagmire."

He then proceeded to ask a rapid-fire series of half a dozen questions, all of which had presumably been discussed already by the secretary and his colleagues. It was a distinctive rhetorical technique that Cheney had used throughout his political career, designed to preempt criticism by demonstrating to potential critics that they had not thought through an issue as thoroughly as Cheney and his staff had, but if they did, then any reasonable person would arrive at the same conclusion.

"Once we got to Baghdad, what would we do? Who would we put in power? What kind of government would we have? Would it be a Sunni government, a Shia government, a Kurdish government? Would it be secular along the lines of the Ba'ath Party? Would it be fundamentalist Islamic?

"I do not think the United States wants to have U.S. military forces accept casualties and accept the responsibility of trying to govern Iraq," Cheney concluded. "I think it makes no sense at all."

●   ●   ●

April 8, 1991, was a balmy evening in the Washington area as the capital prepared for an annual rite as inviolate as the State of the Union and as redolent of springtime as cherry blossoms: the season opener for the

Baltimore Orioles, adopted home team of many a baseball-deprived Washingtonian.

That evening the mood at the ballpark was unusually festive. This would be the last such game in Baltimore's Memorial Stadium. The following season the Orioles would move across town to a sparkling new ballpark in Camden Yards. But at least the venerable old stadium was going out in style. The capital region was feting the recent American triumph in the Persian Gulf and the safe return of many Washington-based service personnel. The roster of dignitaries attending the game included a veritable *Who's Who* of the Bush administration's senior national security officials, many of whom were by now better known than the hometown Orioles. In keeping with the patriotic spirit of the evening, Defense Secretary Cheney had been awarded the signal honor of throwing out the season's first pitch.

Among those with coveted tickets to the game was Robert Kimmitt, serving that evening as acting secretary of state. It was a duty that fell to Kimmitt, the third-ranking official in the Bush State Department, whenever James Baker and Deputy Secretary Lawrence Eagleburger were out of the country. The department would be in seasoned hands while they were away. The six-foot-seven Kimmitt was a former paratrooper who had spent thirteen months in-country, earning a Purple Heart and three Bronze Stars, before being selected to attend Georgetown Law School. Kimmitt's entrée to foreign policy had been an unexpected appointment as a legal adviser to the National Security Council during the Carter administration, where he would wryly tell his old army friends he was "number fifty-five out of fifty-five on the NSC staff." He was being modest. Kimmitt had caught the eye of then–national security adviser Zbigniew Brzezinski, and after the Republican landslide in 1980 had been one of exceedingly few Carter aides to find employment with the Reagan administration. He had been working as general counsel of the Treasury Department when James Baker arrived as secretary of the treasury in 1985. From that point on, Kimmitt was a Baker man, with all that entailed.

After two years together at Treasury, Kimmitt had become one of Baker's top aides during the 1988 Bush presidential campaign. Among other campaign chores, Kimmitt had been charged with interviewing prospective vice presidential candidates for George Bush. He had privately voiced reservations about the selection of Dan Quayle as Bush's running mate, advice that had been rejected by Bush but which earned Kimmitt the undying respect of Baker, who despised Quayle.

Within the walls of the State Department, Kimmitt was known colloquially as Colonel Bob—the honorific as much a commentary on his temperament as on his military background. Kimmitt's job as undersecretary for political affairs was to keep the State Department bureaucracy running smoothly. It was a role that involved fewer high-profile trips overseas, but suited the father of five just fine. Kimmitt was a good fit for the job in other ways as well. As they say at West Point, he had quiet command presence. On those rare occasions when he needed to call an employee at State on the carpet for committing some indiscretion, Kimmitt seldom lost his temper. He seldom needed to. A frown and a few carefully chosen words of reprimand from the imposing ex-soldier were enough. He never had to worry about a repeat offense.

But Kimmitt was a worried man this evening. Throughout the preceding two days he had been in frequent contact with James Baker, who was at that moment visiting Turkey, an indispensable ally during the recent war with Iraq. Ostensibly the visit was to thank the Turkish government and President Turgut Ozal for their steadfast support throughout the Gulf crisis. Kimmitt, however, was one of the few people in Washington who knew the real reason for Baker's stopover in Turkey: to see firsthand whether the United States needed to do something about Saddam Hussein's slaughter of Iraq's Kurdish population.

That very afternoon the secretary of state had visited a Kurdish refugee camp in the remote mountainous region of southeastern Turkey that bordered Iraq, and Kimmitt was expecting to hear back from him later that evening. The press and the human rights organizations in Washington were screaming for the Bush administration to do something soon.

All of these thoughts were weighing on Kimmitt's mind as he and his son Robert Jr. inched their way through Washington traffic toward the ballpark. Cheney will be at that game, he reasoned to himself, so I should be safe to go, too. In the event that Baker needed to contact him, Kimmitt had even taken along his "radios" (which was how the former infantryman thought of the secure satellite communications equipment that senior U.S. officials carried when they traveled). After eight solid months of working sixteen-hour days during the Gulf crisis, he badly wanted this night out with his son.

They had gotten only as far as the Jefferson Memorial, however, when Kimmitt was seized by a premonition of trouble—the sort of instinct that had more than once saved his life in Vietnam and which he had learned never to ignore. "There's just something that tells me I shouldn't be out of the office today," he muttered out loud. Kimmitt turned to his crest-fallen son. "Robert," he apologized, "I hate to do this, but I really think I've got to be in the office." He urged his son to go on to the game without him.

Kimmitt made the short trip from the Tidal Basin to the State Department building in pensive silence. He had just arrived at his office when the telephone rang.

It was Baker. As always, the secretary of state minced no words. "The situation is much, much worse than any of us anticipated," he informed Kimmitt. "I don't care what you have to do," Baker shouted. "Break the bureaucratic logjam, and let's get things moving." And in Baker's mind, there was little doubt about what he himself needed to do to "break the bureaucratic logjam."

"I'm going to call Cheney and the president next," he told Kimmitt.

The beautiful spring evening had been ruined for Bob Kimmitt, and was soon about to be ruined for many other Bush administration officials.

●   ●   ●

It had taken James Baker all of twelve minutes to realize that something needed to be done about the Kurdish refugee catastrophe in northern Iraq, and soon.

Accompanied by Dennis Ross and Morton Abramowitz, the U.S. ambassador to Turkey, Baker walked silently through a squalid, nameless refugee camp on the Turkish side of the Iraqi border. He was horrified by the conditions. There were tens of thousands of Kurdish refugees in this camp alone, with no potable water, no food, and no firewood. Many bore wounds from their encounter with Saddam Hussein's Republican Guard during the pell-mell flight across the border. Worst of all was the cold. Springtime in this part of the world brought no respite from bone-chilling gusts of wind that ripped across the barren hills of this, the most destitute region of Turkey. At one point, to the alarm of his security detail, the secretary of state seized a handheld microphone and leapt onto a small promontory to say a few words directly to the refugees. Although few of them could understand what he was saying, the meaning behind his actions was clear.

Climbing back aboard Baker's official aircraft, the two senior officials traveling with the secretary were struck by the change in his demeanor. Ross was astonished to see that the cool, unsentimental Baker had grown visibly emotional over what he had just seen. Abramowitz found the moment equally memorable. "We clocked it at twelve minutes, but it was a very important twelve minutes. There were Kurds lying all over the mountainsides. You had one of these Dante-like scenes, him holding a microphone, addressing them. And that changed the whole thing."

Even so, the ever-circumspect secretary of state was careful not to commit the Bush administration publicly to any definite course of action. "We are not prepared to go down the slippery slope of being sucked into a civil war," he said to the traveling press contingent aboard the aircraft. "We cannot police what goes on inside Iraq, and we cannot be arbiters of who shall govern Iraq." Consulting briefly with Ross and Abramowitz in his private compartment, it was a different story.

"We've got to use our military to save these guys," Baker told them categorically. Unwilling to wait until the return to Ankara, he began placing heated calls to Washington on the spot.

Later, as he unwound from his harrowing day on the flight back to the Turkish capital, the man who had managed the last four Republican presidential campaigns framed the argument he would use to convince Dick Cheney and George Bush of the need for a new American military intervention in Iraq.

This was not how victory was supposed to look.

●   ●   ●

During the first two weeks of April 1991, one theme emerged with pervasive frequency in the Bush administration's public statements on the

Kurdish refugee crisis: a near paranoia among the administration's leading policymakers about the prospect of "getting bogged down" in a putative Iraqi civil war. President Bush's own views on the subject, in
particular, were so consistent, so frequently expressed, and so forcefully
articulate that they form an extraordinary annal of how this notion informed his reluctance to intervene on behalf of the Kurds.

Even before Baker had left for Turkey, Bush had cited his concerns
about American forces becoming involved in a "civil war" as the primary
rationale for U.S. noninvolvement in the conflict. At a joint press appearance with Japanese prime minister Toshiki Kaifu on April 4, the president expanded on this view at some length. Bush was asked by one
reporter: "Mr. President, the critics are suggesting that you've abandoned
the Kurds to Saddam Hussein's mercy; one has even likened it to your
Bay of Pigs. Could you explain to us why you were willing to do so much
to help liberate Kuwait and why now we are standing on the sidelines
while the Kurds are struggling?"

"Be glad to," Bush replied. "It was never a stated objective of the
Coalition to intervene in the internal affairs of Iraq. Indeed, I made it
very clear that we did not intend to go into Iraq. I condemn Saddam Hussein's brutality against his own people. But I do not want to see United
States forces, who have performed with such skill and dedication, sucked
into a civil war in Iraq. . . . And I don't think there's a single parent of a
single man or woman that has fought in Desert Storm that wants to see
United States forces pushed into this situation."

After Baker had reported back from Turkey, the president had reluctantly consented to the creation of "safe havens" in northern Iraq protected by U.S. and Coalition forces (what would later become known as
Operation Provide Comfort). But he continued to expound on the wisdom of staying out of the "civil war" in Iraq. In a somewhat pedantic exchange on April 11 with the veteran CNN correspondent Charles
Bierbauer, who had inquired about the legal status of the safe havens in
Iraq, the president telegraphed his thinking on the matter.

"Charles, you're off on the wrong track," Bush chided. "If you'd listen
to what I said, you'd be right about this. There is no difference between
these people [on the two sides of the "safe haven" boundary]. And it takes
the United Nations action to do some formalization; that's not what we're

doing. We're going to help these refugees, and please don't try to make a difference when there isn't any. If you don't believe me, do what I did yesterday: Talk to John Major, and you will see that there are no differences.

"And P.S.," the president added, wagging his finger in a scolding gesture. "I am not going to involve any American troops in a civil war in Iraq. They are not going to be going in there to do what some of my severest critics early on now seem to want me to do. I want these kids to come home. And that's what's going to happen. And we are going to do what is right by these refugees, and I think the American people expect that, and they want that. But I don't think they want to see us bogged down in a civil war by sending in the 82nd Airborne or the 101st or the 7th Cavalry."

Two days later, in a speech to the Air War College at Maxwell Air Force Base in Alabama, Bush continued on this theme. "I do not want one single soldier or airman shoved into a civil war in Iraq that has been going on for ages. I'm not going to have that."

The phobia about "getting bogged down" in a putative Iraqi civil war also goes far in explaining the Bush administration's initial refusal to prevent Iraqi helicopter gunships from attacking the Shia and Kurds, until it was too late. Mistakenly or not, George Bush viewed shooting down Iraqi helicopters (a relatively innocuous measure, given the utter supremacy of Coalition air forces over Iraq) as a possible first step toward American involvement in a shooting civil war. Asked point-blank at the same exchange with reporters why he refused to interfere with Iraq's use of helicopters to strafe the Kurds, Bush drew an explicit connection between denying air rights to Saddam's internal security forces and the possibility of U.S. entanglement in Iraq's "civil war":

"Why let their helicopters continue? Because I do not want to see us get sucked into the internal civil war inside Iraq, that's why. I can understand people thinking that [we should shoot down Iraqi helicopters]. I can understand their criticism. And then, how do you take care of the tanks and the riflemen and the other parts of the divisions that remained in northern Iraq? Helicopters is but part of it."

The president was not alone in harboring these views. Other key members of his administration shared the same beliefs about the inadvisability of becoming embroiled in Iraqi internal affairs. Scowcroft and the NSC staff continued to view the prospect of a long-term American commitment in Iraq with alarm. Richard Haass offers this summation of their thinking at the time. "We were reluctant to alter war aims and, even more so, to allow U.S. forces to be drawn into an internal situation with the potential to become a multifront civil war. What we were trying to do was look for ways to address the humanitarian problems without getting dragged into what we viewed as a quote unquote 'quagmire.'"

While virtually all of the leading national security figures of the Bush administration accepted the notion that "getting bogged down" in Iraq's internal difficulties was unwise, the anxiety reigned supreme among senior U.S. Army officers. Robert Zoellick, for instance, recalls the powerful entrenched opposition of the military against any policy response to the Kurdish crisis that might lead to a lengthy postwar occupation of Iraq by U.S. forces. "There was a combination of the political calculation but also the military; the U.S. military was quite strong against establishing an ongoing obligation for what became a safe haven. They had to be pulled into it, and that's understandable. I'm not blaming them, I'm just saying that there was that dimension."

These same officials also accepted the president's rationalization for allowing Saddam Hussein to continue to use his helicopters against the Kurds. When pressed by the conservative commentator George Will on Iraq's use of helicopter gunships during his Sunday morning talk show appearance on April 7, Cheney declared: "I think it's important to emphasize that this isn't just a question of shooting down helicopters. Some people say, well, just take out the helicopters, that'll solve the problem. It's not [just helicopters], as we heard from the Kurds themselves—it's artillery, it's tanks. The only organized military force inside Iraq is the Iraqi force, Saddam Hussein's army, and for the United States to get involved just a little bit, with just a little bit of military action, strikes me as fundamentally a bad idea. If you don't have a clear-cut military objective, if you're not prepared to use overwhelming force to achieve it, then we don't have any business committing U.S. military forces into that civil war."

Throughout the Gulf crisis, no member of the UN Coalition had been more supportive of Bush administration policy than President Turgut Ozal and the government of Turkey. Certainly none had made greater financial sacrifices to support the U.S.-led Coalition. The Turks had been an ally of unique strategic importance during the crisis. As a longtime NATO member that also happened to share a long border with Iraq, Turkey provided the air forces and special operations troops of the United States and other members of the Coalition with an invaluable toehold right in the heart of the combat theater itself. As a Muslim country that was also a member of NATO, Turkey provided unqualified support for the UN Coalition—a powerful symbolic argument against Saddam's claim that the Gulf crisis was a conflict between the West and Islam.

Most important, Iraq's main oil pipeline—Saddam's economic lifeline—ran across Turkish territory and terminated at the Turkish port of Ceyhan on the Mediterranean Sea. The Turks could literally flip the switch on most of Iraq's oil exports. With their support, maintaining an oil embargo against Iraq was a simple matter; without it, there was no oil embargo.

But the pipeline was not only Saddam's economic lifeline, it was also Turkey's: one of the country's single largest sources of foreign currency earnings. Upholding the UN oil embargo for seven months had been a bitter economic pill for Turkey to swallow, but the Turks had gamely done so in the interest of long-term stability in the region.

The Turks' extraordinarily strong support for the U.S.-led Coalition was also the result of another development: the blossoming friendship between Turgut Ozal and George Bush. Unlike most of Bush's "friends" in the Islamic world, Ozal had not known the president well before assuming power, and the two leaders had gotten off to a rocky start. In the summer of 1990 the Bush administration had negotiated a military base agreement with the government of Greece—nominally a NATO ally of Turkey, but in reality a bitter ethnic and military rival of the Turks for centuries. Knowing that any base agreement with the Greeks was sure to raise the ire of Turkey, the administration did not inform Ozal's government until after the negotiations with Greece were complete. The administration also did not inform Morton Abramowitz, the veteran U.S. ambassador in Ankara. When Ozal and his government learned that a military agreement with Greece had been negotiated behind their backs, they collectively went into what Abramowitz described to Washington as "terrible paroxysms of anger." Abramowitz himself was "pissed off" to have been left out of the loop.

It so happened that Secretary of Defense Cheney had been visiting Ankara when news of the Greek base agreement broke. "Cheney got the rudest treatment I've ever seen given any American official," remembers Abramowitz, grimacing at the memory. Shortly before Cheney's departure from the Turkish capital, Abramowitz pulled him aside. "I think it's very important that you go back and ask the president to call Ozal," he said urgently, "and tell him there's nothing in that agreement that in any way is directed at Turkey."

Bush made the call and repeated Abramowitz's formula almost verbatim. A still suspicious Ozal asked, "Would you say that publicly?" The Turkish president was less concerned about the specifics of the Greek base agreement than by the impression that the United States was willing to collaborate secretly with Turkey's traditional rival in the eastern Mediterranean. Bush said that he would, and did.

"That was an episode that changed very much the way our business was done," Abramowitz later said. "The two presidents now had a tie which was very strong, and if necessary could do their business on the phone." The newly forged bond of trust between the two leaders would prove instrumental a month later, when Saddam invaded Kuwait.

During the months preceding Desert Storm, and then during the war itself, Bush and Ozal had conversed over forty times by phone ("even more frequently than Bush and John Major," Abramowitz notes proudly). George Bush had not only made a friend; he had found a true kindred spirit. Like Bush, Ozal had a consuming passion for foreign policy and thought about the Near East in broad, geopolitical terms. Unusual for Turkey, he preferred to conduct diplomacy himself rather than leaving it to the Foreign Ministry or the military general staff, the two traditional arbiters of Turkish foreign policy. Indeed, Ozal had dismissed three of his cabinet ministers during the Gulf crisis so that his would be the only voice on how to manage the confrontation with Iraq. But also like George Bush, Ozal's attention to domestic policy sometimes suffered from his absorption with Turkey's role in world affairs. Among both

American observers in Ankara and the Turkish political elite, he had the reputation of being a man who was frequently bored with the details of Turkish domestic politics.

Ozal had two main strategic priorities in the Gulf crisis. The first was a simple one: He wanted Saddam Hussein removed from power as quickly as possible. When James Baker had paid his first visit to Ankara after the Iraqi invasion of Kuwait, in late August 1990, he had been mildly surprised by Ozal's vehemence on this point. "Are we going to get rid of Saddam Hussein?" the Turkish president had asked.

"Mr. President, we are prevented by law from taking actions to assassinate foreign officials," Baker reminded Ozal. "Our focus now is to strangle him through political and economic sanctions." Ozal remained adamant. "We need to finish him off," he countered. "Every state is vulnerable if Saddam Hussein continues to exist. We will be in perpetual danger. Please tell President Bush that he has to go." During an October 1990 visit to Washington, Ozal had repeated this message in an Oval Office conversation with President Bush. "Saddam is the most dangerous man in the world, and we have to get rid of him," he said earnestly to Bush. "It is up to you to do something about it."

Ozal's insistence on eliminating Saddam's regime was all the more surprising because it did not reflect the views of either the Turkish military (the traditional kingmakers in Turkish politics) or the country's business establishment. Turkey's generals saw in the Iraqi Ba'athists a determinedly secular military regime not dissimilar to their own, one that kept a tight lid on Iraq's Kurdish population, the Turks' main security concern in Iraq. The Turks had a large, restive Kurdish minority of their own, and the Turkish army did not want to see any developments that advanced the Kurdish cause in either country. The Turkish business community was most interested in the huge profits generated from trucking and construction contracts inside Iraq, where Turkish companies were by far the largest foreign contractors. A solid majority of the Turkish public had opposed the war with Iraq.

Ozal's reason for wanting Saddam gone had to do with his second strategic concern: the Iraqi leader's determination to retain his weapons of mass destruction. In every meeting with U.S. officials, Ozal harped on the need to ensure that the outcome of the Gulf crisis included the elimination of Iraq's stocks of chemical weapons and their associated delivery systems. Ironically, though, his insistence did not stem from a fear that Saddam Hussein would one day use these weapons to attack neighboring Turkey. The Turks knew that not even Saddam was foolhardy enough to attack a heavily armed neighbor that was also a NATO member.

Rather, Ozal's concern about Iraqi possession of WMDs was motivated by another consideration. In 1987, Saddam had been confronted with an earlier rebellion by the Iraqi Kurds. In response, he had launched the notorious Anfal campaign to crush the revolt. Saddam had put his most brutal general (and cousin), Ali Hassan al-Majid, in charge of pacifying the Kurdish areas of northern Iraq. Ali promptly resorted to the use of chemical weapons as a means of terrifying the Kurds, earning himself the sobriquet "Chemical Ali" throughout the Middle East. But the Anfal campaign worked. Kurdish resistance crumbled, and tens of thousands of terrified Kurdish refugees fled across the border into Turkey. Ali was later put in charge of the Iraqi occupation forces in Kuwait after the August 1990 invasion and was directly responsible for ordering many of the worst atrocities committed by Iraqi troops in Kuwait.

What resulted from Anfal was a humanitarian crisis that threw the economy of Turkey into a recession and roiled Turkish politics for the better part of a year. Worse from a Turkish perspective, the introduction of so many refugees into the restive Kurdish-populated regions of southeastern Turkey caused ethnic tensions among Turkey's own Kurds to flare up, leading to a season of separatist violence in Turkey. The conventional wisdom on Anfal among both the Turkish political elite and ordinary Turks was that the real fallout from Iraq's use of chemical weapons had not been the residue from the weapons themselves, but rather the Kurdish refugees.

Ozal's nightmare, then, was not the hypothetical possibility that Saddam might one day use chemical weapons against Turkey; but rather, the very real possibility that Saddam might one day again use chemical weapons against his own Kurds. From Ozal's perspective, the worst security threat that Iraq posed to Turkey was another Kurdish refugee crisis. The obvious way to remove this threat was to remove a regime that had already proven that it possessed both the means and the will to instigate such a crisis.

In this context, Saddam's suppression of the Kurdish rebellion in March 1991, and the subsequent flight of Kurdish refugees into Turkey, was nothing short of an unmitigated catastrophe for Ozal. It was history repeating itself all over again, but with one key difference. In 1988 approximately 75,000 Kurdish refugees had fled into Turkey. Now, there were nearly a million.

An increasingly agitated Ozal complained about Saddam's survival on an almost daily basis to Abramowitz. "He was very much against it," the ambassador recalls, "and I think he tried to communicate that, he told me a lot about it, and I was conveying those views [to the White House]. But I don't think he had a shot at the president, because I think that decision was made very quickly. He was very unhappy. He thought that was a major mistake."

Abramowitz empathized with the Turkish leader's predicament over the Kurds. During his time in Turkey, he had come to appreciate Ozal's strategic acuity and pro-American instincts. "It was a big problem for the Turkish government. We felt guilty that they had risen up and we had done nothing. We should have felt guilty—we encouraged it."

●   ●   ●

By April 14, Saddam Hussein felt sufficiently confident of his control over northern Iraq that he could offer a blanket "amnesty" to the hundreds of thousands of Iraqi Kurds who had fled into Turkey. Later that Sunday morning, Dick Cheney was asked about Saddam's offer on the NBC News program *Meet the Press.*

"Mr. Secretary," challenged one of the show's panelists, the conservative columnist Robert Novak, "Saddam Hussein today made an offer to the Kurds. He said, No questions asked, come back, you won't be harmed. If you were a Kurd, would you take him up on that offer?"

Cheney frowned at the question. "Well, I don't think I have any way of putting myself in the position of the Kurds. I don't know precisely what motivated them when they left." Seeing the skeptical reaction this last assertion elicited from the *Meet the Press* panel, Cheney added quickly, "Presumably the fear of Saddam Hussein's forces; and that is clearly what has driven them to the dire circumstances they are now in."

"So you have no advice for them whatsoever?" an incredulous Novak asked.

"Again Bob, I'm reluctant to get into the position of advising those people where to go," Cheney replied. "I don't know what their circumstances are. And I do know that we are prepared to help them where they are."

Novak tried another tack. "Senator Gore of Tennessee, who was one of the few Democrats who supported the original war resolution, says that the Bush administration, President Bush now, have pinned their entire policy in Iraq on the support of Saddam Hussein." Gore, of course, was too good a politician not to have shared key portions of his "private" April 3 letter to Bush with members of the media; especially his charge that Bush was "mortgaging U.S. policy in the Gulf to the success of tyranny in Iraq."

"Isn't it true you would prefer Saddam Hussein to a Kurdish independent state, or to a partition of Iraq between the Sunnis and Shi'ites?" Novak concluded accusingly.

Cheney looked offended at the suggestion. "Bob," he countered, shaking his head grimly, "to suggest after what we've done to Saddam Hussein to drive him out of Kuwait, to destroy his offensive military capability, that somehow we prefer Saddam Hussein, is just silly. It makes no sense at all to make a statement like that."

Later in the program, conversation shifted to another controversy swirling around the Pentagon: Cheney's announcement only weeks after Desert Storm had ended that the Bush administration planned to reduce the size of U.S. conventional forces by 25 percent. With the United States running a massive budget deficit and about to enter a recession, securing the peace dividend from the end of the Cold War was a pressing concern for the administration. Many, however, were disputing the wisdom of reducing the American military so soon after the major conflict that had just taken place in the Gulf.

R. W. "Johnny" Apple, the cherubic, gray-haired Washington bureau chief of the *New York Times*, posed a hypothetical question to explore Cheney's views on the matter.

"Secretary Cheney, five years from now, ten years from now, fifteen years from now, after we've done this drawdown, after we've closed the bases, reduced the numbers, could we respond to a Gulf crisis as we have responded to this one?"

"Yes, we could," Cheney assured him.

"Not exactly in the same way, could we?" Apple persisted.

"It might be slightly different," Cheney allowed, "but the fact is that it's that kind of scenario, the assumption of a major regional contingency, a major problem in southwest Asia, in the Persian Gulf region, that is the planning assumption for the size force we'll have."

Apple remained unconvinced. "Even with this war," he reminded Cheney, "we didn't have enough sealift. We didn't have enough manpower to rotate troops, which could have been a problem if this were a war that lasted two, three, four, five months. And there were a lot of people we had to bring in from the Reserves, some of whom weren't very effective by your own account."

"Well, I would take exception to that," Cheney bristled. "It worked. We did have enough of what we needed. We were able to patch around."

.   .   .

President Bush announced the start of Operation Provide Comfort, the U.S.-led intervention to protect the Kurds, at an April 16 news conference. Besides humanitarian aid to Kurdish refugees who had fled their homes, Provide Comfort included the creation of "safe havens" located around some of the main Kurdish-populated towns of northern Iraq. Within these safe havens, Kurdish civilians would be protected from Iraqi attack by American and Coalition forces. A variation on the idea of "safe enclaves" that had first been advocated by John Major and Turgut Ozal, the safe havens were intended as a short-term measure, to convince Kurdish refugees—especially those who had fled into Turkey—that it was safe to return to their homes. Behind the scenes, though, the Bush White House had been adamant that the politically suggestive term "enclaves" be changed. The president, and Scowcroft especially, were still skittish about doing anything to imply that the United States supported Kurdish aspirations for an autonomous region in northern Iraq.

The Bush administration had also come up with a solution to the long-term threat posed by Saddam Hussein's regime to the Kurds. The

American-led Coalition declared a "no-fly zone" in Iraq north of the 36th Parallel: a large swath of Iraqi territory that would be off-limits to Iraqi aircraft of any kind. Operation Northern Watch, as the no-fly zone was dubbed, was a tacit admission by the Bush administration of just how damaging Iraq's ability to use its helicopters against the Kurds had been from both a military and public relations standpoint. It would later be joined by Operation Southern Watch, a similar no-fly zone to protect the Shia in southern Iraq.

However, even as he announced the beginning of this major new intervention by U.S. forces and admitted for the first time that he had underestimated the scope of the Kurdish refugee crisis, President Bush continued to maintain that his administration bore no responsibility for what had happened inside post–Desert Storm Iraq.

"You're asking me if I foresaw the size of the Kurdish refugee problem?" the president said in response to one reporter's question. "The answer is: No, I did not. But do I think the United States should bear guilt because of suggesting that the Iraqi people take matters into their own hands, with the implication being given by some that the United States would be there to support them militarily? That was not true: We never implied that."

But the unexpected scope of the Kurdish and Shia massacres led to a fundamental shift in the Bush inner circle's views on what to do about Saddam Hussein. Even with his military badly depleted by the Gulf War and his regime in tatters, Saddam had demonstrated an uncanny ability to make trouble for the Bush administration. And it was the worst kind of trouble for any administration: political trouble.

George Bush had reluctantly accepted the possibility of Saddam's survival in power because he had been persuaded by Scowcroft and his NSC staff that it was necessary for restoring regional stability in the Persian Gulf, to the point where a continuing American military presence in the Gulf would not be required. But the broad-based calls for the United States to do something, anything, to end the slaughter inside Iraq had forced his administration to accede to the creation of safe havens inside Iraq protected by U.S. troops; and no-fly zones in northern and southern Iraq patrolled by U.S. aircraft.

"The initial assumption in February and early March of 1991 was that

Saddam wasn't going to survive politically," Richard Haass says in summarizing the NSC staff's thinking during this period. "The rebellions and his ability to repress them, ironically enough, gave him a new lease on life and allowed him to portray himself as the savior of Iraq. It almost erased for some Iraqis the debacle of the war and allowed him a new justification for his continued rule and for his harshness. From our point of view, then, what we had to do was to make two adjustments."

The first of these adjustments was the need to maintain a substantial, long-term U.S. military presence in the region: both to deter future Iraqi aggression against the Gulf states, and to protect Iraq's oppressed minorities. "What became obvious was that what we were talking about was an open-ended policy," Haass admits. "With, then, all of the layers of it: whether it was the sanctions' open-endedness, the [UN Resolution] 688 operation, Northern Watch, and Southern Watch. Essentially the United States had to transition into an open-ended containment policy of Iraq, using the overflights, the sanctions, and so forth. And it wasn't just the containment of Iraq beyond its borders; but also it was putting limits on what Saddam could do inside his borders, so it was 'Containment-Plus.' And U.S. policy had to make that adjustment."

The second adjustment was far more radical. The pre–Gulf War notion that a "demoralized" Saddam Hussein could be left in power, the product of seven months' work by the Bush administration's best foreign policy minds, was abandoned barely seven weeks after the armistice that ended Desert Storm. The strategy that took its place was a far more direct one: Saddam Hussein had to go.

7

A GRINDING IRRITANT

On May 4, Deputy Secretary of State Lawrence Eagleburger sent a NODIS cable previewing the new strategy to the U.S. ambassadors posted in the six most important countries in the Gulf War Coalition: Great Britain, France, Turkey, Egypt, Saudi Arabia, and Syria. The ambassador in each foreign capital was encouraged to urge their host government to adopt a similar confrontational policy toward Iraq. "Bear in mind," Eagleburger reminded the ambassadors, "that we will attempt to preserve certain ambiguities in the policy, including to what lengths we will go to prevent loosening of UN sanctions now in force."

There was nothing ambiguous, though, in the four key elements of the new approach outlined by Eagleburger:

- The U.S./international community continues to support Iraq's territorial integrity, but now wants a new Iraqi leadership. Because of the invasion and occupation of Kuwait and the brutal repression of his own people, Saddam is discredited and cannot be redeemed. His leadership will never be accepted by the world community, and therefore Iraqis will pay the price.

- All possible sanctions will be maintained until he is gone. Any easing of sanctions will be considered only when there is a new government.

- Time is not on Iraq's side so long as Saddam holds on to power. Iraqis will not participate in postcrisis political, economic, and security arrangements until there is a change in regime.

- We are ready to work with a successor government in Baghdad if the Iraqi people change their government. From the outset, we have made clear that our problem is not with the Iraqi people but with their leadership and especially Saddam. This remains the case.

•   •   •

One inevitable ramification of the Bush administration's retooled strategy was the need to maintain a high-profile military presence in the two major Coalition countries bordering on Iraq: Turkey and Saudi Arabia. Both halves of the administration's new strategy depended on it.

The intrusive daily overflight operations and rigid enforcement of sanctions required by "containment-plus" would be possible only with a large U.S. Air Force deployment in Turkey and Saudi Arabia. Incirlik, the joint U.S.-Turkish air base in southern Turkey close to the Iraqi border, had been the principal logistical base from which Operation Provide Comfort had been launched to supply humanitarian aid to the Kurds. With the implementation of a no-fly zone over northern Iraq, Incirlik was soon to become one of the busiest air bases in all of NATO, with U.S. and Coalition aircraft flying hundreds of sorties in the skies of northern Iraq each day. To support these missions the United States greatly augmented the number of personnel and aircraft at the base.

Although the Coalition had not yet declared a formal no-fly zone over southern Iraq, the need for a similar overflight operation to deter Iraqi aggression in the south—whether external aggression against Saudi Arabia and Kuwait, or internal aggression against the Iraqi Shia—meant that the United States would have to maintain a large military footprint in Saudi Arabia as well. During the Gulf War the Air Force had constructed several huge, modern airfields in the Saudi desert to support combat operations against Iraq. These would now become bases for the hundreds of American military aircraft patrolling the skies of southern Iraq on a daily basis. Operations in both northern and southern Iraq would be coordinated out of CENTCOM's state-of-the-art command center in Riyadh, which had been built to conduct Operation Desert Storm. The requirement for a strong deterrent posture in southern Iraq dashed earlier hopes that U.S. forces could be withdrawn entirely from Saudi Arabia immediately following the end of the Gulf War. Instead, tens of thousands of American personnel would now need to remain in the kingdom indefinitely.

A large military presence in Turkey and Saudi Arabia was also necessary to implement the other half of the Bush administration's new strategy: forcing Saddam Hussein from power. During April and May 1991 the White House found itself grappling for ways to exert more pressure on Saddam's regime. A secret May 24 memo quietly being circulated among the NSC staff, titled "Keeping Pressure on Saddam Hussein's Regime: Strategy and Actions," contained a novel suggestion on how to exert such pressure.

"Our objective is to maintain the pressure for Saddam Hussein's removal and continue to impress on other Iraqis in key positions that they and their country are paying a heavy price for Saddam's leadership," the memo declared. It noted that this had become a far more difficult task, given Saddam's newfound support among the Sunni elite inside Iraq: "In focusing on Saddam, we want to avoid actions which could lead to Iraq's break-up or cause the current military and civilian leadership to rally behind him, as happened during the recent Shia and Kurdish revolts. We are actively looking for ways to turn the screw further that would have a high probability of success and hold Coalition support."

The primary recommendation in the memo was to capitalize on the continued presence of American forces in the Persian Gulf, especially the U.S. aircraft conducting overflight operations inside Iraq, as a goad that would provoke a coup against Saddam. The administration was still pinning its hopes on a military coup led by disaffected Ba'athists in the Iraqi army. "Many of our actions, although officially accepted by the GOI [government of Iraq], have the psychological effect of deliberately infringing on Iraq's sovereignty. We believe this is creating a grinding irritant to the highly developed nationalism of Iraq's educated classes and the Ba'athist and military leadership."

It was not Iraq's educated classes who were becoming irritated, however; it was Turkey's and Saudi Arabia's.

In Ankara, public opinion had soured further over the Bush administration's decision to continue economic sanctions against Iraq even after Kuwait had been liberated. Besides the loss of pipeline revenue from Iraqi oil exports, Turkish companies with substantial investments in Iraq were seeing their earnings wither. Many of Turkey's largest construction companies had been left unpaid for major infrastructure projects they had worked on inside Iraq and now had little prospect of ever being paid. Finally, the Turkish military was unhappy with the creation of the no-fly zone in northern Iraq, since it would mean conducting a major ongoing combat operation from Turkish territory. Turkey's generals, who during the Cold War had been among the United States' most accommodating NATO allies, were complaining bitterly to their counterparts in the Pentagon about the growing number of aircraft and U.S. personnel stationed at Incirlik.

President Ozal had been the staunchest advocate of both the war and of Turkey's close alignment with the Bush administration. He now paid the price for his people's disenchantment with both. The Turkish press and opposition parties in the national legislature mercilessly castigated him as a lackey for his unqualified support of U.S. policy toward Iraq. What Ozal had wanted most was for Desert Storm to result in the fall of Saddam Hussein, and a lessening of military tensions along the Turkish-Iraqi border. He had gotten the exact opposite. "For him, the Gulf War did not produce the benefits he would have liked, and he got attacked for it," sympathized Abramowitz.

Later that year, Abramowitz witnessed a striking display of Ozal's fall from grace with the Turkish public. At a cultural event taking place in one of Ankara's largest theaters, an announcement was made that the president of the republic was in attendance that evening. As Ozal rose from his seat in the presidential box to acknowledge the expected applause of the crowd, an ominous silence descended upon the auditorium. To Abramowitz, it was a poignant metaphor for a proud leader who had stood apart in the strength of his support for the United States—one who now stood apart from his people in a tragically literal sense.

But as uncomfortable as the Turks may have been with the Bush administration's arrangements for post–Desert Storm Iraq, at least the increased U.S. military presence in their country would not lead to a major disruption of Turkish society.

While it was one of the world's most important Islamic nations, Turkey was also a decidedly secular nation. The Turks embraced Western popular culture and harbored strongly Western aspirations. Wearing of the *hijab* (the head covering worn by conservative Muslim women) had been banned in Turkey for many years. Having been a NATO member since the 1950s, the Turks were accustomed to American and European troops transiting through their country. The United States had deployed thousands of personnel at Turkish bases during the Cold War, and off-duty U.S. service members were a familiar sight in the many restaurants and bazaars of Istanbul.

By contrast, Saudi Arabia was entirely unprepared for the stresses of hosting a long-term American military presence. The clash of cultures was simply too great. A nation whose official constitution was the Koran; where all religions other than Islam were outlawed; where women went veiled in public and were forbidden to drive; which had not seen foreign troops on its soil since the days of the Ottoman Empire; could not long tolerate the close proximity of so many American troops and so many American influences.

Even during the early days of August 1990, when much of Iraq's army had been poised along the Saudi border, many members of the Saudi royal family had been willing to take their chances with Saddam Hussein rather than allow U.S. troops into the kingdom. Just as Turkey's unstinting support for the Bush administration's strategy during the Gulf crisis had largely reflected the policy outlook of a single individual, Turgut Ozal, so too had Saudi Arabia's allowing of the Desert Storm campaign to be fought from its territory largely been the decision of one man: King Fahd. Convinced of the threat Saddam posed to his nation, and concerned above all about the long-term stability of the Gulf region, the king had swept aside all objections to the deployment of American forces on Saudi soil. He had given the Bush administration a blank check—in the most literal sense—to do whatever was necessary to remove the Iraqi threat and restore the status quo in the Gulf.

But Fahd had always known that the most he could do was buy the

United States some time to deal with the threat posed by Saddam. A significant portion of the Saudi population, and an even larger portion of the country's clerics, had never reconciled themselves to the idea of having non-Muslim troops in the Islamic holy land. As the number of U.S. personnel in the kingdom swelled to nearly half a million in the months immediately preceding Desert Storm, opposition to the American deployment had grown and become more strident. The seven months of the Gulf crisis, from Iraq's initial invasion in August to the conclusion of the Desert Storm campaign in late February, had been the most tumultuous period in the modern history of Saudi Arabia.

For the first time in memory, leading Islamic clerics (whose salaries were subsidized by the Saudi government) had openly criticized the king and the House of Saud. There had been public demonstrations against the purported "lewd behavior" of U.S. servicewomen deployed in Saudi Arabia. Iraq, a fellow Arab country, had dared to attack Saudi territory with Scud missiles during the Gulf War: an outrage that, ironically, many Saudis blamed on the presence of American troops in their country. Fahd had been able to keep the dissent under control only by assuring his subjects, and especially the senior, "establishment" clerics, that all non-Muslim troops would leave Saudi Arabia just as soon as Iraqi forces had been driven out of Kuwait.

Throughout the Gulf crisis, the king and other Saudi officials had constantly tried to impress the urgency of their situation upon the Bush administration. Ambassador Chas Freeman had, of course, dutifully reported Saudi anxieties about an open-ended U.S. military deployment back to Washington. The king had also personally raised the issue with President Bush on numerous occasions, most notably during the president's Thanksgiving 1990 visit to the Gulf.

The top officials of the Bush administration had themselves declared, both publicly and privately, that they shared the Saudi desire for a rapid withdrawal of U.S. forces after the crisis was over. President Bush had promised on numerous occasions that U.S. troops would not remain in the kingdom "one day more than necessary" to complete their mission. During the August 1990 diplomatic mission that had secured King Fahd's permission for American forces to be deployed in the kingdom, Secretary of Defense Cheney had personally pledged that the United

States would seek no permanent bases on Saudi territory. Cheney had subsequently made half a dozen trips to Saudi Arabia, each time repeating the same message.

The inconclusive outcome of Desert Storm thus came as a rude shock to King Fahd and the Saudi government. They had never imagined that Saddam Hussein could survive a crushing military defeat in the Gulf and still remain a long-term threat to the kingdom. But far worse for the Saudis was the unanticipated prospect of a large U.S. military contingent remaining behind in their country indefinitely.

"As far as they were concerned," Freeman observed at the time, "we were there as their guests, on sufferance, on a day-to-day basis, and could be asked to leave at any time." And to the Saudis, the United States was a guest that had long overstayed its welcome. Freeman captured the Saudis' mood with an expressive analogy. "It is not the Saudi or Arab custom to ask guests to leave, but at various points along the way they began to behave like a man who has had a guest over to dinner, and the dinner's over and the man's wife has gone to bed. And then the man takes the dog out for a walk and returns, and the guest is still sitting there. And when you turn the air conditioner off, and turn the lights off, and start going to bed yourself, you sort of expect the guest to leave. We were so dim we didn't understand that."

Freeman did understand, however, and warned Washington that the failure of American forces to withdraw was creating serious domestic problems for King Fahd. Religious hard-liners in Saudi Arabia were furious that two months after the Gulf War had ended, the "infidel soldiers" had still not left. "There was an immediate postwar spike in religious militancy and xenophobic reaction in the kingdom, which was of considerable concern," Freeman noted. The Saudi government itself was so concerned that it had taken the almost unprecedented step of sending some prominent clerics into exile, which, of course, only infuriated the religious community more.

Further complicating matters, the Gulf War had plunged Saudi Arabia into a deep recession. From a purely economic standpoint, the war could not have come at a worse time for the Saudis: It brought to a head a number of unfavorable trends that had been developing for years. Saudi oil revenues had been pinched by the same long-term decline in world oil prices that Saddam Hussein had complained about so bitterly during the summer of 1990, leading to the once unimaginable in Saudi Arabia: a budget deficit. For the first time in its history the Saudi government had been forced to cut spending, and to curtail the generous welfare state to which Saudi citizens had been accustomed for decades. Simultaneously, a baby boom during the OPEC glory years of the early 1970s had created a large population of young adults who were trying to enter the workforce just as the economy and government spending were beginning to experience a painful downturn. Unemployment in the kingdom was skyrocketing, particularly among young adult males.

On top of all this, Saudi Arabia had incurred massive costs during the Gulf War. The Saudis had spent heavily on infrastructure projects during the war to support the nearly six hundred thousand Coalition troops that had taken part in Desert Storm. They had built new roads, ports, and entire new military bases in the desert. The government in Riyadh had also generously rewarded poorer Arab nations like Egypt and Syria, which had committed large numbers of troops to Desert Storm. The Saudis had paid the entire cost of transporting over three divisions' worth of Egyptian and Syrian troops to Saudi Arabia, and had underwritten most of the operating expenses for these troops while they were in the country. Finally, the Saudis had reimbursed the United States for some of the costs it had incurred during the Gulf crisis. On one memorable occasion, during Secretary of State Baker's "tin cup tour" of Coalition capitals to solicit financial support for Coalition military activities in the Gulf, King Fahd had personally pledged $15 billion for the U.S. Treasury.

The common stereotype of the Saudis in the West as plutocrats with an unlimited supply of petrodollars at their disposal masked the fact that Saudi Arabia was a nation of only 18 million people, less than one-twelfth the population of the United States, with an economy that was still relatively small by global standards. The cost of the Gulf War had strained even the economy of the United States. It had strained the economy of Saudi Arabia to the breaking point.

The post–Desert Storm fiscal crisis in Saudi Arabia had ominous political overtones. For three decades the Saudi monarchy had bought social peace in the country by lavishing money on its citizens. Every young

Saudi had come of age entitled by right to a government-funded job. The large population of Islamic clerics had enjoyed government-funded stipends, and the Saudi government had subsidized hundreds of mosques and Islamic schools to provide sinecures for many of the clerics. The unspoken compact between the House of Saud and the clerical community was that in return for unstinting financial support from the government and the right to hold sway over cultural mores in Saudi society, the clerics would agree to keep any criticism of the monarchy muted.

In the wake of the Gulf War, however, government largesse on the same scale was no longer possible, just at the moment when it was needed most. Thousands of young Saudi men found themselves unemployed and angry, making them a ready pool of recruits for radical political and religious movements. Meanwhile, months of encounters between U.S. military personnel and the more socially conservative Saudis had galvanized opposition to the regime from the clerics, even as they saw their accustomed perquisites being curtailed. It was an explosive mixture.

Fairly or not, many Saudis began to blame the continuing presence of U.S. forces in the kingdom for their woes. Word of King Fahd's $15 billion pledge to the United States during the Gulf War had sparked intense discussion among the people; even in Saudi Arabia, $15 billion is an eye-opening sum of money. Now, wildly inflated rumors about how many "infidel soldiers" were still in the kingdom, and how much the king was paying to keep them there, ran through a disenchanted populace like wildfire. The House of Saud, always secretive where finances were concerned, did nothing to dispel the rumors.

"The welfare state began to fall apart," Freeman observed at the time. "Ordinary Saudis had no idea how much the Saudis were spending on the U.S., but imagined that it was more than it actually was. They saw a direct relationship between the decline in their own living standard and the presence of the U.S. Air Force in their country." The ambassador tried to impress on Washington both the scope of the economic crisis confronting the Saudis and the potential political ramifications.

Grappling with its own fiscal crisis, the White House had little sympathy to spare for the Saudis. At the State Department, Secretary Baker vehemently disputed Freeman's assessment that Saudi Arabia was on the verge of insolvency, leading to sharp words between the two. Baker's ability to extract large financial contributions from America's allies during the Gulf War had brought him considerable prestige, and he refused to accept the possibility that the Saudi treasury might be running empty only months after he had charmed $15 billion out of King Fahd.

And even had the Bush administration's principal figures wanted to relieve the domestic pressures on King Fahd, they could not afford to remove the American forces based in Saudi Arabia. Doing so would be tantamount to giving Saddam Hussein carte blanche to dictate events in southern Iraq and along the border with Kuwait.

Nevertheless, some in Washington did sympathize with the Saudi predicament. "Containment was a disaster from their standpoint," acknowledges Dennis Ross. "Huge American presence on their soil, lightning rod, and Saddam still where he is." Richard Haass asserts that the NSC staff was always cognizant of the fact that an open-ended American presence was a potential threat to the House of Saud and the other conservative monarchies in the Persian Gulf. "There was an understanding that any large U.S. presence was risky for those countries. It could be risky for the political stability of the regime."

Surprisingly, few U.S. officials, if any, seem to have worried about another possibility: the potential long-term threat to the United States as a result of American forces remaining in Saudi Arabia. Yet the final version of the post-crisis planning paper drafted by Richard Clarke and the Deputies Committee months earlier, at the height of Operation Desert Storm, contained a chillingly prescient warning:

> A permanent U.S. presence will provide a rationale for, and could become a target for, the terrorist threat which will outlive the war. At home, evidence of hostility to the U.S. in the region— especially terrorist activity—will eventually erode domestic support for active U.S. involvement in Gulf security.
>
> Thus, the U.S. presence must be designed to have as low a profile as possible. It must rely heavily upon temporary presence through combined exercises, prepositioning, and naval forces. Wherever possible, its location should be remote. The appearance of "U.S. bases" must be avoided and, generally, the presence of

U.S. servicemen in the societies should be minimized. Details about the size of U.S. forces should be as vague as possible consistent with U.S. domestic requirements.

Haass, for one, found reassurance in the fact that most of the American military units that remained in Saudi Arabia were composed of Air Force pilots and support personnel stationed at Saudi air bases, rather than more intrusive Army or Marine units. "It was out of the way, it wasn't as if the average Saudi every day was facing an occupation," he maintains. "It was nothing like that. What we're talking about was a presence pretty much at out-of-the-way air bases, far away from the holy sites."

Even Haass, though, recognized that any form of U.S. military presence in the kingdom was a less than desirable outcome. "It was one of the unfortunate consequences of having to have in place something of a containment policy, or 'containment-plus' policy. On the other hand, people always tried to—what's the word—'tailor' it in a way that it caused the least possible offense. Obviously, though, any presence was offense for some in Saudi Arabia."

·   ·   ·

That April, Osama bin Laden left Saudi Arabia for the last time.

The son of Saudi Arabia's wealthiest construction tycoon, the thirty-four-year-old bin Laden had spent most of the preceding decade in Afghanistan, one of hundreds of young, mostly upper-class Arabs from the Gulf states who had taken up arms against the Soviets after the 1979 Soviet invasion of Afghanistan. Motivated by a mix of Islamic zeal and a thirst for adventure, some of these "Afghan Arabs" had become minor celebrities in their home countries, held up by doting Islamic clerics as shining examples of Muslim youth who had rejected a life of easy materialism to take up jihad on behalf of the *Ummah*—the universal brotherhood of Muslims everywhere that is one of the central tenets of the Islamic faith.

Bin Laden was one of these celebrities. After leaving Afghanistan for the Sudan in 1988, he had cofounded an organization to maintain the network of relationships that had developed among the Afghan Arabs during their years together in Afghanistan. His vision was to expand the jihad begun in Afghanistan to include enemies of the *Ummah* anywhere in the world. A civil engineer by training, bin Laden chose a construction term as the name for the new organization: *al-Qaeda* (the Base or Foundation).

He had been back home in Saudi Arabia only a short time when Saddam Hussein invaded Kuwait. Bin Laden sought an audience with King Fahd. To an outsider it might have appeared strange for an ordinary Saudi citizen who was not a member of the government or the royal family to ask for a meeting with the head of state during a major international crisis. Bin Laden, however, was no ordinary Saudi. His stature as one of the heroes from the jihad in Afghanistan had made him a well-known figure inside Saudi Arabia. And even had this not been the case, his status as son of one of the kingdom's wealthiest men would have made him impossible to ignore. Muhammad bin Laden, Osama's father, had built many of the largest public works projects in Saudi Arabia during the 1970s and 1980s. His family's influence was hard to miss: The bin Laden name was plastered (literally) on buildings and construction sites throughout the kingdom.

In Riyadh, bin Laden was offered a meeting not with the king, but with Prince Sultan, the Saudi defense minister and a member of the royal family. Bin Laden had a proposition for the king, he told Sultan. Through al-Qaeda, he would recruit an army of mujahideen to defend the holy soil of Saudi Arabia from an Iraqi invasion. They would also wage a jihad to drive the Iraqi invaders from Kuwait, just as they had driven the Soviets from Afghanistan. The long arms on his gangly six-foot-five frame gesticulating excitedly, bin Laden warmed to his theme. It was a perfect mission for the new al-Qaeda. Saddam's troops would not dare set one foot on Saudi soil, he promised. If they did, millions of Muslims from around the world would rally beneath the green banner of Islam to wage jihad on the Iraqi infidels who dared attack the Custodian of the Two Holy Mosques. It would be Afghanistan all over again, only on a far grander scale.

If Osama bin Laden's offer to raise an army of mujahideen to fight Saddam Hussein hinted at his delusions of grandeur, it also reflected his genuine hatred of the Iraqi regime. Bin Laden despised Saddam, the

Iraqi Ba'ath Party, and everything they represented. From his perspective, Saddam and the Ba'athists were guilty of three unforgivable sins: They were secular socialists (who took inspiration from the fascist ideology of Ba'ath Party founder Michel Aflaq rather than from the Holy Koran); they were nationalists (who wanted Iraq to dominate the Islamic world militarily and politically, not unite the Islamic world in a global jihad against the infidels); and they had been the Soviet Union's most important client in the Arab world during the 1980s (while bin Laden and the other mujahideen had been fighting for their lives against the Soviets in the mountains of Afghanistan). It is difficult to say which of the three Osama bin Laden would have found most offensive.

Saddam's personal behavior was a disgrace in the eyes of any Muslim who considered himself devout. He was known not to pray five times a day, if at all, and to drink Scotch whiskey. Puritanical even by the strict standards of Saudi Arabia, bin Laden considered such behavior to be that of an apostate.

Prince Sultan listened politely to bin Laden's grandiose plans for the better part of an hour before declining his offer. But while bin Laden had merely been disappointed by the House of Saud's refusal of help from al-Qaeda, he was positively enraged several days later when it was announced that King Fahd had invited U.S. troops into Saudi Arabia to defend the kingdom. Bin Laden had been ready to wage jihad at the prospect of *Iraqi* troops setting foot in Saudi Arabia—and the Iraqis were fellow Arabs from a predominantly Muslim country. The prospect of American troops on Saudi soil was simply unthinkable to him.

Although the United States had covertly aided the mujahideen in Afghanistan with weapons and supplies during their guerrilla war against the Soviets, it had been strictly an alliance of convenience. Bin Laden and the membership of al-Qaeda hated the United States for its support of Israel, its perceived hostility toward the Palestinians and other Muslims, and most of all for what they saw as its irredeemably corrupt culture. In accepting the deployment of U.S. troops, King Fahd was bringing that corrupt culture to the birthplace of Islam, and allying Saudi Arabia with a "godless" nation that was Israel's strongest supporter. Hundreds of thousands of Christian "Crusaders"—and even Jews!—would trample on holy ground where the Prophet himself had once walked.

Joining his voice to those of the most reactionary clerics in the kingdom, bin Laden had been one of the most outspoken critics of the House of Saud throughout the seven months of the Gulf crisis.

The continued presence of U.S. military personnel after Desert Storm confirmed his worst suspicions about Fahd's motives—and America's. One prominent jihadist and intimate of Osama bin Laden, Abu Musab al-Suri, revealed how bin Laden's outrage at the continuing presence of American troops on Saudi soil after the 1991 Gulf War was the precipitating event that led him to begin waging a terrorist war against the United States:

> In addition to mingling with jihadists, [it was] the Saudi
> government, its ruling institutions and official clergymen's stance
> about the Kuwait war aftermath and the presence of U.S. troops
> in Saudi Arabia. The changes that followed this war exposed the
> infidel's great role in the Arabian peninsula and the depth of the
> religious institutions' hypocrisy. . . . He was convinced of the
> necessity of focusing his effort on fighting jihad against America.

As far as the al-Qaeda leader was concerned, by allowing impure Western influences to corrupt Islam on the Arabian peninsula, Fahd was abrogating his main royal responsibility, to be the Custodian of the Two Holy Mosques at Mecca and Medina. Bin Laden harbored a deep, almost personal attachment to the two holy sites, one that went beyond ordinary piety: his father's company had been the principal contractor in a massive expansion and rebuilding of the Holy Mosques at Mecca and Medina, arguably the most important construction project in the history of Saudi Arabia. That virtually all of the American personnel remaining in the kingdom would be stationed either in Riyadh or at remote air bases hundreds of miles from either Mecca or Medina was a detail of absolutely no significance to Osama bin Laden. In March 1991 he went beyond merely criticizing the king and began calling openly for devout Saudis to rise up against the monarchy and replace it with an Islamic caliphate that would expel the infidel soldiers from Arabia.

This was going too far. The Saudi government revoked bin Laden's passport and began making quiet plans to place him under some form of internal arrest. Tipped off by an al-Qaeda sympathizer in the government, bin Laden slipped out of Saudi Arabia near the end of April 1991. His first destination was the mountainous region of Pakistan along the border with Afghanistan, where he still had many friends. The leader of al-Qaeda had new enemies to fight.

·　　·　　·

The following month, Dick Cheney arrived in Saudi Arabia with Undersecretary of Defense Paul Wolfowitz to discuss with King Fahd the arrangements that would be necessary to deter a future Iraqi invasion of the kingdom. CENTCOM and the U.S. embassy staff in Riyadh had been thinking about the same problem, and together had come up with an initial plan that reflected the local cultural sensitivities.

But Wolfowitz had his own ideas on what was needed. As far back as 1979, when he had written his Pentagon study with Dennis Ross on possible responses to an Iraqi invasion of Saudi Arabia, Wolfowitz had worried about the threat that Iraq posed to the militarily weak oil states of the Persian Gulf. The main strategic problem identified by Wolfowitz and Ross in their analysis was the length of time that would be needed for U.S. ground forces to arrive in the combat theater after any Iraqi invasion. The two officials had estimated that it would take at least ten to twenty days for a sizable American ground force to arrive in-theater. By then, of course, an Iraqi army would have had more than enough time to overrun the Saudi oilfields and would be in a position to hold the world's oil supply hostage against any attempt to dislodge them.

Wolfowitz believed that the Saudis, the United States, indeed, the entire civilized world had been extraordinarily lucky in August 1990: that Saddam Hussein had made a stupendous strategic blunder by annexing Kuwait, and then stopping his forces at the Saudi border. Iraq's action had raised all of the alarm associated with an actual invasion of Saudi Arabia while reaping none of the benefits. If Saddam had seized the Eastern Province of Saudi Arabia as well as Kuwait, he could have been dislodged only with a military operation far costlier than Desert Storm had been. And even then, without the ability to marshal troops in Saudi Arabia, it might have been militarily impossible to reverse the invasion. They could not rely on Saddam to make the same mistake again.

The key, Wolfowitz had argued as far back as 1979, was to preposition in the Gulf the heavy equipment that U.S. forces would need to stop any large-scale invasion of the region. The United States could fly large numbers of troops anywhere in the world within twenty-four hours. However, the heavy equipment that army and Marine units needed to fight a war—the tanks, artillery, trucks, and tons of ammunition and other supplies—could be sent only by ship. It would take at least several weeks for cargo ships to travel from the U.S. coast to the Persian Gulf—too long.

But if the heavy equipment was already prepositioned in the Gulf, U.S. soldiers and Marines could be flown into the region, "marry up" with their equipment, and engage in combat operations within days. The concept was so strategically sound that during the 1980s the Reagan administration had made it the centerpiece of its Rapid Deployment Force—the forerunner of U.S. Central Command. The United States had built a number of MPS (Maritime Prepositioning Ship) vessels—special, climate-controlled cargo ships designed to store the heavy equipment that American troops would need in a ground war—and stationed them, fully laden, at Diego Garcia, a U.S. base in the Indian Ocean not far from the Persian Gulf.

During the final week of July 1990, when the Pentagon had been monitoring the threatening movement of Iraq's army toward the Kuwaiti border, Wolfowitz had strongly urged Cheney and Colin Powell to order several of the MPS ships into the Persian Gulf as a deterrent. The mere sight of the ships anchored off the coast would send a powerful message to Iraq, Wolfowitz argued, and might prevent Saddam Hussein from taking any rash action. And in the event that the worst actually happened, the MPS ships would be right where they needed to be.

The two Pentagon chieftains had vetoed Wolfowitz's suggestion as being overly provocative. The White House and the State Department also weighed in against the idea: Several of the governments in the Gulf had privately expressed concern to Washington about even implying that American ground troops might be deployed on their territory. The MPS ships were not sent into the Gulf, and did not unload their cargo until weeks later, when the Iraqi conquest of Kuwait was already a fait accompli.

Chastened by the experience, Wolfowitz now believed that the only way a prepositioning strategy could work was for the necessary equipment to be stored not on ships offshore, but in Saudi Arabia itself. It was this idea that Cheney and Wolfowitz planned to discuss with King Fahd.

After the usual round of pleasantries that preceded any meeting in Saudi Arabia, Wolfowitz opened the discussion with a real showstopper.

In order to establish prepositioned equipment here, he announced grandly, we will need from you 10 million square feet of air-conditioned warehouse space. Clearly not sensing the astonishment of his Saudi hosts at this pronouncement, Wolfowitz continued with growing enthusiasm to tick off a detailed list of the other infrastructure items that the United States would need in order to store military equipment in Saudi Arabia.

But the pièce de résistance was where Wolfowitz proposed to get the equipment.

What we will do, he informed the Saudis, is sell you all of 7th Corps' equipment.

The Saudis were familiar with the U.S. Army's 7th Corps. Based in Germany, it had been sent to Saudi Arabia to take part in the Gulf War, where it had provided the "left hook" of Operation Desert Storm: the heavy armored force assigned to attack and destroy Iraq's best-equipped military units, the Republican Guard tank divisions. Consisting of several large armored divisions and their supporting units, 7th Corps boasted more troops and more tanks than the entire standing army of Saudi Arabia.

Wolfowitz had had one final brainstorm, which he now shared. The Saudis would not be permitted to use the equipment they purchased. You'll just be buying it from us, he explained patiently in his pleasant, professorial voice. With the money that you pay us, we will then be able to procure new equipment for U.S. forces. But we'll have the old equipment here, and can come back at any time and use it to defend you, Wolfowitz concluded with a disarming smile.

The worried expression permanently etched on King Fahd's face had been growing deeper and deeper as Wolfowitz spoke. Fahd was certain he had misunderstood the American. Bewildered, he glanced quickly at

Cheney, who had remained impassive during his colleague's remarkable presentation. Finding no succor there, he turned next to his counselors, but they had been struck speechless by what they had just heard.

"You'd better discuss that with Crown Prince Abdullah," the king told Wolfowitz nervously. Abdullah's reaction to the proposal when he heard it was immediate and unequivocal: No way.

"The idea that somehow the Saudis would buy all of the U.S. Army's equipment without being able to use it, and then store it at *their* expense in *their* country for our convenience, this after they had just gone bankrupt in the war, was just nuts," an official familiar with the talks later commented.

Unabashed, the Bush administration dispatched Assistant Secretary of State Richard Clarke to try changing the Saudis' minds about the proposal. The hard-charging Clarke made a strong impression on his Saudi interlocutors, though perhaps not the impression that the administration wanted him to make. The Saudi deputy foreign minister later confided to an American official that the meeting with Clarke was the one time in his life he wished he had been wearing his ceremonial dagger, because he would have had an occasion to use it.

●   ●   ●

As part of the cease-fire terms that had ended Operation Desert Storm, Iraq was required to make a full declaration of any weapons of mass destruction it still possessed to the UN Coalition, as well as turn over its remaining Scud missiles to Coalition forces. All of the weapons were then to be destroyed under the supervision of UN weapons inspectors. These conditions were enshrined in UN Security Council Resolution 687, which passed by a unanimous vote in early April. Among other arrangements, UNSCR 687 created the UN Special Commission (UNSCOM) to oversee weapons inspections inside Iraq.

On April 19, 1991, Iraq made its first WMD declaration, as required under the terms of UNSCR 687. Even after a six-week Coalition air campaign that had targeted Iraq's Scud missiles and suspected WMD facilities, with some being hit numerous times, the inventory of weapons that Iraq claimed had survived the Gulf War was still sobering:

- 105 Scud missiles (30 of them with chemical warheads)

- Several thousand artillery shells containing the nerve gas Sarin

- 650 tons of a more primitive nerve gas called Tabun

- So much mustard gas in munitions and bulk storage that the Iraqis were having difficulty quantifying the exact amount

Reuters reported on April 19 that the Iraqi declaration "set in motion a complicated clock that could see the destruction of these weapons in about two months." This ambitious timetable assumed that Iraq would continue to comply with the terms and the calendar imposed by UNSCR 687.

The real complication, though, was that Saddam Hussein had not declared the most important parts of his WMD program. The April 19 declaration cataloged only Iraq's surviving missiles and some of its chemical munitions. But these were weapons whose existence Saddam was willing to concede, since even if they were destroyed by UNSCOM, reconstituting them in a country with as large an industrial infrastructure and as many chemical engineers as Iraq had would be a simple matter.

The crown jewel of Iraq's WMD program was its advanced nuclear weapons research, which Saddam had not declared to the UN and which he was loath to give up. In June, UN weapons inspectors were shocked to discover that Iraqi progress on designing an atomic bomb had been far more advanced than previously thought. They also uncovered extensive facilities for enriching uranium, of which Western intelligence services had been previously unaware. Most of Iraq's uranium enrichment facilities had been so well hidden that they were left entirely untouched by the Coalition air campaign.

Unfortunately, these discoveries were made just as the United States was desperately looking to extricate its forces from Iraq. At the time the regime in Baghdad had made its April 19 declaration, the American military presence inside Iraq's borders had been extensive. Only two days previously, on April 17, U.S. ground forces had entered northern Iraq as part of Operation Provide Comfort to create safe havens for the Kurds. A significant number of the troops that had taken part in Desert Storm were still in the Gulf region. And the American-led Coalition had just initiated a no-fly zone in northern Iraq. The ability of the United States to threaten military action against the Iraqi regime had thus been fairly high.

As early as April 24, however, President Bush had telephoned UN secretary-general Javier Pérez de Cuéllar and asked for UN peacekeepers to replace the American troops on the ground in northern Iraq. The Bush administration still remained deeply concerned about the possibility of American troops being drawn into a putative civil war inside Iraq. Bush's talking points for the call reflected just how anxious the White House was for the UN to take over the problem of managing post–Desert Storm Iraq.

"I am sorry to say that I am disappointed in the UN's slowness in getting off the ground," Bush told Pérez de Cuéllar. "I know this is a complex problem with many dimensions, but it is really important for the UN to get into Iraq to where the refugees are now, and to the temporary encampments we are building.

"Is there any timetable you can give me?" he further pressed the secretary-general. Ironically, Iraqi foreign minister Tariq Aziz had also written a letter to Pérez de Cuéllar that week making the same request. For its own reasons, the government of Saddam Hussein also wanted to see U.S. forces withdrawn from Iraqi territory as soon as possible and for the UN to take the lead in monitoring Iraq's behavior.

By June the drawdown of U.S. ground forces from Iraq and the larger Gulf region was already well under way. The discovery of Iraq's nuclear weapons program thus presented the Bush administration with a dilemma. Saddam Hussein's failure to reveal the full scope of Iraq's nuclear activities represented a clear violation of both the letter and the spirit of the terms that had ended the Gulf War. But what should be done about the situation? During the three months that had followed the end of Desert Storm, the White House had learned the hard way just how resistant Saddam Hussein was to any form of coercion short of military action. Yet it was reluctant to initiate a new military confrontation with Saddam, even over an issue as important as Iraq's pursuit of nuclear weapons.

Accordingly, the Bush administration fell back on sanctions and the "grinding irritant" effect provided by U.S. overflights of Iraqi territory as its best options for exerting pressure on the Iraqi regime. It continued to hope against hope that a coup against Saddam would still take place. A June 7 State Department cable addressed to Coalition capitals explained the administration's diplomatic strategy:

> The Iraqi leadership appears to believe it can outlast international pressure to remove Saddam Hussein. Moreover, faced with Shia and Kurdish insurgencies, the ruling elites may see continuation of Saddam Hussein in power as the lesser of two evils.
>
> We think that it's important to counter this with sensible, active steps to maintain the diplomatic price of Iraq's loss of status and influence in the world, particularly the Arab world where Iraq aspires to leadership. This will add a psychological dimension to the pressure of economic sanctions.
>
> Our public diplomacy needs to sharpen the distinction between pressure against Saddam Hussein, as opposed to pressure on the Iraqi people, which is not our intention. To this end, there are some positive things we think should be said to the Iraqi people, including the elite groups who can separate their future from Saddam Hussein's political rule.

The cable optimistically asserted that "even after withdrawal of Coalition forces from northern Iraq, the international community will retain significant leverage with Baghdad."

•   •   •

But Baghdad had been quick to recognize that the international community was in fact losing its ability to leverage events inside Iraq. Saddam Hussein aggressively exploited the situation on several fronts. In June, Iraq resumed military operations against both the Kurds and the Shia. In the Kurdish north, Saddam's forces were somewhat constrained by the no-fly zone and the presence of some UN relief personnel on the ground. There were practically no UN or Coalition personnel in the Shia regions of southern Iraq, giving Saddam's forces a virtually free hand there.

Of even greater concern to the Bush administration, during this same period Iraq began to test the limits of the UN weapons inspection regime it had accepted as a condition for ending the Gulf War. It had become patently obvious that the Iraqi government had not made the full declaration of its WMD programs required by UNSCR 687, especially of its nuclear programs. There was also a growing pattern of harassment directed at the UNSCOM weapons inspection teams in Iraq. The Iraqis were far too canny to deny the inspectors access to sites outright, at least for the moment. Instead, they interfered with UNSCOM in other ways. UN personnel would be stranded for hours waiting for Iraqi "transportation" to and from sites. The Iraqi "minders" assigned to escort the UNSCOM teams would routinely tamper with the briefcases and laptop computers of the inspectors.

The White House was torn over how to respond to Saddam Hussein's calculated campaign of defiance. "There was a division of views about this in the administration," recalls Robert Gates. "There were some of us who felt that every time he did this, we should react disproportionately, and that we should go after remaining military forces in a calculated way. It was the strategy of making clear to the Iraqi military that as long as he was there, they were going to pay the price, to try to induce them to take some action against him." However, this hawkish view did not carry the day in Washington. "For a variety of diplomatic and political reasons," Gates observes, "there was reluctance to reengage with the military in a major way."

President Bush himself remained far more concerned about the dangers of the United States being drawn into a civil war in Iraq than about Iraq's cheating on weapons inspections, or its continuing slaughter of its own citizens. At a press conference with foreign correspondents in Washington on July 8, Bush was asked by one journalist: "Given Saddam Hussein's assault on the Shi'ites and the Kurds, and given his deceit over the nuclear weapons research which has now brought the renewed threat of military action by the United States, do you now feel that you stopped the ground war too soon and should have pressed on to either Baghdad or until Saddam was overthrown?"

"No, I don't," the president answered. "And the reason I don't is that much of the legality of the steps we've taken came through international sanction, international will as expressed in twelve resolutions of the Security Council. It was not ever the intent to march to Baghdad and to get bogged down in guerrilla warfare in the city of Baghdad to accomplish that end."

Bush elaborated on why he remained so adamant on the point. "Because what I foresee would have been marching into Baghdad, Coalition forces getting sniped at and maybe not finding Saddam Hussein, and being bogged down in urban guerrilla warfare," he explained. "And so the critics now, some of whom opposed our entry as a Coalition into the war, are saying, well, 'You should have gone into Baghdad.' And I say: 'Yes, and do what?' "

*   *   *

By birth, breeding, and temperament, George Bush had always been a living link to the Wise Men, the legendary Eastern Establishment notables whose vision of an American-led international order after World War II had laid the groundwork for the American Century. Giants like Dean Acheson and John McCloy had been his father's friends from Wall Street and politics. His values, honed on the playing fields of Andover, and in Skull and Bones at Yale, were their values, just as they had been his father's values before him. And in many respects, Bush's vision of a New World Order—characterized by containment of aggression in key regions, strong respect for international law, and empowerment of the United Nations as the principal guarantor of international security—was an homage to the Wise Men's vision of what the postwar world should look like. After all, it was the Wise Men who had created the United Nations.

Despite this background, when a forty-six-year-old George Bush had assumed his first important foreign policy job, as Richard Nixon's UN ambassador in 1971, he possessed surprisingly little firsthand experience with international politics. Bush had spent most of the preceding two decades in rural West Texas building his oil business before moving his family to Houston to run for Congress in 1966. The UN appointment had been a bone tossed to Bush by Richard Nixon after Bush had been defeated in the 1970 U.S. Senate election in Texas—a defeat that many observers believed to have doomed his future political career. During the

1950s, Nixon had enjoyed a decent relationship with Prescott Bush, who had been one of the few members of the establishment who did not look down their noses at Nixon's humble background and Whittier College undergraduate degree. Nixon considered himself a mentor to the younger Bush and had offered him the UN job as a consolation prize.

Bush himself had known that he had much to learn about diplomacy. He had been a little starstruck when Nixon and National Security Adviser Henry Kissinger interviewed him for the UN job. His greatest fear was committing some diplomatic faux pas in New York that might embarrass his country and earn him Nixon and Kissinger's famously biting contempt.

"In time, I hope to move more into the policy end of things. In the meantime, it is better to do my homework, not bother the President or Secretary, and learn the business cold," Bush reminded himself in his diary at the time. It is the mantra of a schoolboy who is afraid of getting into trouble with his teachers. Kissinger himself had not been optimistic about Bush's prospects at the UN; the transplanted Texan had not been his choice for the post. "Absolutely not," Kissinger had told Nixon when they discussed the possibility of Bush serving as UN ambassador. "He is too soft and not sophisticated enough."

But Bush defied expectations and developed into a highly effective and well-liked UN ambassador. With typical energy, he threw himself into the role, familiarizing himself with UN protocol while finding the time to meet personally with an astounding number of delegates from other nations and their families. Kissinger had underestimated George Bush's talent for making valuable friendships in any political setting.

The new ambassador and his wife reconnected effortlessly with the New York society circles into which they had both been born, as if they had never left for Texas. One of the perks of the permanent representative's job is its official residence, a palatial apartment at the Waldorf-Astoria Hotel. This apartment became the scene for a nonstop whirlwind of dinners, parties, and other socializing hosted by the Bushes. Both George and Barbara Bush later looked back on this period as one of the happiest times in their lives.

Reports of Bush's charm and popularity in New York soon reached the

White House. Barely a year after arriving at the UN, Bush received a flattering "attaboy" letter from Nixon himself. One visiting foreign minister had raved to the president that "of all the American ambassadors to the UN he had known you were by far the best," Nixon informed Bush. "Your concern and the concern your wife has shown for their families, finding them places to live, for the small countries as well as the large, has made a very strong favorable impression about you personally and also through you for the country."

Already thinking about a revival of Bush's political career, Nixon urged him to get out of Texas and reestablish his voting residency in the Northeast, where Bush would be back in his element and far more appealing as a Senate candidate. "Keep up the good work," Nixon wrote to his protégé, "and be sure to take my advice and get your roots down in Connecticut as soon as you can conveniently work it out."

Among the many friendships that George Bush formed at the UN, none was more enduring than that with Prince Sadruddin Aga Khan. The prince's father, the reigning Aga Khan, was hereditary ruler of the world's 20 million Ismaili Muslims, a sect of the Shia faith who lived primarily in India and Pakistan, but had large communities throughout the Middle East. Heirs to fabulous wealth, the Aga Khans were celebrated patrons of Islamic art and education. Prince Sadruddin had grown up speaking four languages in an apartment on the Champs-Élysées in Paris. But he shunned the easy life of a playboy prince in favor of a career spent working on philanthropic and human rights causes. After graduating from Harvard, he had been recruited to join the permanent staff of the United Nations. His rise within the organization was meteoric. In 1965, at the age of thirty-two, the prince had been appointed UN High Commissioner for Refugees, the official responsible for managing the UN response to refugee crises in various parts of the world. It is one of the most powerful jobs at the UN. He was still serving as high commissioner when George Bush arrived at the UN as the U.S. permanent representative in 1971.

The two quickly became fast friends. This was not so surprising, as the urbane, athletic, thoroughly Westernized prince had much in common with Bush. Both were members of their respective aristocracies: Bush the son of a U.S. senator, Prince Sadruddin the son of the Aga Khan. One was a Yale man who, as a member of the Yale Development Board, raised funds for his university's endowment; the other a Harvard man whose family had endowed the university museum with a priceless collection of Islamic art. Both George Bush and Sadruddin Aga Khan had been instilled by their parents from an early age with a sense of noblesse oblige that led each to pursue a career in public service. Finally, and perhaps most important, each harbored a burning ambition beneath their affable personalities. George Bush had dreamed of becoming president since his teenage years, and his posting to the UN mission in New York was the latest stop on his *cursus honorum* to the White House. Prince Sadruddin had long expressed a desire to become UN secretary-general and in 1981 would actually be offered the position, only to see his candidacy vetoed by the Soviet Union.

So warm was the relationship that when Ambassador Bush made a weeklong official visit to the UN offices in Geneva during the summer of 1972, the prince invited Bush to stay with him and his wife at Bellerive, the Aga Khan's elegant château on the shores of Lake Geneva. Not content for his dear friend George to make the short daily trip from Bellerive into Geneva by limousine, he scribbled on the invitation: *I can also provide you with a boat which you can use to go to the UN. Yours, Sadri.* The prince was only being practical. That way, there might even be time during Bush's visit for the two of them to get in a few sets of tennis.

It had seemed like a stroke of good luck for the Bush White House, then, when the man who had beat out Prince Sadruddin for the job of UN secretary-general, Javier Pérez de Cuéllar, appointed the prince as his special envoy for refugee issues in Iraq after the Gulf War. Eager to wash his hands of Iraq as quickly as possible, George Bush had been confident that his old friend and tennis partner Sadri could be persuaded to endorse the quickest possible transfer of responsibility for safe havens in northern Iraq from the United States to the UN.

However, after inspecting conditions in northern Iraq firsthand, the prince began calling for a far more extensive effort by Coalition forces to protect the Kurds. He also grew increasingly vocal about the plight of his fellow Shi'ites in southern Iraq. Unlike the situation in northern Iraq, there were no safe havens in the southern part of the country. Many terrified Iraqi Shi'ites had fled into the dense marshes at the delta of the Tigris and Euphrates Rivers to take refuge from Saddam's security forces. The UN was having great difficulty getting any humanitarian workers at all into the marshes, and on several occasions UN aid workers had been blocked from entering the region by Iraqi troops.

In the absence of any international oversight, Saddam was continuing his purge of the Shia population with a degree of brutality unusual even for his regime. From sketchy reports on the ground, the UN had been able to estimate that up to 100,000 Iraqi Shi'ites were trapped in the marshes by Iraqi troops and were sure to face certain slaughter when they tried to leave. This was on top of the approximately 50,000 Shi'ites who had already been killed since the end of the Gulf War, over 30,000 in the city of Basra alone.

During the second week of July, Prince Sadruddin traveled to southern Iraq to see conditions there for himself. While he was touring the region, the Iraqi government made a clumsy attempt at Potemkin-like deception. Whenever the prince's delegation entered a particular section of the marshes, the Iraqis would withdraw their troops and security personnel from that area, only to return and conduct reprisals against the local population after the UN visitors had left.

The prince was nobody's fool and soon realized what was taking place. On July 16 he sent an angry letter to Iraqi foreign minister Aziz, complaining: "As soon as my mission had left the area, and especially on the 12th and 13th of July, a heavy military presence was redeployed to take up the same positions which had obviously been vacated merely for the duration of my visit." The prince demanded an immediate cessation of military attacks against the Iraqi Shia and establishment of a "humanitarian center" in southern Iraq to function as a base for UN relief efforts.

Prince Sadruddin's spirited advocacy on behalf of Iraq's Kurdish and Shia communities galvanized several members of the Gulf War Coalition to take diplomatic action against Iraq. At UN headquarters, Tom Pickering and his counterparts from France and the United Kingdom collared Iraqi UN ambassador Mohammed al-Anbari for a private meeting. Citing the prince's reports of conditions inside Iraq, they warned al-Anbari that Iraq's government must desist from further violence against its own people, or face serious consequences.

The NSC staff at the White House was already beginning to consider what some of those consequences might be. A three-page memo from Haass to Scowcroft that week discussing various policy options bore a portentous title: "Rethinking the Use of Force Against Iraq."

8

"WE CANNOT LET THIS CRAZY MAN THUMB HIS NOSE AT THE WORLD"

The collapse of the Iron Curtain in Europe during George Bush's first year in office had led to an outpouring of national sentiment in the formerly communist countries of Eastern Europe. Nowhere was this more true than in the Balkans. In Yugoslavia, itself a construct from an earlier American president's vision of New World Order, events were transpiring during the summer of 1991 that would soon confront Bush and his advisers with a daunting moral dilemma. They would also greatly complicate his administration's ability to contain Saddam Hussein.

On June 25, Croatia—previously one of the six republics that made up Yugoslavia—declared its independence in a plebiscite. Within twenty-four hours the neighboring republic of Slovenia followed suit. The defection of these two polities from the Yugoslav federation represented the failure of two years' efforts to preserve the federation and the bonds between its constituent peoples. In a corner of the world characterized by ethnic, religious, linguistic, and historical cleavages potentially as stark and forbidding as the local topography, the ties fostered by federal union had served as the bridges that permitted cultural and economic exchanges among the peoples of the region to flow, and even to thrive. The secessions of Croatia and Slovenia were a clear sign that those bridges were collapsing. They were not the only bridges that would collapse in Yugoslavia.

The day after Croatia's declaration of independence, the Serb minority population of the newly independent republic rebelled. By July 1991 the situation had escalated into all-out war between Croatia and Serbia proper.

Amazingly, in light of later events, the outbreak of war in the Balkans attracted scant public concern in Western Europe and the United States. But this was not perhaps so surprising. After all, "the rebirth of history" had come off remarkably well elsewhere in Eastern Europe: Germany was reunited, Hungary and Poland had emerged from the Cold War with their ancient cultures intact, and Prague was becoming the Paris of the 1990s. Few would have guessed that the same historical forces that produced a Václav Havel or a Lech Walesa would shortly disgorge Slobodan Milošević and Radovan Karadzić. While unfortunate, the violence in Yugoslavia seemed to be the inevitable pangs that accompany a rebirth of history.

Wisely, the Bush administration's position on the future status of the Balkans remained the territorial integrity of the Yugoslav federation, at least for the time being. As early as December 1989 the Bush administration's ambassador in Belgrade, Warren Zimmermann, had advocated: "The United States should support a combination of 'unity and democracy.' The two have to go together. If we encourage the breakup of Yugoslavia in support of Slovenian (and later Croatian) democracy and self-determination, then democracy as well as unity would be lost."

By spring 1991, however, it had become clear that Croatia was intent on seceding from the Yugoslav union at whatever cost. On June 21, four days before the plebiscite in Croatia, the administration made one final high-profile effort to stave off the fragmentation of Yugoslavia. The president dispatched James Baker to Belgrade to meet with the prime minister of the Yugoslav federation, Ante Marković, as well as the presidents of all six Yugoslav republics. During nine consecutive hours of meetings, a cordial, unflappable Baker implored each politician he met with to maintain the federal structure of Yugoslavia until an orderly plan for secession could be negotiated. Baker's special target was Franjo Tudjman, the president of Croatia, the republic most intent on secession. "If Yugoslavia fragments," he asked Tudjman rhetorically, "who will preserve the rights of minorities? The United States will not recognize unilateral secession," Baker warned, "which can only trigger violence and bloodshed. Those who fail to negotiate will be responsible if violence breaks out."

However, Baker's last-minute mission to Belgrade represented the limit to which President Bush wished to become involved in the Balkan crisis. Writing in his diary on July 2, 1991, Bush rejected any American role in mediating the conflict between Serbia and Croatia:

> Yugoslavia is poised on the brink of civil war. This is one where I've told our top people, "We don't want to put a dog in this fight." It's not one that we have to mastermind. The concept that we have to work out every problem, everywhere in the world, is crazy. I think the American people understand it. I don't want to look isolationistic; I don't want to turn my back on the desires of many ethnic Americans that come from that part of the world; but I don't think that we can be looked to for solving every problem every place in the world.

As it happened, the two most experienced Yugoslavia experts in the administration were two senior officials who had been longtime intimates of George Bush dating back to the 1970s: Deputy Secretary of State Lawrence Eagleburger, a career diplomat who had served for seven years at the U.S. embassy in Belgrade, four of them as ambassador; and Brent Scowcroft, who had served as a U.S. Air Force attaché in Belgrade and who, like Eagleburger, was still fluent in Serbo-Croat. Both men strongly urged Bush to allow the European Union to mediate an end to the war.

Robert Kimmitt suggests that the president was saturated with other foreign policy concerns at the time, especially the ongoing turmoil in Iraq, and was only too willing to let Europe take the lead on Yugoslavia.

"Going back to that 'victory fatigue' that we had to some degree after the Gulf, I think George Bush, advised of course by Scowcroft, who had been military attaché in Belgrade, and Eagleburger, who had been ambassador, basically said, 'If the Europeans want to have that one, let them take it.' "

Even as the Bush administration surrendered the lead role in the Balkans to the European Union, however, Lawrence Eagleburger—arguably the most seasoned Yugoslavia hand in any of the Western democracies—recognized that this was a formula for disaster: not because the Europeans lacked sincere motives or skilled diplomats (they had a surfeit of both); but because they had tragically underestimated the potential for a major conflict to erupt in the region.

"There was in Europe, much more than here, a real belief that this could all be managed without a lot of bloodshed," Eagleburger later remarked. "From the very beginning, I said, 'When it goes, it's going to be a bloody mess.' Even I didn't think it would be as bloody as it eventually was. But I thought it would be a bloody mess."

On August 18, hard-liners in the Soviet military attempted to seize power in a coup against Soviet leader Mikhail Gorbachev. For the next four days a mesmerized global audience watched the dramatic events play out in Moscow and witnessed the survival of a shaken Gorbachev and the emergence of Boris Yeltsin as Russia's future democratic leader.

With almost palpable relief, the Bush administration briefly turned its attention from the terra incognita of the New World Order back to the familiar terrain of the Cold War. The president and his national security team were almost perfectly suited to handle this kind of crisis, and during the four days of the coup both their morale and the administration's approval ratings briefly soared.

The outcome of the crisis was everything they could have hoped for, and more. Back in power, Gorbachev announced the dissolution of the Soviet Union and the birth of a new, democratic Russian Federation. The Bush White House was exultant at the news. George Herbert Walker Bush had forever made his mark in the history of American foreign policy. He had presided over the fall of the Soviet empire without a shot being fired; just as he had presided over the peaceful reunification of Germany in 1990 and the peaceful end of the Cold War in Europe in 1989. Fourteen months away from reelection, he could legitimately claim to be a liberator on three continents.

The crisis in Moscow had been like a tonic to George Bush. During the weeks that followed, staffers noticed a spring in the president's step, and he exuded a renewed sense of purpose. With Mikhail Gorbachev safely back in power and the Cold War now officially over, a reenergized Bush decided that the time had come to do something once and for all about the still-simmering aftermath of the Gulf War.

And that September, a stroke of good luck inside Iraq seemed to provide him with the perfect opportunity.

It had a name that perfectly captured both its function and its low profile: Petrochemical Complex 3. An unassuming cluster of five modern office buildings in one of the nicer sections of downtown Baghdad, it housed offices and research laboratories for Iraq's large petroleum engineering industry. And something else. In September 1991 a team of UNSCOM weapons inspectors led by American David Kay staged an unannounced inspection at the complex and discovered a massive cache of documents related to Iraq's nuclear weapons program: sixty thousand pages of blueprints, technical schematics, and testing data.

Clearly a subscriber to the "hide in plain sight" school of weapons proliferation, Saddam Hussein had hidden the blueprints for his planned nuclear arsenal not in some secret underground bunker in the desert, but in an office park across the street from the al-Rashid Hotel in Baghdad — the luxury hotel where most Western journalists and diplomats stayed when they visited the Iraqi capital.

The importance of the UN inspectors' discovery was best gauged by the Iraqi government's response. Baghdad announced that in the future, UNSCOM inspectors would no longer be permitted to take documents away with them when they conducted an inspection of a site. Coming on the heels of months of previous harassment against the inspectors, this was all the justification the White House needed to take action.

On September 24, Bush telephoned French president François Mitterrand and British prime minister John Major from the Oval Office to enlist their support for a punitive military campaign against Saddam Hussein. He spoke with Mitterrand first.

"I believe we both agree that Iraq's interference with the inspection teams is a challenge to the entire cease-fire regime and to the UN," Bush began. After suggesting that Saddam should be given several more days "to allow the inspectors to leave with their documents," the president continued: "We believe that the appropriate response under these circumstances would be carefully targeted air strikes. Obviously, we'll leave the targeting to the military experts, but we would probably combine sites of suspected weapons of mass destruction capability and perhaps another target.

"We are talking about a limited objective," he assured Mitterrand. "We want Saddam to comply with all the UNSC resolutions. The objective would not go beyond that—for example, targeting Saddam. It is my view this action on our part would convince Saddam to moderate his behavior. If not, we would have to be prepared to take further steps.

"I believe that this is a reasonable and relatively constrained approach and that this would meet with international understanding and support," concluded Bush. "The reason I feel this way is because it's wholly consistent, both legally and politically, with existing Security Council resolutions. Moreover, all this comes after months of Iraqi noncompliance and trying to frustrate the world community."

"I agree with this way of handling things," Mitterrand said gravely. "I think you're right about what must be done. It is difficult but we must meet our responsibility."

Several hours later, the president spoke with John Major.

"We simply cannot let this crazy man thumb his nose at the world," Bush railed. "I want to get your advice on this. Mitterrand has come through as fully supportive."

"I don't have any difficulty at all," Major assured him. "We want to get the inspection team out so they do not become hostages." Saddam's use of British subjects in Iraq as "human shields" during the Gulf crisis still rankled in Britain. "There ought not to be too large a gap between the team's leaving and a strike. It will be difficult if people leave without documents. We will be criticized by public opinion. But I don't want to give Saddam time to move people near sites."

Major added another condition of his support. "I don't want any air strike to be postponed; I would want the strike to be as soon as practical after the people are out."

Bush was impressed by his British counterpart's reasoning. "I agree. That's a good point, right on target."

"The other point is, it is time to teach him a lesson," Major continued. There was an additional issue that the president had not addressed, so

Major raised it himself. "You didn't mention it," the prime minister said with a hint of amusement in his voice, "but we would like to take part if you wish."

Bush was, of course, pleased by this idea. "I very much would like this. It would send a good signal. Our two militaries should continue to talk. We don't think, by the way, we need any new resolution to do this."

"Neither do we," Major concurred. "We agree we have cover under existing resolutions."

·   ·   ·

Just as planning for the air strikes was getting under way, another crisis of direct concern to all three countries intervened. On October 6 a tenuous cease-fire in the three-month-old war between Serbia and Croatia came apart. The next day the Serb-controlled Yugoslav National Army launched a major new offensive against Croatia, which included an artillery bombardment of the famous Croatian tourist city of Dubrovnik.

To this point the Balkan conflict had attracted scant attention from the public in the United States and even in nearby Europe, though the Balkans had been an area of concern for governments on both sides of the Atlantic for months. The shelling of Dubrovnik, a city familiar to millions of North American and European tourists, and the wanton destruction of priceless architectural treasures in that famous port, were the first developments in the Serbo-Croatian war that truly registered on the public consciousness of the United States, and especially of Western Europe.

The escalation of the war in the Balkans prompted talk for the first time of using NATO military assets to force a temporary cease-fire in the vicinity of Dubrovnik. In retrospect, the failure to do so must be regarded as a catastrophic missed opportunity. With access to the powerful air and naval forces of Allied Forces Southern Europe (AFSOUTH) based in nearby Italy, NATO had more than enough military power to shield Dubrovnik. And a demonstration of NATO power, even if limited only to Dubrovnik, might have introduced an element of uncertainty into the calculations of the Serb leadership and made them far more reluctant to pursue a policy of total war in Bosnia the following summer.

Indeed, some Bush administration officials were internally advocating precisely this course of action. At the State Department, Robert Kimmitt tried to convince his colleagues: "We should take a page from our Iraq experience. What NATO should do is to say, 'What happens inside Yugoslavia is up to the Yugoslavs to work out, but because we have two NATO countries, Greece and Italy, bordered by the former Yugoslavia, we can't run the risk of it slipping over.' "

Kimmitt's proposed solution was the same one that had been adopted by the Bush administration to contain Saddam's "internal aggression" against the Kurds: imposing a no-fly zone over the region.

"I wish NATO had put a no-fly zone over then-Yugoslavia," Kimmitt later said, "because I think that would have raised a question in the minds of Milošević and others about what these 'crazy Americans' might do next, and I think it would have given a real impetus to the EU diplomatic effort on the ground."

In the absence of any form of military response from the United States and its European allies, however, the aggressors in the Balkans drew the correct conclusion that the West could not muster the political will to intervene militarily in the region. "Because it looked like the U.S. and NATO and everybody else were stepping back, I don't think we ever put any ambiguity into our policy that leapt out in the mind-set of the bad guys," Kimmitt asserts. "Therefore a lot of what happened, happened on an unconstrained basis, and I think the diplomacy, because it didn't have any effective military arm to it, never had much of a chance."

.   .   .

One bad guy had been watching the American response to the Balkan crisis with particular interest. As the Bush administration scrambled to devise a strategy for dealing with the escalation of the war in the former Yugoslavia, plans for taking military action against Saddam Hussein were postponed until things could settle down in the Balkans.

The Iraqi dictator interpreted the Bush administration's anemic response to the crisis in the Balkans as a telling sign that it was losing its stomach for military action. Saddam capitalized on this situation by launching his own new offensive against the Kurds, only days after the

Serbs had begun their offensive against Croatia. For the first time since April, the Iraqi assault included a large-scale artillery bombardment of Kurdish towns. By mid-October, over two hundred thousand Kurdish refugees had been driven once again from their homes.

At the Pentagon the Joint Chiefs of Staff had abruptly transitioned from contingency planning for combat operations against Iraq to contingency planning for possible combat operations against the Serbs. "I think we began to get distracted a little bit," admits one of the Joint Chiefs in retrospect. "Things were starting to get going in the Balkans, the focus shifted over there, and in doing that it actually prevented us from implementing a more aggressive policy in the Middle East." The end result was that no military action took place in either the Balkans or Iraq.

•   •   •

A number of congressional leaders had for some time been watching the deterioration of the Bush administration's Iraq policy with dismay. Among them was Pennsylvania congressman John Murtha. A Democrat from a rural, working-class district outside of Pittsburgh, Murtha had been one of President Bush's key allies in Congress during the months leading up to Desert Storm. A plainspoken former Marine and Vietnam veteran who was one of the most conservative members of the Democratic caucus, Murtha had strongly supported the use of force in the Gulf. During the House debate on the Gulf resolution, he had been instrumental in mobilizing support for the measure among like-minded Democratic hawks. Without these key swing votes, it is doubtful that the House would have authorized the use of force by the president.

Murtha enjoyed a warm relationship with George Bush: He was the sort of uncomplicated, patriotic politician that Bush instinctively liked. Murtha was also one of the few members of Congress trusted by Scowcroft. During the Gulf crisis, Murtha had been one of only a handful of congressional leaders who had visited U.S. troops once combat in the Gulf had gotten under way.

Like the president and his national security adviser, Murtha had expected Saddam Hussein to be overthrown by his own people in the immediate aftermath of the Gulf War. Unlike them, however, he believed that the United States should be doing more to encourage opposition movements inside Iraq now that Saddam had survived the war.

During one of his visits to the Gulf, Murtha and several members of the congressional delegation had been granted an audience with King Fahd. At one point in the conversation, the king leaned forward and urgently asked the visiting legislators to persuade President Bush to withdraw U.S. military personnel from Saudi Arabia "the minute the war was over." As long as American forces were quartered in his country, the king said seriously, they would always be at risk of a terrorist attack like the one that had taken place in Beirut. Murtha took the advice to heart. The 1983 bombing of the Marine barracks in Beirut that had claimed the lives of 241 of his fellow Marines still resonated with him.

The congressman thought that the best way to get American personnel out of harm's way in the Gulf was to support the Iraqi opposition's efforts to take Saddam out. He did not share the president's and Scowcroft's concerns about a successful uprising in Iraq leading to instability. As far as he was concerned, Saddam was a greater threat to stability than anyone. He also worried about the long-term financial cost of containing Saddam. The subcommittee that Murtha chaired in the House was responsible for approving every dollar that the United States spent on defense. He knew down to the penny just what all of the post–Desert Storm military deployments in the Gulf were costing, and Murtha was troubled that American taxpayers were footing the bill for elaborate military operations just to contain Saddam. From Murtha's perspective, it would be a far more efficient use of resources to support the Iraqi opposition to do the dirty work instead of paying to keep tens of thousands of American troops in the Gulf.

Saddam's successful October offensive against the Kurds was the last straw for Murtha. What had been the point of Operation Provide Comfort, and of having a no-fly zone in northern Iraq, if Saddam could do to the Kurds exactly what he had done back in March and April? The administration clearly needed to be doing much more to support opposition groups like the Kurds. Murtha raised this issue in an October 31 letter to the president. In particular, he asked why more was not being done to establish contacts with Iraqi opposition groups working together to oust Saddam.

Murtha was not the only member of Congress complaining about Iraq policy to the president. On November 5 the White House received a letter from the House Select Committee on Intelligence, the bipartisan oversight group whose members are all cleared to see the same sensitive intelligence as the president and the Pentagon. The letter was signed by all fourteen members of the committee—a traditional means of communicating to the White House that its contents reflected strong bipartisan consensus on an issue.

"In our judgment, the current policy towards Iraq does not seem to be working," the letter read. "We note with concern the growing consensus in both the intelligence and policy communities that Saddam has made major strides in consolidating his power in Iraq since the end of the war."

As usual, though, the Capitol Hill denizen that the White House was most worried about was Al Gore.

The Tennessee senator had remained a vociferous critic of the administration's policies in post–Desert Storm Iraq. Of greater concern, however, was that Gore had latched onto a novel idea for raising awareness about the plight of the Kurds. On November 25 he shared his idea in a letter to the White House, making sure to copy James Baker and Dick Cheney as well as the president and Scowcroft (as any Washington insider knew, sending the same letter to three different Executive Branch departments was the surest way to avoid having it "buried").

Gore had given up hope that Saddam Hussein would fall from power anytime soon. The most that the United States could do, therefore, was document his many atrocities against the Iraqi people. "If we cannot destroy his regime," Gore argued smoothly in his letter, "we can destroy his image."

It appears that Kurdish forces are in possession of extensive documentation of atrocities committed against Kurds by Iraqi security forces. Specifically, there are detailed logs itemizing methods of torture and ultimate disposition of victims, prepared by the torturers. And there are videotapes, made by the torturers.

Kurdish representatives here have approached the administration at lower levels seeking agreement to help evacuate these documents from Iraq while the opportunity is ripe. They would be turned over to an American university for translation on an urgent basis, collation, and released.

Gore had just the university in mind. "I have been told that discussions are under way with Harvard to this effect, and I have written to the president of that university urging him to embrace the project.

"Saddam Hussein is attempting to strangle the Kurds by slow degrees," the letter concluded, "operating just under the threshold that might force a response from us—calculating, I am certain, on the odds that you may feel politically inhibited by the state of play in Middle East peace talks, or even," Gore added archly, "by domestic considerations." The four men to whom he was writing did not need to be reminded that the presidential election was less than a year away.

The White House was concerned by Gore's latest gambit. In Washington, even the most public-spirited initiatives are political, and coming less than a year before the 1992 election, this initiative had obvious and potentially dangerous political overtones. The last thing the administration needed as it kicked off George Bush's reelection campaign was more attention being drawn to the plight of the Kurds.

As was the case with most politically sensitive foreign policy matters raised by members of Congress, Scowcroft dealt with this one. His reply to Gore was appropriately receptive, but brief:

We are deeply interested in this issue, and are willing to assist in transporting the documents out of Iraq. As your letter states, the significance of these documents could be enormous. In particular, they could make a major contribution to efforts by the UN to document human rights abuses by the Iraqi regime.

●   ●   ●

The White House had another sensitive political matter to consider that autumn. On December 1, 1991, UN secretary-general Pérez de Cuéllar would retire from his post after ten years in office. The field of possible successors to replace him as secretary-general had been winnowed down to two candidates. As one of the five permanent members of the UN, the United States would have the right to veto any candidate it found unacceptable. Moreover, as the largest contributor to the UN budget, the United States' opinion on which of the candidates it preferred would carry great weight with many UN members.

The first candidate was George Bush's friend Sadruddin Aga Khan. The prince, of course, had already won the job once, only to be vetoed by the Soviets for being too pro-Western in his views. This time, however, with Washington's support and no more Cold War posturing by the former Soviet Union to worry about, it was assumed that he was a shoo-in for the post. The prince's twenty-year friendship with President Bush was perceived as an added mark in his favor.

The other candidate was Boutros Boutros-Ghali, an Egyptian diplomat who had been a member of Anwar Sadat's delegation during the signing of the 1978 Camp David peace accords. He was seen as the preferred candidate of non-Western countries in the Third World, especially the Arab bloc.

Ordinarily George Bush should have been ecstatic at the prospect of installing a strongly pro-Western official in such an important post—especially given their long personal friendship and the fact that they had once worked together at the UN. But in the late autumn of 1991 the Bush White House had other considerations to think about. Bush and Scowcroft had been alarmed by how forcefully Prince Aga Khan had called attention to the refugee crisis in Iraq during his visits to that country. Since then the prince had continued to call for a larger international presence in both northern and southern Iraq.

They were even more alarmed by something else the prince had been advocating. Convinced that economic sanctions were harming the Iraqi people far more than Saddam Hussein, Prince Aga Khan had called for UN sanctions on nonmilitary goods to be lifted. As an alternative, the prince had proposed some form of oil-for-food arrangement in which Iraq would be permitted to sell some of its oil outside the UN embargo if the proceeds were used to buy food and medicine for the Iraqi people.

This proposal clashed directly with the Bush administration's post–Desert Storm strategy for containing Saddam Hussein. Given the inability of the administration to undertake concerted military action against Iraq, economic sanctions were the only tool it had left for keeping the pressure on Saddam's regime. The White House could not tolerate any serious proposal to end sanctions against Iraq, or allow the country to sell more oil for any purposes. Bush and Scowcroft had come to recognize the validity of Richard Darman's observation from over a year earlier: that in a battle of economic wills between a democracy and a dictatorship, the ability of the dictatorship to keep its people well fed was a strategic weapon.

In his brief time as UN special envoy for Iraq, Prince Aga Khan had demonstrated that he intended to be an activist in confronting the Iraqi regime over its internal policies. Given his lifelong passion for human rights and his strong personal ties to the Shia community, this was not at all surprising. But the prospect of an activist secretary-general frightened the White House at a time when it was desperately trying to minimize the attention being paid to the failed aftermath of the Iraq War.

Accordingly, the United States announced at the United Nations that it had not been able to arrive at a decision on which candidate to endorse—an announcement widely seen as a stunning repudiation of Prince Aga Khan's candidacy. Boutros Boutros-Ghali was elected secretary-general.

*　　　*　　　*

The Bush administration soon received disturbing confirmation of just how badly economic sanctions were failing to achieve their goal of pressuring Saddam Hussein.

On December 3, two representatives of the Harvard Study Group on Iraq met quietly with the staff of the U.S. Mission at the UN. The purpose of the meeting was to preview the contents of a report that had been commissioned by the UN Sanctions Committee and was soon to be released. Conducted by academic experts in the fields of nutrition and humanitarian aid operations, the report provided an unbiased assessment of the effectiveness of UN sanctions in Iraq since the end of the Gulf War. It confirmed trends that the NSC and the U.S. intelligence community had suspected for months but had not been able to verify.

The report pulled no punches in its conclusion: Saddam Hussein had taken advantage of the economic sanctions against Iraq to strengthen his control over the country. "Saddam has used a siege mentality since the cease-fire to replace former high-level government officials with his own close supporters," the report noted. The regime was also using food rations to extend its control over ordinary Iraqis' daily lives. "Most people are almost totally dependent on the government's distribution system for their food supplies," the report warned. It went without saying, of course, that Saddam's regime could withhold these supplies from its internal opponents at any time.

·   ·   ·

Jalal Talabani did not look like anyone's idea of a successful guerrilla leader. A short, rotund man who favored the baggy white cotton trousers worn by many Iraqi Kurds, he could have easily been mistaken for a successful merchant bartering with customers in one of Iraq's countless open-air souks. The impression would have been strengthened by Talabani's gregarious, backslapping personality and the sanguine grin he sported beneath a large moustache.

In fact, Talabani was the leader of the Patriotic Union of Kurdistan (PUK), one of the two main Kurdish opposition movements in Iraq. For decades the PUK had waged an intermittent guerrilla war against the Ba'ath regime in Baghdad along with a rival Kurdish sect, the Kurdish Democratic Party (KDP), which was headed by Talabani's occasional ally and longtime archrival Massoud Barzani. Each of the two Kurdish leaders commanded their own force of *pesh merga*, which they alternately used to launch attacks on the Iraqi army and each other. Despite his somewhat shopworn appearance, Talabani was a tough, battle-hardened commander entirely at home climbing through the mountains of northern Iraq with his men. As the most famous proverb in the Kurdish language maintains, Kurds have no friends but the mountains.

That age-old bit of folk wisdom had been powerfully vindicated yet again after the Gulf War. 1991 had been a very bad year for Talabani and his people. For a few brief, shining weeks in March, the Iraqi Kurds had come close to realizing their longtime dream of carving an autonomous republic out of their ancestral homeland in northern Iraq. The Kurds had expelled Saddam Hussein's forces from the entire region. More important, they had captured Kirkuk, a northern Iraqi city with a mixed Kurdish-Arab population which was the symbolic center of Kurdish national identity. Conveniently, Kirkuk also sat atop one of the world's richest oilfields.

This momentary triumph had been shattered by Saddam Hussein's massive counterattack against the Kurds in March and April. Talabani had pled with the United States to intervene, to no avail. So desperate had the situation been that the Kurdish leader had made the ultimate sacrifice to save his people. On April 20, Talabani had traveled to Baghdad and appeared on Iraqi state television with Saddam Hussein. Wearing a forced smile, the Kurdish leader had embraced Saddam, literally, in return for the promise of a cease-fire.

But neither this humiliation nor the creation of safe havens in northern Iraq during Operation Provide Comfort had been enough to forestall Saddam's repression of the Kurds for very long. Once U.S. troops had withdrawn from the safe havens, the Iraqi army had renewed limited operations against the Kurds. Then, in October, Saddam had launched his major new offensive against the Kurds. In tandem with the assault, the Iraqi regime had imposed a systematic blockade on the major Kurdish towns and agricultural areas of northern Iraq. With winter approaching, Talabani's people found themselves in the same desperate straits they had seen in April. As disillusioned as he had become with George Bush and the Americans, Talabani felt he had no choice but to reach out to the United States for help.

On December 9, Talabani faxed a plaintive "letter to the international community" to the U.S. embassy in Turkey, his channel for communicating with the U.S. government.

A tragedy of immense proportions is unfolding in Iraqi Kurdistan. It is now over five weeks since the Iraqi regime has imposed a blockade on much of the Kurdish region. Basic supplies of food, medicine, and fuel have been severely rationed. . . . Furthermore, since October, more than 200,000 people have been driven from their homes as a result of indiscriminate Iraqi shelling of Kurdish towns and villages. Now, an estimated total of 800,000 refugees are

faced with destitute horror from the encroaching bitter winter. . . .
As in such cases, it is the children and the elderly who are the
most vulnerable, succumbing to the cold, hunger, and disease.

Referring bitterly to his April reconciliation with Saddam, Talabani added:

The Kurdish leadership has attempted to defuse the situation and
arrive at a compromise solution with the Iraqi regime. However,
despite recent "agreements" and Iraqi public pronouncements,
the blockade and the policy of military encroachment continue
unabated.

Talabani's letter made two specific requests. The first was for the
United States to extend the existing no-fly zone over northern Iraq further south, from the 36th Parallel to the 35th. This would effectively
deny most of the airspace in Iraq north of the city limits of Baghdad to
Iraqi forces. The second request was for UN forces to drive the Iraqi army
out of the city of Kirkuk. The Kurdish leader did not specify where these
forces would come from. According to Talabani, there was "a justifiable
case for the UN to force the Iraqi army to withdraw from the oil city of
Kirkuk, and resume oil production." The oil revenues from Kirkuk,
claimed Talabani, "are to be used to help all the Iraqi people." Knowing
that the United States (to say nothing of neighboring Turkey) was likely
to be skeptical about this claim, Talabani addressed it head-on.

There will undoubtedly be concern that this may lead to Kurdish
control over the contested city of Kirkuk. The Kurdish movement
will offer every possible assurance to refrain from taking
advantage of this proposal, should it be pursued, to advance our
claims to Kirkuk. The Kurdish leadership will accept a
demilitarized zone into which the Kurdish forces will not enter.

The Bush administration did not respond to Talabani's letter. For the
administration, the communiqué contained nothing but bad news. If
nothing else, it was a reminder that as far as containing Saddam Hussein's behavior inside Iraq went, they were back where they had started

immediately after the Gulf War. Still, it was a rude way to treat the future president of Iraq.

•   •   •

But the worst news of all for the White House that month came on the next day, December 10.

Standing on the steps of the New Hampshire statehouse in the picturesque town of Concord, right-wing commentator Pat Buchanan announced to a cheering crowd his intention to challenge George Bush for the Republican presidential nomination.

A veteran of the Nixon White House with a record of advocating divisive, controversial views on social issues, Buchanan had found his niche as one of the few prominent Republicans to vehemently oppose Operation Desert Storm. A longtime isolationist, he considered American involvement in the Gulf War to have been a huge mistake, the work of a cabal of Washington insiders who hoped to use the war to enhance Israel's security interests.

During one pre–Gulf War appearance on the television news roundtable *The McLaughlin Group*, Buchanan had made national headlines by claiming, "There are only two groups that are beating the drums for war in the Middle East—the Israeli Defense Ministry and its amen corner in the United States." The remark had been widely seen as anti-Semitic, especially after Buchanan elaborated on his theme by naming four prominent Jewish supporters of military action against Iraq—former *New York Times* editor A. M. Rosenthal, former Reagan Pentagon official Richard Perle, syndicated columnist Charles Krauthammer, and Henry Kissinger—as being the ones responsible for formulating U.S. policy in the Gulf.

During the Gulf crisis, Buchanan's criticism of President Bush had represented a fringe position within the Republican Party. But with the unresolved outcome in the Gulf, there were now many Republicans asking questions about George Bush's foreign policy. Combined with lingering anger against Bush among some conservative Republicans over his broken "No new taxes" pledge, it made for a potent political platform.

"Why am I running?" Buchanan shouted to his supporters. "Because we Republicans can no longer say it is all the liberals' fault. It was not some liberal Democrat who declared 'Read my lips! No new taxes!' then broke his word to cut a backroom budget deal with the big spenders. What is the White House answer to the recession caused by its own breach of faith? It is to deny we even have a recession."

But Buchanan reserved his most withering criticism for Bush's foreign policy.

"He is yesterday and we are tomorrow. He is a globalist and we are nationalists. He believes in some Pax Universalis; we believe in the Old Republic. He would put America's wealth and power at the service of some vague New World Order; we will put America first. So to take our party back and take our country back, I am today declaring my candidacy for the Republican nomination for the president of the United States."

•   •   •

For George Bush, Buchanan's candidacy was a political disaster, one whose true dimensions would become apparent only much later. What Buchanan's announcement did immediately, though, was to expose Bush's weakened domestic position for the rest of the world to see—and in presidents, the perception of weakness invites challenges of many kinds.

Less than nine months earlier, President Bush had enjoyed an approval rating in the ninetieth percentile. Most of his leading Democratic rivals for the presidency had been frightened out of entering the 1992 race by Bush's laurels from the Gulf War. The Bush White House had been laying the groundwork for a second term, and for the Republican Party to reclaim control of Congress.

Now, the president faced a serious uprising in his own party and a contested Republican primary against a candidate whose foreign policy views symbolized everything George Bush had opposed for much of his career.

•   •   •

Given all of the aggravation that Iraq had caused for the president and his national security team during the preceding year, they could have been forgiven for looking forward to January 17, 1992, with special anticipation.

That evening, the senior members of the Bush administration were glued to their TV sets. The Discovery Channel was broadcasting the first episode in a three-part television series on the Gulf War. "The Gulf Crisis: The Road to War" was one of the most expensively produced and heavily promoted documentary programs ever shown on public television. The highlight from the six hours of programming was a series of in-depth, on-camera interviews with the principals themselves: Cheney, Powell, Baker, Scowcroft. For one evening at least, the members of George Bush's war Cabinet could forget the months of bad news from Iraq, and the fact that the internal situation in the country was on the verge of spinning out of control yet again. Instead, they could spend the first anniversary of the start of Operation Desert Storm reliving some of their greatest moments from the Gulf crisis. And for a White House suddenly concerned about the 1992 election and badly needing to reclaim the mantle of victory from Desert Storm, it was must-see TV.

"The Gulf Crisis: The Road to War" was a documentary with a definite point of view. As one reviewer commented, "The series makes no pretense of journalistic balance. It is, by and large, a forum for the administration's key policymakers during the war to present one view—theirs—of a controversial war whose final lessons remain unclear."

There would be no uncomfortable questions raised about the failure of war-termination planning in Iraq; no questions about the ongoing humanitarian catastrophes in northern and southern Iraq; no questions about the survival of Saddam Hussein's WMD programs and his increasingly brazen defiance of UN weapons inspectors: no unpleasant surprises of any kind.

Perhaps the only surprising part of the program was the organization that had commissioned it. "The Gulf Crisis: The Road to War" had not been the idea of one of the Big Three networks, or of CNN, or even PBS. Instead, the idea for the documentary series had come from the American Enterprise Institute, the most important and well-connected neoconservative think tank in Washington. AEI had already been planning to hold a scholarly conference on the first anniversary of the Gulf War. "I thought, 'Why don't we do it with television in mind?' " said the senior AEI official who was responsible for shepherding the project. "Get a producer and do it right."

That individual was former Reagan-era defense official Richard Perle. One of the most influential neoconservative thinkers in Washington, Perle had served as assistant secretary of defense at the Pentagon during the 1980s, where his many admirers considered him the real architect behind the resurgence of U.S. military power under Ronald Reagan. Even Perle's critics at the Pentagon—and they were also many—acknowledged the importance of his role. They had dubbed Perle "the Prince of Darkness": the nickname a testimony to both his Hobbesian view of international politics and his effectiveness at working behind the scenes to achieve his policy goals. Since leaving government, Perle had continued to exercise influence through his position as senior fellow at AEI and his work as a defense lobbyist. His real influence, though, stemmed primarily from his role as mentor and father-confessor to many of the most prominent and rising young neoconservatives in Washington, a number of whom had gotten their start in Republican politics working for Perle at the Pentagon.

Perle's most recent contribution to the Republican foreign policy cause was that of television interviewer. Unwilling to entrust the principal officials of the Bush administration to the tender mercies of some unknown journalist, he had decided to conduct the most important interviews himself.

The undisputed star of the first night's episode was Dick Cheney. With his well-modulated baritone and reassuring country doctor's manner, Cheney was ideally suited for this sort of platform. In pleasant, conversational tones he shared with Perle for the better part of an hour the story of the Bush administration's response to the invasion of Kuwait. No one who heard him could have failed to come away impressed with Cheney, or with the administration's handling of the crisis in the Gulf.

Naturally enough, the defense secretary spent some time recounting the details of his dramatic August 1990 diplomatic mission to Saudi Arabia. "One of the things I had promised the king was that we would deploy forces, we'd deploy a lot of forces, but that once the need for them was ended, we would remove those forces," Cheney declared. "We were not looking for permanent bases. That carried great weight with them."

Perle revealed himself to be an attentive listener and a diffident questioner. Only once in the entire interview did he raise what might have been considered a controversial issue. Toward the end of his session with Cheney, he asked simply, "Did we stop too soon?"

Cheney nodded, as if he had been expecting the question.

"I don't think so," he said. "I think it's important for a president to make a decision about when we use force. He needs to know when to use force and when not to, when to send troops into combat and when not to. I think he got it right both times."

Cheney dismissed the criticism from Republican hawks and some Democrats that American forces should have continued their advance to Baghdad itself.

"If we had gone on to Baghdad, we would have had to send in a very large force. We might well have been involved in intensive combat inside the city of Baghdad, which is a whole different proposition than the kind of desert warfare we've done so successfully, where the range of our artillery and tanks and airpower was so useful. It would not have been very useful in that kind of combat inside a major city."

The secretary of defense reiterated his most frequently used objection to the notion of regime change in Baghdad. "We would have had, once we toppled Saddam Hussein's government, to put another government in its place. The question is what kind of government—a Sunni government, a Shia government, a Kurdish government? There would have been a question about how long you would have had to leave U.S. forces there to prop it up.

"My guess," Cheney concluded, "is that if we had gone on to Baghdad, that I'd still have U.S. forces in Iraq today. I think that was a quagmire we did not want to get involved in. I think we did achieve our objectives, and I think the president got it right when we decided to stop operations when we did."

Perle beamed, clearly pleased by Cheney's response.

"You said something when we talked before that I found particularly poignant, that had to do with asking our guys to inflict enormous casualties beyond the point that we stopped," Perle reminded Cheney, referring to an earlier off-camera conversation between the two to prep for the interview. "Do you want to say that again?" he prompted.

Cheney obliged. "The photographs of American Marines and GIs taking care of thousands of surrendering Iraqi prisoners was one of the most poignant memories I have of the war. . . . They very quickly made the transition from being warriors to being angels of mercy. It's part of our character. That's the way we are."

.   .   .

By February 1992 the consequences of Saddam Hussein's internal embargo against the Kurds were becoming too serious to ignore. Much of northern Iraq was on the verge of starvation. With the embargo, Saddam had finally discovered the perfect means of waging war on the Kurds without provoking an American military response. If he could not crush the Kurds militarily, he could starve and freeze them out. U.S. aircraft in the no-fly zone could intercept Saddam's helicopters and monitor the movements of his army to their hearts' content. They could not force him to allow deliveries of food, medicine, and fuel to his own people.

The human impact was staggering. UN ambassador Tom Pickering spelled out some of the details in a February 14 cable to Washington:

- Progressive cuts in food deliveries to the north to a rate equal to half the government ration—far less than other areas in Iraq. Food is in extremely short supply, with some northern cities having received no government food shipments at all for months.

- Drastic curtailment of fuel deliveries, to a level approximately 25 percent of the pre-October level. Acute fuel shortages have made it virtually impossible for thousands of families to heat their homes.

- A total cutoff of government medical supplies to Kurdish areas.

- Confiscation of even the smallest quantities of privately purchased food carried by civilians arriving from the south.

Several days later, on February 18, the UN Human Rights Commission released the findings from the most comprehensive attempt ever undertaken to investigate and document the crimes of the Iraqi regime. The eighty-six-page report was titled simply "Iraq: A Compendium of Horrors."

·　·　·

The Bush White House had a crisis far closer to home about which to worry. That evening the results were tallied from New Hampshire's first-in-the-nation presidential primary.

Fifty-three percent.

George Bush, a sitting Republican president who had presided over the peaceful end of the Cold War, had received only 53 *percent* of the votes in the Republican primary. Barely half the *Republican* primary voters in New Hampshire, one of the most politically conservative states in the nation, wanted to see Bush receive a second term.

The Bush campaign offices in Manchester and Washington tried to put the best possible spin on his thin margin of victory, but Bush's opponents could smell the blood in the water. At his New Hampshire headquarters, a crowing Pat Buchanan celebrated his strong second-place showing in the Republican primary and vowed to continue his campaign to the floor of the Republican Convention itself. On the other side of town, the Democratic victor, Massachusetts senator Paul Tsongas, was already envisioning his wife as first lady. "America," he gushed to the media, "you're going to love Nikki Tsongas."

But no candidate's headquarters was more jubilant than that of the Democrat who had finished third in his party's primary. Thrilled that he had survived last-minute revelations of his adultery with Gennifer Flowers, Arkansas governor Bill Clinton christened himself the "Comeback Kid" and prepared to take his campaign south.

·　·　·

Like many famous men throughout history, George Bush possessed a bold, distinctive handwriting style that bordered on the illegible. Consequently, for most of his life Bush had used a typewriter for much of his personal correspondence, even when writing his trademark rambling letters to family and friends. This had not changed in the White House. The president always had access to a typewriter in both the Residence and the Oval Office, and when he felt the need to convey important instructions directly to his staff, he usually sent them a typed memo. Although Bush was a notoriously bad typist, his typing was at least legible. His secretaries made sure there was always a stock of blank memo forms—each bearing their distinctive FROM THE PRESIDENT legend—near his typewriters for him to use.

The White House staff, and even senior officials like James Baker and Brent Scowcroft, had long since learned that when they received one of Bush's memos, it involved a matter that the president considered important and wanted action taken on immediately. They had also learned that the number of memos emanating from the president was an excellent barometer of his mood. When Bush was anxious about the way his administration was handling things, the frequency of memos would increase sharply.

It was not a good sign for the Bush reelection campaign, then, that by the spring of 1992 the president was writing an increasing number of memos to his staff about campaign-related matters. March had been a very bad month. The U.S. economy was still mired in a deep recession. Iraq was still a shambles. The president's poll numbers were down. Contrary to expectations, the Democrats had coalesced around a single candidate, and that candidate was not Paul Tsongas—a dour Greek-American liberal from Massachusetts in the mold of Michael Dukakis, the Democrat whom Bush had beaten handily in 1988. Instead, Governor Bill Clinton had ridden his impressive showing in the March 7 Super Tuesday primary to become the Democratic frontrunner. The Bush campaign did not quite know what to make of Clinton yet, which was a concern.

Worst of all, the field of potential challengers to Bush had gotten even more crowded. On March 20, Texas billionaire Ross Perot had stunned the White House and the entire nation by announcing on the *Larry King Live* show that he was running for president. Bush, of course, had known Perot for years: in the narrow circles of the Texas aristocracy during the 1960s and 1970s, it would have been difficult for two men of such obvious future promise not to have known each other. He had even considered Perot a friend of a sort, though after Perot had paid a courtesy call on then-Ambassador Bush in New York in 1971, Bush had confided to his diary: "He is a difficult fellow to figure out. He has always been very friendly to me, and he and his wife Margo are great, but he is a very complicated man. I think he now pictures himself as totally non-partisan." But Perot running against him as a third-party candidate for president was assuredly not the kind of non-partisan Bush had in mind.

George Bush was now being barraged with criticism on a daily basis from three different rivals for the White House. And while it was difficult to imagine three presidential candidates with less in common than Bill Clinton, Pat Buchanan, and Ross Perot, they could all agree on one thing at least. As the campaign intensified, criticism of Bush's handling of the aftermath to the Gulf War had become a staple of all three men's rhetoric.

Bush was unhappy that his opponents were being allowed to make critical statements unchallenged about what he still considered his greatest triumph as president. He wanted it stopped. The president had decided on the stock response he wanted used by his campaign to any questions about the way Desert Storm had ended.

On March 25, Bush sent a memo to his aide Phil Brady containing his instructions on the matter.

FROM THE PRESIDENT
TO: Phil Brady

Send the attached response on the end of
Desert Storm to:

Speech writers at EOB* and
at Campaign.

Surrogates should be given this answer—advise
campaign of that.

gb

* The Executive Office Building across the street from the White House, where most presidential staff had their offices.

The attachment was a single typewritten page that bore the heading:

Q. Why did you end the war when you did, instead of going on to Baghdad to get Saddam Hussein?

Beneath was a nearly verbatim transcript of Dick Cheney's response to this question from Richard Perle, on "The Gulf Crisis: The Road to War," two months earlier.

•   •   •

On April 1, Bill Clinton arrived in Manhattan to make the first important speech on foreign policy of his campaign. That afternoon Clinton addressed the Foreign Policy Association, a prestigious group of academic experts and other opinion-leaders on U.S. foreign relations. The centerpiece of Clinton's speech was his critique of how the Bush administration had handled Iraq both before and after the Gulf War.

"In the Persian Gulf, first the Bush administration made misguided attempts to purchase Saddam Hussein's goodwill through American assistance," Clinton charged. "Then, after America's smashing victory over Iraq, he left Saddam Hussein with enough military force to remain in power and savagely suppress uprisings by Shi'ites and the Kurds." No one in the audience had any doubt about who the "he" was. "Who rose up after the president's promptings to do so."

Clinton's speech received a standing ovation in New York. The next day, newspaper editorials across the country commented favorably on his impressive debut in foreign policy.

•   •   •

As badly as the White House needed to focus its attention on domestic issues and the campaign, two foreign crises escalated during the first week of April on which key decisions could not be put off any longer.

The first was Iraq. During the preceding several weeks, U.S. aircraft enforcing the no-fly zone in northern Iraq had noticed an alarming new development: Besides helicopters, now Iraqi fixed-wing aircraft—jet fighters and troop transports—were routinely violating the no-fly zone by crossing the 36th Parallel into northern Iraq. It was the first major use by Iraq of its air force since the Gulf War. Not only did fixed-wing aircraft greatly enhance Iraq's ability to mount attacks against the Kurds, but the presence of Iraqi fighter aircraft in the skies of northern Iraq were also a direct threat to the safety of American aircraft patrolling the no-fly zone, and to UN humanitarian workers flying into and out of Iraq.

On April 6, after days of discussion in Washington on how this latest Iraqi escalation should be handled, UN ambassador Pickering was instructed to begin laying the groundwork among the Perm-5 members of the Security Council to take up the matter of Iraq's violations.

The second and far more pressing issue was what to do about the breakup of Yugoslavia.

In December 1991 the European Analysis Sub-Directorate of the CIA had produced an intelligence forecast that had some frightening implications: "Bosnia-Hercegovina: On the Edge of the Abyss."

By the early months of 1992 it had become abundantly clear to the Bush administration that only a significant ground peacekeeping force could prevent further escalation of the crisis in the Balkans—at that point a very bad situation, but not yet one irreversibly lost. While attending a conference to discuss Yugoslavia with other leaders at The Hague on November 9, 1991, President Bush had been asked about the possibility of using a UN peacekeeping force. "With respect to the United Nations," one reporter had asked, "do you support the idea of possibly forming a peacekeeping force to intervene in Yugoslavia, assuming that your European partners agree?"

"You're too far ahead of the power curve," Bush had replied, clearly troubled by the suggestion. "We're not talking about force. We're talking about economic sanctions. And thus, I cannot answer a hypothetical question of that nature. We're just not there yet."

But momentum for creating a Balkan peacekeeping force was growing. On November 27 the UN Security Council had voted unanimously to explore the possibility of ending the war between Serbia and Croatia by deploying UN peacekeepers in Croatia. The United States had joined the vote to pressure the UN into taking action in the Balkans. But the

Bush White House remained convinced that the American people would not support U.S. participation in such a peacekeeping force.

The desire to farm out the necessary task of fielding peacekeepers in the former Yugoslavia led to a fundamental shift in American policy toward the region, one that would have tragic and far-reaching consequences for later events in the Balkans. Preservation of Yugoslavia's territorial integrity and some vestige of a federal structure for the country, the sound positions that had been the linchpin of American policy in the Balkans for seventy years, were abandoned. Instead, the United States was now willing to pay almost any diplomatic price to get someone else's troops on the ground in the former Yugoslavia.

In this case the price of getting someone else's troops on the ground was U.S. acquiescence to the diplomatic recognition of breakaway Yugoslav republics. On January 13 the European Union had formally recognized Croatia and Slovenia as independent nations. The Bush administration did not follow suit and, publicly, continued to support the idea of a Yugoslav federal union as U.S. policy. Behind the scenes, however, the administration was beginning to contemplate the idea of granting recognition to the breakaway Yugoslav republics in return for a European commitment to undertake peacekeeping operations in the Balkans.

The decision to grant diplomatic recognition to Slovenia and Croatia was inextricably linked with the question of extending similar recognition to Bosnia-Herzegovina. The most cosmopolitan of the former Yugoslav republics, in all senses of the term, Bosnia had been essentially untouched by the fighting between Serbia and Croatia, despite having an unenviable geographic position squarely between the two combatants. Moreover, the Serb and Croat minority communities living in Bosnia were far more extensively integrated with the region's majority population—the Muslims—than had been the case with the Serb minority in Croatia. In Sarajevo, the Bosnian capital, the intermarriage rate among the three communities was 30 percent. Even many Balkan observers questioned whether the large Serb and Croat minority communities of Bosnia would risk their own livelihoods to engage in a pointless ethnic war.

Lord David Owen, later the UN special envoy for the Balkans, squarely blames the Bush administration's policy for the spread of the Balkan conflict to Bosnia. "The U.S., who had opposed recognition of Croatia in December 1991, became very active in pushing for recognition of Bosnia-Herzegovina in the spring of 1992," Owen would write. "Yet it should not have been judged inevitable, nor indeed was it logical, to push ahead and recognize Bosnia-Herzegovina, an internal republic of Yugoslavia that contained three large constituent peoples with very different views on independence. To do so without the prior presence of a UN Prevention Force was foolhardy in the extreme."

Suffice it to say that as a point of American credibility (to say nothing of common sense), the administration should have never nourished the nationalist hopes of the Bosnians when it was so patently unwilling to address the inevitable consequences of Bosnian secession. In practical terms, official recognition of the three breakaway republics only served to accelerate and render irrevocable the collapse of Yugoslavia while raising unrealistic expectations within Croatia and Bosnia that the United States would take the necessary steps to preserve the integrity of these new republics' borders.

Moreover, in a move that predictably infuriated both Belgrade and the Bosnian Serbs, the Bush administration timed its announcement of diplomatic relations with Bosnia-Herzegovina to take place on April 7, twenty-four hours after it accorded similar recognition to Croatia. Twenty-four hours after that, the Bosnian Serbs declared their own independent republic.

The newly recognized Bosnian government was not long in seeking help from Washington. On April 9, two days after his nation had been formally recognized by the United States, Bosnian president Alija Izetbegović sent two telegrams to the White House. The first acknowledged a personal message President Bush had sent to Izetbegović two days earlier, extending American diplomatic recognition to the government in Sarajevo.

Dear Mr. President:

With great satisfaction I have received news that the United States recognized Bosnia-Herzegovina. I appreciate particularly that you

have informed me about it personally. It has special importance
in this critical situation for Bosnia-Herzegovina, for the future
cordial relations of our two countries, and for the peace and
security in the region. Bosnia-Herzegovina is grateful to the great
American nation and to its President.

The second telegram raised a more delicate issue.

Dear Mr. President:

I am sorry that I have to write to you for a second time in a day
after the recognition of Bosnia-Herzegovina. Unfortunately, war
operations have been undertaken in our country. The Federal
Yugoslav Army (JNA) is bombarding cities in West Herzegovina.
Serbian forces are shelling Sarajevo from the hills around. . . .
Being unable to defend our citizens, since we do not dispose of
our own army, we are forced to request an international political
and military support.

⁘

If help for the Bosnian Muslims was not immediately forthcoming from
Washington, it soon came from another source. Osama bin Laden had
spent much of the preceding year shuttling between Pakistan and the
Horn of Africa, building centers for his new al-Qaeda network in a number of countries. In April 1992, al-Qaeda opened its first European field
office in Bosnia, to aid the virtually defenseless local Muslim population
in their conflict against the Serbs. Bin Laden's interest in coming to the
defense of his coreligionists was genuine, though the secular, *slivovitsa-*
sipping Muslims of Sarajevo, with their democratic aspirations and European lifestyle, were hardly his kind of Muslims.

But bin Laden soon recognized some of the other advantages that the
Balkan conflict offered for his nascent organization. Accustomed to operating in some of the most lawless regions on earth—Afghanistan, the
Sudan, the mountainous reaches of Pakistan—bin Laden saw in the
growing anomie of Bosnia not only a fertile recruiting ground, but an

ideal transit point for men, money, and weapons between Europe and the Islamic countries of the Middle East. As the great historian of the Balkan Wars, Misha Glenny, would later remark, it was the sort of place "where $30 buys you not just a counterfeit passport, but a real one."

Osama bin Laden certainly thought so. For much of the ensuing decade, he would travel on a Bosnian passport.

•　　•　　•

Like many Harvard faculty members, Martin Peretz wore two hats. Peretz was a longtime lecturer in the Harvard Social Studies program, a demanding interdisciplinary degree that attracted some of the university's brightest undergraduates. He was also publisher of *The New Republic*, the most influential liberal-leaning political magazine in the United States. There was more overlap between these two jobs than one might have thought, since the undergraduate tutorial rooms at Harvard had long furnished the lion's share of writers for Peretz's magazine.

As the 1992 presidential campaign got under way, Peretz had added a third role to his busy repertoire: full-time promoter of Al Gore's future presidential aspirations.

Peretz had taught Gore while the Tennessee senator had been an undergraduate at Harvard and had raved for years that Gore was one of the most impressive students he had ever encountered, surely destined to become president one day. Gore, of course, shared this assessment.

Peretz had been disappointed when Gore had chosen to sit out the 1992 race after his abortive run for the White House in 1988. He was therefore gratified when rumors emerged that Bill Clinton was thinking of defying conventional wisdom and picking his fellow Southerner from Tennessee to be his running mate. Peretz was determined to use the platform provided by his magazine to do everything possible to advance the prospects for a Clinton-Gore ticket.

The editorial staff of *The New Republic* had never been admirers of George Bush (a recurring feature in the magazine parodied Bush with a less flattering pseudonym—Shrub). It was not only that Bush was a Republican. The president and his administration were considered pro-Arab and hostile to Israel, and especially to Israeli settlement policy, while Peretz and many of his editors proudly considered themselves Zionists. There had been a brief truce between the White House and *The New Republic* during the 1991 Gulf War, which Peretz and his magazine had supported. The inconclusive aftermath of the conflict had since then provided them with much grist for criticism of the Bush White House.

With Gore being part of the Democratic ticket now a distinct possibility, *The New Republic* ratcheted up its criticism of Bush's foreign policy throughout the spring of 1992. On June 1 the magazine ran a cover story by Mark Hosenball questioning the Bush administration's prewar handling of Iraq and its ability to confront a resurgent Saddam Hussein.

Even by the standards of American presidents, George Bush was unusually sensitive about his foreign policy judgment being called into question. Incensed, he sent a memo to Scowcroft with the offending magazine attached:

FROM THE PRESIDENT

June 2, 1992

Brent:
   Please have someone review cover story and send in letter to ed.
   We must keep knocking this trash down with the truth.
   Your op-ed was great!

                                          gb.

PS: also a similar story attached in today's POST (NY)
Same thing . . .   gb

·   ·   ·

Throughout the spring of 1992 the ethnic conflict in Bosnia grew steadily worse. By May, Sarajevo itself had come under siege. As had been the case in Croatia the previous year, the virtually unarmed Bosnian Muslims were woefully unprepared to confront the militias of the Bosnian Serbs, who had ready access to the armories of the Serb-dominated

Yugoslav National Army (JNA). Adding to the difficult position of the Bosnian Muslims was the overt military cooperation between Bosnian Serb militias and JNA regulars. An American decision to impose an arms embargo against all of the former Yugoslav republics, including Bosnia (a decision made, ironically enough, on the grounds that the introduction of more arms to the region would endanger any peacekeeping forces stationed there), only had the effect of reinforcing the Serbs' existing military advantage.

The "internationalization" of the Balkan crisis and introduction of UN observers into the region, the two developments in which the Bush administration had invested such hope, proved useless in moderating the conflict. In fact, both Serbian and Bosnian Serb forces were growing openly brazen in hijacking UN humanitarian aid convoys and harassing the small cadre of UN personnel deployed in Bosnia itself.

Questions about the possibility of American intervention in Bosnia were increasingly dominating President Bush's interactions with the press. This was not the topic that the president wanted to discuss only five months before the election. But even Bush could see that the hands-off policy of his administration in the Balkans was eroding some of his stature as a decisive leader in international affairs. At a press conference on June 4 the president was asked about the contrast between his active engagement during the early months of the Gulf crisis and his seeming passivity about the escalating crisis in the former Yugoslavia.

"Sir, you say that you have a strong international leadership role. But the New World Order that you are promoting is being challenged in Yugoslavia these days. It appears that the sanctions are not working against Serbia. When are you going to take the lead of an international coalition to force Milošević out of Bosnia, the way you did with Saddam Hussein out of Iraq?"

Bush looked uncomfortable at the question. He did not see the two as analogous. "I think the sanctions—I'm not prepared to give up on the sanctions at all," he said. "They've only been in effect for a few days."

But others whose opinion mattered far more to George Bush were also dismayed by the contrast. The plight of the Bosnian Muslims had resonated deeply throughout much of the Islamic world, especially in the two countries that had been indispensable allies in the war against Iraq: Turkey and Saudi Arabia. The Ottoman Turks had once ruled the lands that constituted much of the former Yugoslavia, and they retained especially strong cultural ties to the Muslim community of Bosnia, the oldest in Europe, which was a remnant of Ottoman rule. The Turkish government had pressed the United States and its other NATO allies to take action in Bosnia. Besides their historic ties to the Bosnian Muslims, the Turks had a concrete national security interest in not seeing a full-scale ethnic war break out in the Balkans just across their borders.

King Fahd's role as Custodian of the Two Holy Mosques in Saudi Arabia conferred on him a symbolic responsibility as protector of the *Ummah,* the worldwide Muslim community (in much the same way that the kings and queens of England have retained the title Defender of the Faith for the worldwide Anglican Communion). Scenes of Bosnian Muslims being driven from their homes and the Serb siege of Sarajevo televised each evening in newscasts around the globe had prompted an outcry throughout the Islamic world. Fahd was coming under enormous pressure to do something, not only from his own people but from Islamic clerics in other nations.

On June 7, Prince Bandar bin Sultan, the influential Saudi ambassador in Washington, notified Secretary of State Baker that he had an urgent letter for President Bush from King Fahd. A legend in Washington for his access to top U.S. officials, Bandar had developed unusually strong ties to Bush and his inner circle during the 1990–91 Gulf War. He was one of the few foreign diplomats in the capital who could command immediate attention from the White House. The original letter from the king, handwritten in beautiful Arabic script on embossed paper, was promptly relayed to the White House along with a typed translation.

Fahd made no bones about drawing a correlation between the crisis in Bosnia and the earlier crisis in Iraq.

Dear President Bush:
I am aware that you are following closely, and with great concern, the brutal massacres being perpetrated against the Muslim population in the Republic of Bosnia-Hercegovina by the

armed forces of the Republic of Serbia. I am also aware that you are personally upset by what is occurring because it stands in stark contrast to the manners and principles which I, and the rest of the world, know you personally stand for. You, Mr. President, have in the past taken noble and just positions to champion the cause of justice, and have stood firmly in the face of oppression and aggression. The position you took in the face of Iraq's naked aggression against Kuwait has not been lost on us. It was a strong and resolute position of which you can be proud, as we are, and without which Kuwait would not have been liberated.

We are now, less than two years after one aggression, witnessing another ugly aggression which does not differ from the previous one. Children, women, and elderly are being indiscriminately killed in the Republic of Bosnia-Hercegovina. They are being subjected to the most brutal form of oppression and humiliation. This is a matter which brings great pain and sorrow to me, but it is not the only matter. The inability of the nations of the world to bring an end to this oppression and violence magnifies my pain and sorrow.

Based on my personal relationship with you, and based on my understanding of the brave and resolute positions which you have taken in the face of aggression and oppression, I call upon you personally, and on behalf of the Saudi people, as well as on behalf of the rest of the world, to help put an end to the massacres to which the Muslim population in the Republic of Bosnia-Hercegovina is subjected, and to take a firm stand towards what is occurring there. You, Mr. President, have previously taken firm and noble positions to support victims, and to restore justice. We strongly believe that force can only be contained by force.

But the king was not only asking for help; he was also offering it.

I wish to take this opportunity to assure you, Mr. President, that the Kingdom of Saudi Arabia will support, with all its strength, any positions taken by you to end the oppression and put an end to the violent massacres which the people of Bosnia-Hercegovina are subjected to. My government is also prepared to offer them any humanitarian assistance.

Your friend,
Fahd bin Abdulaziz Al-Saud
Custodian of the Two Holy Mosques
King of the Kingdom of Saudi Arabia

Given the importance that George Bush attached to his personal relationships with other world leaders, this gentle rebuke by a close ally like King Fahd would have stung far worse than a forest full of newsprint denouncing his administration's policy in Bosnia.

●   ●   ●

That same week, the king was also voicing his displeasure about the Bush administration's handling of another crisis.

Iraqi violations of the no-fly zone in northern Iraq had been going on unabated since April. During the early days of June 1992, however, Baghdad had added a new twist: Iraqi aircraft, including jet attack planes, began straying dangerously close to the Saudi border with southern Iraq. While there was no formal no-fly zone yet in southern Iraq, the overflights were a direct violation of the cease-fire terms that had ended the Gulf War, which forbade Iraq to operate fixed-wing military aircraft anywhere south of Baghdad. The flights appear to have been part of Saddam Hussein's continuing campaign against the Iraqi Shia in the south. However, they were also a test of U.S.-Saudi air defenses along the border, barely eighteen months after Iraq had fired Scud missiles into Saudi Arabia during the Gulf War.

But more than a test of American and Saudi air defenses, they were a test of the Gulf War Coalition's remaining resolve. Since the end of Desert Storm, Saddam Hussein had violated on a massive scale both the letter and the spirit of the conditions that ended the conflict. He had not, however, done anything to challenge the military forces of the Coalition. Thus far, Saddam's defiance of the international community had been limited to brutal onslaughts against Iraq's own Shia and Kurdish communities, and interference with the work of UN weapons inspectors inside

Iraq. Having seen that none of these outrages had provoked a military response from the U.S.-led Coalition, Saddam determined that the time had come to begin probing the collective will of his enemies.

The Saudis were understandably upset by the situation and began complaining to their American contacts at every level. The CIA station chief in Jeddah sent a telegram to Langley on June 6 warning of Saudi intelligence's concern over Iraq's use of fixed-wing aircraft. Fahd had his own channels of communication with Washington. He called Ambassador Freeman in to demand that the United States do something. It was bad enough that the U.S. Air Force was maintaining a large presence in the kingdom; but to endure both internal criticism about the presence of the U.S. Air Force and provocative actions by the Iraqi air force was just too much. On June 8, the day after Fahd sent his letter to Bush on Bosnia, Freeman sent a cable to Secretary Baker conveying the king's personal concern over the Iraqi flights.

·　　　·　　　·

It came, however, at an especially tense moment in the Balkans. The siege of Sarajevo had reached a critical juncture. Bosnian Serb forces, supported by regular army units from the rump Serbian republic, had commenced artillery shelling of Sarajevo and its airport (the city's only lifeline to the outside world) to bring the siege to a final resolution. Not only did the shelling pose a danger to the besieged population of Sarajevo; the attacks on the airport were a direct threat to the safety of unarmed humanitarian workers from the UN and other international organizations as well as to the tiny UN Protection Force (UNPROFOR) guarding the airport itself. Compared to the tense standoff in the outskirts of Sarajevo, Saddam Hussein's use of fixed-wing aircraft in southern Iraq was seen as a comparatively minor problem that could be dealt with later.

At James Baker's insistence, a working group at the State Department had crafted an integrated politico-military strategy—labeled the "game plan"—to at least protect the delivery of humanitarian aid to Bosnia. Of all the senior officials in the Bush administration, Baker was perhaps the most open to making some show of force in the Balkans. The game plan called for the United States, acting in concert with other nations, to impose a naval blockade on the ports of the rump Serbian federation, and "demonstrate willingness to conduct multilateral airstrikes [for example, against Serb artillery positions in the hills surrounding Sarajevo] as necessary to create the conditions for delivery of humanitarian relief." A key proviso of the plan was that U.S. forces were under no circumstances to act alone, or for that matter on the ground in Bosnia itself.

Even this proposal for a narrowly delineated use of U.S. military force in Bosnia met with sharp objections from the Pentagon, on the grounds that it would lead to a "quagmire" in the Balkans. Baker later recorded in his memoirs the strong opposition of Defense Secretary Dick Cheney and JCS chairman Colin Powell to the game plan: "I knew both Powell and Cheney would be vehemently opposed to this initiative, fearing that it would put us on a slippery slope leading to greater military involvement down the line. Their model for using force was, understandably, the Gulf War; and Bosnia had more characteristics of Vietnam than Iraq. . . . Cheney and Powell went through the dangers associated with any use of military force, even just for delivery of humanitarian relief."

On June 28, French president François Mitterrand made a dramatic surprise visit to Sarajevo, where he toured the city with Bosnian president Izetbegović. At a joint press conference with Izetbegović, Mitterrand declared that the international community must not equate those who attack Sarajevo with those who defend it—a pointed warning to the Bosnian Serbs besieging the city.

The siege of Sarajevo—a city familiar to many Americans from its having hosted the 1984 Winter Olympics—had also captured the imagination of the American public. Editorial pages throughout the country were calling for the Bush administration to intervene in the crisis. Many in Congress were also calling for action. Even so, at a news conference on July 2, Bush maintained that there was no domestic support for a more proactive U.S. role in the crisis.

"Under our system, the president of the United States makes those decisions on the commitment of forces or not to commit forces," he declared. "That's one of the decisions that rest with me, not with anybody else, not the Congress, not anybody else. So no decision has been taken on that. And I have had no pressure to try to respond fully, from the United States Congress or any citizens here, to say why aren't we putting more troops into Sarajevo right now, for example. I haven't had any feeling that there's a great demand for that."

That would change the next day.

•   •   •

On July 3, 1992, American journalist Roy Gutman, a reporter for *Newsday*, a daily newspaper with a circulation of over a million in New York City and Long Island, broke the story that Serb forces in Bosnia were engaged in a calculated campaign of genocide against the Muslim population of Bosnia. Over the course of the ensuing months, Gutman and other Western journalists would chronicle in words and unforgettable pictures the first attempt by a European nation since the Second World War to obliterate the identity of an entire people. In describing their campaign to drive the Muslim population from Bosnia, Serb leaders unwittingly added a new term to the twentieth century's lexicon of shame: ethnic cleansing.

It is important to note that the events in Bosnia that would soon give pause to the entire world community were not the ordinary atrocities and human misery to be expected in any hard-fought civil war, saddening as those might be. Rather, ethnic cleansing represented a deliberate, systematic attempt by one group (initially the Bosnian Serbs, although later the Croats of Herzegovina would commit atrocities against their Muslim neighbors that differed from those of the Serbs only in the particulars) to drive another from their midst on no other basis than a difference in religion or surname.

With stunning disregard for the sensibilities of Europe (and equally stunning disregard for their own history of victimization at the hands of fascism), the Serbs created an apparatus of murder and intimidation in Bosnia eerily reminiscent, on a petty scale, of Nazi predations in Eastern Europe during the Second World War. Entire households were massacred after all of their portable wealth had been stolen. Entire male populations of remote mountain villages were herded off, never to be seen again until their corpses were uncovered in shallow pit graves. Then there were the concentration camps.

Ethnic cleansing transcended mere mass murder, to encompass the worst form of genocide: the attempted degradation of an entire people and their culture. The graceful mosques and libraries of a hundred Bosnian towns—as distinctive a part of Europe's cultural landscape as the *Kölner Dom* of Germany or the Synagogue of Florence—were razed to the ground in an orgy of religious bigotry. Schools, courthouses, and any other buildings that might serve as a repository of the past were set ablaze in an attempt to remove any record that Muslims had lived in Bosnia for seven centuries. Most abhorrent was the practice of mass rape—not as the detritus of war, but as part of a deliberate policy to wipe out the bloodlines of Muslim families—on a scale rivaled only by Soviet ravages on the Eastern Front in 1945.

Some of the headlines alone from Gutman's dispatches that summer and fall were enough to capture the full extent of the horrors:

Like Auschwitz—Serbs Pack Muslims into Freight Cars
Death Camps—Survivors Tell of Captivity, Mass Slaughters in
  Bosnia
The Rapes of Bosnia—"We Want the World to Know"
Slow Reaction to Biggest Refugee Crisis Since World War II

To this point, the conflict in Bosnia had been indistinguishable in its essentials from the earlier fighting in Croatia and was processed as such by both official Washington and the American people. The irrefutable evidence of genocide emerging from Bosnia changed all of that. Distaste for foreign entanglements runs deep in the American soul; but contempt for mass murderers and empathy for their victims runs deeper, and the American people responded to the horrors they were shown with that curious, uniquely American mixture of outrage and compassion.

The chambers of Congress reverberated with calls from the people's elected representatives to take active measures to end the genocide. Every major editorial page in the country exhorted President Bush to lead the world community to do its duty in the Balkans, as he had done in the Persian Gulf. Elie Wiesel, who had only the previous year conferred the award that bore his name upon President Bush, now compared ethnic cleansing in Bosnia to the early stages of the Holocaust: not the sort of comparison Wiesel would make lightly. After the first week of July

1992, the Bush administration could no longer advance the argument that "no domestic support" existed for Western intervention in Bosnia, since a broad cross-section of the American public now demanded action to end the slaughter.

But President Bush remained adamant in opposing the use of military force to rectify the situation. "I am not interested in seeing one single United States soldier pinned down in some kind of guerilla environment," he maintained. "And I could certify to the American people that's what would happen."

9

"SADDAM HUSSEIN IS WINNING THE PEACE"

Iraqi cooperation with UNSCOM weapons inspections had begun and ended with Iraq's first and only weapons declaration, in April 1991—and even that declaration, of course, had omitted mention of Saddam Hussein's advanced nuclear research program.

Since then the Iraqi regime had pursued a calculated and ambitious strategy of impeding the UNSCOM inspections. By July 1992 the litany of violations that Iraq had committed against the terms of UN Security Council Resolution 687 was extensive and ranged from the relatively minor (like leaving UNSCOM inspectors stranded at sites with no transportation) to the fairly serious (like Baghdad's September 1991 announcement that UNSCOM personnel could inspect any building they liked as long as they removed no documents).

UNSCOM personnel, as required by their charter, reported every violation of UNSCR 687 to the Security Council. The United States, as one of the permanent five members of the UN and leader of the Coalition that had fought the Gulf War, also lodged its own protests against Iraq's behavior on a regular basis. In September 1991 the Bush administration had come close to conducting punitive air strikes against Iraq to force Iraqi compliance with UNSCOM, only to see the outbreak of a fresh round of fighting in the Balkans prevent the air strikes from taking place. Since then, Iraq's lack of cooperation had, if anything, become even worse.

But as intransigent as Iraq's conduct had been, there was one line that Saddam Hussein had yet to cross. Iraq had never actually denied access to a suspected weapons site to an UNSCOM inspections team. Even Saddam seemed to recognize that doing so was a violation in an entirely different category from having his security services rifle through the suitcases of UNSCOM personnel, or refusing to allow them to cart away documents. Denying access to a site would constitute a "material breach" of the entire cease-fire arrangement that had ended the Gulf War, almost requiring the UN Security Council to take action in response. A material breach could mean war.

For this reason, denying access to a site was not a decision that could be taken lightly by Saddam. His own personal survival might very well be put at risk by such a decision. Indeed, a less ambitious despot might have eschewed the risk and focused his attention on cementing his hold over his embittered populace. But Saddam was nothing if not supremely ambitious.

Moreover, he had been greatly emboldened by the events of the preceding sixteen months. His control over Iraq was stronger than it had been before he invaded Kuwait. Based on the Bush administration's failure to take punitive military action against him, despite numerous provocations, he had concluded that the White House was losing its stomach for another major military intervention overseas. Washington's vacillating response to the crisis in the Balkans, NATO's own backyard, confirmed this impression. Most of all, he had correctly gauged that the political winds in the United States were blowing against his nemesis, George Bush. While prone to astonishing miscalculations in the foreign policy realm, Saddam was a shrewd observer of American domestic politics. He did not need his intelligence services to tell him that Bush's popularity had waned and that the president's reelection campaign was in deep trouble during the summer of 1992. They get CNN in Baghdad, too.

At 9:30 A.M. on the morning of Sunday, July 5, an UNSCOM team arrived at the Iraqi Agriculture Ministry in downtown Baghdad to conduct an unannounced inspection. In the Kafkaesque logic of Saddam Hussein's regime, the Agriculture Ministry building housed facilities for nuclear and biological weapons research.

They were denied access. As the UNSCOM team waited with their vehicles in the parking lot, the Iraqi regime launched a carefully choreographed diplomatic offensive. The Foreign Ministry released a statement declaring that the inspection request was an insult, and that the inspection of "civilian" government buildings was not required by Iraq under the terms of UNSCR 687.

The next day, with the UNSCOM inspectors still parked in their vehicles outside, the Foreign Ministry arranged a tour of the "besieged" building by diplomats from a handful of friendly Arab countries who still had diplomatic relations with Iraq. Also that day, a UN humanitarian aid convoy in northern Iraq came under attack by Iraqi forces. Among the members of the UN party was French president Mitterrand's wife, Danielle, who was a prominent human rights activist in France. It is not entirely clear whether the Iraqi forces knew that Mme. Mitterrand was in the convoy when they attacked, though news of her visit to Iraq had been widely reported in the international media.

Later that afternoon, in New York, the president of the UN Security Council declared Iraq's denial of access to the building "a material and unacceptable breach of the provisions of Resolution 687."

Iraq's action had caught the Bush administration at an awkward moment. President Bush, along with James Baker and Brent Scowcroft, had been on a state visit to Poland, and all three were now in Munich for the annual G-8 summit of major economic powers. On July 8 the president had his first news conference with reporters in over a week. Bush did not mention the brewing crisis inside Iraq. Neither did the traveling White House press corps, which instead peppered the president with questions about the worsening situation in the former Yugoslavia.

•   •   •

In Washington, the first formal meeting on how to respond to the standoff did not take place until July 8. Richard Haass chaired the meeting in the White House Situation Room. It was decided to issue a demarche to the Iraqi government demanding that it cease blocking access to the Agriculture Ministry building. No answer was forthcoming from Baghdad for two days. On July 11 most of the UNSCOM team, which had remained staked out in the Agriculture Ministry parking lot throughout this period, departed from Iraq. The six inspectors who remained behind had the tires of their vehicles slashed by the Iraqis.

Ordinarily, news of a major standoff with Saddam Hussein would have been the top news item in the American media, but that week there were other exciting developments in the headlines. On July 9, Democratic frontrunner Bill Clinton defied conventional wisdom by announcing a fellow Southerner, Tennessee senator Al Gore, as his running mate for November. While unconventional, Clinton's choice was politically astute. The presence of Gore contributed instant gravitas to the Clinton campaign on foreign policy and national security issues, Clinton's greatest vulnerability. It also further enhanced his appeal among moderates and independents in the South.

For the next several days, political pundits debated the wisdom of Clinton's choice of Gore while media attention focused on every aspect of the two youthful candidates and their wives. On July 13, all attention shifted to New York, where the Democratic National Convention was beginning. The Southern theme was continued in the choice of prime-time speakers for the convention. The keynote address was given by former Texas congresswoman Barbara Jordan, who was famous for her eloquent cadences. But it was agreed by most attendees that the best speech of the convention was given by Georgia governor Zell Miller, a Democratic moderate well known for his country-fried sense of humor. Miller could not resist taking a playful shot at George Bush's seeming ineptitude in the face of the escalating crises in Iraq and the Balkans. "Our commander in chief talks like Dirty Harry," Miller told a boisterous convention audience, "but acts like Barney Fife."

Al Gore added his own critique. "If President Bush and Vice President Quayle are such whizzes in foreign policy," Gore asked, "why is it that Saddam Hussein is thumbing his nose at the world?" Unwittingly, he had used the exact same description of Saddam's behavior that President Bush had used with British prime minister Major nearly a year earlier.

Despite the fact that the Iraqi regime was in material breach of one UN resolution and had violated the terms of a dozen others, Iraq remained a member state in good standing of the United Nations. One unusual consequence was that the country continued to maintain a large diplomatic delegation at UN headquarters in New York. This situation created some awkward moments for the U.S. diplomats posted in New York, since the Americans could not avoid occasionally bumping into their Iraqi counterparts in the hallways, the delegates' dining room, even the restrooms.

However, the presence of the Iraqis in New York was a huge convenience for other reasons. The Bush administration had pulled Joseph Wilson and his team out of Baghdad shortly before the launch of Operation Desert Storm, and there had been no American diplomats in Iraq since then. Iraq's ambassador to Washington had been expelled, and only a skeleton staff remained at the Iraqi embassy in Washington. Thus, Iraqi UN ambassador Mohammed al-Anbari had become the administration's principal channel for delivering messages to the government of Saddam Hussein—no easy task when dealing with a regime in which "shooting the messenger" was not always just a figure of speech.

But Iraq's UN delegation was not only capable of receiving messages. It was also capable of delivering them.

On July 14, al-Anbari told the president of the Security Council, Cape Verdean ambassador de Jesus, that Iraq would not allow UN inspectors into its Agriculture Ministry under any circumstances. "The Government of Iraq has concluded that the Security Council is paralyzed and cannot exercise its mandate," al-Anbari boasted. He also dropped a new bombshell. Iraq saw little value in continuing to comply with the UN sanctions imposed after the invasion of Kuwait. In keeping with this position, he continued, Iraqi foreign minister Aziz had sent a letter to UN secretary-general Boutros-Ghali demanding that Iraq be allowed to export oil at "pre-August 1990 levels."

However, the most unexpected and ominous development was a third point. The Iraqi ambassador informed the Security Council president that Iraq would no longer participate in the UN boundary commission demarcating the final border between Iraq and Kuwait. The commission's next meeting was to have taken place in New York the next day, July 15. The Iraqi government had given its reasons for walking out of the border talks in an insulting letter to Boutros-Ghali. "The outcome of the commission's work is a purely political decision imposed by the powers that today control the Security Council and the United Nations; in particular, the governments of the United States and the United Kingdom."

Edward Perkins, who had replaced Tom Pickering as UN ambassador a few months earlier, summarized the net impact of the news in a cable for Washington: "Iraq Challenges the Security Council across the Board."

.   .   .

More than the standoff with UN weapon inspectors, Iraq's withdrawal from negotiations on the border with Kuwait raised alarm in Washington. Even after his defeat in Desert Storm, Saddam Hussein had never renounced his claims to Kuwaiti territory, especially the Rumailah oil-field and the islands of Warbah and Bubiyan in the Contested Zone. At least the Iraqi government had been willing to negotiate on the issue, however. Iraq's sudden rejection of the UN boundary commission's jurisdiction meant that Saddam Hussein might be intending to act on his claims in the relatively near future. Unlike Saddam's WMD programs, which represented a long-term strategic threat that might take years to materialize, the ability of his reconstituted army to threaten Kuwait was entirely tangible. And for obvious reasons, the Bush White House would have never been able to live down a *second* Iraqi invasion of Kuwait.

A NODIS cable was sent from the State Department to Ambassador Perkins in New York, and to U.S. ambassadors in the main Coalition capitals, detailing the Bush administration's strategy for dealing with the Agriculture Ministry standoff. "Continued Iraqi defiance is unacceptable, and we are prepared to use force if necessary to persuade Saddam to meet the requirements of the relevant UN resolutions." The cable further acknowledged that "while there is every likelihood that any documentation relating to weapons of mass destruction which may have been located within the ministry has been removed or destroyed, this blatant attempt to limit the scope of UNSCOM's mandate in Iraq cannot be allowed to stand."

.   .   .

Further complicating matters, on July 11 Serb forces in Bosnia had launched a massive new offensive. Tens of thousands of new Bosnian refugees had fled to neighboring republics in panic. On July 12 a stricken President Franjo Tudjman of Croatia sent a letter to the White House.

"Due to the most recent avalanche of refugees from Bosnia and Hercegovina that was set in motion on 11 July, the Republic of Croatia is now facing insurmountable difficulties in its effort to provide shelter and food for these people. Only in the course of the last 24 hours, 20,700 refugees crossed the Croatian border. The extent to which these people are panic stricken is best illustrated by the fact that many of them (even women and children) swim across the Sava River seeking shelter on the Croatian side. . . . The events taking place along the Sava River are particularly dramatic: We are faced with a massive exodus of the Moslem and Croatian population from Bosnia across the river, while Croatian towns are being destroyed."

The humanitarian nightmare in Bosnia, not the diplomatic standoff in Iraq, dominated the headlines and the nightly newscasts. President Bush soon received a painful personal indication of how his failure to act in the Balkans was sapping his political support even among the most loyal Republicans. On July 15 former Reagan national security adviser William Clark sent a private note to Bush, withdrawing his support for the president in the 1992 election because of Bush's failure to respond to the allegations of genocide in Bosnia. For Bush, it was like a body blow.

Bill Clark was an upstanding California judge who had been a long-time member of Ronald Reagan's "California Mafia." Although he had brought little formal background in foreign policy to his job as national security adviser and served in the position only a few years, Clark had left Washington with his reputation for probity intact. During his time in the White House, Clark had enjoyed a warm working relationship with then–Vice President Bush. He had been an early supporter of Bush's presidential candidacy in 1988.

The president sent Clark a note asking him to reconsider. "We're terribly troubled by all of this and without throwing a lot of troops into the fray, we're trying to bring about peace in the area."

•   •   •

On July 17, the two-year anniversary of the National Day speech in which Saddam Hussein had issued his veiled threat against Kuwait just weeks before invading the country, the Iraqi dictator again took to the airwaves. In a podium-pounding address, he vowed never to let UN inspectors search the Agriculture Ministry for documents on Iraqi missiles; though why there would be documents on missiles at an Agriculture Ministry, he did not say. Apparently inspired by his leader's fervor, Iraq's agriculture minister announced to a news conference later that day that he and his staff were determined not to let the "UN scoundrels" desecrate his ministry.

The next day, July 18, UNSCOM chief Rolf Ekeus traveled to Baghdad in a last-ditch attempt to negotiate a workable deal on inspections. After two days of fruitless discussions, the talks ended deadlocked. Citing "threats of physical pressure," the final six members of the UNSCOM team evacuated Iraq on July 22.

The Iraqi regime was quick to celebrate the lifting of the "siege" at the Agriculture Ministry. The next morning the Ba'ath Party's official newspaper, *al-Thawra*, proclaimed: "The team of spies and scoundrels left their position without being able to defile the sanctity of the Agriculture and Irrigation Ministry!" Tariq Aziz declared that the inspections were at an end for good, as far as the Iraqi government was concerned. "Nothing is required from Iraq anymore, as Iraq has honored all of its commitments in accordance with UNSC Resolution 687."

•   •   •

Iraq was the topic of a rare Saturday morning NSC meeting held at Camp David on July 25. The president was joined by Vice President Quayle, Brent Scowcroft, Dick Cheney, Colin Powell, Robert Gates (now CIA director), White House spokesman Marlin Fitzwater, Chief of Staff Samuel Skinner, Lawrence Eagleburger, who was sitting in for a traveling James Baker, and Scowcroft's new deputy, retired navy admiral Jonathan Howe. For the better part of two hours the group discussed how to handle both the diplomatic and public relations aspects of the crisis. Cheney had volunteered to make the rounds of the Sunday talk shows on July 26, and much of the group's time was spent coming to agreement on the talking points that he would use. It was a thankless assignment for the defense secretary; there was no way of knowing whether he would be asked primarily about Iraq or the equally pressing crisis in the Balkans.

In fact, he was challenged on the administration response to both crises. Appearing on NBC News' *Meet the Press*, Cheney was asked about Saddam Hussein by moderator Tim Russert.

"Hasn't he won, in a sense?" Russert asked. "For seventeen days, he kept the UN inspectors away from the Agricultural Ministry. The inspectors have now left. Any documents that were in the ministry may very well be gone."

"I think it would be a mistake to focus on just the Agriculture Ministry question," Cheney replied. "What's at stake here is really whether or not the United Nations can effectively carry through on the sanctions that were imposed at the end of the Gulf War, and are we going to be able to be as successful as we have.

"The inspections have worked well; they've uncovered a lot of new information about his weapons of mass destruction, destroyed a lot of facilities. But now he has drawn a line in the sand, so to speak, and we'll have to see whether or not the UN is up to the task of being able to successfully implement those sanctions. To say that he's won I think would be totally inappropriate. I don't think that's true. I think the jury is still out on that question."

Another panelist, *Washington Post* columnist David Broder continued in the same vein. "With the advantage of hindsight, wouldn't you say that the United States and the United Nations made a mistake in not identifying him as the problem and making a specific objective the removal of Saddam Hussein in that regime?"

Cheney gave a grim smile. "I'm asked that question repeatedly, and I think we made the right decision when we decided not to proceed. It would have involved putting a lot of additional Americans into Iraq. It would have involved combat in places like Baghdad, a very different situation than the desert. And while it was a cheap war in terms of casualties—we only had 146 Americans killed in action—for those 146 Americans and their families, it wasn't a low-cost war.

"The question," Cheney concluded, "boils down to how many additional American casualties would we have been willing to accept to get

Saddam Hussein. And my answer was then, and is now, not very damn many."

One week later it was more of the same skeptical treatment for the secretary of defense; only the venue had changed. Cheney appeared on the CNN program *Newsmaker Saturday*. The show began with a dramatic voiceover by the announcer: "Are U.S. ground troops heading to Kuwait just for the exercise?" That morning's *Washington Post* had run a headline that the Bush administration was dispatching nearly three thousand U.S. troops to Kuwait for "exercises" along the Kuwaiti border with Iraq.

One of the CNN panelists, Wolf Blitzer, asked Cheney about a new rumor that was circulating in Washington. "What about those who argue here, back home, that the timing is just too coincidental, given the fact that President Bush is in the midst of a political campaign? Is there anything to that?" Blitzer asked.

"No, there really isn't, because of course we haven't determined the timing with respect to the latest controversy over Iraq," Cheney replied. "That's something they determined."

The defense secretary pronounced himself somewhat mystified as to why Saddam had chosen to challenge the Bush administration at this particular juncture.

"Saddam Hussein, for whatever reason, decided that this was the month that he wanted to confront the UN over this inspection regime," Cheney said. "And this current situation in Iraq is a situation that developed independently of anything that we caused or created."

Later in the program, Cheney was asked by the program's host, Charles Bierbauer, to contrast the Bush administration's willingness to use force again in Iraq with its unwillingness to do so in the Balkan republics. The distinction was clear in the defense secretary's mind.

"I think the situation in Yugoslavia is radically different than what it was in Iraq and Kuwait," he explained. "In the Gulf we had a situation where Saddam Hussein's Iraqi government invaded another government and went across international boundaries, committed aggression—a clear-cut situation. In Yugoslavia, we've got an internal civil war: a conflict between various ethnic and nationality groups; between different republics inside Yugoslavia. It's a dramatically different set of circumstances."

There was a moment of awkward silence after this explanation. Both

Bierbauer and Blitzer knew instantly that Cheney had just committed a major gaffe in stating official U.S. policy—a rare blunder for the always self-possessed, carefully briefed defense secretary.

"Mr. Secretary, there is no Yugoslavia anymore," Bierbauer reminded him. "Those are independent nations that your government recognizes in Bosnia and Croatia."

Cheney was taken aback for a moment. But he was less concerned with arguing the niceties of sovereignty and diplomatic recognition than advancing the Bush administration's preferred case for why there should be no U.S. intervention in the Balkans.

"Charles, the problem—the thing to keep in mind in Yugoslavia is its history and the amount of violence that historically characterized the relationships between a lot of those groups that make up Yugoslavia. In World War II, for example: There were some 1,750,000 Yugoslavs who were killed—11 percent of the population. Thirty German divisions were in Yugoslavia trying to pacify the country. The point is, over half of those Yugoslavs who were killed in World War II were killed by other Yugoslavs. Even in the midst of World War II. Even with German occupation, there was still an amazing level of violence between the various groups that make up Yugoslavia. Now I think we ought to do everything we can to try to bring that civil war to an end. . . . But I don't think we want to put U.S. forces on the ground in Yugoslavia with a mission of trying to end the war."

●   ●   ●

Dick Cheney may have been mystified as to why Saddam Hussein had chosen to confront the international community in July 1992, but the rest of the Bush inner circle was laboring under no such impediment. There was a growing realization inside the White House that Saddam had timed his escalation in Iraq to coincide with the deteriorating situation in the Balkans and the U.S. presidential election. At the July G-8 summit in Munich, President Bush had openly discussed the growing entanglement of the two crises with European leaders, especially French president Mitterrand. Several weeks later Bush sent a private letter to Mitterrand at the Élysée Palace recapping their conversation:

I want to share with you my assessment of the serious situation we face in Iraq and particularly Saddam Hussein's determination to resist UN authority. Unlike previous problems with Iraq since the end of hostilities, Baghdad's defiance of UN authority is across the board and uniformly bold. We are not sure if this is because Saddam thinks we are distracted by Yugoslavia and domestic concerns.

Sharing his thoughts with a trusted allied head of state, Bush gave a pessimistic assessment of developments in Iraq, raising a litany of concerns that he never spoke about in public with American audiences.

We believe Iraq is still concealing dozens of Scud missiles and its biological warfare program, for example. If Iraq is able to preserve its weapons of mass destruction, much of what we worked for and fought for will be undermined.

Beyond this issue is a wide pattern of defiance which leads us to believe that Saddam intends to return to past practices. Iraq has refused to participate in the work of the Iraq-Kuwait Boundary Commission. . . . Attacks on Shia opposition targets in southern Iraq have escalated sharply this month, including use of jet aircraft for the first time since the Gulf War. In the North, Iraqi use of terror tactics against the Kurds has become flagrant. . . . I know that Madame Mitterrand recently had a firsthand experience with the horrors of that situation, and we are grateful she was unharmed by the attack on her motorcade.

If military action is needed, I very much hope that France— and the United Kingdom—will join us again. . . . We, as well as our diplomatic and military advisers, must stay in close contact as we decide how to respond to Iraq's behavior.

•   •   •

On August 4, senior diplomats from France and the United Kingdom arrived in Washington for secret consultations on how the "Perm-3" countries should handle Iraq. The meeting was hosted at the State Department.

The department itself was in transition. President Bush had already asked James Baker to return to the White House as chief of staff to rescue Bush's sinking presidential campaign. Baker would be bringing his top cadre of aides—Dennis Ross, Undersecretary of State Robert Zoellick, and departmental spokesperson Margaret Tutwiler—with him. Undersecretary of State for Political Affairs Robert Kimmitt had also left, accepting the president's offer to be the first U.S. ambassador to the new, unified Germany.

The August 4 meeting was run by Kimmitt's replacement, Arnold Kanter. A veteran State Department official with a PhD from Harvard, Kanter had worked closely with Brent Scowcroft during the Nixon and Ford years and was a protégé of the national security adviser. Naturally, then, Kanter had consulted extensively with Scowcroft on the main points of his presentation to the visiting diplomats.

"Thank you for coming here on such short notice," Kanter began. "The fact that you've come—and in August—suggests that your governments attach as much importance to the subject of our discussion this morning as does mine. Let me try to put the proposition as simply as I can.

"Saddam Hussein is winning the peace. Or at least that argument can be made—and is being made. His trophies are his steadily accumulating successes in violating every single UNSC resolution passed since August 1990. I don't think anyone in this room will argue with the statement that Saddam's recent behavior shows he learned nothing from the war, and that he is determined to reestablish Iraq as a major regional power."

There was no argument, so Kanter went on.

"The pattern of his violations makes clear that that is the centerpiece of his strategy. The pace and boldness of his recent moves suggests he believes he is succeeding."

Kanter then launched into a depressing recitation of Iraqi misdeeds during the preceding year. "What we are facing," he concluded, "is a comprehensive, across-the-board challenge to the authority of the UN. Up to now we have been dealing with the problem on a largely ad hoc basis. I would submit that unless the Coalition, starting with the countries here today, are prepared to meet Saddam's strategy with a comprehensive, coordinated, and resolute approach of its own, the trend lines are not going to get better.

"Saddam is thinking big. So should we."

• • • •

It was a sign of just how concerned the Bush White House was about the situation in Iraq that during that same week it agreed to meet with the Iraqi opposition to discuss ways of toppling Saddam Hussein's regime.

James Baker, Brent Scowcroft, and Paul Wolfowitz met in Washington with representatives of the Iraqi National Congress (INC), the umbrella group encompassing the largest Iraqi opposition groups. Of course, this inevitably meant dealing with the leading Kurdish and Shia groups that represented the strongest opposition forces inside Iraq—a prospect once unimaginable to the three senior administration officials in the room.

Perhaps the most impressive figure at the meeting was Kurdish leader Massoud Barzani. Jalal Talabani's longtime rival for preeminence among the Kurds, Barzani also hated Saddam with a passion, as well he should have. The Iraqi dictator had perpetrated a crime of almost biblical proportions on the Barzani clan, murdering five thousand male relatives of Barzani in cold blood to punish Barzani and his people for taking part in the 1987 Kurdish uprising.

Although there were a handful of Sunni opposition figures present, Scowcroft recognized that the majority of those at the meeting were Shi'ites and Kurds who were understandably suspicious of the Bush administration's motives after being "abandoned" in the wake of Desert Storm. The national security adviser went out of his way to cultivate Barzani in the discussion that followed. "We won't let you down," he assured the Kurdish leader at one point.

Given the strained history between the administration and the Iraqi opposition, the meeting was going surprisingly well until the issue of war crimes trials for Saddam and the leading figures of his regime came up. Scowcroft immediately grew wary. The Bush administration's ideal scenario was still a coup by one of Saddam Hussein's generals, who would necessarily be a Sunni and a Ba'ath Party member. The administration remained opposed to the idea of holding war crimes trials since these might discourage members of Saddam's inner circle from trying to seize power in Iraq.

There was an angry reaction to the U.S. position. The worst suspicions of many in the room about American motives had just been confirmed.

Worse still, the INC representatives understood exactly the outcome the White House was hoping for in Iraq and knew that it reflected a naïve lack of understanding about the nature of Saddam's regime. One of the Sunni opposition figures in the room was Gen. Arif Abd-al-Raqazz, who had been head of the Iraqi air force and the figurehead prime minister of Iraq under Saddam before defecting. Arif flatly informed the Americans that Saddam's internal security was so good that a coup would not take place, and that even if it did, replacing Saddam with a senior Ba'ath Party official would achieve nothing.

Scowcroft remained unconvinced. The following month the NSC staff on his instructions drafted a position paper entitled "Potential Iraqi and Regional Downside to a War Crimes Trial of Saddam."

.   .   .

Like a bad cold, the persisent rumors among the Washington press corps that the Bush administration had engineered a military showdown with Iraq in order to help the president's poll numbers simply would not go away. It was not difficult to understand why the rumors took hold during the summer of 1992. Saddam Hussein had violated so many UN resolutions on so many occasions during the preceding two years that it was hard for those outside the Bush inner circle to grasp why his actions during July represented a sharp escalation or merited the threat of a military response. Reporters saw George Bush's sagging poll numbers, heard his threatening rhetoric against Saddam, and connected the dots as they saw them.

Few reporters, if any, were privy to details on the full scope of Saddam's challenge to the international community in July. And for a variety of reasons, the Bush administration was unwilling to share many of the details. The White House was hardly going to announce, for example, that Iraq's abrupt departure from the Iraq-Kuwait boundary talks, coupled with the presence of Iraqi jet fighters along its southern border, raised the real possibility (however remote) that Saddam Hussein was intending to attack Kuwait again.

It was President Bush's bad fortune, however, that the rumors of an "October surprise" being planned by the White House reached a crescendo at the absolute worst possible moment. On August 16, the eve of the Republican National Convention in Houston, the *New York Times* called Richard Haass for comment about an article it was planning to run the next morning. The article would claim that "Pentagon sources" had revealed that the United States was planning a major punitive bombing campaign to coincide with the Republican Convention, so that the president would "look strong" as he accepted the nomination.

Haass was horrified. Better than anyone, he knew that planning for possible military action against Saddam Hussein had begun as a direct response to Iraq's serious, across-the-board escalation during July. Haass was certain of this, because he was the one doing most of the planning. Although he worked on the policy, not political, side of the White House, Haass recognized that publication of such an article on the first day of the Republican Convention would be a devastating blow to George Bush's reelection campaign. Worse, once this charge was leveled against the president, it would be next to impossible for the Bush administration to muster domestic support for military action against Iraq during the remainder of the campaign—and Saddam Hussein would know this.

Haass called the *Times* Washington bureau and demanded to speak with the bureau chief, Howell Raines.

"You shouldn't go with the story for two reasons," Haass argued to Raines. "One, the president is in no way motivated by the politics. To the contrary, because he's worried that some people will think this, he's actually disinclined to do this, but he's prepared to do it anyhow because it's the right thing to do."

Raines was accustomed to dealing with government officials who were outraged by stories that the *Times* was planning to run. "I've got someone in the Pentagon saying he's politically motivated," he revealed.

Haass snorted derisively. "Look, the Pentagon has about thirty thousand people in it. You may have some colonel in the Pentagon who's saying it's politically motivated, but there is no one in the Pentagon who has access to the actual meetings saying that." What he did not tell Raines was that, at that moment, there were fewer than ten people within the Bush administration who were aware that planning for possible military action against Iraq was under way. Because of the unusually sensitive nature of the Iraq issue for the White House, the decision-making circle had been kept deliberately small.

"Anyone who had access to the president would know he's not politically motivated," Haass continued, his voice rising. "Just because you have someone saying something doesn't make that person a source. This is one of the worst examples of irresponsible journalism I have ever been associated with," he shouted over the phone.

Having failed to appeal to Raines's journalistic instincts, Haass tried to make the national security case for not running the story. "You know, if you run the story, the United States won't be able to bomb, and this is really bad for American national security," he reasoned. "The UN will blink, they will basically get spooked by this, because it will look like they are in cahoots with the United States. This is bad journalism, and it's bad for U.S. national security."

These arguments failed to make a dent. The next morning, August 17, the *Times* ran the story on page one. Nor were they the only newspaper to do so. Journalist Gerald Seib published a similar story in the *Wall Street Journal*. That evening, the president asked Dick Cheney to go on public broadcasting's *MacNeil/Lehrer Newshour* to defend him from the charge. Seib was also scheduled to appear.

"Secretary Cheney," asked anchor Judy Woodruff, "you heard what Gerry Seib was saying. Would this administration not be unhappy, as he put it, if there were a confrontation at this point with Saddam Hussein?"

Cheney was barely controlling his temper. "Judy, first of all let me try to restrain myself so I don't use the kind of language I'd like to use to describe the story that I've just listened to over the airwaves. The notion that somehow we would cobble together a military strike for partisan political purposes, or listen to Mr. Seib or whatever his name is spin on endless theories about how the United States military is opposed to insisting that Saddam Hussein comply with UN Security Council resolutions is just plain wrong.

"The fact that things got ratcheted up a bit in July had nothing to do with the Bush administration or the United States government. That was a choice that was made by Saddam Hussein. He's the one who decided that he would not allow inspectors into the Agriculture Ministry. . . . We've continued to insist that he must comply with those UN resolutions. We've indicated continuously that we have sufficient force, if called upon to do so, to compel his compliance. That was our policy in 1990, that was our policy in 1991, and that's our policy in 1992. And it has not changed or been affected in any way by the fact that there is a convention under way in Houston.

"The thing I find most galling of all, most objectionable of all, is the suggestion by the *New York Times* or anybody else that President Bush or I or General Powell would think so lightly of our responsibilities for the young men and women under our command that we would mount some kind of a military operation to achieve a gain in the polls in a partisan campaign."

Then, for the first time, Cheney acknowledged that Saddam's escalation of the crisis throughout the summer of 1992 had not been an impulsive decision by the Iraqi dictator, but a calculated attempt to capitalize on a White House distracted by a presidential campaign that was going badly.

"They've flown some missions with aircraft this summer that they had not done previously against the Shia in the south," the defense secretary admitted. "It's a sense on our part, as we look at the situation, that Saddam Hussein has made a decision—perhaps we are in the middle of a political campaign—that he wants to ratchet up the level of activity as he confronts the United Nations and the Coalition."

*   *   *

The unflattering articles that ran on the opening day of the convention were a bad omen. The 1992 Republican National Convention was a disaster for George Bush. On the opening night of the convention, Pat Buchanan delivered a harsh prime-time address designed to appeal to his followers. Later dubbed the "culture wars" speech, Buchanan's diatribe attacked the Democratic ticket in such divisive tones that it alienated even many Republican convention delegates. It was a harbinger of an entire convention that seemed off key. By the time the president left Houston, he faced a double-digit deficit in the polls.

Even Mother Nature appeared to be conspiring against the Bush campaign that summer. On August 24, Hurricane Andrew—a Category Five hurricane bearing winds of 165 miles per hour—swept through south Florida, causing over $20 billion in damage before veering toward the Louisiana coast and causing an additional $5 billion in damage. At the time, it was the costliest hurricane in U.S. history. In Florida, tens of thousands were left homeless and trapped by rising waters. Armed bands of looters roamed the streets.

President Bush had made a brief trip to Florida to inspect the damage the day after the hurricane. For three days, however, no federal troops were sent to Florida, as conditions in the greater Miami area steadily deteriorated. Finally, on August 27, the emergency management director for Miami-Dade County made an impassioned plea on national television.

"Where in the hell is the cavalry on this one?" she demanded tearfully. "They keep saying we're going to get supplies. For God's sake, where are they? We're going to have more casualties because we're going to have more people dehydrated. People without water. People without food. Babies without formula. I am not the disaster czar down here. President Bush was down here. I'd like him to follow up on the commitments he made." The Bush administration's failure to respond to the disaster more quickly was widely criticized on editorial pages across the country, yet another blow to a teetering White House.

But George Bush had been in this situation once before. In 1988 he had trailed Michael Dukakis by 17 percentage points after Dukakis's "bounce" after the Democratic National Convention, only to recover and cruise to an easy victory in the fall election. As he returned to Washington to kick off the campaign in earnest, Bush was determined that just as in 1988, the key to victory in 1992 would be to highlight his and the Republican Party's vast edge over the Democrats in maintaining America's national security.

The first priority of the Bush campaign was restoring the president's Gulf War laurels. After two years' worth of uninterrupted bad news from Iraq, Bush's opponents had succeeded in recasting the conflict in terms of the decision to stop the war with Saddam Hussein still in power. The president was determined to seize the mantle of victory from the Gulf once again. Fortunately, he had the perfect opportunity to do so.

On August 25, four days after accepting the GOP nomination, Bush flew to Chicago to address the American Legion national convention. It had always been a receptive audience for George Bush, who not only identified with the Legionnaires, but was a Legionnaire. The president devoted most of the speech to defending his administration's performance during the Gulf War.

"Now, let's get straight what was at stake," Bush reminded his audience. "A madman with missiles and chemical weapons stood on the brink of a choke-hold on much of the world's energy supplies, threatening to overrun our allies. We destroyed that threat, liberated Kuwait, and locked up a tyrant in the prison of his own country. We know now Saddam Hussein was developing the weapons to destroy Israel. Tens of millions of deaths of Arabs or Israelis would not matter to this killer. The Middle East could well have become a nuclear apocalypse. That is what was at stake."

The president next defended the controversial ending of the war.

"Now, some who were faint-hearted and stood in the way of crushing Saddam's aggression now have the gall to say, 'You stopped the war too soon.' Some also say that General Norman Schwarzkopf wanted to march into Baghdad and get Saddam. False! I'll never forget—this is a true story and history has it recorded on film—sitting in the Oval Office on February 27, 1991, our troops having performed so magnificently in the field. And with me in the room was General Scowcroft and the Secretary of Defense, Dick Cheney, the Chairman of the Joint Chiefs of Staff, Colin Powell. They recommended to me, as president who has the responsibility for this, that we stop the slaughter; our mission was accomplished. I asked, are you sure that our field commanders feel this way? They both said yes.

"But to double-check, Colin Powell got up from the couch in our office—you all have seen pictures of it—walked over to the desk that you see pictures of, reached into the front right-hand corner of the desk, and there was a secure telephone; picked up that secure phone, and got General Schwarzkopf on the line in my presence. And General Powell looked up at me after he had talked to Schwarzkopf, and he said, 'Mission accomplished.'"

Bush had discovered a new enemy: "revisionist historians" who challenged his administration's account of how the Iraq War had ended.

"And I don't like this historical revision," the president complained. "We did the right thing; we did the compassionate thing in the end as well."

Though he did not mention the ongoing plight of the Shia or the Kurds in Iraq, Bush repeated his stock rationale for not coming to their aid after Desert Storm. "If we'd continued, hundreds of thousands of American troops would be on the ground in Iraq today attempting to pull warring factions together or bogged down in some guerrilla warfare. . . . History shows us the danger of losing sight of our objectives. Liberators can easily become occupiers. A Commander-in-Chief has to know not only when his objectives have been reached but when to consolidate his gains.

"We've seen too many situations where we asked those kids to fight with one hand tied behind their back. Not as long as I am Commander-in-Chief."

* * *

Colin Powell remained the most popular figure in the Bush administration. Unlike President Bush or Secretary of Defense Cheney, who had seen their personal popularity soar in the immediate aftermath of Desert Storm, only to deteriorate as Saddam Hussein survived and consolidated his power in Iraq, Powell's stature had only grown since the Gulf War. He was seen by many as an Eisenhower-like figure, one who transcended mere partisan politics. Indeed, speculation about the JCS chairman's future plans had become a popular parlor game in Washington. It was commonly assumed that Powell was considering a presidential run in 1996.

The White House was not unaware of Powell's broad appeal among large segments of the American public. Indeed, some within George Bush's inner circle were urging the president to capitalize upon it before it was too late, by dumping Vice President Dan Quayle from the ticket and replacing him with Powell. Bush himself recognized the immense credibility Powell possessed on national security matters. As the situations in Iraq and the Balkans had grown more and more untenable, the president had increasingly tried to cloak himself in the mantle of Powell's popularity when attempting to justify his policies in both regions. References to the advice of "my respected JCS chairman, Colin Powell" had become a fixture of Bush's responses to hostile questions from the press about why his administration was not doing more in Iraq and Bosnia. And unfortunately for George Bush, hostile questions from the press about these two crises had become a depressingly frequent occurrence during the eighteen months that had followed Desert Storm.

Far from expressing discomfort at becoming a lightning rod for deflecting criticism about the Bush administration's early termination of the Gulf War, or its unwillingness to intervene in Bosnia, Powell seemed to almost relish the role. Partly, this was a function of how he viewed his own role. The JCS chairman had long believed that one of his primary responsibilities was to inform deliberations on the use of military force with the "real world" perspective of the combat soldier. Powell was convinced that his predecessors' failure to do so during the Vietnam War had been a contributing factor to the war's outcome. "As a corporate entity, the military failed to talk straight to its political superiors or to itself," he would later write in his memoirs. "The top leadership never went to the secretary of defense or the president and said, 'This war is unwinnable the way we are fighting it.' " This failure had been the animating principle of Powell's subsequent career. "Many of my generation, the career captains, majors, lieutenant colonels seasoned in that war, vowed that when our turn came to call the shots, we would not quietly acquiesce in half-hearted warfare for half-baked reasons the American people could not understand or support." Powell had codified these beliefs in the so-called "Powell Doctrine": the JCS chairman's oft-stated view that the United States should not engage in military action except as a last resort, in the face of a clear threat to American national security, and then only with overwhelming force.

Just as important, though, was Powell's evolving relationship with George Bush. During Ronald Reagan's second term, when he served as Reagan's national security adviser, Powell had enjoyed a cordial relationship with Bush but had not been particularly close to the then–vice president. This changed during the first two years of the Bush presidency, when the Bush national security team conducted two large military interventions—in Panama and the Gulf—and dealt with the epochal events in Eastern Europe. Of necessity, Powell found himself interacting with the president on a regular basis, and the more he saw of George Bush the more he liked.

In many respects, Bush conformed to Powell's ideal of how the commander in chief of the armed forces should act. When it came to national security matters, the president was an engaged, "hands on" crisis manager who was nonetheless also a careful listener, open to suggestions from his advisers. Bush had a solid working knowledge of defense and foreign policy from his many years in the executive branch. Most of all, he possessed an innate caution about risking the lives of American troops abroad that mirrored Powell's own. Of the senior figures on the Bush national security team, only the president and Powell had actually seen combat, and Powell believed that this experience had made the two of them responsible stewards of the U.S. armed forces, each in his own way.

Although the term was anathema in a Republican Party increasingly dominated by social conservatives from the South and West, Powell knew that George Bush was, like himself, a quintessential "Rockefeller Republican": a pro-business moderate from the Northeast who supported a strong foreign policy, but was fairly liberal on social issues. Bush had tacked hard to the right during the 1988 presidential campaign, but in private, his essentially centrist political views were not difficult to discern. In this respect, Bush was markedly different from the other senior civilian for whom Powell worked, defense secretary Dick Cheney, whose low-key style masked the fact that he was one of the most conservative Republicans in Washington.

While he tried to maintain an Olympian detachment from partisan politics (and had discreetly but firmly disassociated himself from the campaign to draft him onto the Bush ticket), Powell recognized that George Bush's reelection campaign was in deep trouble as autumn began. In private, he had voiced his support for the president, and his desire to see Bush win a second term was sincere. As a serving military officer, Powell could not publicly campaign for the president. But there were other ways he could try to help.

On October 8, 1992—just three days before the first presidential debate—Powell wrote an op-ed piece in the *New York Times* defending the Bush administration's failure to intervene to stop the genocide in the

Balkans. Powell had written the article in response to a *Times* editorial from several days earlier that had lambasted both Bush and Powell for being too cautious in their use of military force. Entitled "Why Generals Get Nervous," Powell's article contained a ringing endorsement of George Bush:

> President Bush, more than any other recent President, understands the proper use of military force. In every instance, he has made sure that the objective was clear and that we knew what we were getting into. We owe it to the men and women who go in harm's way to make sure that their lives are not squandered for unclear purposes. . . . So you bet I get nervous when so-called experts suggest that all we need is a little surgical bombing or a limited attack.

That same month, Powell wrote a longer essay in the prestigious journal *Foreign Affairs*, defending the Bush administration's decision to leave Saddam Hussein in power at the end of the Gulf War. "The Gulf War was a limited-objective war," he wrote. "If it had not been, we would be ruling Baghdad today—at an unpardonable expense in terms of money, lives lost and ruined regional relationships." Powell ridiculed those, especially in his own party, who lamented that President Bush had not given the order for U.S. troops to march all the way to Baghdad after the liberation of Kuwait.

> We must assume that the political objective of such an order would have been capturing Saddam Hussein. . . . What purpose would it have served? And would serving that purpose have been worth the many more casualties that would have occurred? Would it have been worth the inevitable follow-up: major occupation forces in Iraq for years to come and a very expensive and complex American proconsulship in Baghdad? Fortunately for America, reasonable people at the time thought not. They still do.

It is not clear whether Powell changed many minds with his defense of administration policy. By any standard, though, his attempt to deflect criticism away from the president and onto himself was an extraordinary act of loyalty toward a president wounded and at bay—one that the elder George Bush would never forget.

But others would not forget, either. In arguing that the Bush administration had not erred by leaving Saddam Hussein in power at the end of the Gulf War, Powell was advancing a position little different from the one that George Bush, and Brent Scowcroft, and James Baker, and of course Dick Cheney had been advocating for eighteen months. In doing so, however, Powell had cemented his own growing reputation as the administration's "reluctant warrior." Those in Republican foreign policy circles who were dissatisfied with how the Gulf War had turned out— and already there were many—came to see him as their nemesis. A belief took root among the discontents that it had been Powell, with his formidable bureaucratic skills and eponymous doctrine, who had forced an end to Desert Storm "one day too soon" and had denied the United States a total victory over Saddam Hussein.

·　　·　　·

Despite the president's reinvigorated campaigning, the autumn began with George Bush still trailing Bill Clinton by a double-digit margin in the polls. The president's last chance to make up ground were the three presidential debates scheduled for mid-October. Despite the fact that the Bush campaign had discovered to its dismay that the Arkansas governor was a natural in front of any audience, Bush was eager for the debates to begin. The president was convinced that once he was on the same stage with the Arkansas governor, the American people would be reminded of Bush's stature and past achievements as a world leader, and would come to the right conclusion about which of the two candidates was better qualified to be president. "Let's get it on!" Bush clapped when the debate conditions had been agreed upon.

The one piece of good luck for the Bush campaign had been that Ross Perot had dropped out of the presidential race as abruptly as he had entered it. On July 29, muttering cryptic comments about "Republican operatives" trying to ruin his daughter's wedding, Perot had declared he was no longer running for president.

He qualified for the ballot in all fifty states, however. On October 1, just in time for the debates, Perot reentered the race.

•   •   •

George Bush planned to go on the attack in the first debate, held October 11 on the campus of Washington University in St. Louis. His issue of choice was Bill Clinton's activities protesting the Vietnam War while Clinton had been a Rhodes Scholar at Oxford. Although the issue had been chosen by the Bush campaign staff because of its likely resonance with the Republican base, the president needed no encouragement to use this line of attack. He genuinely was offended by Clinton's actions.

As luck would have it, midway through the debate Bush was asked a question about presidential character. The former captain of the Yale baseball team prepared to hit this hanging curveball out of the ballpark.

"I think the American people should be the judge of that," he said. "I think character is a very important question. I said something the other day where I was accused of being like Joe McCarthy because I questioned— put it this way—I think it's wrong to demonstrate against your own country or organize demonstrations against your own country in foreign soil. I just think it's wrong. Maybe, they say, well, it was a youthful indiscretion. I was nineteen or twenty, flying off an aircraft carrier, and that shaped me to be commander in chief of the armed forces. And I'm sorry, but demonstrating—it's not a question of patriotism. It's a question of character and judgment.

"They get on me, Bill's gotten on me, about 'Read my lips.' When I make a mistake, I'll admit it. But he has not admitted the mistake. And I just find it impossible to understand how an American can demonstrate against his own country in a foreign land, organizing demonstrations against it, when young men are held prisoner in Hanoi or kids out of the ghetto were drafted. Some say, well, you're a little old-fashioned. Maybe I am, but I just don't think that's right. Now, whether it's character or judgment, whatever it is, I have a big difference here on this issue. And so we'll just have to see how it plays out. But I couldn't do that. And I don't think most Americans could do that."

But if there was one question that Clinton had been carefully prepped on how to answer, it was this one.

"I've got to respond directly to Mr. Bush," he said when his turn came. "You have questioned my patriotism. You even brought some right-wing congressmen into the White House to plot how to attack me for going to Russia in 1969 to 1970, when over fifty thousand other Americans did.

"Now, I honor your service in World War II. I honor Mr. Perot's service in uniform and the service of every man and woman who ever served, including Admiral Crowe, who was your chairman of the Joint Chiefs and who's supporting me. But when Joe McCarthy went around this country attacking people's patriotism, he was wrong. He was wrong."

Clinton paused for a moment, then played his trump card. "And a senator from Connecticut stood up to him, named Prescott Bush," he reminded the audience. Clinton turned to address Bush directly.

"Your father was right to stand up to Joe McCarthy. You were wrong to attack my patriotism. I was opposed to the war, but I love my country. And we need a president who will bring this country together, not divide it. We've had enough division. I want to lead a unified country."

Anyone watching the debate could see that the point had scored. The president was clearly surprised and more than a little angry that Clinton had dragged his father's good name into this business.

.   .   .

Bush fumed for days over Clinton's "dirty trick." Four days later, at the second presidential debate in Richmond, the president had a chance to come to his father's defense. Asked another "character" question, Bush brought up Clinton's mention of Prescott Bush at the first debate:

"The other night, Governor Clinton raised—I don't know if you saw the debate the other night, suffered through that. Well, he raised a question of my father. It was a good line, well rehearsed and well delivered. But he raised a question of my father and said, 'Well, your father, Prescott Bush, was against McCarthy.' You should be ashamed of yourself."

.   .   .

If the president had been eager for the first debate to begin and spoiling for a fight during the second, he was anxious before the third and final debate, at Michigan State University on the evening of October 19. The previous two debates had done little to erode Bill Clinton's lead in the polls. There were only two weeks left until election day. The president knew he could not afford just to do well in Michigan. He needed to win the debate outright.

The final debate had been billed as the "economic policy" debate, and for this reason among others there seemed to be fewer fireworks than in the previous two encounters. By now the three candidates had all become accustomed to each other's quirks. For the first seventy minutes of the ninety-minute debate they traded statistics on the dry minutiae of trade policy and the number of jobs created in Arkansas. None of the three candidates landed a knockout blow on either of the others.

Toward the end of the debate, Ross Perot was given one minute to rebut a routine question on the advancement of female executives in his corporation. Perot dispensed with this issue in twenty seconds, then wheeled triumphantly on Bush.

"For the rest of my minute, I want to make a very brief comment here in terms of Saddam Hussein. We told him that we wouldn't get involved with this border dispute, and we've never revealed those papers that were given to Ambassador Glaspie on July 25. I suggest, in the sense of taking responsibility for your actions, we lay those papers on the table. They're not the secrets to the nuclear bomb.

"Secondly, we got upset when he took the whole thing, but to the ordinary American out there who doesn't know where the oilfields are in Kuwait, they're near the border. We told him he could take the northern part of Kuwait, and when he took the whole thing, we went nuts. And if we didn't tell him that, why won't we even let the Senate Foreign Relations Committee and the Senate Intelligence Committee see the written instructions for Ambassador Glaspie?"

For a moment, George Bush's jaw literally dropped. He was stunned by what Perot had just said, as much over the substance of the charge as by the fact that Perot had raised the issue of Iraq completely out of the blue. Nevertheless, the president did rather well under the circumstances, sustained momentarily by his anger at Perot.

"I'd like to reply on that," Bush snapped. "That gets to the national honor. We did not say to Saddam Hussein, Ross, 'You can take the northern part of Kuwait.' That is absolutely absurd. Glaspie has testified . . ."

"Where are the papers?" Perot interrupted shrilly.

"Glaspie's papers have been presented to the United States Senate. So please . . ."

"If you have time," Perot interrupted again, looking straight into the camera, "go through NEXIS and LEXIS, pull all the old news articles. Look at what Ambassador Glaspie said all through the fall and what have you, and then look at what she and Kelly* and all the others in State said at the end when they were trying to clean it up. And talk to any head of any of those key committees in the Senate. They will not let them see the written instructions given to Ambassador Glaspie. And I suggest that in a free society owned by the people, the American people ought to know what we told Ambassador Glaspie to tell Saddam Hussein. Because we spent a lot of money and risked lives and lost lives in that effort, and did not accomplish most of our objectives. We got Kuwait back to the emir; but he's still got his nuclear, his chemical, his bacteriological, and he's still over there, right? I'd like to see those written instructions. Sorry."

The moderator of the debate, Jim Lehrer of PBS, intervened. "Mr. President, when you—just to make sure that everybody knows what's going on here. When you responded directly to Mr. Perot then, you violated the rule, your rules. Now, I'm willing . . ."

"I apologize," the president said. "When I make a mistake, I say . . ."

"No, no, no," interjected Lehrer, "I just want to make sure that everybody understands. If you all want to change the rules, we can do it."

"No, I don't. I apologize for it. But that one got right to the national honor," said Bush, still peeved.

There was a sixty-second reprieve while Clinton gave his answer to the original question on women's opportunity in the workplace. It was Bush's great misfortune that the next question came from Helen Thomas, the famous White House correspondent for UPI, who had tormented Bush and five previous U.S. presidents. If Helen Thomas knew one thing, it was how to spot a question the White House did not want asked.

---

* Assistant Secretary of State John Kelly, who had testified before Congress with Glaspie.

"Mr. Perot, what proof do you have that Saddam Hussein was told that he could have—do you have any actual proof, or are you asking for the papers?" Thomas asked. "And also, I really came in with another question. What is this penchant you have to investigate everyone? Are those accusations correct, investigating your staff, investigating the leaders of the grassroots movement, investigating associates of your family?"

After denying he had a penchant for obsessive investigations, Perot retuned to the topic of Iraq:

> Now, let's go back to Saddam Hussein. We gave Ambassador Glaspie written instructions. That's a fact. We've never let the Congress and these Foreign Relations—Senate Intelligence Committee see them. That's a fact. Ambassador Glaspie did a lot of talking, right after July the 25th, and that's a fact, and it saw the newspapers. You pull all of it at once and read it, and I did, and it's pretty clear what she and Kelly and the other key guys around that thing thought they were doing.
>
> Then, at the end of the war when they had to go testify about it, their stories are a total disconnect from what they said in August, September, and October. So I say, this is very simple: Saddam Hussein released a tape, as you know, claiming it was a transcript of their meeting, where she said, "We will not become involved in your border dispute," and in effect, "You can take the northern part of the country."
>
> We later said, No, that's not true. I said, Well, this is simple. What were her written instructions? We guard those like the secrets to the atomic bomb, literally. Now, I say: Whose country is this? This is ours. Who will get hurt if we lay those papers on the table? The worst thing is, again, it's a mistake. Nobody did any of this with evil intent. I just object to the fact that we cover up and hide things, whether it's Iran-contra, Iraqgate, or you name it. It's a steady stream.

No one familiar with recent Washington history could fail to notice that Perot had mentioned a steady stream of scandals in which George Bush was implicated at one time or another.

"Governor Clinton, you have one minute," Lehrer intoned.

Clinton was also surprised that Perot had raised the issue of Iraq without warning, but he took a statesmanlike tack, all too happy to allow the unelectable Perot to smear Bush while he remained above the fray.

"Let's take Mr. Bush for the moment at his word," Clinton allowed. "I mean, he's right, we don't have any evidence, at least, that our government did tell Saddam Hussein he could have that part of Kuwait. And let's give him the credit he deserves for organizing Operation Desert Storm and Desert Shield. It was a remarkable event." He continued:

> But let's look at where, I think, the real mistake was made. In 1988, when the war between Iraq and Iran ended, we knew Saddam Hussein was a tyrant. We had dealt with him because he was against Iran. The enemy of my enemy maybe is my friend.
>
> All right, the war is over. We know he's dropping mustard gas on his own people. We know he's threatened to incinerate half of Israel. Several government departments, several, had information that he was converting our aid to military purposes and trying to develop weapons of mass destruction. But in late '89, the President signed a secret policy saying we were going to continue to try to improve relations with him, and we sent him some sort of communication on the eve of his invasion of Kuwait that we still wanted better relations.
>
> So I think what was wrong—I give credit where credit is due, but the responsibility was in coddling Saddam Hussein when there was no reason to do it and when people at high levels in our government knew he was trying to do things that were outrageous.

"Mr. President, you have a moment—a minute, I'm sorry," said Lehrer.

"It's awful easy when you're dealing with 90/90 hindsight," Bush replied. "We did try to bring Saddam Hussein into the family of nations. He did have the fourth largest army. All our Arab allies out there thought we ought to do just exactly that. When he crossed the line, I stood up and looked into the camera and I said, 'This aggression will not stand.' We formed a historic coalition, and we brought him down. We destroyed the fourth largest army, and the battlefield was searched, and there wasn't one single iota of evidence that any U.S. weapons were on that battle-field. The nuclear capability has been searched by the United Nations, and there hasn't been one single scintilla of evidence that there's any U.S. technology involved in it.

"What you're seeing on all this Iraqgate is a bunch of people who were wrong on the war trying to cover their necks here and try to do a little re-visionism. I cannot let that stand, because it isn't true. Yes, we had grain credits for Iraq, and there isn't any evidence that those grain credits were diverted into weaponry, none, none whatsoever. And so I just have to say it's fine. You can't stand there, Governor Clinton, and say, 'Well, I think I have supported the minority—let sanctions work or wish that it would go away—but I would have voted with the majority.' Come on, that's not leadership."

The debate ended five minutes later. All in all, it was not the way George Bush would have wanted to discuss Iraq in the final minutes of the final debate of his final election.

•   •   •

On November 3, Bill Clinton was elected president, winning a 43 per-cent plurality in the three-way race. For George Bush it was a bitter dis-appointment, one that would trigger a long period of introspection and second-guessing within the Bush inner circle. But this second-guessing was nothing compared to that which would take place within the larger Republican Party.

Saddam had proved to be so skilled at timing his provocations to ex-ploit Bush's political vulnerability that many soon were asking if the United States had won a great military battle in the Gulf but perhaps lost the war. Against the backdrop of withering criticism over its apathy in Bosnia, failing domestic policies, and a formidable presidential chal-lenger, the Bush White House found itself unable to muster the will, or the allies, to mount an effective response to Saddam's defiance. The once-mighty Bush foreign policy machine had suddenly appeared impo-tent in responding to major international security crises. The time was right, and Saddam knew it. An emboldened Saddam took note, hedged his bets, and began defying the world.

The bitter conclusion that many would draw was that Saddam Hussein may have lost the Gulf War, but he had "won the peace." Within the Republican Party, some officials quietly began to question whether a "Realist" approach to managing the Gulf crisis had yielded an unmanageable and politically damaging outcome. As a result, onetime "true believers" in Realpolitik would steadily become "converts" to the cause of regime change in Iraq.

And Dick Cheney had drawn his own conclusion from 1992. If ever a confrontation with Saddam Hussein became necessary again, it would be best not to do it in an election year.

10

THE OLD GUARD DIES,
BUT DOES NOT SURRENDER

On January 20, 1993, only minutes before Marine One arrived at the White House for the final flight that all presidents dread, George Bush honored a long-standing tradition among the small fraternity of former presidents by leaving a quick note to his successor, Bill Clinton. "You won't have any trouble from me," Bush assured the incoming president in his brief missive.

The other senior figures of the Bush administration had made no such promise. And far from slipping quietly into private life, the fiercely loyal cast of advisers who had shared the world stage with George Bush would continue to advocate a vision of U.S. foreign policy that reflected their own beliefs—beliefs inevitably at odds with those of the Clinton White House. Over the eight years of the Clinton presidency, these individuals' dislike of President Clinton would coalesce into something more: a virtual government-in-exile, with its own policy positions, clearly defined roles, and designated spokespersons. This shadow administration capitalized on a complex network of friendly editorial pages, think tank affiliations, and Capitol Hill alliances to advance its cause during nearly a decade spent out of power.

Two attributes defined the Bush inner circle during this period and kept them united during what were for them wilderness years. The first was a visceral loathing of President Clinton that went far beyond the usual antipathies of Washington politics. To the veterans of the first Bush White House, the new president's perceived ineptitude in world affairs threatened to undo what they saw as their own uninterrupted string of foreign policy achievements. The second attribute was the unusual degree of cohesion among those who had held senior foreign policy posts during the Bush years. To an extent unprecedented in American history, the members of a defeated administration remained in constant close contact with each other and astonishingly disciplined in the policies they continued to articulate—almost as if they expected to return to power one day. Many were indeed seeking to position themselves for future Republican administrations, in the time-honored Washington way. Never before, though, had such a large group of senior officials from a previous administration remained so focused in their opposition, and over so long a period of time.

Both of these attributes—strident contempt for Bill Clinton, and extraordinary internal cohesion even as an opposition faction—sustained the Republican shadow government through eight long years of rule by a popular, politically canny Democratic president. However, the Republican establishment that emerged eight years later was very different from the Republican cohort that had served in the first Bush administration. Instead of reflecting the cautious, Vietnam-tempered worldview of former President Bush and his contemporaries, the new thought leaders of Republican foreign policy had been shaped most of all by their participation in the early successes of the Bush administration, and by the experience of being in opposition during the Clinton years. Supreme self-assurance in the rightness of their own vision of the U.S. national interest, coupled with a reflexive hostility to Bill Clinton's policy positions, became the animating spirit of their policy. The consequences of this transformation within the Republican establishment, for both American foreign policy and the Republican Party itself, would not become fully apparent until the unexpected accession of George W. Bush returned them once again to power.

●   ●   ●

No incumbent president likes to lose his bid for a second term, but George Bush took his defeat in 1992 especially hard. Longtime acquaintances of the president, even those familiar with his melancholic side, were shocked at his listless demeanor during his final two and a half months in office as a lame duck.

The mood in the West Wing during this period was equally funereal.

Many White House staffers were not only mourning the imminent loss of their own jobs, they were also mourning with George Bush over the loss of his. Unusual for an occupant of the Oval Office, Bush had been almost universally adored by his staff. His innate courtesy and gravitas had defined for many of them how a president should look and act. "He just exuded a sense of presidential and American leadership," Richard Haass would say years later, struggling to put into words how he felt about Bush after serving through all four years of the Bush presidency. "The best of presidential and the best of American." There was a palpable sense of lost opportunity among the Bush foreign policy team. Most of the president's advisers shared his sentiment that the American electorate had not given the Bush administration sufficient credit for its skillful handling of the Cold War in Europe, and above all, for marshaling the nations of the world to liberate Kuwait.

Fortunately, the Kuwaitis themselves knew that they owed their country to George Bush, and in the spring of 1993 they wanted to show their thanks. The emir of Kuwait invited the former president, his entire family, and the principal officials of his administration during Desert Storm for a three-day celebration in Bush's honor, to be held in Kuwait City from April 15 to 18.

The invitation was exactly the restorative that Bush needed. For the first time since the election, he returned to his usual gregarious self: ironing out the details of the trip with the Kuwaiti embassy and his Secret Service detail, working the phones with family and friends to invite them along, calling his many acquaintances in the Persian Gulf to inform them that he was visiting the region. It was perhaps an indication of how much those who loved George Bush had been worried about his emotional state of mind after the election that the entourage accompanying the former president was an unusually large one. Besides Barbara Bush and Brent Scowcroft, his two inseparable companions, it included Bush's sons Marvin and Neil, Neil's wife Sharon, and Laura Bush, the wife of George W. Bush, who would not be making the trip. A number of Cabinet officials from the Gulf War—including James Baker and John Sununu—also accompanied the former president.

Bush was greeted like a rock star in Kuwait. Crowds of people lined the route of his motorcade, strewing flowers in his path in the same way that the citizens of Kuwait City had on the day they were liberated. Bush was visibly moved by the display of gratitude. He reveled in every minute of the first two days, speaking with hundreds of dignitaries from Kuwait and the other Gulf countries, clearly back in his element.

On the final day of his visit, Bush was awarded an honorary degree at Kuwait University. Just hours before the former president was scheduled to accept his degree, Kuwaiti security forces intercepted an Iraqi national named Wali al-Ghazali near the university's campus, driving a sport utility vehicle outfitted as a massive truck bomb. Among other incriminating items, al-Ghazali carried on his person a map of the building in which Bush was to speak. Under rigorous interrogation, al-Ghazali confessed that the plot to assassinate Bush, much of his family, and several of his former Cabinet colleagues had been conceived by the Mukhabarat—Iraq's secret intelligence service.

The Clinton administration took the news of Iraq's involvement in the plot to assassinate George Bush seriously. More than the strong trail of circumstantial evidence pointing back to Iraq, intelligence experts agreed, the shocking nature of the planned crime itself bore Saddam Hussein's distinctive signature. A defining trait of Saddam's psychotic personality was his tendency to personalize conflicts against his enemies. Consequently, when Saddam took revenge against an enemy who had threatened his rule, it was not enough for him merely to torture or kill the enemy alone. Rather, the Iraqi dictator had an almost primal need to take revenge against an enemy's extended family or clan: having his security forces kill a man's sons or rape his wife and daughters before executing him was standard practice for Saddam. It was this same instinct that had led Saddam to order the murder of five thousand male members of the Barzani clan as an object lesson to Kurdish leader Massoud Barzani during the 1987 Kurdish rebellion.

Few nations, or even terrorist groups, would dare risk making an assassination attempt on a former U.S. president; the potential retribution for doing so was just too great. But there was only one nation that would try to wipe out a former president's entire family as well.

President Clinton discussed options for punishing Iraq with his new national security adviser, Anthony Lake. A genial man with a scholarly mien, Lake looked the part of the New England college professor and gentleman farmer he had once been. Lake had begun his career in government as a Foreign Service officer during the 1960s, when he had served at the U.S. embassy in Saigon at the height of the Vietnam War. Both he and Clinton were outraged at the planned attack and agreed that a strong message needed to be sent to Saddam Hussein.

They also agreed that given the unusually serious threat against the life of a former U.S. president, it would be appropriate to share the best available intelligence on the incident with George Bush himself. Lake had known his predecessor as national security adviser, Brent Scowcroft, since the 1960s, when the two men had worked together in the Nixon administration. They had since encountered each other at a number of academic foreign policy conferences. While they worked for different political parties, Lake enjoyed a cordial relationship with his Republican counterpart: They shared the same cautious, moderate worldview.

With President Clinton's approval, Lake contacted his predecessor and offered to set up a special intelligence briefing on the incident for Scowcroft and Bush. Both men, obviously, were cleared to see even the most sensitive raw intelligence data. After Scowcroft had consulted with Bush, the offer was declined. Lake was surprised. George Bush's extensive background in intelligence was well known, as was Scowcroft's intense interest in all matters pertaining to national security. The national security adviser had been expecting Bush and Scowcroft to leap at the opportunity to be brought "into the loop."

On June 26 the United States launched two dozen Tomahawk cruise missiles against the headquarters of the Mukhabarat in downtown Baghdad. The building was leveled to the ground, destroying many of the Iraqi government's espionage files. As far as is known, Saddam Hussein got the message: Iraq made no further attempts to take revenge on the Bush family. Nevertheless, for years afterward, some Republican pundits close to the former president would complain about Bill Clinton's "weak" response to the attempt on his predecessor's life.

.   .   .

Saddam Hussein had one thing in common at least with George Bush: Like the former president, the Iraqi dictator viewed his legacy in terms of the 1991 Gulf War. For Saddam, however, the Gulf War had never ended, and its final outcome remained very much in doubt. After Iraq had walked out of the UN Boundary Commission talks in July 1992, it had never returned to the talks. The Iraqi regime had also never renounced its territorial claims to Kuwait.

Saddam had witnessed firsthand in 1992 that the White House—any White House—was at its most vulnerable in the months preceding an election. His first "across the board" challenge to the will of the international community in July of that year had been timed to capitalize on a Bush White House distracted by a reelection campaign in free-fall and by the crisis in Bosnia. As the fall 1994 midterm elections in the United States approached, Saddam believed that it was time to test the resolve of the United States once again.

The Clinton administration had been in political trouble almost from its first days in power. The Clinton domestic agenda had been derailed by the failure of the president's health care initiative and by a financial scandal surrounding the White House Travel Office. In the foreign policy realm, the continuing ethnic warfare in the Balkans still occupied much of the West's attention, and there was still no concerted response from the United States and its NATO allies. On October 3, 1993, Somali insurgents shot down two U.S. Army Blackhawk helicopters in Mogadishu, where President Bush had dispatched a large U.S. peacekeeping force the previous year to provide humanitarian aid during a famine. Eighteen American soldiers were killed, with some having their dead bodies dragged through the streets of the Somali capital. The remaining 30,000 U.S. troops in Somalia had been withdrawn by the Clinton administration soon after, creating the impression that the United States had been driven out of Somalia by tribesmen armed with rifles and a few rocket-propelled grenades.

The Republicans were poised to make major gains in the November 1994 election. Throughout that autumn the American media was filled with commentary on the president's political troubles. Saddam thought he smelled weakness.

On October 2, 1994, the U.S. intelligence community observed a disturbing series of developments along the Iraqi border with Kuwait. In an eerie reprise of Iraqi troop movements in the weeks preceding the 1990 invasion of Kuwait, 80,000 Iraqi troops—including two full Republican Guard tank divisions—were deployed along with all of their equipment to a marshaling area just north of the border. The deployment of 80,000 Iraqi troops and hundreds of tanks to the Kuwaiti border was a real and imminent threat to Kuwaiti security. Even after the massive destruction of Iraqi military equipment during Desert Storm, Iraq still maintained the largest and most powerful army in the Gulf region. Despite being chastened by the 1990 invasion, Kuwait was still far too weak militarily to stop a serious assault by the heavy mechanized forces of the Republican Guard.

In Washington, the threat that Saddam Hussein might try to invade Kuwait again was seen as serious. At the time the only American forces in the Gulf region were the U.S. Air Force units based in Saudi Arabia, and a small training detachment of the U.S. Army in Kuwait itself. Neither would be enough to stop Iraq's armored divisions on the border if Saddam were actually intent on invading Kuwait. Accordingly, on October 14 the United States launched Operation Vigilant Warrior, a rapid deployment of ground troops and aircraft to the Kuwaiti theater. Besides dispatching the 24th Mechanized Infantry Division of Desert Storm fame back to Kuwait, the Clinton administration also dispatched several hundred fresh combat aircraft to the Gulf, including tank-killing A-10 Warthogs.

Vigilant Warrior was a success. Saddam Hussein soon withdrew his forces from along the border, and on December 21 Vigilant Warrior was officially terminated, having served its purpose. But CENTCOM and the White House had been sufficiently concerned that they took precautions for the future. For the first time, U.S. Army units were deployed to Kuwait on a permanent basis—5,000 American troops to act as a "trip-wire" force in the event that Iraq crossed the border. Some A-10 squadrons were also rotated to Kuwait on a permanent basis.

Naturally, though, the entire episode reopened the debate on whether the Bush administration had made the right decision by not going to Baghdad and leaving Saddam Hussein in power after the Gulf War. Although Saddam's continuing designs on Kuwaiti territory were well known to officials of both parties in Washington, until Vigilant Warrior most Americans had not been aware that even after Desert Storm, Iraq remained a serious conventional threat to the security of the Gulf region. Former members of the Bush national security team suddenly found themselves subjected once again to sharp criticism over their handling of the Gulf War's aftermath.

In response, those officials most loyal to former President Bush mounted a spirited campaign in leading editorial pages to defend Bush's decision not to topple Saddam Hussein. One of these was Richard Haass. On October 12, Haass wrote in the *Washington Post:* "What are the consequences of this history for the present? If we use force against Iraq, the temptation will arise to make the removal of Saddam Hussein a specific objective. Like most temptations, it should be resisted. The problem is not one of desirability but feasibility. Again, it is not possible to design a military operation at an affordable cost that would achieve this goal. We cannot sustain—politically, economically or militarily—an operation in Iraq that sets as its goal a change of regimes, not any more today than three and a half years ago."

Haass suggested an alternative strategy. "If Iraq invades Kuwait," he wrote, "a more appropriate and achievable objective would be the destruction of much of what remains of Iraq's military capability—its aircraft, tanks, artillery and command and control—and not just those forces near Kuwait. This could be carried out using aircraft and cruise missiles. The result would be an Iraq led by Saddam unable to threaten its neighbors—and possibly a Saddam too weak to hold on to power."

●   ●   ●

The Republican landslide came two years too late to help George Bush. On November 6, 1994, the Republican Party captured both houses of Congress in a historic electoral victory. Republicans took eight new seats in the Senate, regaining control for the first time since the mid-1980s. But the more epochal transformation took place in the House. With a loss of 54 seats, the Democrats lost control of the chamber for the first time in forty years.

The undisputed architect of the Republican triumph was Newt Gingrich, who was suitably rewarded by his colleagues by being elected the new House Speaker. Gingrich had been the driving force behind the creation of the Contract with America, a campaign manifesto of ten "promises to the American people" that had essentially turned the 1994 election into a national referendum on the Clinton administration's policies. The American electorate had resoundingly rejected the Clinton administration's policies. Even the Democrats in Washington were marveling at how successfully Gingrich and the Republicans had succeeded in nationalizing the 1994 election.

The ten promises contained within the Contract with America reflected traditional Republican concerns on social and economic policy: lower taxes, less crime on the streets, more religion in public life. Perhaps the most controversial plank was its sole foreign policy provision. The Contract with America called for passage of a "National Security Restoration Act," which would forbid U.S. troops from serving under UN command and cut American payments to the United Nations, especially the peacekeeping budget. That was it as far as foreign policy was concerned: nothing about Saddam Hussein; nothing about the Balkans; nothing about the Middle East peace process; nothing about America's relations with superpowers like Russia or China; nothing about the proliferation of weapons of mass destruction, whether in Iraq or elsewhere; nothing about the growing terrorist threat to the United States during the 1980s and early 1990s.

In its heavy emphasis on domestic concerns over foreign policy, the Contract with America reflected a striking transformation taking place within the Republican Party. For decades the Republican leadership in Congress had been dominated by traditional "Main Street" Republicans from the American heartland: men like Senator Bob Dole of Kansas, or Congressman Bob Michel of Illinois. These individuals were more attached to Congress as an institution than to any specific ideology or set of policies. In domestic policy they sought bipartisan consensus with their Democratic counterparts. In foreign policy they exhibited the cautious internationalism of the Greatest Generation, to which nearly all of them belonged. Most had served overseas in the U.S. military during the Second World War; some, like Dole, were highly decorated heroes from that conflict.

The new Republican majority was far younger, far more Southern, and far more politically conservative than the Republican opposition it had replaced. The new majority believed they had been elected to stage a Republican revolution in Washington, not to master the arcane traditions of the Capitol building. Many of the new Republicans on Capitol Hill were young enough to have avoided Vietnam entirely; and most of those who had not been young enough had received deferments. Never before had the American people elected a congressional majority so few of whose members had served in the military. Perhaps the most striking attribute of the new House membership, though, was its startling lack of familiarity with the world outside America's borders. Fully a third of the new Republican House members had never set foot outside the United States. In the main, many of them considered that a good thing; or if not, then certainly not a deficiency to be rectified. The deep suspicion of the UN reflected in the Contract with America was an accurate reflection of these individuals' deep distrust of the foreign, in all senses of that term. Still, overall it was a sanguine and self-confident group. Given all that they would face over the next decade, they would need to be.

The lack of substantive knowledge about world affairs within the new Republican caucus did arouse the concern of some, however. Anthony Lake, for one, recognized that conducting a bipartisan foreign policy would be tough sledding with the new Congress. Lake was concerned enough that he raised the issue with the one person who was perhaps in a position to do something about it: Newt Gingrich. Although the two men were worlds apart in political ideology, Lake had always respected Gingrich's intellect and openness to creative thinking. Unlike many in his caucus, the House speaker himself was deeply interested in broad international trends, with a particular penchant for the futurist writings of Alvin Toffler.

As tactfully as he knew how, Lake proposed that the Clinton NSC staff and the House Republican leadership might conduct a series of seminars for the new membership of the House, to familiarize them with key issues facing U.S. foreign policy in various parts of the world. Somewhat to Lake's surprise, Gingrich was not only open to the suggestion; he was enthusiastic about it. It turned out that Gingrich harbored his own concerns about the lack of international experience among some of his own members and had been thinking of putting together an orientation program similar to what Lake was proposing. Gingrich promised to take up the issue within the Republican caucus at the first opportunity.

For all their knowledge about world affairs, perhaps both men were a little naïve about human nature. When the possibility of discussing foreign policy with the staff of the Clinton White House was raised in caucus, the House Republicans angrily kiboshed the very notion.

* * *

The foreign policy issue that dominated the 1992 Clinton campaign had not been Iraq, but Bosnia. Reflecting the deep concern that the Bush administration's failure to respond to the "ethnic cleansing" of Bosnia had raised in many quarters of the Democratic Party, Bill Clinton had made U.S. military intervention to end the genocide in the Balkans one of the central planks of his foreign policy platform.

In an October 1992 speech to the Institute of World Affairs in Milwaukee, Clinton had said: "When I argued that the United States, in cooperation with international community efforts, should be prepared to use military force to help the UN relief effort in Bosnia, Mr. Bush's spokesman quickly denounced me as reckless. Yet, a few days later the administration adopted the very same position. While the administration goes back and forth, more lives are being lost and the situation grows more desperate by the day."

Once in office, however, the Clinton administration backed away from its pledge to intervene. Especially after the debacle at Mogadishu, the administration had grown skittish about U.S. intervention in the midst of sectarian conflicts. Compounding the president's difficulties in contemplating the use of force was his uneasy relationship with the U.S. military. Bill Clinton had never served in the military, and his Vietnam draft history was well known to the American public—indeed, it had been one of the major issues of the 1992 campaign. As the historian David Halberstam memorably phrased it, even his salute was sloppy. Clinton had retained Colin Powell as chairman of the Joint Chiefs of Staff, in the hopes that the presence of the most popular American military leader since Eisenhower would enhance his standing on military issues. During the first months of his presidency, however, the president experienced a public falling-out with Powell over his controversial proposal to allow openly gay people to serve in the U.S. military, an initiative that Powell adamantly opposed.

As a result, during the first two years of the Clinton presidency, U.S. policy in the Balkans remained largely a continuation of the Bush administration's earlier hands-off policy. The UN had thus taken the lead in the Balkans, creating "safe havens" protected by a small force of UN peacekeepers in a number of Balkan towns. But just as with the safe havens that had been created in the Kurdish areas of northern Iraq after the Gulf War, safe havens in Bosnia were intended only as a temporary expedient, and were truly "safe" only as long as the international community was committed to protecting them.

In June 1995, Bosnian Serb forces launched a major new offensive against the Muslim community in Bosnia, with the goal of bringing their "ethnic cleansing" of Bosnia to its final conclusion. On July 6 the Bosnian Serbs began laying siege to the safe haven in the town of Srebrenica, and started shelling the town and the outmanned garrison of Dutch UN peacekeepers defending it. As over 40,000 Muslims from the surrounding areas crowded into the Srebrenica safe haven, the commander of the Dutch garrison beseeched NATO for air support and additional troops, to no avail. On July 11 the commander of the Bosnian Serb militia, Gen. Ratko Mladić, met with the Dutch commander and demanded that the Dutch peacekeepers abandon the town. He also demanded that the unarmed Muslims of Srebrenica surrender themselves into his custody.

On July 16 the last Dutch troops withdrew. The female residents of the town were bused away. During the week that followed, Bosnian Serb troops killed at least 7,000 unarmed Muslim male prisoners.

The dramatic ten-day standoff at Srebrenica dominated news coverage night after night in Western Europe and the United States. It was the most serious escalation of the Balkan conflict since the outbreak of ethnic cleansing in the summer of 1992. Nevertheless, despite the fact that news of mass executions of Muslim civilians was being reported as early as July 16 by the BBC and other global news networks, neither the United States nor the European Union could muster the political will for military intervention.

*   *   *

Just as he had in 1992, Saddam Hussein saw in the West's distraction with the Balkans a perfect occasion to challenge the will of the international community to continue sanctions and weapons inspections against Iraq. And just as in 1992, he waited barely twenty-four hours for word of a mass slaughter in Bosnia to reach the West before striking. Conveniently for Saddam, the Bosnian Serbs had chosen to begin their mass killing of Srebrenica's Muslims twenty-four hours before Iraq's National Day.

On July 17, 1995, Saddam made his customary televised speech to the Iraqi people to celebrate the anniversary of the Ba'ath Party's rise to power. As in each of the previous five years, the speech furnished the occasion for the Iraqi dictator to lay down a defiant ultimatum. This time Saddam threatened to end all cooperation with UNSCOM weapons inspections unless all UN sanctions against Iraq were lifted within a month. It was a farcical demand, which the UN promptly rejected. But as events soon revealed, Saddam had good reason for wanting an end to UN weapons inspections in Iraq.

Sometime during the evening of August 6, Saddam's son-in-law Hussein Kamel defected from Iraq by slipping across the Jordanian border with Saddam's daughter in tow. On August 8, Kamel appeared on Jordanian television calling for a national uprising against his father-in-law. For Saddam, it was a serious blow, and not only because Kamel was family. Hussein Kamel had been the de facto head of Saddam's so-called Concealment Committee, whose name was an accurate description of its sole purpose: to conceal Iraq's WMD programs from UNSCOM. The committee's work was so important to Saddam that it could have been entrusted only to a family member. That made Kamel's defection all the more damaging.

The Iraq regime made a clumsy attempt at damage control by turning over a large cache of WMD-related documents to UNSCOM, claiming that they had been hidden by Kamel himself. But Kamel was quite simply "the man who knew too much." In extensive debriefings with UNSCOM officials over the next four months, the Iraqi defector revealed the sorts of secrets that only an insider would know about the true extent of Saddam's nuclear, chemical, and biological weapons research.

It was perhaps the busiest and most productive four months of UN nonproliferation efforts during the entire post–Desert Storm period.

.   .   .

It was also a busy autumn for William Kristol. In September 1995, Kristol had launched a new political magazine, *The Weekly Standard*, with longtime Washington political pundit Fred Barnes. In some respects Kristol was returning to his family's roots. His father, Irving Kristol, had for many years been editor of *Commentary*, perhaps the most respected monthly journal of conservative thought in America, which was read by academics and lay readers alike.

Kristol had a very different model in mind for his new magazine. In article length and tone, if not in editorial outlook, *The Weekly Standard* was intended to offer a neoconservative alternative to *The New Republic*, Martin Peretz's liberal-leaning publication. Kristol of course knew Peretz and many of the editors at *The New Republic* well. Having done both his undergraduate work and doctoral work in government at Harvard, he had more than once locked horns in a good-natured way with Peretz and some of his editors in seminars and at speaker events.

Still, Kristol had always been impressed by the platform that *The New Republic* had provided for Peretz to advance his political views. During the 1992 election the magazine's sharp critiques of the Bush White House, especially its policies in Iraq and Bosnia, had played no small part in helping elect the Clinton-Gore ticket. It was well known in Washington that *The New Republic* was avidly read inside the Clinton White House, despite the fact that the magazine's coverage of President Clinton was by no means always flattering. Why couldn't a similar magazine exist for sophisticated political commentary by neoconservatives? Kristol had asked himself.

While *The Weekly Standard* was very much a labor of love for him, Bill Kristol was no dilettante. He was determined that the new magazine would be a success. Besides assembling a talented staff of contributors—including future *New York Times* columnist David Brooks, and John Podhoretz, son of *Commentary* founder Norman Podhoretz—Kristol and Barnes had secured a powerful financial backer: Rupert Murdoch, the

Australian media titan who owned the *New York Post* and the FOX television network. Murdoch was interested in assembling a collection of media properties in the United States that reflected his conservative political views, and *The Weekly Standard* fit nicely into his vision.

That same autumn, Kristol was also working on a publication for another magazine. Together with Robert Kagan, a fellow neoconservative and alumnus of the Reagan administration, Kristol had begun thinking about the long-term future of Republican foreign policy. The success of the Contract with America the previous year had set the domestic agenda for the Republican Party for years to come. But like Newt Gingrich, Kristol knew that the contract was light on foreign policy specifics. What was needed was a similar document to set the future foreign policy agenda for the GOP. The two neoconservative intellectuals set out to write one.

Because Kristol and Kagan wanted their foreign policy manifesto to receive the widest possible airing within Republican circles, they did not publish it in *Commentary*, or even in *The Weekly Standard*, many of whose readers would be fellow neoconservatives who already shared most of the authors' core beliefs. Instead, they published their essay in the March–April 1996 edition of *Foreign Affairs*, the nonpartisan magazine whose pages defined establishment opinion on U.S. foreign relations. The choice of publication hinted at their ambition for the piece. The two authors were not looking to offer an alternative to the Republican foreign policy mainstream; they were looking to define what the Republican foreign policy mainstream should be.

Titled "Towards a Neo-Reaganite Foreign Policy," the essay made no bones about its core argument: that the assertive foreign policy of the Reagan era had represented a golden age for the Republican Party in world affairs. In their view, Ronald Reagan's visionary attempts to promote democracy and American values throughout the world had directly led to the collapse of the Soviet empire and the emergence of the United States as the world's sole superpower. In case the reader missed the logical corollary, that there had been a falling off since then, Kristol and Kagan made the point explicit. While the Clinton administration came in for its share of criticism, Kristol and Kagan were equally harsh on the Bush administration, "where self-proclaimed pragmatists like James

Baker found it easier to justify the Gulf War to the American people in terms of 'jobs' than as a defense of a world order shaped to suit American interests and principles."

Rather than capitalizing on the historic opportunity represented by the end of the Cold War, the essay argued, the Bush and Clinton administrations had squandered it with a "tepid" foreign policy approach that did not reflect the transformed global landscape. Instead of relying on traditional Realist concepts like balance of power, the piece argued, the United States should pursue a form of "benevolent global hegemony" in which American military and economic predominance would be used "to preserve and enhance that predominance."

If the intention of the two authors had been to launch a debate on the future direction of Republican foreign policy, they succeeded. In the next issue of *Foreign Affairs*, the Letters to the Editor section was flooded with letters from members of the Republican Party's "Old Guard": officials who had served during the Nixon and Ford years, who represented the voice of traditional Republican foreign policy.

Nevertheless, the ideological battle had only just been joined. In a war of words that would play itself out in dozens of scholarly articles and op-ed pieces over the next decade, the two sides would come to attack each other's worldviews—and motives—in ever more acrimonious terms. For while it may have seemed to some like a highbrow intellectual feud among Republican foreign policy wonks, both sides correctly saw the contest as nothing less than a battle for the very soul of the Republican Party.

●   ●   ●

During the five years that followed the end of Desert Storm, the U.S. Air Force presence in Saudi Arabia had only grown in size and strategic importance. The need to maintain the no-fly zone in southern Iraq coupled with Saddam's frequent provocations along the border, such as his October 1994 deployment of eighty thousand troops near Kuwait, made the deterrence provided by American airpower more essential than ever.

The American presence in Saudi Arabia had taken on the trappings of a semi-permanent deployment. Air Force squadrons and personnel rotated in and out of Saudi Arabia on a routine basis. Because enforcing the no-fly zone was considered a combat duty assignment, it was an important ticket for Air Force pilots to punch in terms of career advancement. Many U.S. Air Force personnel no longer lived in temporary air-conditioned tents near the flight lines, as they had during the Gulf War. Instead, like the thousands of foreign contractors who worked in the Saudi oil industry, they were housed in large, self-contained apartment compounds on the outskirts of Saudi towns.

Saudi society had never reconciled itself to having an American military presence in the country. If anything, resentment of the United States had grown even more intense. Most knowledgeable observers agreed that it was only a matter of time before this resentment erupted into open violence.

In November 1995, five U.S. members of a joint military training mission with the Saudis were killed in a terrorist bombing. It was believed to be al-Qaeda's first terrorist operation against American military personnel. The following year, however, al-Qaeda was upstaged by an older terrorist foe of the United States. On June 25, 1996, the Iranian-inspired Hezbollah terrorist group detonated a large suicide truck bomb at the Khobar Towers residential complex outside Riyadh, which was being used to house U.S. Air Force personnel. Nineteen Americans were killed and 76 wounded in Hezbollah's most deadly attack against American service members since the 1983 bombing of the Marine barracks in Beirut.

Like al-Qaeda, Hezbollah claimed to be motivated by the presence of infidel Americans living near Islamic holy places. Not to be outdone, several months later Osama bin Laden issued a fatwa (religious decree)* calling on all Muslims to join in a jihad to drive the Americans out of Saudi Arabia.

.   .   .

That summer, the long-awaited coup attempt against Saddam Hussein by Iraq's generals finally took place. A new opposition group, al-Wifaq,

---

* This was a purely symbolic gesture, as only imams or scholars affiliated with certain Islamic educational institutions are permitted to issue a fatwa.

made up largely of Iraqi military officers who had grown disillusioned with Saddam, had been collaborating with the CIA for months on a bold plan to seize control of the army units and security forces based in the Iraqi capital. Unfortunately, as former Iraqi air force chief Arif Abd-al-Raqazz had glumly predicted to the Bush administration four years earlier, Saddam's internal security was simply too good for a military coup to work. In June 1996 the Mukhabarat got wind of the al-Wifaq plot and executed several hundred actual or suspected conspirators. Confident about the security of his grip on power, Saddam promptly ordered his government to start denying UNSCOM inspectors access to suspected weapons sites, for the first time since the Agriculture Ministry standoff in 1992.

Several months later a bitter armed conflict broke out between the two leading Kurdish factions: the PUK headed by Jalal Talabani and the KDP headed by Massoud Barzani. The issue was not Saddam Hussein, but control of the lucrative oil smuggling business along the border with Turkey, which was the main source of the Kurds' finances. Talabani's forces were gaining the upper hand until Barzani brought in an additional partner. In 1991 it had been Talabani who traveled to Baghdad to cut a deal with Saddam. This time it was Barzani. On August 17 he agreed to a cease-fire between the KDP and the regime in Baghdad in return for a promise from Saddam that the Iraqi army would attack Talabani.

The Iraqi dictator was as good as his word. On August 31 the Republican Guard crossed the 36th Parallel in Iraq (the boundary of the U.S.-patrolled no-fly zone in northern Iraq) and captured the key Kurdish town of Arbil, which was the center of Talabani's power base. Arbil was also the headquarters of the Iraqi National Congress, the main coalition of opposition groups in Iraq. That night Saddam's security forces executed over two hundred members of the Iraqi opposition captured in Arbil.

•   •   •

The Clinton administration was in a state of collective shock at what had happened inside Iraq. At the beginning of June there had actually been reason for optimism on the Iraq front, based on the imminent possibility of a military coup and the progress that had been made on weapons inspections the previous year. Just two months later, U.S. policy toward Iraq was in a shambles. The best opportunity in years for a coup against Saddam had been crushed; the Iraqi regime had initiated a major standoff with the UN over weapons inspections; the Kurds, the largest, best-armed, and most reliably anti-Saddam group in Iraq, were at each other's throats; and Saddam's Republican Guard troops had conducted a successful military operation in an area of Iraq that was supposedly off-limits to them.

Nevertheless, the administration recognized that it needed to take action, and fast. The best available military option was a major campaign of punitive air strikes against the Iraqi military, to be conducted by the U.S. aircraft based in Turkey and Saudi Arabia.

Unfortunately, there was more bad news to come: Both the Turks and the Saudis refused to allow offensive strikes to be launched against Iraq from the bases on their territory. The Turks, as always, were deeply concerned by any strife involving the Iraqi Kurds that might spill over onto their territory. The Saudi government was still reeling from the Khobar Towers bombing two months earlier and was looking to lower the profile of American forces in the kingdom. It was the first time that the Saudis had refused to allow the United States to strike Iraq from their territory.

Accordingly, President Clinton ordered the only feasible military option available to him. On the night of September 3, the United States launched forty Tomahawk cruise missiles at Iraqi air defense installations in the southern no-fly zone—five hundred miles from Arbil.

· · ·

The Republican-controlled Congress was also dismayed at what was happening. Some of the newer members of the Republican majority were openly calling for American military action to finish off Saddam once and for all. Democrats retorted by reminding them that it was George Bush who had left Saddam in power in the first place. Shortly after Congress returned from its Labor Day recess, several congressional committees convened hearings on U.S. policy in Iraq. Because the Republicans now controlled both houses of Congress and thus the hearings, the witnesses invited to testify had a decidedly Republican cast.

On September 12, former secretary of state James Baker was scheduled to testify before the Senate Armed Services Committee. A seasoned Washington hand, Baker knew from long experience the value of previewing his testimony by publishing it in major newspapers a few days in advance of his appearance. On September 10 he wrote an op-ed piece for the *New York Times* and other newspapers discussing the main issue that he planned to address at the hearings: defending the Bush administration from fresh charges that it had erred in not removing Saddam Hussein when it had the chance. Under the headline "On to Baghdad Would Have Been U.S. Disaster," the piece read:

> President George Bush's judgment to end the war when he did was the absolutely correct one—even with the benefit of 20/20 hindsight. For a host of reasons—strategic, political, military and diplomatic—the marching-to-Baghdad canard is as nonsensical now as it was then. All our political and war aims, as enunciated by the Bush administration throughout the crisis, had been achieved. Our strategic objective was accomplished: Kuwait was liberated, and Saddam's ability to threaten his neighbors in the future was substantially diminished.

Baker's article went on to enumerate in detail the five "compelling reasons" why the Bush administration's decision to stop the war had been the correct one: 1. loss of life; 2. military occupation; 3. bolstering Iran; 4. fracturing the Coalition; and 5. destroying the foundations for postwar peace.

In his Senate testimony, Baker further suggested that Bill Clinton was to blame for the outbreak of factional fighting between the Kurds. "This represents a defeat for U.S. policy that, like the demise of the Coalition, is attributable at least in part to a failure of leadership," Baker alleged.

One week later it was Paul Wolfowitz's turn to testify. On September 19 the former undersecretary of defense appeared before the Senate Foreign Relations Committee. Wolfowitz now occupied one of the most prestigious academic foreign policy jobs in Washington: dean of the

Johns Hopkins Nitze School of Advanced International Studies, the graduate program that trained many future U.S. diplomats. He had become a familiar sight testifying on Capitol Hill.

If anything, Wolfowitz was even more categorical than Baker in blaming Bill Clinton for the collapse of the Gulf War Coalition. Wolfowitz began his testimony with a ringing commendation of former president Bush's handling of the Gulf War. "The amazing Coalition that President Bush assembled to defeat Saddam Hussein and drive him out of Kuwait five years ago was built on the president's promise that we would finish the job of liberating Kuwait," he declared. "If the Saudis had not believed in that promise, they would never have agreed to the deployment of American forces because doing so entailed great risks for them." Wolfowitz said nothing about his own unease at the time over how the Gulf War had ended, or the failure of the Bush administration to respond to the humanitarian plight of the Iraqi Shi'ites and Kurds. Instead, Wolfowitz preferred to reserve all of his fire for the Clinton White House.

Deriding the Tomahawk strikes as "pinprick bombing attacks," he continued: "President Clinton and his aides have the audacity to claim that the events of the last three weeks have been a great foreign policy success and a demonstration of the president's ability to lead." The reality, Wolfowitz charged, was that the Clinton administration had "betrayed" the Kurds of northern Iraq by not intervening in the tribal feud between Talabani and Barzani over who would control the oil smuggling out of Iraq. The gist of Wolfowitz's argument was that by not doing so, the Clinton administration had lost some of America's most valuable allies in the struggle to topple Saddam.

The claim that it was Bill Clinton who had "betrayed" the Kurds was ironic. Indeed, Wolfowitz's next words could have just as easily been read as an indictment of the Bush administration's policy toward the Kurds five years earlier, in the aftermath of Desert Storm.

"They pretend that no promises were made to the people of northern Iraq or to the people whom we enlisted in the effort to oppose Saddam Hussein. Such statements go beyond merely auguring that nothing could be done to fulfill our promises. They claim that no promises were ever made. Such statements amount to simple betrayal, and that is one reason why the Coalition against Saddam Hussein is in tatters."

A week later Wolfowitz published a transcript of his testimony in the *Wall Street Journal* under the headline "Clinton's Bay of Pigs." At the end of the piece, Wolfowitz for the first time hinted that the strategy of containing Saddam Hussein in Iraq was not enough, and that the United States would need to move "beyond containment":

> Saddam Hussein is a convicted killer still in possession of a loaded gun and it's pointed at us. Saddam is driven by a thirst for revenge in his personal struggles with individuals . . . as well as with countries. He never forgets and is determined to get his enemies, however long it takes. Should we idly sit by with our passive containment policy, our inept covert operations, and wait till a man with large quantities of WMD and sophisticated delivery systems strikes out at us at a time of his choosing?

As always, though, George Bush's strongest partisan remained Brent Scowcroft. The former national security adviser was incensed that the breakdown of American policy in Iraq during the summer of 1996 had become a fresh occasion to criticize President Bush's war-termination strategy in the Gulf.

"We have been listening to the same sad refrain for five years," Scowcroft complained in a guest column for *Newsweek*. "If only George Bush had finished off Saddam Hussein when he had the chance at the end of the Gulf War, we wouldn't be in this mess today. There are two things wrong with this reinterpretation of history. The first is that we never had the objective of destroying Saddam's regime during Desert Storm. The second is that had we continued the war and overthrown Saddam, we might be worse off today."

Scowcroft elaborated on his second point. "If we had pressed on to Baghdad in 1991, we would have been on our own. And if we had succeeded in overthrowing Saddam, we would have confronted a choice between occupying Iraq with thousands of American troops for the indefinite future, and creating a gaping power vacuum in the Persian

Gulf for Iran to fill. There was no support among the American people for the first alternative in 1991, and even less so today."

·   ·   ·

There was also a presidential election under way in the autumn of 1996. The Republican candidate was Kansas senator Bob Dole, making his final run for the White House after thirty years in public life. The Senate majority leader and Republican warhorse had already announced that he was not running for reelection to the Senate. One way or another, this would be his last campaign.

Historians may one day remember the 1996 race as the most cordial presidential contest of the twentieth century. Certainly it was the least confrontational. Bill Clinton, apparently convinced that the only way he could lose the election was to be accused of showing insufficient respect for Dole's distinguished military service during World War II, went out of his way to praise Dole's war record at every opportunity. Bob Dole, apparently having been told by media consultants that his famously crusty demeanor was not a part of his appeal, went out of his way to smile at every turn. It made for an oddly discordant campaign.

On paper, there were significant differences between the candidates and their platforms, but one would have been hard-pressed to realize this from watching the three presidential debates. To a surprising degree, the two men found themselves agreeing with each other, especially on foreign policy questions. In a sense, Clinton had already neutralized Dole's most important foreign policy issue. During the three years following the outbreak of "ethnic cleansing" in the Balkans, Dole had been perhaps the most forceful advocate in the Senate of U.S. military intervention to end the genocide. It had not been a universally shared position, especially among Republicans. But the Kansas senator had persevered, first with George Bush and then with Bill Clinton, never abandoning the issue. At last, in autumn 1995, after the collapse of the UN safe havens policy at Srebrenica, the Clinton administration had negotiated the Dayton peace accord with the three warring republics of Serbia, Croatia, and Bosnia, bringing a temporary respite to the Balkans. As part of the Dayton accord, the United States had deployed twenty-five thousand peacekeeping troops to Bosnia. Some admirers of the Kansas Republican said that Dole had shamed the White House into finally doing something about "ethnic cleansing."

But with the Balkans temporarily at peace, there was little else to divide the two candidates in foreign policy. Both were innately cautious in their view of the world, especially where the use of American troops was concerned. And Dole offered the American electorate no stirring vision of the future; it was not his style. Support for his candidacy even among Republicans was more dutiful than enthusiastic.

The candidate himself sometimes seemed at a loss to explain how American foreign policy in a Dole administration would differ from that in a second Clinton administration. "There really are differences between us," Dole protested on one occasion. Even he did not sound convinced.

11

SPEAKING WITH TWO VOICES

After Bill Clinton's easy victory over Bob Dole in the 1996 election, the internal debate within GOP circles over the future direction of Republican foreign policy intensified and took on an entirely new cast.

To a large extent this development was a direct consequence of Clinton's mastery over the domestic political scene. After the 1994 Republican landslide, many within the GOP had been optimistic that a weakened Democratic Party in Congress would hamstring the president's 1996 reelection campaign. But threatened by a Republican ascendancy, Clinton rallied and showed why he was such a formidable politician. In rapid succession he co-opted Newt Gingrich by offering him a pseudo-presidential platform at their 1995 "summit" in New Hampshire; pushed for the rapid negotiation of the Dayton peace accord in the Balkans; and handily won a budget showdown with the Republican Congress by briefly allowing a government shutdown to occur.

The constant tailwind to all of these political victories was the explosive growth of the U.S. economy. Partly because of the Internet boom, and partly because the Clinton White House had finally closed the budget deficits of the Bush years, the U.S. economy now entered the greatest sustained period of growth in its history. Bill Clinton had waged his 1992 campaign on the mantra, "It's the economy, stupid," to highlight the sluggish performance of the economy under President Bush. Now, amidst the unprecedented prosperity of the late 1990s, the mantra took on an entirely new meaning.

1997 was a very bad year for the Republicans, but a very good year for

President Clinton. America was at peace, and ordinary Americans were optimistic about the future. The scandals that had plagued the Clinton White House in its early years appeared to have dissipated. The two major international crises that had been boiling since the end of the Bush years—Iraq and the Balkans—had both entered a quiet phase. The Clinton administration was finally devoting attention to its two main foreign policy priorities: improving relations with Russia, and crafting a comprehensive peace settlement between Israel and the Palestinians. Progress was being made in both areas, the latter thanks to Dennis Ross, who was now serving as the president's chief Middle East envoy. President Clinton's approval rating hovered near 60 percent. The Nasdaq that year gained 22 percent; it would gain nearly twice that in 1998, and an astonishing 85 percent in 1999.

Many Republicans were frustrated and demoralized. The prospect of four more years out of power was a dreary and disquieting one to them. How to create the conditions for an eventual Republican restoration was the question of the hour. They could hardly fault the president on his stewardship of the American economy. They turned, then, to his stewardship of American foreign policy, and to the theme that the Clinton administration was failing to confront the emerging national security threats of tomorrow.

·　　·　　·

On June 3, William Kristol announced the opening of a new think tank in Washington. The Project for a New American Century (PNAC to its friends) had a list of backers almost as impressive as its somewhat grandiose name. Among those who signed PNAC's "Statement of Principles" that day were former defense secretaries Dick Cheney and Donald Rumsfeld; former vice president Dan Quayle; Jeb Bush; Steve Forbes; and a veritable *Who's Who* of Washington neoconservatives, including William Bennett, Zalmay Khalilzad, Lewis "Scooter" Libby, and Paul Wolfowitz.

PNAC had been Kristol's brainchild, intended to become a neoconservative policy shop similar to the much larger American Enterprise Institute. Unlike AEI, however, PNAC would focus exclusively on national security policy. It was intended to become a center of policy research for the "neo-Reaganite" foreign policy that Kristol had called for in his essay with Robert Kagan the previous year. The Statement of Principles made PNAC's intellectual debt to the Reagan years explicit:

> We seem to have forgotten the essential elements of the Reagan Administration's success: a military that is strong and ready to meet both present and future challenges; a foreign policy that boldly and purposefully promotes American principles abroad; and national leadership that accepts the United States' global responsibilities.
>
> Such a Reaganite policy of military strength and moral clarity may not be fashionable today. But it is necessary if the United States is to build on the successes of this past century and to ensure our security and our greatness in the next.

The more assertive brand of foreign policy coming from some quarters of the Republican Party soon became apparent. During the first week of November, Saddam Hussein ordered the expulsion of all American officials from the UNSCOM teams conducting weapons inspections in Iraq. He also threatened to shoot down American U-2 spy planes conducting reconnaissance flights over Iraq to assist UNSCOM. Kristol and several other neoconservatives seized upon this latest outrage by the Iraqi dictator as an opportunity to broach publicly an idea they had long been discussing.

On November 9, 1997, Kristol and Zalmay Khalilzad published an editorial in the *Washington Post* beneath an eye-catching headline: "We Must Lead the Way in Deposing Saddam." The editorial marked the first time that a major Republican figure had openly called for the United States itself to topple the Iraqi regime through military action (as opposed to working through a surrogate like the Iraqi National Congress). Kristol provided a rationale for this policy in "Saddam Must Go," a longer article he and Robert Kagan wrote for *The Weekly Standard* the following week. The two neoconservatives were adamant that only a ground invasion could do the job. "The only sure way to take Saddam out is on the ground. We know it seems unthinkable to propose another ground attack to take Baghdad. But it's time to start thinking the unthinkable."

The article also crossed another line: For the first time, it assigned equal blame for the situation in Iraq to the Bush administration. Since the beginning of the Clinton years, it had been almost an unwritten rule among the Republican officials who had served under President Bush that while Bill Clinton's Iraq policy was fair game, it was not permissible to raise questions about George Bush's decisions in the aftermath of Desert Storm, only to defend them. But helping preserve George Bush's historical legacy was now the least of the two authors' concerns.

"It has become increasingly clear ever since the Gulf War ended that the Gulf War ended badly," they wrote. "The decision to leave Saddam in control of Iraq, and to hope vainly that he would be overthrown or assassinated by his own people, was a mistake. The only decent thing the former president could do under the circumstances, Kristol and Kagan suggested, was to apologize and "acknowledge his error."

The views expressed in "Saddam Must Go" reflected a far broader consensus within Republican foreign policy circles than had been previously thought. That became clear on January 26, 1998, when the Project for a New American Century released an "open letter" to President Clinton on the need to topple Saddam Hussein's regime. PNAC's letter ran as a full-page ad in the *New York Times*, the *Wall Street Journal*, and other major newspapers.

The letter repeated many arguments that Kristol and Kagan had made in their "Saddam Must Go" essay two months earlier. But while the letter may have been addressed to Bill Clinton, its real target was Republicans who still subscribed to the view that containment could work in Iraq.

The publication of this letter marked the beginning of an irreversible schism in Republican foreign policy ranks. It was one thing for a few neoconservative intellectuals to advance a provocative new approach to Iraq in the pages of *The Weekly Standard*. But running a full-page notice in major newspapers is quite another thing: a public and highly political act that cannot be ignored. For the first time, the wider American public became aware of serious divisions within the Republican Party over Iraq. More important than the content of the letter was the list of individuals who had signed it. Besides Kristol, Kagan, Khalilzad, Wolfowitz, and other prominent neoconservatives, there were some surprising names from the Republican mainstream: former defense secretary Donald Rumsfeld; Richard Armitage; and Robert Zoellick, Secretary of State James Baker's top aide during the Bush years, who had been assumed to share his boss's views on Iraq. Only the previous year Zoellick had seemed to offer a strong defense of the Bush administration's original decision to contain Iraq rather than march to Baghdad. "Having follow-up [policies] that constrained and limited Iraq were objectives that can, have been, and are continued to be achieved," he told one interviewer. "The potential implications of 'total victory' were outweighed by the risks and costs. I think the decision was right today as well, because, I think part of the challenge, that this is what life is about, is that one has to continue to box in Saddam Hussein. And that is a cheaper and less expensive choice than trying to conquer a country and occupy it."

Of course, the signatories to the PNAC letter still represented only a tiny minority of the Republican establishment. Few outside the charmed inner circle had even been asked to sign the letter. Richard Haass was friendly with several of the former Republican officials who signed the letter, but does not remember being approached about signing it himself.

"I remember talking about it," he recalls. "I knew about it, and I talked to several people who signed it, and I don't know if they assumed I wouldn't sign it, or I made it clear I wouldn't sign it." Haass personally thought the letter was a waste of time and a distraction from the true strategic issues with respect to Iraq. "The issue wasn't whether one wanted Saddam out—of course one did. My concern at the time was whether that was where to put the emphasis. If people were convinced that the ouster of Saddam was the U.S. aim, it concerned me that it would make it more difficult to get international support for all of the sanctions that were meant to be enforced.

"Secondly, it wasn't very clear to me that the United States had many tools available at the time, short of an all-out war and occupation of Iraq, that would enable us to realize that goal. So while I sympathized with the goal, I didn't understand it as a matter of policy."

The Clinton White House had more pressing concerns to worry about that week than unsolicited advice from the Republicans on how to deal with Iraq. The major news of the week was that President Clinton had been accused of misleading a federal grand jury about his relationship with a White House intern, Monica Lewinsky.

.   .   .

The two sides in the Iraq debate may have been the only people in Washington with something other than the Lewinsky scandal on their minds. On February 26, William Kristol and Robert Kagan had written on op-ed essay in the *Washington Post* declaring that the containment of Iraq was a failure. Resurrecting a favorite neoconservative hobbyhorse, the two authors also drew a comparison between the policy of containing Saddam Hussein and the policy of détente that Henry Kissinger had pursued with the Soviet Union during the 1970s. Among neoconservatives, "détente" was a dirty word.

But not among Realists. The next day James Baker furnished a quick rebuttal to Kristol and Kagan. "There is nothing wrong with containment of Iraq's weapons programs as a policy, provided that it is sufficiently robust and sustained," he wrote in the *New York Times*. "It worked against the Soviet Union for more than 40 years. It has worked against Saddam's conventional force, nuclear, chemical, and missile capabilities for the last seven years. It can be made to work against his biological weapons capabilities."

Brent Scowcroft was almost beside himself with anger. As a close associate of Kissinger throughout the entire eight years of the Nixon and Ford administrations—first as Kissinger's deputy national security adviser, later his peer as national security adviser under Gerald Ford—Scowcroft himself had been one of the architects of the détente policy. He had also, obviously, been the primary advocate of pursuing a containment strategy against Iraq after the Gulf War. In a real sense, Kristol and Kagan were denigrating the two most important policy initiatives of his career.

On March 1, Scowcroft wrote a *Washington Post* opinion piece denouncing their argument. He called his essay "The Power of Containment."

Scowcroft was especially annoyed that the two neoconservative authors had dredged up the old 1970s debate over détente to make their point. As Scowcroft well knew, William Kristol carried his own personal baggage from that debate: His father Irving had been one of the harshest critics of Kissinger and the détente policy. Scowcroft believed that the peaceful outcome of the Cold War had conclusively shown which side had been right in that debate.

"These critics argued that since a war was inevitable and containment only served to strengthen the position of our enemies, we should attack them preemptively and destroy them while we could. Our victory in the Cold War proved these critics wrong," he wrote. Scowcroft did not specify who the critics were, but both he and Bill Kristol knew who he was talking about. "And if containment could produce a peaceful end to the Cold War on our terms, surely it can be sufficient to deal with threats posed by Saddam Hussein."

Having defended his strategy for Iraq, Scowcroft now attacked Kristol and Kagan's as "a recipe for throwing the region into chaos of unknown dimensions, the outcome of which we cannot even dimly perceive beyond knowing that our national security interests would likely be gravely damaged."

·　　·　　·

President Clinton's legal troubles over the Monica Lewinsky incident continued to mount all through the summer of 1998. On August 6 the president testified to a federal grand jury and that evening made a televised statement apologizing to the American people.

It was a piece of immense bad fortune for Bill Clinton, the American people, and the world that al-Qaeda had already chosen the next day to stage its largest terrorist operation yet. On August 7, truck bombs were used to attack the U.S. embassies in Nairobi, Kenya, and Dar es Salaam, Tanzania. The Nairobi bombing was especially horrific, with 12 Americans and over 200 Kenyans killed; 5,000 were wounded.

There was absolutely no doubt in Washington over who was responsible: By coincidence, U.S. intelligence had been monitoring the communications of al-Qaeda's Nairobi cell. The Clinton White House ordered an attack on al-Qaeda's redoubt in Afghanistan. On August 20 the United States launched Tomahawk missiles at the Tarnak Farms complex in

Afghanistan and a chemical plant in the Sudan suspected of producing precursor chemicals for chemical weapons. Unfortunately, in light of President Clinton's legal troubles, many in the United States questioned the timing of the missile strikes. Late-night comedians made arch references to the 1997 Dustin Hoffman movie *Wag the Dog*, in which a scandal-plagued president launches a military operation overseas to divert attention from his problems at home.

Even the Taliban wanted to talk about Monica Lewinsky. On August 22, two days after the Tomahawk strikes on Tarnak Farms, the U.S. government had its one and only direct contact with the reclusive leader of the Taliban regime in Afghanistan, Mullah Omar. A senior official in the Clinton State Department was contacted by an intermediary, who asked if he wished to speak by phone with a "senior Taliban official." When the U.S. official cautiously said that he did, a conference call was arranged. Omar himself came on the line.

Omar said he had no specific message to convey to the U.S. government, just some general advice. Because of what Omar delicately termed Clinton's "domestic difficulties," the American Congress should force him to resign, the Taliban leader said, laughing mirthlessly. This would also improve America's standing with the Islamic world. He claimed there was no evidence that Osama bin Laden had committed terrorist acts from Afghan soil. Omar urged that the United States withdraw its forces from the Gulf region, since they were considered a threat to Islam's Holy Sites. If the United States did not withdraw, Omar claimed, the Saudi people would rebel against their government and force the Americans out.

•   •   •

In presidents, the perception of weakness invites challenges of many kinds. In Congress, House Republicans began drawing up plans to impeach Bill Clinton. Meanwhile, with a weakened president at the other end of Pennsylvania Avenue, the Republican majority in Congress now attempted to force passage of one of its most controversial pieces of legislation. The Iraq Liberation Act was intended to codify into U.S. law the desire among many in Congress for a regime change in Iraq. It called for the president to designate opposition groups in Iraq that were committed to the fall of Saddam Hussein as recipients of U.S. aid. It further called for the creation of a war crimes tribunal to try Saddam Hussein and other Iraqi officials for genocide and crimes against humanity. Finally, the act urged the U.S. government to support Iraq's "transition to democracy" after the fall of Saddam Hussein. Although the Iraq Liberation Act expressly forbade the use of the U.S. military to bring about the fall of Saddam Hussein, it was nonetheless a favorite pet issue among neoconservatives, because it finally made the fall of Saddam Hussein an explicit goal of U.S. foreign policy.

But many considered the act a mischievous and potentially dangerous piece of legislation. With the exception of making regime change in Iraq a formal requirement of U.S. foreign policy, there was nothing in the act that required a new law, critics charged. The United States already had plenty of overt and covert means for funneling aid to the Iraqi opposition—all of them legal. The convening body for a war crimes tribunal would be the UN or the International Court of Justice at The Hague, not the United States Congress. Finally, the suggestion that future U.S. administrations should support Iraq's "transition to democracy" was not even a requirement, but merely a "sense of the Congress" resolution that had been tacked on to the end of the bill. There was a danger that the language in the preface of the Iraq Liberation Act could be used to justify actions being taken against the Iraqi regime that were not actually contemplated by the act itself. For all of these reasons, the Clinton administration had opposed its passage.

However, with Bill Clinton's fate now in the hands of the Republican Congress, standing on these symbolic points was of minor concern to the White House. The president quietly withdrew his threat to veto the bill. On October 5 it passed in the House, and two days later it sailed through the Senate by a unanimous vote. On October 31, President Clinton signed it into law.

Saddam Hussein himself was apparently unconcerned by the provisions of the act. That month, he expelled the ten American members of an UNSCOM inspection team.

·   ·   ·

November 3, 1998, was election day in the United States. While most of the focus was on Washington, to see if voters would punish congressional Democrats at the polls for the president's difficulties, some Republicans could have been forgiven for paying more attention to the polls in Texas. At the Governor's Mansion in Austin, George W. Bush's campaign staff was anxiously waiting for results from the exit polls. Not to see if Bush would win reelection to a second term as governor—a landslide victory was assured for the popular incumbent—but to gauge the breadth of the governor's support among minority and independent voters.

By 9:00 P.M. the outcome was clear. George W. Bush had been elected to a second term by a historic margin. He had drawn unprecedented levels of support from across the political spectrum, even among traditionally Democratic constituencies. Bush's staff and supporters were ecstatic. After six years in the wilderness, the Republicans had finally found their champion.

●   ●   ●

UN weapons inspectors left Iraq during the second week of December 1998. They were not to return again for four years. On December 15 the head of UNSCOM, Australian diplomat Richard Butler (who had replaced Rolf Ekeus the previous year), reported to the Security Council that Iraq was engaged in a systematic attempt to interfere with inspections and mislead the international community about its WMD programs.

The following day, the Clinton administration ordered the launch of Operation Desert Fox, a four-day campaign of punitive air strikes. It was the largest air campaign against Iraq since Desert Storm. On the third day of Desert Fox, President Clinton made a national radio address to the American people, declaring that regime change in Iraq as described in the Iraq Liberation Act was now the official policy of the U.S. government. Ironically, that same day, former secretary of state Baker wrote an op-ed piece stating that Clinton had pursued the correct policy with Desert Fox, and reiterated that it would be a mistake to topple Saddam Hussein.

●   ●   ●

For George W. Bush, the 2000 presidential campaign kicked off in earnest on November 19, 1999. That evening the Texas governor addressed a standing-room-only crowd at the Ronald Reagan Library outside Los Angeles. The speech had been billed as Bush's first major address on foreign policy.

There was a good deal of curiosity about George H. W. Bush's son among the assembled Republican dignitaries, who included Nancy Reagan and former secretary of state George Shultz. It was obvious that many had come to kick the tires on the candidate. Many of those in the room either knew or had worked with his father at one time or another. The elder George Bush was a known commodity in foreign policy. His son had made an impressive record as a large-state governor, but his views on world affairs were largely unknown.

The audience was pleased by what they heard. Bush delivered a speech that reflected traditional Republican foreign themes. Most of his remarks were devoted to just two countries: Russia and China. Bush criticized some aspects of the Clinton administration's policy toward both nations and called for a more circumspect approach by the next administration. The rest of the speech was similarly restrained and sober—exactly the sort of speech that would resonate with the Republican power elite. Bush did not mention Iraq. Afterward he received a standing ovation from the crowd, as he had just passed an important test.

Bush's Reagan Library speech had been written by Condoleezza Rice. The former provost of Stanford University, now serving full-time as Bush's principal foreign policy adviser, the forty-five-year-old Rice was already a well-known figure in Republican foreign policy circles. The 2000 presidential campaign would be her national coming-out party.

Rice was a child of pre–civil rights Alabama, who had grown up in the shadow of the Birmingham church bombing—one of the most infamous terrorist acts ever perpetrated on American soil. A Democrat earlier in her career, she had been a prize pupil of Josef Korbel, the father of Clinton secretary of state Madeleine Albright, and had briefly worked for the presidential campaign of Gary Hart. Plucked from a junior faculty post at Stanford by Brent Scowcroft to become the Sovietologist on his NSC staff, she soon became a favorite of both Scowcroft and the elder George

Bush, who treated her more like an overachieving daughter than a junior NSC staffer.

Rice's meteoric rise within the councils of the Bush family was emblematic of both the strengths and weaknesses of her approach to foreign policy. Like virtually all of the rising young national security officials who had thrived during the first Bush administration, she had been an exceptionally disciplined thinker, adept at face-to-face diplomacy with foreign leaders and fiercely loyal to the former president. Rice espoused a dogmatic vision of balance-of-power politics that dovetailed perfectly with that of her bosses. As the Bush White House's Soviet expert during the watershed events that took place in the former Soviet bloc from 1989 to 1991, she would forever be associated with the end of the Cold War in Europe and the peaceful reunification of Germany: two of the great, unmitigated triumphs of twentieth-century American foreign policy. The importance of these issues at the beginning of George Bush's presidency had afforded Rice a priceless opportunity to see and be seen at the highest levels of his administration, leapfrogging her past more seasoned contemporaries and making her a member of the Bush family's private brain trust.

At the same time she could be impatient to the point of callousness with issues that fell outside her relatively narrow range of expertise. Rice had left government service after barely two years, leaving behind a trail of unalloyed accomplishments. Though she could not have known it at the time, this spared her from association with the meltdown of Bush administration policy in the Balkans during the disastrous summer of 1992—which, as the White House expert on East European security affairs, would have fallen squarely on her plate. Rice's apathy toward the ethnic conflict raging in the former Yugoslavia throughout the 1990s was as much a product of this fortuitous coincidence as it was of a worldview that saw "civil wars" and smaller countries as lesser concerns for a great power. She would later show the same impatience with the Clinton administration's fixation on a little-known terrorist faction called al-Qaeda.

Rice was the best-known member of an influential cadre of Republican foreign policy strategists who in the fall of 1999 took upon themselves the task of tutoring George W. Bush in the complex nuances of statecraft. Dubbed the Vulcans, this group was dominated by Rice herself and by Robert Zoellick, an attorney and former executive of the finance company Fannie Mae, who had been James Baker's top aide at the State Department. Together they were the outstanding figures from a generation of young holdovers from the first Bush administration—most of whom had been in their thirties at the time—who had played key roles in managing the end of the Cold War in Europe.

The beliefs of the Vulcans exerted an unusual degree of influence during the 2000 presidential campaign, owing to the younger George Bush's relative inexperience at world affairs. The candidate absorbed all of their pet themes and all of their prejudices: above all, an instinctive mistrust of any foreign policy initiative that had been undertaken by the Clinton White House. At this stage in his foreign policy education, George W. Bush's worldview could be distilled into a simple dichotomy: national interest *good*, nation-building *bad*. Egged on by the Vulcans, Bush would incessantly criticize the Clinton administration's intervention in the Balkans as a use of American military force that violated both precepts. Withdrawal of U.S. peacekeeping troops from the Balkans thus became one of the few points of differentiation in the foreign policy positions of Bush and his eventual opponent, Vice President Al Gore.

•   •   •

The cast of foreign policy advisers assembled by George W. Bush far outclassed the relatively unknown group advising Vice President Gore in name recognition and star power. Besides the Vulcans and Rice herself, already preselected to become national security adviser in a second Bush White House, it included former JCS chairman Colin Powell, former defense secretary Donald Rumsfeld, and Dick Cheney, whom Bush chose as his running mate.

Still, even surrounded by this glittering cast of luminaries, George W. Bush was widely expected to lose ground to Al Gore on the foreign policy issue. Both the vice president and his running mate, Senator Joseph Lieberman, were among the Democratic Party figures most knowledgeable about world affairs. Moreover, Gore was uniquely well positioned to criticize the first Bush administration's policies in such places as Iraq and

Bosnia. Not only had he been one of relatively few Democrats to support the Gulf War, but in the aftermath of Desert Storm, Gore had urged the first George Bush to pursue a more muscular containment of Saddam Hussein long before this issue became a Republican rallying cry. He and Lieberman had also been early advocates of U.S. action to end ethnic cleansing in the Balkans.

However, on foreign policy, as on so many other issues, Gore found himself constrained by his long association with Bill Clinton. To have pressed George W. Bush on crises that had been allowed to fester because of questionable decisions made by the first Bush administration would have meant attacking his opponent's father, at a time when the Clinton scandals had created a warm nostalgia for the dignified White House of the elder George Bush. The Gore campaign's failure to exploit the foreign policy record of an earlier Bush White House, combined with the relentless exertions of the Vulcans on George W. Bush's behalf, effectively neutralized what was to have been a decisive issue for the Democrats in the 2000 presidential election.

Less than one month before election day, al-Qaeda carried out a deadly bombing on the USS *Cole*, a U.S. warship making a port call in the Middle East. Distracted by the tightest presidential race in American history, neither candidate paid sufficient attention to this latest attack in an undeclared war against the United States. Less than a year later, one would have to.

＊　　　＊　　　＊

The 2000 presidential race ended in a contested outcome. For five weeks, partisans of both candidates watched breathlessly as the future direction of American history rested on the vagaries of hanging chads, then progressed through the courts. On December 16, George W. Bush emerged victorious.

For most Republicans it was a moment for celebration and restoration after eight long years shut out from the corridors of executive power.

For others, however, it was a time for reflection about the future ahead. Some in the new president's inner circle viewed the previous eight years as a historical accident, one that had interrupted the grand plans for a Republican future that had briefly glimmered in the early days following the 1991 Gulf War.

At a private dinner with a few close friends to celebrate his victory, Vice President–elect Cheney shared his belief that the Republican triumph in 2000 had opened up a whole range of new opportunities in foreign policy: opportunities to pursue a new vision of the future, and opportunities to settle scores with old enemies. Now was finally the time, Cheney concluded, to do something about Saddam Hussein.

12

UNFINISHED BUSINESS

Never had a new administration slipped so comfortably into the corridors of power. The national security team that George W. Bush brought with him in January 2001 was remarkable for its seasoning and breadth of experience. Individuals who had worked in two or more previous Republican administrations were the norm. Indeed, some senior officials could boast of foreign policy experience dating back to the 1960s.

Their task was clear in their own minds. They would bring procedural excellence, and if not conceptual brilliance then at least conceptual consistency, back to American foreign policy. Realism would reign supreme once again. The day-to-day grist of diplomacy would run flawlessly. All of the indignities—real or imagined—of the Clinton years would be put behind them, replaced by the formal, hierarchical style of policymaking to which this group of officials was accustomed. James Baker had once sneeringly characterized the Clinton White House as a place where "foreign policy was decided in late-night bull sessions over pizza." There would be none of that in *this* administration.

Because the national security team surrounding George W. Bush far overshadowed him in their substantive knowledge of world affairs, it was commonly assumed that the new president would be unduly influenced by these foreign policy veterans in his administration. But the common assumption was wrong. At the time of his inauguration, Bush knew exactly what he wanted in the international arena. He wanted his father's foreign policy: which is to say, a foreign policy in which the United States would have good relations with the "important" countries; in which

America would react decisively, even violently, to assaults on its citizens abroad; and most of all, a foreign policy in which "evil regimes" would be diplomatically isolated.

And the sense of gratitude felt toward the new president by the veterans of the first Bush administration who now occupied key posts in the present one—Dick Cheney, Colin Powell, and Condoleezza Rice foremost among them—was almost palpable. He was the unquestioned champion of their camp, in an almost Homeric sense. At a time when the Nasdaq had hovered near 5000; when Bill Clinton had stained the Oval Office only to see his approval ratings soar; when the world was seemingly at peace, and the American people had seemingly lost interest in the sort of great power diplomacy they longed to practice; George W. Bush had swaggered forth from his Texas ranch to avenge his father's loss—their loss—in 1992. He had outlasted their hated adversaries in the Clinton-Gore camp, and restored all of them to the life they loved like no other.

So much of their behavior toward the new president—their fierce protectiveness about his image, their lavish praise of virtues that went unnoticed by the larger public, their singular lack of humor about the shortcomings he did possess—were attributable to the gratitude they still felt for what the older Bush had accomplished. He was their Achilles; and they would form his phalanx, shields and spears pointed outward.

·　　·　　·

Among the first decisions faced by the new Bush White House was what to do about the archetypical evil regime, Saddam Hussein's Iraq. The president knew that regime change in Iraq was a bellwether issue for the neoconservative wing of the Republican Party, much of which had labored so tirelessly on his behalf during the recent election. And he had not forgotten that Saddam, as the president occasionally reminded audiences, "tried to kill my dad." George W. Bush himself, however, was not fixated on Saddam Hussein. Asked in a pre-inauguration interview with the New York Times whether Iraq had "bedeviled" his father's administration, Bush replied: "I wouldn't say it bedeviled the past Bush administration. I think the past Bush administration dealt with it very firmly and left a regime in place that isolated Saddam."

The younger Bush had campaigned on the idea of a "humble" foreign policy for the United States, and his natural instinct was one of retrenchment from overseas military commitments. This instinct was shared by most of the president's national security team. National Security Adviser Condoleezza Rice, his closest adviser on foreign policy matters, saw Iraq as a relatively minor issue compared to the reshaping of relations with Russia and China, whom Rice had labeled on numerous occasions a "strategic competitor" of the United States. An expert on strategic arms negotiations with the Soviets during the 1980s, she was also keenly interested in moving forward on national missile defense, the Bush campaign's signature national security issue in 2000. In an essay in the January–February 2000 issue of *Foreign Affairs*, which was widely seen as the foreign policy manifesto of George W. Bush's administration, Rice had written of the WMD threat from Iraq and North Korea: "These regimes are living on borrowed time, so there need be no sense of panic about them. Rather, the first line of defense should be a clear and classical statement of deterrence—if they do acquire WMD, their weapons will be unusable because any attempt to use them will bring national obliteration."

National missile defense, not Iraq, was also Secretary of Defense Donald Rumsfeld's top priority. During the late 1990s, Rumsfeld had chaired a bipartisan commission that examined the ballistic missile threat to the United States from emerging powers and rogue states in the Third World. The group had included Stephen Hadley, now Rice's deputy national security adviser, and Stephen Cambone, whom Rumsfeld had appointed to a top Pentagon post. Their report urged that the United States build a national missile defense system similar to the Strategic Defense Initiative first proposed during the Reagan era. The release of the commission's report in July 1998 was sandwiched between two events that accentuated the threat of nuclear-armed missiles from the Third World: the Indian and Pakistani nuclear tests of May 1998, and the provocative test-firing of a ballistic missile by North Korea over Japanese airspace in August 1998.

Rumsfeld had signed the Project for a New American Century's January 1998 letter to President Clinton calling for the removal of Saddam Hussein. He appeared, however, to have been mollified by passage of the

Iraq Liberation Act later that year, which reflected most of the letter's goals. Indeed, the new defense secretary had unwittingly latched onto the 1991-vintage policy of using enforcement by American aircraft of the no-fly zones in Iraq as a potential "grinding irritant" to weaken the Iraqi regime. Rumsfeld was convinced that if Iraqi troops fired on Coalition aircraft, it would provide an excuse for the United States to launch retaliatory strikes against Saddam's already demoralized military.

The Bush Cabinet member with the greatest initial interest in the Iraq issue was Secretary of State Colin Powell. Powell believed that the UN sanctions policy that had been in place against Iraq since the invasion of Kuwait in 1990 had become self-defeating. He wanted to replace it with a program of "smart sanctions" that would ease the strain on Iraqi civilians while still preventing the export of military material to Iraq. His interest in this issue was shared by Richard Haass, whom Powell had asked to head the Policy Planning Staff at the State Department. During his time out of government service during the 1990s, Haass had written a scholarly book criticizing the UN sanctions policy.

Iraq was the subject of the Bush administration's first full NSC meeting, on January 30. The meeting arrived at an Iraq strategy that balanced the need to focus on other foreign policy priorities against the need to demonstrate to "Iraq hawks" within the Republican Party that the new administration was serious about taking a harder line against Saddam Hussein. Powell was given the green light to proceed with smart sanctions. At the same time, planning began for a new campaign of punitive air strikes against Iraq that would be far more severe than the "pinpricks" of the Clinton administration, to be implemented in the event that Iraq committed violations in the northern or southern no-fly zones. Since Iraqi air defense batteries targeted or fired at Coalition aircraft in the two no-fly zones on an almost daily basis (an action that violated the terms of several UN Security Council resolutions), this was tantamount to ordering the strikes to take place in a matter of weeks.

Most important, the Bush administration was determined to greatly strengthen its ties to the Iraqi opposition. After Operation Desert Fox in December 1998 and his impeachment the following month, President Clinton had lost interest in Iraq, the Bush White House believed. It was almost an article of faith among the president and his advisers that they could do a much better job than Clinton of exerting pressure on Saddam's regime by working more closely with the Iraqi opposition. Two of the principals of the new administration, Dick Cheney and Donald Rumsfeld, already had close ties to leading Iraqi opposition figures, especially Ahmed Chalabi, head of the Iraqi National Congress.

*   *   *

On February 16, 2001, the planned air strikes took place. Coalition aircraft destroyed a number of radars and command centers used by Iraq's air defense network. It was the most significant military response to Iraq since Desert Fox, over two years earlier.

Nevertheless, there was already growing disillusionment within the ranks of the neoconservatives at the foreign policy direction the new administration was taking. This disillusionment had begun even before President Bush was inaugurated. In December 2000, Robert Kagan had written a scathing critique of Condoleezza Rice and the national security team surrounding the new president-elect. "Rice thinks we cannot afford four more years of Clinton and Gore coddling China," Kagan had written. "Her alternative: four years of Republicans coddling China." Kagan saw little difference between the foreign policy of the Bush administration and that of the Clinton administration it was replacing. "We know that on a number of big issues, most of Bush's vaunted advisers agree with Clinton and Gore. On the biggest issue where they don't agree, American intervention abroad, Gore is probably more right than they are."

Neoconservative dissatisfaction stemmed from two sources: people and policy. Neoconservatives regarded some of the principal officials of the new administration with suspicion. Colin Powell had been a figure of loathing among neoconservatives since his days as the "reluctant warrior" during the first Bush administration. Rice was a self-professed Realist and viewed as the alter ego of Brent Scowcroft, one of the nemeses of neoconservative foreign policy. Even George W. Bush would not have been their first choice for president; the *Weekly Standard* had endorsed Sen. John McCain. With the exception of Donald Rumsfeld's Pentagon, there were few Executive Branch departments where neoconservatives occupied the senior policymaking roles.

But their dissatisfaction with policy was even greater. Kagan's critique of Condoleezza Rice's approach to world affairs captured the essence of neoconservative dissatisfaction with Bush administration foreign policy: It was "weak"; and in many areas it was essentially a continuation of the Clinton administration's foreign policy. With the exception of national missile defense, the Bush White House had embraced none of the causes dear to neoconservatives. Above all, the administration's Iraq policy was a huge disappointment. With the election of a Republican White House, neoconservatives had been hoping for a confrontational new stance against the regime in Baghdad. Instead, with each passing month, Iraq seemed to slip further and further down the list of the Bush administration's national security priorities. Even the Republicans in Congress were surprised and dismayed by the administration's seeming lack of interest in fomenting a confrontation with Saddam Hussein. On March 7, Colin Powell appeared on Capitol Hill to testify about the plan to enact "smart sanctions" against Iraq. A number of Republican lawmakers accused Powell and the administration of having little interest in implementing the provisions of the Iraq Liberation Act.

• • •

Matters came to a head in April 2001. The crew of an American EP-3 reconnaissance aircraft was taken prisoner in China after its plane collided with a Chinese fighter jet. Prominent neoconservatives urged an aggressive U.S. response to the incident. The threat posed by communist China was a favorite bogeyman among neoconservatives. Many had argued during the 1990s that China was the most likely national security challenge facing the United States in the twenty-first century. "The rise of China looms over Asia," Paul Wolfowitz had warned in one article on this topic. Virtually the entire Bush foreign policy team was on record as favoring a more confrontational posture toward China. Bill Clinton's purported "weakness" in dealing with China had been a frequent neoconservative charge for the preceding eight years. Even the first President Bush's measured response to the 1989 Tiananmen Square massacre had never sat well with the neoconservatives.

In his handling of the crisis, however, President Bush turned to the one figure in his administration who adamantly opposed taking a hard line with China, and who possessed the stature to achieve a negotiated solution: Colin Powell. Powell pushed the idea of a carefully worded "non-apology" to the Chinese leadership, which secured the release of the American aircrew. The Bush White House considered its handling of the crisis a diplomatic and public relations coup, but the "apology" to the Chinese was bitter gall to the neoconservatives.

On July 30, 2001, former CIA officer and neoconservative author Reuel Marc Gerecht wrote a bitter denunciation of the Bush administration's Iraq policy in *The Weekly Standard*. The title of the essay was "A Cowering Superpower."

"From the spring of 1996, the Clinton Administration's Iraq policy was in meltdown; under the Bush Administration, it has completely liquefied," Gerecht charged, in a comparison that surely rankled the Bush White House. "It would be better to see the Administration start explaining how we will live with Saddam and his nuclear weapons than to see senior Bush officials, in the manner of the Clintonites, fib to themselves and the public."

Ironically, the main subject of Gerecht's essay was not Iraq, but the Bush administration's tepid response to another threat: Osama bin Laden and al-Qaeda.

"The Butcher of Baghdad has checked, if not checkmated, the United States. Only against this backdrop can we properly assess the threat bin Laden poses. The Saudi militant is unquestionably going to come at us again. Then the Bush Administration will have to make a defining decision."

•   •   •

Rage. The rage of America.

By the afternoon of 9/11, the American people were sick to death of the Islamic world. For three decades it had been a source of nothing but grief for the United States. They were sick of the 1973 and 1979 oil shocks, sick of corrupt emirs and pan-Arabist generals, sick of hijacked airliners and terrorist bombings, sick of Iranian mullahs, sick of Yasser Arafat. They were sick of suicide bombers in Beirut and Riyadh and Lower Manhattan.

And always Americans died: They died in the Marine barracks in Beirut, and the army barracks in Dharan, and the air force barracks in Riyadh. They died on the *Stark* and they died on the *Cole*. They died in U.S. embassies. They died on Pan Am jetliners and TWA jetliners and American jetliners and United jetliners. They died in the parking garage of the World Trade Center, and eight years later, they died everywhere in the World Trade Center. They died at their posts in the Pentagon.

This, in a country were Muslims lived in peace and prosperity.

Even so, they might have accepted the losses were it not for the atrocities: the hostage-taking; the violation of embassies; the hurling of a crippled old man in a wheelchair over the railing of a cruise ship; the bombing of civilian airliners; the indiscriminate mass murder of thousands in skyscrapers.

In all that happened afterward, the rage, the righteous anger, of the American people was the catalyst and key ingredient.

And in George W. Bush, the American people had found the perfect vessel for their limitless rage. Had the attacks occurred on his father's watch, the elder Bush would have responded decisively, even violently, to them. No one familiar with his neuralgic attitudes about terrorism and hostage-taking could have any doubts about that. Ultimately, though, Bush senior would have restrained himself out of concern for the long-term stability of America's relationships in the world. His instinct would have been to reach out to America's friends, especially America's friends in the Islamic world (many of whom happened to be personal friends of his), and to capitalize on the tremendous outpouring of support for the United States after 9/11. This most worldly of men would have used the attacks and the global response to them as an occasion to build an even grander Coalition than the one he had built after the invasion of Iraq. His overarching goal would have been to demonstrate that the entire civilized world stood united against such behavior.

The younger George Bush and those surrounding him were interested in demonstration of a very different sort. For three decades, whether the weapon was oil or terror, the Islamic world had demonstrated that it wanted asymmetrical conflict with the United States. And as General Sherman might have phrased it, the most powerful nation in history now meant to let them have their fill of it.

In the 1970s they were constrained by the overhanging shadow of Vietnam. In the 1980s, they were constrained by the mortal struggle with the Soviet Union for influence in the region. In the 1990s they were constrained by having lost the White House during a decade of intense American self-absorption. Now, in September 2001, there suddenly were no more constraints.

.   .   .

There would have to be a response worthy of the event, but what?

As a shaken Bush national security team gathered at Camp David for a war council on the morning of Saturday, September 15, four days after the 9/11 attacks, there was little doubt about who was culpable. Throughout the preceding summer there had been ominous intelligence warnings that bin Laden was determined to attack inside the United States. The U.S. intelligence community had since confirmed that al-Qaeda had conducted the operation.

Even so, Iraq had been on the minds of many during the preceding four days. On the afternoon of September 11, Donald Rumsfeld had confided to Gen. Richard Myers, vice chairman of the JCS, at the still-smoldering Pentagon, "My instinct is to hit Saddam at the same time, not just bin Laden." On September 12 a sharp discussion had taken place at the White House over whether to attack Iraq, with Rumsfeld and his deputy Paul Wolfowitz arguing for such an attack, and Colin Powell and his deputy Rich Armitage arguing against. Later that same evening, in a famous exchange, President Bush himself had ordered his NSC counterterrorism chief, Richard Clarke, "See if Saddam did this. See if he's linked in any way."

At Camp David the Iraq question came to a head. Deputy Secretary of Defense Paul Wolfowitz made an impassioned case that war against Iraq should be part of "this round" of the administration's war on terror. Colin Powell would later tell the National 9/11 Commission investigating the attacks: "Paul was always of the view that Iraq was a problem that had to be dealt with. And he saw this as one way of using this event to deal with the Iraq problem."

Most of the others in the room, including President Bush, were skeptical that Iraq was involved in the attacks. But there was another concern related to Iraq. Since the end of the Gulf War ten years earlier, Saddam Hussein had exhibited a consistent pattern of capitalizing on major crises involving the United States in order to challenge the will of the international community. Many in the room—including Vice President Cheney, Secretary Powell, and Wolfowitz himself—had had bitter first-hand experience of this during the summer of 1992, when Saddam Hussein capitalized on a White House distracted by the outbreak of ethnic war in the Balkans to mount an "across the board" challenge to the UN regime imposed on Iraq after the Gulf War. Now, in the aftermath of the worst attack ever on American soil, there was concern that Saddam might "take advantage" of the situation. Such a challenge might take the form of a concerted attempt to shoot down U.S. aircraft patrolling the no-fly zones in Iraq, a ground offensive to recapture territory from the Iraqi Kurds, or even an attempt to annex all or part of Kuwait again. All were gambits that Saddam had tried before when a White House had been distracted by more pressing domestic or international crises.

After some discussion, the meeting concluded with a presidential directive to focus exclusively on attacking al-Qaeda in its redoubt in Afghanistan. By the end of the day on September 15, the focus of planning in the group had shifted entirely to al-Qaeda and Afghanistan. Still, President Bush remained concerned about the possibility of Iraq taking hostile action at a moment of perceived American weakness. On September 16 he privately instructed Condoleezza Rice to have the NSC staff draw up contingency plans for military action against Iraq if warranted. The following day, at a plenary NSC meeting back at the White House, the president repeated this instruction, specifically requesting a plan to seize Iraqi oilfields if Saddam acted against American interests.

· · ·

If the matter of Iraq had been settled for the time being at the White House, the debate elsewhere was just beginning. Within days of the attacks, William Kristol had convened a special two-day conference at the Project for a New American Century's offices ten blocks away. On September 19, PNAC sent George W. Bush a letter declaring the conference's finding: that failing to remove Saddam Hussein from power would be a "decisive surrender in the war on terrorism." That same day, the Defense Policy Board, a group of outside advisers to the Pentagon that functions much like a university's board of trustees, began its own two-day conference at the Pentagon. The board included such Republican heavy-hitters as Newt Gingrich (now retired from Congress) and Richard Perle. Donald Rumsfeld and Paul Wolfowitz sat in on many of the board's discussions over the two days. After nineteen hours of meetings, Gingrich summed up the conclusion of the board: "If we don't use this as the moment to replace Saddam after we replace the Taliban, we are setting the stage for disaster."

Nor were these sentiments limited to Washington alone. Despite the fact that the shock from 9/11 had barely receded in New York, and the embers of the World Trade Center site were still smoldering, a number of New York–based newspapers were actively calling for a war to remove Saddam Hussein throughout the month of September. On September 24 columnist William Safire of the *New York Times* wrote a column describing Saddam, not Osama bin Laden, as "the ultimate enemy." Four days later, on September 28, *National Review* editor Rich Lowry wrote an essay for the *New York Post* that began:

> If Saddam Hussein escapes the full wrath of the U.S. war on
> terrorism, he will once more have Colin Powell and the dictates
> of a great international Coalition to thank. It was to preserve the
> Gulf War Coalition—for what, exactly, no one knows—that
> Powell, as Chairman of the Joint Chiefs, urged the first President
> Bush to stop short of Baghdad.

Lowry's account of war termination in 1991 left out a number of critical details—not least of which was the fact that Powell's civilian superior at the time, Dick Cheney, had also argued for ending the war, and had defended the decision to do so in the strongest language for years afterward. But one of the most bizarre relics of that period was the sudden venting of the collective neoconservative spleen against Colin Powell. Lowry was not the only one to take issue with the secretary of state. That same week, William Kristol added another charge. "Powell did his best to persuade

President Bush not to wage war against Saddam [in 1991]," Kristol wrote in the *Washington Post*. If anyone thought it odd that so many Republican pundits were seizing on the 9/11 attacks to criticize the ending of the 1991 Gulf War ten years later, few at the time said so.

One of the few who did, though, was former president George Bush. Bush was livid at the sudden flurry of attacks on Powell: partly out of loyalty to one of the principals of his administration, and partly because Bush recognized that it was his legacy and reputation that were being attacked also. As the father of a sitting president in the midst of a major crisis, Bush could not—and would not—engage in a public debate with Powell's critics. He did, however, enlist Brent Scowcroft to come to Powell's defense.

On October 16 the former national security adviser wrote an article for the *Post* defending yet again the Bush administration's decision to end Desert Storm—this time in the context of Osama bin Laden:

> It's interesting to speculate, in the light of our current circumstances, how the situation might now be different had we added occupation of Iraq and removal of Saddam Hussein to those objectives. . . . The United States' being in hostile occupation of an Arab land might well have spawned scores of Osama bin Ladens.

Scowcroft's article did not consider another possibility: that the unplanned presence of U.S. troops in Saudi Arabia after the Gulf War may have helped spawn the original Osama bin Laden.

.   .   .

The war of words over Iraq was so fierce that one might have easily forgotten that there was a real shooting war under way in Afghanistan. In the days immediately following 9/11, the Bush administration had conveyed a stern ultimatum to the Taliban regime in Afghanistan: Turn over Osama bin Laden. When this ultimatum was refused, the United States proceeded with Operation Enduring Freedom, military action to topple the Taliban and destroy al-Qaeda's training camps and infrastructure inside Afghanistan. On September 27 the first CIA special operations teams had entered the country. Several days later, American and British forces began a campaign of carefully targeted bombing in tandem with a deployment of special operations "boots on the ground."

By any objective standard the campaign was stunningly innovative and successful. Part of the reason the Taliban may have felt comfortable in resisting demands for Osama bin Laden's arrest may have been their experience fighting the Soviets in the 1980s. They had assumed that any major power that attempted to invade Afghanistan would repeat many of the same mistakes the Soviets had made.

Instead, the United States employed a brilliant and flexible war plan that maximized the technological and firepower advantages of American troops while making use of assistance from local anti-Taliban sects, such as the Afghan Northern Alliance. Within a month the Taliban regime of Mullah Omar and its Qaeda sympathizers, including Osama bin Laden and the top leadership of al-Qaeda, had fled into the mountainous region of Afghanistan known as Tora Bora for one final stand.

·　　·　　·

The American people were still recovering from the shock of the 9/11 attacks when the first cases of anthrax were reported several weeks later. On October 5, an employee of the tabloid newspaper *National Enquirer* died in Florida after coming into contact with an anthrax-laced letter. During the next several weeks, letters containing anthrax spores were sent to the New York offices of all three of the major television networks: ABC, CBS, and NBC. On October 15, an anthrax letter was sent to the office of Senate Minority Leader Tom Daschle. The Senate office buildings were promptly evacuated for decontamination. A week later, two postal employees in the Washington, D.C., area died of anthrax after handling tainted mail.

Like all terrorists, the perpetrator of this crime sought not just to take innocent life, but to do so in a highly public way that terrorized civil society. From this standpoint, the attacks had an impact far out of proportion to the number of deaths they caused. For the first time since 9/11, cracks of fear and self-interestedness began to show beneath the steely resolve that the American people had exhibited since the attacks. They would have met another "conventional" terrorist attack with defiance; but some seemed to cower in the face of a terrorist threat that came in the form of a dreaded and invisible plague. Even in New York, whose citizens had stunned the entire world with their valor and selflessness after 9/11, there were reports of some individuals hoarding antibiotics or bribing physicians to receive special treatment, even though only a handful of people actually came into contact with the disease.

The anthrax threat soon disappeared as mysteriously as it had emerged, and the perpetrator was never found. This tended to confirm the speculation among law enforcement officials that the attacks had been carried out by a lone sociopath, rather than a terrorist organization. But the long-term effects for American foreign policy were significant. Coming so soon on the heels of 9/11, the anthrax attacks contributed to a general sense among an already-shaken populace that there were terrorists in their midst, and that the threat of death from plague or other weapons of mass destruction was an imminent one. In so doing, the attacks created fertile ground for any who might wish to cultivate these fears.

.   .   .

Even while the fighting was still going on in Afghanistan, prominent neoconservatives in Washington were thinking about the future of the war on terror.

At the American Enterprise Institute, Richard Perle had convened a panel of heavy hitters on October 29 to discuss the subject. Besides his AEI colleagues Newt Gingrich and Michael Ledeen, Perle had also enlisted former Clinton CIA director James Woolsey and Deputy Prime Minister Natan Sharansky of Israel, who was a hero to many neoconservatives for his resistance to oppression in the former Soviet Union.

While the panel had been billed as "The Battle for Ideas in the U.S. War on Terrorism," the casual visitor could have been forgiven for mistakenly believing that they had stumbled into a panel discussion of Iraq.

The recent anthrax scare was very much on Newt Gingrich's mind. He opened his presentation by directing the audience to an article in that morning's *Wall Street Journal* stating that Iraq had produced 2,300 gallons of anthrax. His recommended solution was for the United States to take on Afghanistan and Iraq simultaneously, much as it had fought Germany and Japan at the same time during World War II.

Woolsey went next, bitterly criticizing the first Bush administration for allowing the Kurds and the Shia to be slaughtered in the aftermath of the 1991 Gulf War.

But the most hawkish views were those of Ledeen, who argued that the American campaign against terror could not just stop with Iraq. "No stages," he declared. "This is a total war. We are fighting a variety of enemies. There are lots of them out there. And all this talk about, well, first we are going to do Afghanistan, then we will do Iraq, then we will take a look around and see how things stand, that is entirely the wrong way to go about it. Because these guys all talk to each other and are all working with one another."

Ledeen was less concerned about the United States possibly biting off more than it could chew than by the prospect of "diplomatic solutions" interfering with the total war he and his colleagues were advocating.

"If we just let our own vision of the world go forth, and we embrace it entirely and we don't try to be clever and piece together clever 'diplomatic solutions' to this thing, but just wage a total war against these tyrants, I think we will do very well," he assured the audience. "And our children will sing great songs about us years from now."

·　　·　　·

The large community of Iraqi opposition figures in the United States had recognized that the constant drumbeat of martial talk about Iraq represented an extraordinary opportunity, perhaps their only opportunity, to have the U.S. military topple Saddam Hussein. And many were strategically sophisticated enough to realize that the Iraq Liberation Act notwithstanding, only an outside army could change the regime in Baghdad. Accordingly, within weeks of the 9/11 attacks, many of the leading Iraqi opposition figures had begun talking up the idea of an invasion with their contacts in the U.S. government. None was more active than Ahmed Chalabi, the flamboyant head of the Iraqi National Congress, who was experienced in the ways of Washington from years of making the rounds of Congress and the think tank circuit. Chalabi was also close to prominent figures in the Bush administration like Cheney, Rumsfeld, and Wolfowitz, all of whom saw him as a future president of Iraq. However, Chalabi was regarded with suspicion by the State Department, which considered him a professional intriguer.

But the Iraqi opposition figure with the greatest credibility among the exiles themselves was Kanan Makiya. As private a man as Chalabi was public, Makiya's stature rested on *Republic of Fear*, a book he had written during the 1980s under a pseudonym. Perhaps the definitive account of the brutal nature of Saddam Hussein's regime, the book had become an instant best-seller during the 1991 Gulf War.

On November 21, sensing that the war in Afghanistan was winding to a close and that the Bush administration might be evaluating its next options, Makiya wrote an essay in the *New York Times* calling for a U.S.-led invasion of Iraq. First reminding his American audience of the U.S. "abandonments" of the Iraqi people in 1991 and 1996, Makiya made the case that Iraq was an ideal candidate to become a pro-American bastion in the Middle East once it was liberated: "Iraq's infrastructure, its middle class, its secular intelligentsia, its high levels of education are all reasons for thinking that a new westward-looking political order can, with the help of the west, be set up in Iraq just as it was set up in Japan and Germany after World War II. And unlike Afghanistan, Iraq can pay for its own reconstruction." Makiya was adamant, though, on one point. "That will not come about through bombing. Iraq has been bombed enough. . . . What is desperately needed is an iron American resolve to end the existing regime." By which he meant a ground invasion.

•   •   •   •

By this time there was plenty of American resolve to end the existing regime in Iraq. What was beginning to erode was American resolve to bring a final end to al-Qaeda in Afghanistan.

By the first week of December 2001, U.S. troops had achieved a great victory in Afghanistan. The senior figures of the Taliban had fled Kabul. Large swaths of the country were now under the control of the pro-Western Northern Alliance. Al-Qaeda's network of training camps in the country had been destroyed. Perhaps most impressively, American troops had fought in numerous close-quarters battles with Taliban and al-Qaeda fighters, and the tough, battle-hardened mujahideen had proven no match for Americans aroused by a righteous anger at what had been done to their country—some of whom went into battle wearing NYPD and FDNY baseball caps.

The remnants of al-Qaeda, approximately eight hundred fighters including a wounded Osama bin Laden and his Taliban ally Mullah Omar, were trapped in the mountain pass of Tora Bora, in the remote eastern region of Afghanistan. Finishing them off was sure to be a dangerous and costly mission for U.S. troops, but, given the overwhelming superiority of U.S. special operations forces and the lay of the land, it was a mission that would result in a certain outcome.

Inexplicably, however, the U.S. assault was held back. Instead, Northern Alliance troops were committed to the battle. The United States and its Northern Alliance allies held every advantage at Tora Bora except one: time. It was December in Afghanistan and the fierce mountain winter had arrived. As al-Qaeda fighters fought a desperate holding action, much of the organization's senior leadership slipped away, and each day the battle became more difficult because of the weather. Osama bin Laden was among those who escaped.

One senior official from the first Bush White House who had remained prominent in foreign policy circles blamed a misplaced sense of priorities among some of the administration's top officials for allowing Osama bin Laden to slip away: "The biggest tragedy was Afghanistan. Wolfowitz somehow convinced Cheney that Iraq was more important. There were several arguments. But above all, what motivated them was a belief that having a friendly government in Baghdad would help American companies secure access to Iraq's oil reserves."

Nevertheless, despite the fact that the malevolent genius behind the 9/11 attacks had been allowed to escape, the Bush national security team considered Enduring Freedom a resounding success, and in many aspects it was. Not only was this conflict a prototype for the sort of short, violent, and decisive wars that the Bush administration expected to fight in the future. It also showed how 9/11 had upended the traditional platitudes of Republican foreign policy.

For the American role in Afghanistan would not end with the defeat of the Taliban and their terrorist allies. Rather, the U.S. troops would be committed to remaking Afghani society so that the country could never again serve as a sanctuary for terrorist groups. In short, America was back in the nation-building business.

In the months immediately following the numbing shock of 9/11, few questioned the proposition that failed Islamic states like Afghanistan represented a security threat to the United States. Few even within the Republican establishment questioned the validity of nation-building as the solution to the problem, even though it flew in the face of everything the Bush inner circle had believed for two decades. But nation-building was a strategy that required an entirely new way of thinking about America's role in the world. A national debate on what this role should be would take place only later.

The most immediate impact of the campaign against the Taliban in Afghanistan was that an enormous aura of trust and prestige enveloped the Bush administration in the national security arena, with important consequences for the future. George W. Bush emerged from three months following 9/11 as one of the most powerful presidents in American history. What he chose to do next with that power would be the real defining decision of his presidency.

·　　　·　　　·

The failure to account for Osama bin Laden and the other senior leaders of al-Qaeda only accentuated one of the main rationales for pursuing regime change against Iraq: that a White House preoccupied by an open-ended war on terror would be unable to contain Saddam Hussein over the long term.

This consideration weighed especially heavily on Vice President Dick Cheney. Unlike his thirty-year friend and Cabinet colleague Donald Rumsfeld, Cheney had served in the first Bush White House and had witnessed firsthand the difficulty of maintaining a containment regime against Saddam. Cheney had absorbed two bitter lessons from the first Bush administration's failed confrontation with Iraq in 1992. The first was that Saddam invariably grew more aggressive when the United States was distracted by other security crises. The second was that it was impossible to muster the domestic and international support for major U.S. military action during a presidential election year.

"Cheney is the real enigma in all of this," said a retired official who worked closely with him in the first Bush administration. "People identify him with the neocons, but that's not where he was in 1991–92. He is the real surprise. I ran into him in March 2002, when he made a trip to the Gulf region. I happened to be out there at the same time. He was already talking about Iraq, and people in the region were getting concerned."

In Cheney's mind there were two necessary predicates to these lessons: a final showdown with Iraq would have to take place in 2002 or 2003, not during the election year of 2004; and because Saddam's entire strategy for survival would be based on delaying U.S. action until 2004, no accommodation by Iraq, not even acceptance of robust UN weapons inspections, could be allowed to forestall American military action.

The new urgency became apparent on January 29, 2002, during a provocative State of the Union address by President Bush. The president stunned many by describing Iraq as part of an "axis of evil" that threatened the United States. The decision to launch a crusade against Saddam Hussein had already been reached. All that remained was to determine when and how.

●   ●   ●

As it framed a strategy to wage war on Saddam Hussein, the Bush White House envisioned that a unique set of circumstances would present it with an extraordinary window of opportunity during the six weeks preceding the November 2002 midterm election.

The one-year anniversary of the 9/11 tragedy would inevitably focus all eyes on the president while he led the nation's memorial activities. As they relived the horror and heroism of that day, the American people would never be more susceptible to an appeal for decisive action against another "evildoer" who had a proven capacity for ill will toward the United States. The outpouring of international sympathy that could be expected from around the world during this period would make it the ideal time to build another international coalition in support of military action against Iraq.

This would be especially true at the Manhattan-based UN Security Council, where diplomats of many nations had lived firsthand through the awful events of September 2001. Finally, the looming November elections would preempt criticism from congressional Democrats terrified of being branded as unpatriotic, or worse, weak on terrorism.

This rare alignment of historical forces fell perfectly into orbit with the political and military requirements of any war against Iraq. From a political standpoint, the White House favored a war that would be over by the spring of 2003—well before the beginning of the presidential primary season. From a military standpoint, six months would be needed to move all of the necessary forces into the Iraqi theater. This timetable would allow ground combat to take place before the blistering heat of the Iraqi summer, a practical necessity should U.S. troops be forced to fight wearing chemical protective gear. The Bush administration's plan for going to war with Iraq in the spring of 2003 reflected all of these considerations.

.   .   .

Of the many beliefs that drove the Bush administration and its neoconservative allies to pursue regime change in Iraq, none had greater impact than the unwavering perception that Saddam Hussein was pursuing a massive clandestine program to develop weapons of mass destruction. Just as this belief served as the main public argument used for garnering support both domestically and abroad, it also served an important function *within* the administration. The threat of weapons proliferation became the main bureaucratic "weapon" wielded by advocates of regime change in Iraq against counterparts who favored a more cautious approach toward the Iraqi state.

The persuasive power of this belief was a product of many factors: the difficulties that the first Bush administration had experienced imposing a weapons inspection program on Iraq after an earlier Gulf War; lingering frustration with President Clinton's handling of Saddam Hussein; and the background of the policymakers closest to George W. Bush as strategic arms experts, which led them to overstate the immediacy of the threat posed by nonconventional weapons proliferation. One consequence of the Bush administration's reliance on Iraq's weapons program as a rationale for going to war, though, was that the administration could not afford to abandon this rationale under any circumstances—even when much of the U.S. intelligence community flatly disputed the validity of the belief.

This dissonance underlay the extraordinary antagonism between the Bush White House and the UN Security Council throughout the months leading up to Operation Iraqi Freedom. The Bush administration had accepted a new round of UN weapons inspections in Iraq only because it assumed that inspections would serve as an incremental step on the road to regime change. Since weapons of mass destruction were believed to be present in Iraq, inspections would either locate the weapons or force Saddam Hussein to deny access to the inspectors. Either outcome would constitute an airtight casus belli. When UN inspectors failed to turn up any weapons, however, a surprised Bush administration found itself with no real counter to French proposals for expanding the UN inspections mandate. Rather than debate the issue or rethink its underlying beliefs, the Bush White House skillfully redefined the debate by making support for the American position a test of loyalty toward the United States. This obfuscated the issue, but at the cost of fracturing the Atlantic Alliance.

One other belief about Iraq occupied a position nearly as prominent in the administration's war planning—its rosy expectations about the reception American troops would receive in the wake of a successful invasion. In a phrase favored by Donald Rumsfeld, and later by President Bush himself, U.S. forces would be "greeted as liberators" everywhere they went in Iraq. The frequent voicing of this belief as a regular feature of the Bush administration's public diplomacy served many purposes: to convince a wary Islamic world that Iraqi Freedom was a just war of liberation; to suggest that all segments of the Iraqi populace would embrace an American-style secular democracy; and most of all, to reassure the American people that civil strife in postwar Iraq would pose little long-term danger to U.S. occupying forces.

The unqualified acceptance of these views by many within the administration gave rise to serious shortcomings in planning for the aftermath in Iraq. Incessant guerrilla attacks on American troops dashed early hopes that the reconstruction of Iraq would be an easy or bloodless process. Senior U.S. officials expressed surprise and alarm at the quick consolidation of power by pro-Iranian Shi'ite clerics in southern Iraq. And unlike the first Bush administration, which had viewed Kurdish aspirations in northern Iraq with perhaps excessive trepidation, this administration blithely assumed that Kurdish autonomy was an issue that could be finessed away.

•   •   •

In many respects the ideological debate between the Realists like Brent Scowcroft or Richard Haass and the neoconservatives had been a battle of whether the containment of Iraq would work. Scowcroft, Haass, and other Realists had maintained for nearly a decade that Saddam Hussein could be contained by an administration with the political will to do so. The neoconservatives had vilified containment for a decade, maintaining that Saddam was such a uniquely cunning and evil dictator that he could not be contained by any administration.

So it was ironic that as the Bush administration's intent to invade Iraq became clear in the autumn of 2002, the original architect of Containment shared his views on Iraq. From his perch at the Institute for Advanced Study in New Jersey, ninety-eight-year-old George Kennan remained an astute observer of American foreign policy, though he was now limited to making only the occasional Delphic pronouncement. Kennan had lived to see the peaceful collapse of communism and the triumph of American values, as he had predicted in his famous 1947 Long Telegram from Moscow to Washington.

So his assessment of the forthcoming invasion of Iraq might have given some in Washington pause. On October 14, 2002, Kennan declared:

> The apparently imminent use of American armed forces to drive Saddam Hussein from power . . . seems to me well out of proportion to the dangers involved. I have seen no evidence that we have any realistic plans for dealing with the great state of confusion in Iraqian affairs which would presumably follow even after the successful elimination of the dictator.

The Oracle had spoken.

On February 26, 2003, George W. Bush repaid an important debt. For the preceding eighteen months, no organization had done more to support the White House or provide intellectual ammunition for its planned war with Iraq than the American Enterprise Institute. AEI's influence was at its zenith: no other Washington think tank enjoyed such extensive ties to senior Bush administration officials. Dick Cheney had briefly been in residence at AEI before becoming CEO of the oil services giant Halliburton. His wife, Lynne, an expert on education policy, was still a senior fellow there. Former House Speaker Newt Gingrich had joined AEI after leaving Congress, giving the organization unique clout with the Republican majority on Capitol Hill. Finally, virtually every senior figure in Donald Rumsfeld's Pentagon had close ties to Richard Perle, a longtime fixture at AEI.

Thus, it was only fitting that Bush should give one of his most important speeches on Iraq policy there. Speaking before this most receptive of audiences, the president delivered a bellicose address that left no doubt about Saddam Hussein's fate. Others in Washington and around the world might have been hoping for a last-second breakthrough that would allow war with Iraq to be avoided. But everyone in this room already knew that war with Iraq was, as they say in Texas, a done deal.

"A new regime in Iraq would serve as a dramatic and inspiring example of freedom for other nations in the region," the president declared. Not surprisingly, it was the signature applause line of his speech.

That same day, four hundred miles north of AEI's stately headquarters building on Massachusetts Avenue, another President Bush was giving a very different speech. During the run-up to war with Iraq thus far, George Herbert Walker Bush had kept a low profile. It is considered inappropriate for former presidents to take an active role in criticizing the policies of their successors, and Bush senior was nothing if not a man who observed the proprieties. He had held his tongue during the eight years of the *Clinton* administration; he was even less likely to break a rule where his own son was concerned.

But privately, Bush had been growing increasingly anxious about the imminent conflict with Iraq. He fretted over the likelihood of more serious casualties than in Gulf War I. The casual references among his son's supporters to the "mistake" he had made in not finishing off Saddam Hussein in 1991 were a bitter insult for him to swallow. Most of all, he chafed a little enviously at his enforced inactivity while his son and one-time members of his own national security team—Cheney, Powell, Rice—were engaged in trying to build another coalition against Iraq. Bush senior's own views were no secret in Washington. Although he had not spoken out publicly about the war, Brent Scowcroft had, vociferously, and it was widely (and correctly) believed that Scowcroft would never have done so without first consulting with his best friend.

All of these emotions came to a head on the evening of February 26. Speaking on the majestic hilltop campus of Tufts University in Massachusetts, the first President Bush gamely tried to defend, one last time, his decision to end the Gulf War with Saddam Hussein's regime still in power. "If we had tried to go in there and then create just more instability in Iraq, I think it would have been very bad for the neighborhood," Bush said in response to one audience question during the Q&A session that followed his speech. "Vis-à-vis Iran, for example. And so, if there's a perception that we said, 'You go and rise up and we'll help you,' that's an erroneous perception.

"Frankly I, and most other leaders . . . all felt that the people from within would take care of Hussein. That he couldn't exist, you see. So, I was wrong in that. But, not wrong in going to continue the battle. And not wrong in taking military action that might destabilize Iraq in the center, and that very important center in the neighborhood there.

"And so, there is this misperception," Bush concluded. "And I'm glad to have a chance to clear it up."

Unlike his son and the audience at AEI, this George Bush admitted that he still hoped for a peaceful solution to the standoff with Iraq. "The more pressure there is," he explained to his audience, "the more chance this matter will be resolved in a peaceful matter."

●   ●   ●

Perhaps appropriately, Operation Iraqi Freedom, the U.S. invasion of Iraq, began with an attempt to kill Saddam Hussein. On March 20, 2003,

Coalition forces launched forty Tomahawk cruise missiles at the Dora Farms complex in suburban Baghdad, where "reliable intelligence" had indicated Saddam was spending the night. The Tomahawks completely leveled the area and killed a number of Iraqis, but Saddam escaped. It was later unclear whether the Iraqi dictator had been there at all. Several days later Saddam appeared unexpectedly at a Baghdad street corner, clearly intent on demonstrating that he was still the man in charge.

But Dora Farms had been only the opening salvo of the campaign. Over the next two weeks, U.S.-led forces marched inexorably toward the Iraqi capital. This time there was no talk, as during the first Bush administration, about Iraq complying with UN resolutions or cease-fire terms. Every American service member in the combat theater, from CENT-COM commander Gen. Tommy Franks to the greenest army private, knew that this time the war would not end until U.S. forces had captured Baghdad.

Just as they had during Operation Desert Storm twelve years earlier, U.S. forces performed magnificently. If anything, the pace of their advance exceeded even that of Coalition forces during the first Gulf War; this, despite the fact that there were many fewer American and allied troops than in 1991. By the first week of April 2003, U.S. forces had captured Baghdad International Airport and were carefully probing the defenses of the teeming Iraqi capital itself. Saddam Hussein had been warning for decades that if ever a foreign army threatened to enter Baghdad, Iraq's generals had standing orders to fire chemical weapons at the interlopers.

Fortunately, this boast proved to be an empty one. On the evening of April 8, U.S. forces occupied central Baghdad. The next day produced one of the iconic images of the war. On April 9 a large mob of Baghdad residents congregated around the grandiose statue of Saddam that towered over Firdos Square—the symbolic center of Saddam's regime. With the help of an obliging U.S. Army vehicle and a length of heavy chain, the Iraqis toppled the statue from the pillar on which it stood. The frenzied crowd took turns jeering and striking the shattered bust of the dictator with the soles of their shoes—in the Arab world, the ultimate insult. No one who witnessed the abuse heaped upon the deposed statue could have doubted that their hatred for Saddam was genuine.

But the real Saddam was nowhere to be found. As many of the officials who had fought the first Gulf War with George H. W. Bush had predicted, the Iraqi dictator had gone to ground long before U.S. forces were anywhere near Baghdad. And finding a single person in a country the size of Iraq was still no easy matter.

·　　　·　　　·

The Bush White House was almost transported with joy at the events being televised from Baghdad. The outcome of Operation Iraqi Freedom had conformed perfectly to every expectation that the architects of the conflict had voiced in the months leading up to it. The Iraqi army had collapsed like the paper tiger that Dick Cheney, Donald Rumsfeld, Paul Wolfowitz, and others had long believed it to be. U.S. troops were being greeted as liberators in the streets of Baghdad—the symbolism of American GIs helping Iraqis themselves topple Saddam's statue was impossible for any observer to miss. The approval rating of the president had soared again to post-9/11 levels. Defense Secretary Rumsfeld, who had personally overseen every military detail of the operation, from the number of troops to the timing of the campaign, was being hailed as a strategic visionary. The most pleasant surprise was that Saddam Hussein had not unleashed chemical weapons against U.S. troops when confronted with the imminent loss of power. The Bush administration was convinced that this outcome was the result of the extensive psychological warfare campaign directed at Iraq's generals, persuading them to disassociate themselves from Saddam's regime and disobey the dictator's standing order to fire. The Pentagon was confident that now that American troops had the run of the country, they would quickly uncover the remnants of Saddam's WMD programs that had eluded UN weapons inspectors. Even the discovery of a single bunker's worth of obsolescent chemical munitions left over from the first Gulf War would be enough to demonstrate the WMD threat that Saddam had posed to the American people.

Victory fever was sweeping the entire capital that week. Even the "reluctant warrior" himself, Colin Powell, was not immune. Asked by reporters whether the Bush administration was now contemplating taking military action against Syria and Iran, the secretary of state and former JCS chairman gave his famous grin. "There is no war plan for Syria and Iran," he replied. "Right now."

●   ●   ●

In this atmosphere it was perhaps understandable then that the outbreak of looting and rioting throughout Iraq almost immediately upon news of the fall of Saddam Hussein was initially viewed as only a minor inconvenience: the afterbirth that accompanied the emergence of a new democratic Iraq. Bush administration officials were visibly peeved when the Washington press corps turned its attention away from the historic victory in the Gulf and toward the looting. At a Pentagon briefing on April 10, an irate Donald Rumsfeld berated the "Chicken Littles" in the press.

"I read eight headlines that talked about chaos, violence, unrest. And it just was Henny Penny, 'The sky is falling.' I've never seen anything like it!" the defense secretary exclaimed. "The images you are seeing on television you are seeing over and over and over, and it's the same picture of some person walking out of some building with a vase, and you see it twenty times and you think, 'My goodness, were there that many vases?'

"The task we've got ahead of us now is an awkward one," Rumsfeld continued. "It's untidy. And freedom's untidy. And free people are free to make mistakes and commit crimes and do bad things. They're also free to live their lives and do wonderful things. And that's what's going to happen here," Rumsfeld said. "And for suddenly the biggest problem in the world to be looting is really notable.

"Think what's happened in our cities when we've had riots and problems and looting," Rumsfeld reminded his audience. "Stuff happens!"

●   ●   ●

U.S. troops never did find weapons of mass destruction in Iraq. On April 15, 2003, a team of inspectors led by David Kay returned to Petrochemical Complex 3 in Baghdad, the site where Kay and UNSCOM had discovered the plans for Saddam Hussein's nuclear arsenal twelve years earlier, one of the most important nonproliferation triumphs of the 1990s. Perhaps they had gone to the well once too often. The offices and labs were barren, looted even of their drywall.

The Bush White House was initially not concerned when no WMDs were uncovered in Iraq. Saddam Hussein had been such a master of deception, of "cheat and retreat," that any restricted WMD facilities were sure to be hidden with fiendish cleverness—something really devious. But with each passing day, as first the most suspicious sites and then the secondary and tertiary sites were turned upside down, a growing suspicion began to dawn among the inspectors on the ground that during his final years in power, Saddam may have committed his greatest deception of all.

Still, even without a major WMD find, the liberation of Iraq would have remained an unqualified triumph in the eyes of the American people and the world had not American troops started taking casualties after the fall of Saddam Hussein. Nothing had prepared the senior figures of the Bush administration for this outcome. Even during the chaotic aftermath of the first Gulf War, which had been so politically costly for George H. W. Bush, the casualties had stopped the day the war had stopped.

As the chaos inside Iraq worsened, there began to be whispered comparisons to the aftermath of the first Iraq War.

President George W. Bush and his advisers were determined that he would not share his father's fate. There were many lessons they could have learned from the first Iraq War, but did not. But one lesson that they had learned was the importance of owning the narrative of what had happened in the war. In 1992 they had witnessed George H. W. Bush lose control of the Iraq narrative to his political opponents. It became less a story about presidential leadership and the liberation of Kuwait than a story about the prewar "coddling" of Saddam Hussein, refugee crises, UN resolutions, and weapons inspections. George W. Bush was determined to let no such thing happen to him. His vice president, Dick Cheney, who had borne the brunt of defending the first Bush administration's failed policy in Iraq during the two years following Desert Storm, was perhaps the most adamant on the point. So the Bush White House launched a preemptive campaign against his critics, telling the Iraq story the way it wanted it to be told: as one of Mission Accomplished. As it had discovered in the 2002 campaign to create support for this war among the American people, a good line, a good background shot, and a good audience were the keys to a convincing story. Iraq would remain a story about terrorism and weapons of mass destruction, regardless of the cost.

On June 16, 2003, the president made an appearance in Elizabeth, New Jersey, to make a speech. It was a carefully chosen Republican audience in a carefully chosen venue: hardworking, patriotic business owners living in the shadow of the New York City skyline. The sort of people who would accept without question the claim of a link between 9/11 and the war in Iraq.

It was obvious that the president still wore the laurels of victory with this constituency. After a rousing welcome, George W. Bush spoke to the crowd. He did not speak of military occupation, or civil war, or missing weapons of mass destruction. Instead, he spoke of security and victory and freedom for the people of Iraq. He then warned his audience against those who would deny him and them this story.

"This nation acted to a threat from the dictator of Iraq," the president said. "Now there are some who would like to rewrite history. Revisionist historians is what I like to call them."

In a sense, he had come full circle with his father.

EPILOGUE

Historians sometimes speak of a "Great Man" theory of history: the belief that the presence of a single strong-willed individual with a bold vision of the future can, at critical moments, change the entire course of history. Julius Caesar, Napoleon, Lincoln—all at one time or another have been cited as examples of the Great Man theory.

In the immediate aftermath of the 9/11 attacks on the United States, and then throughout the eighteen months leading to the invasion of Iraq, many Americans came to accept a variation on the Great Man theory—what might be termed the "Right Man" theory. A nation traumatized by the shock and monstrous evil of 9/11 sought strength and reassurance where Americans have always sought strength and reassurance in time of national crisis: from the Oval Office. And among many, a belief took hold that when this time of national testing came, America had been fortunate to have the Right Man in the Oval Office. "Thank God George W. Bush is president," New York mayor Rudolph Giuliani is said to have told his police commissioner in the immediate aftermath of the attacks. Indeed, so prevalent was this belief within the president's inner circle that the neoconservative David Frum (who as one of President George W. Bush's speechwriters had helped coin the phrase "axis of evil") chose *The Right Man* as the title for his memoir of the Bush White House.

For a time this belief was not limited to supporters of the president or Republican partisans alone. So decisive was George W. Bush's leadership in the weeks following 9/11, so intuitive his grasp of what the American people were thinking and feeling at the time, that even longtime critics of the president rallied behind him in the wave of patriotism and national unity that swept through the country after 9/11.

There was, however, one respect in which George W. Bush could not have been any more the Wrong Man. The president was not just any U.S. president. He was the son of George Herbert Walker Bush. It was only natural then that the younger Bush would view the world through the prism of his father's experiences in office. Unfortunately, the Bush dynasty's personal history and historical legacy was entangled in the very two crises that would come to consume George W. Bush's presidency.

The first, surprisingly, was the emergence of al-Qaeda during the 1990s. "They hate us for our freedoms," the president would say to countless American audiences after 9/11 in trying to explain the sudden appearance of a global terrorist group bent on committing mass murder against Americans. The statement is certainly true. He is still saying it. But it was not why they attacked us. The precipitating event that had led al-Qaeda to start attacking Americans, the cause for which Osama bin Laden exchanged his private jet for a private jihad against the United States, was the continued presence of U.S. forces in Saudi Arabia after the 1991 Gulf War. Those forces were not originally intended to be there. Their presence was due solely to the first Bush White House's disastrous handling of the aftermath of Desert Storm: the failure to produce a plan for "managing the endgame" in Iraq; the unrealistic expectation that a Sunni general would topple Saddam Hussein and pacify the country; and above all, the failure to protect Iraq's Shia and Kurdish populations from Saddam's forces, which led to a far greater entanglement of U.S. forces in the region than protecting them probably would have. Intentionally or not, American military personnel remained in Saudi Arabia over the next decade, primarily because just across the Saudi border Saddam remained in power over the next decade.

Osama bin Laden himself had declared on numerous occasions that the specific political goal of al-Qaeda was to drive United States forces out of the Islamic world: first out of Saudi Arabia, then out of other countries in the Middle East. If George W. Bush and his national security team recognized that the chain of events resulting in 9/11 led directly back to the first Bush administration's decisions in the wake of Desert Storm, they never acknowledged the fact. At least not publicly. But privately, officials like Dick Cheney, Colin Powell, Paul Wolfowitz, and others who had served under the first President Bush must have recognized in hindsight the unforeseen consequences of keeping U.S. military personnel in Saudi Arabia to contain Saddam. In April 2003, while most of America's and the world's attention was focused on the fall of Saddam Hussein's regime several weeks earlier, Defense Secretary Donald Rumsfeld quietly announced that the five thousand U.S. Air Force personnel in Saudi Arabia were finally being withdrawn from the kingdom. Never was there a better illustration of closing the barn door once the horse had bolted.

The second international crisis to which George W. Bush and his advisers brought a conflicted personal history was, of course, Iraq. The Bush national security team, and especially Dick Cheney, were indeed fixated on Saddam Hussein, but not in the manner commonly supposed. The 2003 invasion of Iraq to remove Saddam Hussein is often seen as the inevitable end result of a neoconservative ascendancy over Republican foreign policy. In fact, however, during its first eight months in office the administration of George W. Bush had made Iraq an issue of secondary importance in its foreign policy—a cause of considerable dismay for many neoconservatives at the time. Certainly the Bush administration was far more committed than the Clinton administration had been to supporting active measures to bring about the conditions for a coup by the Iraqi opposition. There was nothing remotely sinister or irresponsible in this stance. In trying to help the Iraqi people rid themselves of Saddam Hussein, the administration was pursuing a sound policy that conformed to both the letter and spirit of American law. But staging an actual invasion of Iraq by U.S. troops, as neoconservatives like William Kristol, Robert Kagan, and Richard Perle had been advocating since the mid-1990s, was an entirely different matter.

The 9/11 attacks changed the entire decision-making framework of the Bush White House with respect to Iraq, though again not in the manner commonly supposed. In building the case for war with Iraq after September 2001, President Bush and Vice President Cheney, among other officials, frequently made the argument that the 9/11 attacks had awakened them to the intertwined threats of WMD proliferation and large-scale terrorist attacks on American citizens. If so, then the president and his senior advisers must have been sleeping especially soundly during the 1990s, when these two threats had preoccupied the Clinton national security team. The theory they advanced to the American people was that Saddam Hussein's thirst for revenge against the United States—and the Bush inner circle specifically—was so intense that he was the most likely candidate to transfer WMDs to terrorist groups like al-Qaeda. That Saddam actually had an active WMD program in place was to them a matter of almost biblical certainty.

But while Saddam's hatred of the United States was an established fact, even the Bush White House was aware that Iraq's purported WMD capabilities lagged behind those of Pakistan, North Korea, and Iran. They already had reason to suspect that North Korea and Pakistan were serial proliferators of nuclear and missile technology. And they were certainly cognizant that Iraq's activities as a state sponsor of terrorism paled in comparison with those of Iran and Syria.

There was, however, one area where Saddam Hussein had proven himself time and again a uniquely dangerous menace. In the decade since the end of the 1991 Gulf War, Saddam had shown on numerous occasions his ability to capitalize on a White House distracted by other international crises or domestic political troubles to achieve his own goals. As one senior official in the first Bush White House had phrased it, the Iraqi dictator possessed "mythical powers" when it came to defying the United States. Saddam had first demonstrated these mythical powers during the final two years of George H. W. Bush's presidency, when he had taken advantage of the outbreak of ethnic war in the Balkans and the first President Bush's failing reelection campaign to successfully erode the UN containment regime imposed on Iraq at the end of the Gulf War. The many veterans of that administration who now served under George W. Bush remembered well that while President Bush may have won the war, Saddam Hussein had won the peace. It was an article of faith within Republican foreign policy circles that the eight years of the Clinton administration had afforded Saddam even greater room for maneuver, owing to President Clinton's "weakness" in foreign policy and his domestic political difficulties.

As they contemplated a world transformed by 9/11, Saddam's "mythical powers" to embarrass the United States once again loomed large in the minds of the Bush administration's leading figures. With its military forces and attention dispersed worldwide to wage a truly global war on terror, the United States might lack the means and the political will to respond to a major challenge by Saddam Hussein, just as the first President Bush had in 1992; or as President Clinton had in 1998.

This consideration weighed especially heavily on the mind of Vice President Dick Cheney. During his time as the elder George Bush's defense secretary, Cheney had found himself thrust into the role of principal apologist for the administration's policies in Iraq; especially the president's questionable decision to end the Gulf War with Saddam Hussein still in power. It had been a searing experience for him. In particular, he had witnessed firsthand the difficulty of mounting any kind of effective military action against Saddam amidst the Sturm und Drang of an American presidential campaign.

As Cheney and the other principals of George W. Bush's administration looked to the future after the campaign to topple the Taliban in Afghanistan, this consideration was never far from their minds. If Saddam's carefully timed response to the first George Bush's reelection bid was merely shutting out UN weapons inspections, what might it have been during a second Bush's bid for reelection, after years of assumed WMD proliferation and in the shadow of 9/11? George W. Bush and his advisers—most of whom were there in 1992 to experience firsthand both Saddam's maneuvers and their own inability to counter them—weren't about to wait until 2004 to find out.

They had no idea what form a challenge from Saddam might take in 2004. They didn't need to. For a Bush dynasty already hypersensitive about its record vis-à-vis Iraq, any bad news datelined "Baghdad 2004" would have been a painful flashback to the implosion of an earlier Bush White House.

All wars are inherently political acts. But the Bush administration's decision to invade Iraq in 2003 was more political than most, a war of choice waged by a generation of officials who had been indelibly scarred by their experiences in an earlier Bush administration. After the 9/11 attacks on American soil, taking military action against the perpetrators of this crime was the primary imperative of U.S. foreign policy. The war against the Taliban and al-Qaeda in Afghanistan was a just, necessary, and proportionate response to 9/11. The war in Iraq was none of these things.

It would be far easier for us as citizens to assign blame for America's entanglement in Iraq to faulty intelligence about weapons of mass destruction; or to the machinations of a small cabal of neoconservative think tank officials in Washington. But to do so would be to misstate the central dynamic of the Iraq war. What made the invasion of Iraq inevitable was Saddam Hussein's triumph over the Bush national security team in 1992, and the fear that he would repeat the triumph in 2004. This fixation on Saddam ran through the Bush dynasty like a malignant strain of DNA, a pathogen always a threat to appear under the right conditions of crisis. On the eve of September 11, staging an invasion of Iraq was the last thought on the minds of George W. Bush and the principals of his administration. Forty-eight hours later, their thoughts were consumed by Iraq, almost to the point of crowding out serious deliberation about the real perpetrators of the 9/11 attacks. Once this pathogen had been released into the American body politic, the views of the neoconservatives about regime change in Iraq provided a foreign policy rationale for the war, and faulty intelligence about weapons of mass destruction provided a political rationale that resonated with the American people.

It is with us, the American people, where blame for this war must ultimately lie. Amidst the shock and horror of 9/11, we turned for security to the Bush White House. We wanted Them to protect Us from the threats of the present and the future. Thus we granted extraordinary latitude to one administration and one political family to define what those threats were. But the lesson of the two Iraq wars is that even in a democracy, leaders may perceive threats differently than the people who elected them, and sometimes may fail to perceive certain threats at all. We would do well to remember that in a democracy, leaders are elected to promote the national interest, not to define what it is. That task is left to us.

ACKNOWLEDGMENTS

If any person wishes to learn how many friends they have, I say let them write a book. In researching and writing this book, I incurred a debt of gratitude to many individuals whom I am fortunate to consider friends.

Circle in the Sand first took shape as a Harvard doctoral thesis, and thus I owe particular thanks to the three Harvard faculty members who guided my research from its inception. Stanley Hoffmann, my principal adviser, shaped the development of this book and my overall approach to foreign policy analysis in ways I cannot begin to enumerate. For a half century, he has enriched the lives of his students and elevated the level of discourse on American foreign policy with his unique blend of erudition, moral conviction, and gentle humor.

I was fortunate to have one of America's most distinguished historians, Ernest R. May, as another adviser. No one has done more to educate foreign policy analysts—and foreign policy practitioners—about the complexities of looking to the "lessons" of the past to guide choices in the present. He is a gentleman and scholar, in an era that has too few of either.

Finally, Louise Richardson has been an invaluable source of knowledge and good advice at every stage of this project. Her incisive research and elegant writing about international relations provide a worthy example to emulate. I consider her a role model, both as a scholar and as a human being.

It would have been impossible to write *Circle in the Sand* without the recollections shared by dozens of senior officials who agreed to be interviewed for the book. Those whom I can acknowledge publicly include Morton Abramowitz, Sandra Charles, Dick Cheney, Lawrence Eagleburger, Chas Freeman, John Galvin, Robert Gates, Richard Haass, David Jeremiah, Robert Kimmitt, Anthony Lake, Thomas Pickering, Dennis Ross, Brent Scowcroft, John Sununu, Dan Quayle, Paul Wolfowitz, and Robert Zoellick. Former President George H. W. Bush graciously agreed to answer a number of questions submitted to him in writing.

In the course of seemingly innumerable research trips to the George Bush Presidential Library in Texas, I benefited greatly from the expert and professional assistance of the archival team at the Bush Library. Particular thanks are owed to Dr. Robert Holzweiss, Senior Archivist, as well as to Debbie Carter and Matt Lee. I am also indebted to Ambassador Peter Galbraith for directing me to some important sources on the aftermath of the 1991 Gulf War, a crisis on which he possesses a unique firsthand perspective.

My colleagues at Young & Rubicam Brands went out of their way to express their enthusiasm about my undertaking this project. I am especially grateful to my bosses, Nancy Jaffe, Len Ellis, and Jonathan Perloe, for making my transition from advertising executive to full-time author such a seamless one.

Throughout the period when I was writing this book, a number of friends were unstinting in providing me with encouragement. George Scribner and Mark Andersen, friends and professional colleagues of long standing, offered sound advice on numerous occasions. Other friends who have been supportive include Dr. Bob Deutsch, Susan Lee, David Lipovitch, Chris McCarthy, Amy Meyers, Elizabeth Miller, Matthew Pereira, Keren Perry-Shamir, Heath Podvesker, Howard Seibel, Georganne Shirk, and Diana Villamarin.

In bringing this book to fruition, I was lucky to have the best publishing team in the business working on my behalf. Doubleday "brought the house" to our very first meeting, and *Circle in the Sand* has benefited from the talents of an extraordinary array of individuals. From our first brief telephone conversation, and through countless conversations afterward, I was thrilled to have Gerry Howard as my editor. His candor, perceptiveness, and creative vision manifest themselves in every sentence he speaks. In the course of working together over many months, I also came to appreciate his great ear for narrative and grace under pressure.

Other members of the Doubleday team to whom I owe my thanks include Bette Alexander, Michael Collica, Nicole Dewey, Diana Foster, Lorraine Hyland, Gretchen Koss, John Pitts, Louise Quayle, Alison Rich, and Rakesh Satyal. Dean Curtis copyedited a complex manuscript with flair and precision. John Fulbrook and Umi Kenyon created the stunning cover that told the story of the book in an image.

My agent, Susan Rabiner, successfully brought this book to market. From the beginning, she immediately recognized the potential for this project. I am very grateful for her strategic counsel and perseverance in seeing it through. My attorney, Bob Zielinski, provided skilled legal advice on contractual matters.

For their love and support, I owe my parents, Eldora and Eric Alfonsi, a debt of gratitude that can never be repaid. They have helped me come full circle in my own life. My grandparents, Benjamin and Attilia DiBiase, remain a constant source of inspiration, each in their own way.

Finally, I would speak of the person to whom this book is dedicated, my brother Benjamin. He was my most unfailing source of advice and encouragement in the writing of this book. Barely a day went by when I did not turn to him to bounce a phrase or idea, or just to share an occasional laugh. An astute observer of human nature, gifted writer, and true Renaissance man, he remains my first and best friend.

NOTES

Introduction

3   "the best and the brightest": David Halberstam, *The Best and the Brightest* (New York: Random House, 1972).

Chapter 1

12   "the hanging of British journalist Farzad Bazoft": Thirteen years later, after the fall of Saddam Hussein in 2003, Bazoft's newspaper in Britain, the *Observer*, sent a correspondent to Iraq to track down the man who had arrested and interrogated him, former Iraqi intelligence colonel Kadem Askar. The Iraqi admitted that there had been no credible evidence that Bazoft was spying, and that the execution had been personally ordered by Saddam for political purposes. Ed Vulliamy, "Presumed Innocent," *The Observer*, May 18, 2003.

12   "Before leaving Washington, Dole had been briefed": In her cable to Washington summarizing the meeting, Ambassador Glaspie noted, "From our side, Senator Dole masterfully covered the points suggested to him by the Secretary"; Baghdad #02186, "CODEL Dole: Meeting with Saddam Hussein," Embassy Baghdad to Washington, April 12, 1990.

13   "Saddam must have attached great importance to this meeting": Ibid.

13   "Saddam was using the formal, polite form of the language": Ibid.

13   "Saddam produced a thick dossier": Ibid.

13   "If there is a campaign against Iraq": Ibid.

14   "the Iraqi leader even offered something akin to an apology": Ibid.

14   "I believe your problem is with the Western media": Saddam Hussein had a transcript made of the senators' remarks during the meeting; it was subsequently broadcast on Iraqi state radio. See Foreign Broadcast Information Service, FBIS-NES-90-074, April 17, 1990. See also Douglas Waller, "Glass House," *The New Republic*, November 5, 1990. Dole and

his colleagues' obsequious treatment of Saddam was the subject of a blistering series of columns by *New York Times* columnist William Safire. See, for instance, "Broadcast to Baghdad," *New York Times*, September 10, 1990, p. A23.

14   "Even if Baghdad is pulverized": Quoted in Baghdad #02186, cited earlier.

17   "Normal relations between the United States": National Security Directive 26, "U.S. Policy Towards the Persian Gulf," October 2, 1989.

17   "When Saddam gave his speech": Dennis Ross interview.

18   "As a young Pentagon staffer": Dennis Ross and Paul Wolfowitz, "Capabilities for Limited Contingencies in the Persian Gulf" (1979); for excerpts from the memorandum, see Michael R. Gordon and Bernard E. Trainor, *The Generals' War: The Inside Story of the Conflict in the Gulf* (Boston: Little, Brown, 1994), p. 480, n. 2.

18   "If Iraq precipitated a crisis with Kuwait": Ibid.

18   "The more he examined Saddam's record": Ross interview.

19   "In 1956, shortly after the United States": For a definitive account of the 1956 Suez crisis, with particular emphasis on the strains the crisis caused between the United States and Britain, see Louise M. Richardson, *When Allies Differ: Anglo-American Relations in the Suez and Falkland Crises* (New York: St. Martin's Press, 1996).

20   "this was not the kind of foreign leader": Ross interview.

20   "The whole thing about giving this guy credits": Ibid.

21   "The sheikh did not seem overly concerned": Baghdad #02914, "NSC/NEA Senior Director Haass' Meeting with Minister of Petroleum," Embassy Baghdad to Washington, May 20, 1990.

21   "Haass traveled to Baghdad to hear the Iraqi side": Ibid.

22   "Haass called on an old acquaintance": Ibid.

22   "the top U.S. diplomats posted to capitals": Chas Freeman interview.

23   "Kennan had written his famous 'Long Telegram' ": Kennan's telegram was subsequently published as a landmark 1947 article in the journal *Foreign Affairs*, "The Sources of Soviet Conduct," under the pseudonym 'X'.

23   "the Woolly Mammoth cables": Freeman interview.

24   "The only person at the conference": Freeman interview.

Chapter 2

25   "Saddam accused 'Western imperialists' ": Baghdad #04089, "Saddam's National Day Speech: Warning to OPEC Over-producers," Embassy Baghdad to Washington, July 18, 1990.

26   "Now they want to cut off the livelihood of the Arabs": Ibid.

26   "Saddam's speech, as it dealt with the oil price issue": Ibid.

27   "The letter described Kuwait's 'theft' of oil revenue": Baghdad #04130, "Iraqi Letter to Arab League," Embassy Baghdad to Washington, July 19, 1990.

27 "On July 18, Iraq's ambassador to the United States": State Department #241042, "U.S. Reaction to Iraqi Threats in the Gulf," Secretary of State Baker to Embassy Baghdad and other embassies, July 24, 1990.

27 "Glaspie handed Hamdun a copy": Baghdad #04130, cited earlier.

27 "We have never taken a position on bilateral issues": Ibid.

27 "the preemptive attack that destroyed the Osirak nuclear reactor": For a detailed account of the events surrounding the Israeli raid on Osirak and the issues of preemption that it raised, see Beth N. Polebaum, "National Self-Defense in International Law: An Emerging Standard for a Nuclear Age," in *New York University Law Review* 59:1, April 1984, pp. 187–229.

28 "We believe that disputes must be resolved by peaceful means": Baghdad #04130, cited earlier.

28 "Glaspie now realized that Hamdun must be under strict orders": Ibid.

28 "Hamdun finally spoke": Ibid.

28 "That same day in Washington": Brian Shellum, *A Chronology of Defense Intelligence in the Gulf War: An Aid for Analysts* (Washington: Defense Intelligence Agency History Office, July 1997), p. 7; in Jeffrey T. Richelson, ed., *Operation Desert Storm: Ten Years After* (Washington: National Security Archive, 2001), Document 16. For a narrative account of DIA warnings and Lang's actions in the weeks leading up to the Iraqi invasion, see Bob Woodward, *The Commanders* (New York: Simon & Schuster, 1991), pp. 205–21.

29 "The next morning, July 20": Ibid.

29 "U.S. spy satellites had detected tank transporters": Ibid.

29 "The U.S. defense attaché stationed in Baghdad": *A Chronology of Defense Intelligence in the Gulf War*, pp. 6ff.

29 "three thousand Iraqi military vehicles on the road to Kuwait": Ibid.

30 "Every morning from 8:00 to 9:30 A.M.": John Sununu interview.

30 "the morning conversations among Bush and his two top aides": Ibid.

31 "Unnerved by Saddam's July 17 speech": *The Generals' War*, pp. 16ff.

31 "At 12:30 A.M. on the morning of July 25": Baghdad #04221, "Iraqi Query RE: US/UAE 'Manoeuvers' [*sic*]," Embassy Baghdad to Washington, July 24, 1990.

31 "Without preamble, Hamdun said": Ibid.

31 "Glaspie calmly replied": Ibid.

32 "You know full well we do not want clarification": Ibid.

32 "Who are these 'attachés' ": Ibid.

32 "Glaspie was stunned": The July 25, 1990, meeting between U.S. Ambassador April Glaspie and Saddam Hussein has often been regarded as a critical turning point in the 1990 Gulf crisis. Critics subsequently charged that at this meeting Saddam was given a "green light" to invade Kuwait by the Bush administration. Contributing to the impression that the administration had something to hide, the Bush State Department refused to release an official American transcript of the meeting, leaving

the transcript published by the government of Iraq as the only extant account for the next fifteen years. Called to testify about this meeting with Saddam before Congress on March 20–21, 1991, Glaspie and her immediate superior at the State Department, Assistant Secretary of State for Near East and South Asian Affairs John Kelly, claimed that the Iraqi transcript was accurate as far as it went, but omitted several key statements made by Glaspie. The critical portions from the Iraqi transcript were published, among other places, in the *New York Times*. See "Excerpts from Iraqi Document on Meeting with U.S. Envoy," in *New York Times* (International Edition), September 23, 1990, p. 19.

In 2003, Glaspie's cable to the State Department summarizing her conversation with Saddam was finally declassified. See Baghdad #04237, "Saddam's Message of Friendship to President Bush," Embassy Baghdad to Washington, July 25, 1990. There are only minor discrepancies between the Iraqi account of what was said at the meeting and Glaspie's own reporting of events. However, Glaspie's cable is an invaluable historical record for another reason. It captures in real time her own impressions of Saddam's intentions and motivations based on the Iraqi dictator's words and demeanor during their conversation. What the cable reveals is that the focus on whether Glaspie and the U.S. government gave a "green light" to Saddam (and there is no clear evidence that they did, or intended to do so) may have diverted attention away from the real issues: Saddam's unprecedented behavior in requesting the meeting with Glaspie, and his bizarre, melodramatic rhetoric during the meeting itself. In hindsight, both were highly out of character for the Iraqi ruler, and it is clear that this should have raised the alarm of Glaspie or her superiors in Washington about Saddam's intentions. Unfortunately, as Glaspie's cable to Washington the next day revealed, she interpreted the July 25 meeting as a sign that "Saddam has blinked"—a spectacularly flawed assessment she did not amend until several days later.

The account of the July 25 meeting in this book is based on both sources, but Glaspie's cable should be considered the definitive record of the event by historians.

36   "The next morning Glaspie sent a jubilant cable": Baghdad #04277, "Iraq Blinks—Provisionally," Embassy Baghdad to Washington, July 26, 1990.

36   "Her message noted one other curious fact": Ibid.

37   "on July 25 the DIA had gone to WATCHCON II": A *Chronology of Defense Intelligence in the Gulf War*, pp. 6ff.

37   "Also on July 25, Pat Lang and his staff": Ibid.

37   "On Friday, July 27, even as intelligence": Ibid.

38   "That afternoon, in a secure conference room": Ibid.

38   "An innovation first proposed": In an interview with the author, Cheney attributes the creation of the Deputies Committee to the Bush administration's bungled response to an October 1990 coup attempt against Panamanian strongman Manuel Noriega:

When we went through that exercise on the first of October [1990], what came out of that was that we'd been pretty sloppy inside the Administration in terms of how we dealt with that. Things had happened without conscious decisions being made and so forth. . . . By the time we got untracked, the coup plotters were dead. But out of that emerged the Deputies Committee, the coordinating committee that really began to get our act together in terms of how we dealt with these sorts of crises.

Undersecretary of State Robert Kimmitt, an habitué at Deputies Committee meetings, emphasizes the high degree of cooperation among the Deputies:

The crisis management team was sort of interesting at the Deputies Committee level in guys like Wolfowitz, Gates, Jeremiah, Kerr, Richard Haass in the Gulf, myself. These are all guys who have worked here for years, including the eight years of the Reagan administration. We had long ago figured out whether or not we liked each other, so there was no BS in our meetings. We just got right to work. (Robert Kimmitt interview)

39   "Ordinarily, the fifth person in attendance": Robert Gates interview.
39   "the deputies' consensus was that Saddam would likely seize": Memorandum, Sandra Charles to Brent Scowcroft, July 27, 1990, Case No. 98-0099-F/2, Richard Haass Files, Bush Presidential Records, George Bush Presidential Library.
39   "The agency was reporting": Interview with a senior Bush administration official.
39   "Kessem described Kuwait": The best firsthand account of the 1961 Iraq-Kuwait border incident is that of the Western leader who marshaled a military response to Iraq's gambit, British prime minister Harold Macmillan. See Harold Macmillan, *Pointing the Way, 1959–1961* (London: Macmillan London, 1972), pp. 383ff.
40   "Irredentism is always a popular battle cry": Ibid.
40   "Shortly after the 1968 presidential election": Henry Kissinger, *White House Years* (Boston: Little, Brown, 1999), p. 51.
41   "Charles was surprised": Sandra Charles interview.
41   "Analysts believe that a shallow incursion": Memorandum, Sandra Charles to Brent Scowcroft, July 27, 1990, Case No. 98-0099-F/2, Richard Haass Files, Bush Presidential Records, George Bush Presidential Library.
41   "In Tel Aviv, Israeli energy minister": Foreign Broadcast Information

Service, FBIS-JN 2907090890. See also State Department #251879, "Request for Clarification on Israel's Chemical Weapons Capability," Washington to Embassy Tel Aviv and other embassies, August 1, 1990.

42 "On the evening of July 28, Ambassador Glaspie was summoned": Baghdad #04343, "GOI Requests Official USG Reaction on Israeli CW Admission," Embassy Baghdad to Washington, July 30, 1990.

42 "The Government of Iraq does not approve of loose talk": Baghdad #04355, "Demarche on Israeli Statement on CW," Embassy Baghdad to Washington, July 30, 1990.

42 "Later that evening, Iraqi state television": Baghdad #04343, cited earlier.

43 "Samuel Lewis, the U.S. ambassador to Israel": State Department #251879, cited earlier.

44 "Shortly after her meeting with Saddam on July 25": Baghdad #04277, cited earlier.

44 "She offered two suggestions directly": Baghdad #04326, "President Bush's Response to Saddam's Message—Next Steps," Embassy Baghdad to Washington, July 29, 1990.

45 "We have defined our national interest": Ibid.

45 "Saddam and the Iraqis, all of them": Ibid.

45 "Just so there was no confusion in Washington": Ibid.

46 "On July 28 the president had responded": State Department #247900, "President Bush's Response to Saddam Hussein's Message," Washington to Embassy Baghdad, July 28, 1990.

46 "At CIA, I learned firsthand what intelligence can and cannot do": George Bush, personal letter to the author, April 26, 1996.

46 "For that reason, he would later admit privately": Ibid.

48 "Bush admitted that he had been 'very anxious to get this call' ": Memorandum of Telephone Conversation, George Bush and King Hussein (C. David Welch, Notetaker), July 27, 1990, OA/ID CF 01043, Richard Haass Files, Working Files—Iraq Pre 8/2/90, Bush Presidential Records, George Bush Presidential Library.

48 "Hussein immediately sought to reassure the president": Ibid.

48 "I appreciate the recent exchange of messages we have had": Talking Points, "Points to Be Made with Iraqi President Saddam Hussein" (unused), August 1, 1990, Case No. 98-0099-F/2, Richard Haass Files, Bush Presidential Records, George Bush Presidential Library.

Chapter 3

50 "Iraq invaded Kuwait in the predawn hours": For a firsthand account of the invasion from inside Kuwait, see H. Norman Schwarzkopf, *It Doesn't Take a Hero* (New York: Linda Grey Bantam Books, 1992), pp. 295–98.

51 "They have conducted a highly professional operation": Woodward, *The Commanders*, p. 227.

51 "Pickering's first thought was to notify": Thomas Pickering interview.

52 "You might try the Russian Tea Room": Ibid.

52 "The Kuwaiti ambassador said that night": Ibid.

52 "Shortly after the 1988 election": Ibid.

53 "By a vote of 14-0": UN Security Council Resolution 660, August 2, 1990.

53 "After he reported the good news to Brent Scowcroft": Pickering interview.

53 "We're not discussing intervention": George Bush, "Remarks and an Exchange with Reporters on the Iraqi Invasion of Kuwait," *Public Papers of the President*, August 2, 1990.

54 "There was a tendency on the part of the military": Pickering interview.

54 "I was frankly appalled": George Bush and Brent Scowcroft, *A World Transformed* (New York: Alfred A. Knopf, 1998), p. 321.

54 "You must kick Saddam out of Kuwait": Lawrence Eagleburger interview.

54 "Mr. President, I don't think your policy is sustainable": Pickering interview.

55 "I was dismayed": Paul Wolfowitz interview.

56 "It is difficult to overstate the depth": Baghdad #04277, cited earlier. In the same analysis, Glaspie elaborated on some of the reasons why many Iraqis held such negative perceptions of the Kuwaitis: "The Kuwaitis who come to Iraq with pockets full of Iraqi dinars (purchased at the black market rate, which is less than one-tenth the official rate) and which they ostentatiously spend, . . . who can be seen in Basra and in the northern summer resorts, often drunk, sometimes disorderly. . . . They also come to Baghdad in droves, providing the clientele for cheap nightclubs and call girls.

   "Iraqis deeply feel that the Kuwaitis are immensely stingy shylocks, living high while Iraq, which made such terrible sacrifices during the war, is still suffering," Glaspie concluded.

56 "He overreached": Sununu interview.

56 "Rewinding the clock on history": Gates interview.

56 "Nobody anticipated a wholesale invasion": Charles interview.

57 "I know he's a thug": Quoted in James A. Baker III, *The Politics of Diplomacy: Revolution, War, and Peace, 1989–1992* (New York: G. P. Putnam's Sons, 1995), pp. 5–6.

58 "Any attempt by any outside force": Jimmy Carter, "The President's State of the Union Address," *Public Papers of the President*, January 23, 1980.

58 "Not insignificantly, the Saudis": See for instance Daniel Yergin, *The Prize: The Epic Quest for Oil, Money, and Power* (New York: Simon & Schuster, 1991), p. 690. According to Yergin, adding to the Saudis' importance in this regard was their general preference for stable, long-term prices—of all the major oil producers, the Saudis were the least hawkish on price. By contrast, the regimes most antagonistic toward the U.S., such as Iraq, Iran, and Libya, were notorious "price hawks" who constantly sought to extract greater revenue and pricing concessions from their customers in the West—as Saddam tried to do, for example, in the months leading up to the invasion of Kuwait.

58   "The most tangible indication": It should be noted here that George Bush and James Baker had both played key roles in the AWACS negotiations. Baker, for instance, recalls in his memoirs that "as White House Chief of Staff, I'd led the legislative strategy effort to support President Reagan's decision to allow the sale of AWACS radar planes to Saudi Arabia in 1981." In *The Politics of Diplomacy*, p. 118.

60   "During the Reagan years, Bush had functioned": This perceptive observation was made by Daniel Yergin. See *The Prize*, pp. 755–58.

61   "An Iraqi-instigated oil crisis": This was not only a theoretical possibility. While the 1973 OPEC oil embargo had imposed severe economic hardships on citizens of the United States and Western Europe, it had literally represented a death sentence for millions of impoverished people throughout the Third World, who could no longer afford to purchase tractor fuel and petrochemical fertilizer, the two basic raw materials of modern agriculture.

61   "It's been a remarkable twenty-four hours": Minutes from NSC meeting, August 3, 1990, on the Persian Gulf, Case No. 98-0099-F, Bush Presidential Records, George Bush Presidential Library.

61   "King Fahd, King Hussein, Mubarak": Ibid.

62   "Diplomatic efforts are under way": Ibid.

62   "We don't expect the Arabs to confront Iraq": *A World Transformed*, p. 323.

62   "It would be useful to take a minute": Minutes from NSC meeting, August 3, 1990, on the Persian Gulf, Case No. 98-0099-F, Bush Presidential Records, George Bush Presidential Library.

63   "Beyond that, the consequences": Ibid.

63   "Scowcroft's eruption was a planned one": *A World Transformed*, p. 322.

63   "This is the first test": Eagleburger interview; see also minutes from NSC meeting, August 3, 1990, on the Persian Gulf, Case No. 98-0099-F, Bush Presidential Records, George Bush Presidential Library.

64   "The last day or so": Ibid.

64   "Recognizing that this topic was political dynamite": Ibid.

64   "Sununu was concerned": Ibid., Sununu interview.

64   "Even without that, he would be in control": Ibid.

65   "We should introduce a bold statement": Ibid.

65   "According to the Kuwaiti ambassador": Ibid.

65   "On the Iranian border": Ibid., Richard Haass interview.

66   "What about on the other side, with Syria?": Ibid.

66   "They want an 'Arab solution' ": Ibid.

67   "We are concerned about the aircraft on the carrier": Ibid.

67   "This would be the NFL, not a scrimmage": Ibid.

67   "But why weren't they able to kick Iran?": Ibid.

68   "One question is how individualized is this aggression?": Ibid.

68   "Iraq could fall apart": Ibid., Brent Scowcroft interview.

68   "Haass promptly seconded his boss's observation": Ibid., Haass interview.

68 "There are thirty-eight hundred U.S. citizens in Kuwait": Ibid.

69 "This would change the ball game": Ibid.

69 "Bush's period of service as UN ambassador": For a sense of the tension that the Munich Olympic massacres created at the UN and in the surrounding New York community during this period, see George Bush Personal Papers, United Nations Files—Jewish File, Folders 1–3, George Bush Presidential Library.

70 "the prototype of a successful operation": Scowcroft interview.

70 "cheap shot at the *Mayaguez* incident": Brent Scowcroft, letter to the editor, *Washington Post*, April 9, 1980.

71 "This will help": George Bush Personal Diary, May 14, 1975; George Bush Personal Papers, China File—Peking Diary, George Bush Presidential Library.

71 "Though I supported Jimmy Carter's rescue mission": George Bush, personal letter to the author, April 26, 1996.

72 "a president must go the extra mile": Ibid.

72 "Bush had already gone the extra mile": In this context, it is significant that Bush later identified the crimes committed by Panamanian troops against U.S. citizens as the specific "precipitating event" that led him to order military intervention in Panama, when only a few months earlier he had been reluctant to take even minor actions in support of a coup attempt against Noriega.

Asked to account for the dramatic reversal of policy, Bush explicitly cited the threat to the safety of American personnel as the decisive factor: "I think what changed my mind was the events I cited in briefing the American people on this yesterday: the death of the Marine; the brutalizing, really obscene torture of the navy lieutenant; and the threat of sexual abuse and the terror inflicted on that lieutenant's wife; the declaration of war by Noriega; the fact that our people down there didn't know where this was going—they weren't sure what all that meant and whether that meant we could guarantee the safety of Americans down there." George Bush, "The President's News Conference," *Public Papers of the President*, December 21, 1989.

Dick Cheney, who served as Bush's defense secretary during the Panama invasion, confirmed that it was the perceived threat to American lives in Panama that prompted the president's hand. "I think there are precipitating events that do force a president's hand. Clearly, [armed intervention] is a decision no president ever takes lightly, and I think most of the time they will do everything they can to find ways diplomatically to deal with the problem, and not reach for military force as always the first option. So what happens lots of times, as in Panama, you've got an ongoing problem you've been working at diplomatically, and through sanctions, and every other way you can think of, and then all of a sudden the relationship gets bad enough, that something truly bad happens, that people start getting hurt, and then I think all presidents feel a special obligation, at least the ones I worked for, any time there's a threat to American lives" (Cheney interview).

73 "That brings up the question of what if Iraqi troops": Minutes from NSC meeting, August 3, 1990, on the Persian Gulf, Case No. 98-0099-F, Bush Presidential Records, George Bush Presidential Library.

73 "I think to an extraordinary degree": Wolfowitz interview.

73 "Only a dozen officials": For a list of attendees, see Minutes of NSC Meeting on Iraqi Invasion of Kuwait, August 5, 1990, Case No. 98-0099-F, Bush Presidential Records, George Bush Presidential Library.

74 "The original reason for this meeting": Ibid.

75 "There is not factual disagreement between CIA and DIA": Ibid.

75 "Baker quickly concurred": Ibid.

75 "We would need to see more missiles": Ibid.

75 "The next day a chastened Webster": Minutes of NSC Meeting on Iraqi Invasion of Kuwait, August 6, 1990, Case No. 98-0099-F/3, Bush Presidential Records, George Bush Presidential Library.

75 "My sense is that Iraq": Minutes of NSC Meeting on Iraqi Invasion of Kuwait, August 5, 1990, Case No. 98-0099-F, Bush Presidential Records, George Bush Presidential Library.

75 "Maybe if he sees it is not business as usual": Ibid.

75 "We don't want to appear to be negotiating": Ibid.

76 "This is a Catch-22": Ibid.

77 "I am concerned that if we put forces in Saudi Arabia": Ibid.

78 "Its reputation was one of inveterate cronyism": On the charges of cronyism leveled at the Carlyle Group, see Dan Briody, *The Iron Triangle: Inside the Secret World of the Carlyle Group* (New York: John Wiley and Sons, 2004).

85 "Never before in American history": Perhaps the only close parallel would be President Woodrow Wilson's close relationship with Colonel Edward House, a Democratic Party "wise man" during the early years of the twentieth century who acted as Wilson's adviser on foreign policy matters. House later played a key role in helping develop Wilson's famous Fourteen Points peace plan at the end of World War I. For a penetrating account of their relationship, see Alexander L. George and Juliette L. George, *Woodrow Wilson and Colonel House: A Personality Study* (Dover Publications, 1964).

87 "During the long flight to Saudi Arabia": Freeman interview.

87 "Though based on essentially the same raw intelligence": For published firsthand accounts of the meeting, see Schwarzkopf, *It Doesn't Take a Hero*, pp. 302–6; Woodward, *The Commanders*, pp. 263–73.

88 "Freeman thought this was an inspired gesture": Freeman interview.

88 "His most important point": See Woodward, *The Commanders*, p. 264. Over a year later, interviewed for the PBS television documentary "The Gulf Crisis: The Road to War," Cheney would repeat the claim that the

United States had promised King Fahd that all U.S. forces would be withdrawn from Saudi Arabia after the Iraqi threat to the kingdom was removed: "One of the things I had promised [Fahd] at the direction of the president was that we would deploy forces, we would deploy a lot of forces, but that once the need for them was ended, we would remove those forces. We were not looking for permanent bases."

88 "Fahd was clearly relieved by this pledge": Freeman interview.

89 "Fahd cut him off": Ibid. For a similar account, see Schwarzkopf, *It Doesn't Take a Hero*, pp. 305–6.

89 "The president wants you to stop in Egypt": Gates interview.

90 "The six men boarded": Ibid.

90 "The Americans met with Mubarak": Ibid.

90 "Saddam broke his word to me": Ibid.

91 "The president thinks he may want": Ibid.

92 "What I wanted to do was get a quick update": Minutes of NSC Meeting on Iraqi Invasion of Kuwait, August 6, 1990, Case No. 98-0099-F/3, Bush Presidential Records, George Bush Presidential Library.

92 "In the last twenty-four hours the situation has stabilized": Ibid.

92 "The Federal Reserve has a similar study": Ibid.

93 "How long can Iraq withstand the pain": Ibid.

93 "Iraqi oil will only get to market": Ibid.

93 "We also need to discuss cheating": Ibid.

94 "With time, cheating will go up": Ibid.

95 "We need to assess what it takes to starve them": Ibid.

95 "Darman is making a point I agree with": Ibid.

Chapter 4

96 "alliance bandwagoning": On the concept of alliance bandwagoning, see Stephen Walt, *The Origins of Alliances* (Ithaca, NY: Cornell University Press, 1987).

97 "In the life of a nation": George Bush, "Address to the Nation Announcing the Deployment of United States Armed Forces to Saudi Arabia," *Public Papers of the President*, August 8, 1990.

97 "Bush enunciated the 'four simple principles' ": Ibid.

97 "I can't think of an individual, specific thing": Ibid.

98 "No, I don't feel let down by the intelligence": Ibid.

98 "I have not been advised of that": Ibid. See also pp. 119–20 above.

99 "A line has been drawn in the sand": Ibid.

99 "A half century ago our nation": George Bush, "Remarks to Department of Defense Employees," in *Public Papers of the President*, August 15, 1990.

99 "The armies and air forces": Ibid.

100 "What ensued was a heated debate": For differing perspectives on the tanker incident, cf. Bush and Scowcroft, *A World Transformed*, pp. 351–53;

Baker, *The Politics of Diplomacy*, pp. 285–86; and Schwarzkopf, *It Doesn't Take a Hero*, pp. 321–23.

101   "Pickering was needed back at the UN": Pickering interview.

101   "Dick Cheney and the Pentagon": Ibid.

101   "The problem, as Pickering saw it": Ibid.

102   "two NODIS cables": U.S. Mission UN #02425, "Iraq-Kuwait Settlement Ideas," U.S. Mission UN to Washington (NODIS), August 30, 1990; and U.S. Mission UN #02436, "U.S. Objectives—Iraq-Kuwait Settlement," U.S. Mission UN to Washington (NODIS), August 30, 1990.

102   "Our stated goals": U.S. Mission UN #02436, cited earlier.

102   "We need to begin to find a way": Ibid.

103   "Pickering had been struck at the time": Pickering interview.

104   "Pickering's plan called for an exclusionary zone": U.S. Mission UN #02425, cited earlier.

104   "Pickering recognized that Iraq had": Ibid.

104   "Enforcing the exclusionary zone": Ibid.

105   "Our ideas . . . are based": Ibid.

105   "We were in a position to err": Pickering interview.

106   "Pickering proposed limiting the size": U.S. Mission UN #02425, cited earlier.

106   "The principal problem": U.S. Mission UN #02436, cited earlier.

107   "On his personal copy of the Pickering document": OA/ID CFO1518, Richard Haass Files, Working Files—Iraq 8/2/90-12/90 [6 of 8], Bush Presidential Records, George Bush Presidential Library.

107   "This is a tall order": U.S. Mission UN #02425, cited earlier.

109   "Scowcroft changed this to": Memorandum with Attached Speech Draft, William F. Sittman to James Cicconi, September 11, 1990, OA/ID 53762 [2], Box 66, Speech File Drafts—Address to Joint Session of Congress 9/11/90, White House Office of Speechwriting, Bush Presidential Records, George Bush Presidential Library.

110   "No longer will the machinery": Ibid.

110   "We stand today": Ibid.

111   "Attached is the edited version of the speech": Ibid.

111   "Wilson reread the message flimsy in his hand": Memorandum, Richard Haass to Robert Kimmitt, September 11, 1990, OA/ID CF1478, Richard Haass Files, Working Files—Iraq September 1990 [2 of 4], Bush Presidential Records, George Bush Presidential Library.

113   "Convey to President Bush": *A World Transformed*, p. 337.

115   "a team from U.S. Central Command headquarters": Virtually every major account of the 1991 Gulf War has emphasized the deep dissatisfaction of the president and his principal advisers with the October 11 briefing. For Scowcroft's own description of his dissatisfaction, see *A World Transformed*, pp. 380–81.

115   "It was the B-52s that did it": Freeman interview.

116 "he received a 'frag order' ": Ibid.
116 "If Washington puts a single B-52": Ibid.
116 "Freeman disputed the necessity": Ibid.
117 "You don't appear to have read my previous response": Ibid.
117 "If you want to pull me out of here": Ibid.
118 "Do you want these things?": Ibid.
118 "Mr. President, I don't think your staff": Ibid.
120 "the issue of Saudi sensitivities about foreign troops": Ibid.
120 "against whom Saudi clerics railed in their Friday sermons": On the deep hostility toward the U.S. deployment among some segments of the Saudi clerical population, see Daniel Benjamin and Steven Simon, *The Age of Sacred Terror: Radical Islam's War Against America* (New York: Random House Trade Paperbacks, 2003), pp. 107–8.
121 "Freeman had been peppering them with telegrams": Ibid.
121 "Testifying to the House Foreign Affairs Committee": "Progress Report on the Gulf Crisis" (prepared statement by Secretary of State Baker, October 18, 1990), in *Crisis in the Persian Gulf: Hearings and Markup before the Committee on Foreign Affairs, House of Representatives* (Washington, 1990), pp. 63–72.
121 "Baker sent a special 'Eyes Only' cable": State Department #355801, "UNSC Resolution and Military Action to Liberate Kuwait—Talking Points to Use with King Fahd," Secretary of State to Consulate Jeddah (Eyes Only for the Ambassador), October 22, 1990.
121 "Until the necessary forces are in place": Ibid.
122 "the ambassador sent a NODIS cable to Bush and Baker": Riyadh #09445, "Examining Our Military Options," Embassy Riyadh to Washington (NODIS), October 29, 1990.
122 "Due largely to the weather": Ibid.
123 "Initiation of offensive operations": Ibid.
123 "Continued deployment of foreign troops": Ibid.
123 "Both we and Saddam": Ibid.
124 "Given the lead times": Ibid.
125 "Freeman highlighted the next-to-last sentence": Ibid.
125 "When he came to the White House": *A World Transformed*, p. 375.
126 "It was my impression": Ibid, p. 382.
126 "I am very much concerned": George Bush, "The President's News Conference," *Public Papers of the President*, October 9, 1990.
126 "Shortly after the invasion of Kuwait, the exiled emir of Kuwait": The size of the Kuwaiti retainer paid to Hill & Knowlton and its surrogates was reported at the time in the leading trade journal for public relations professionals. See *O'Dwyer's FARA Report* 1:9, October 1991, p. 2.
127 "A senior executive of the firm's Washington office": For details on Fuller's role, see *O'Dwyer's PR Services Report* 5:1, January 1991, pp. 8, 10.
127 "The theme that struck the deepest emotional chord": Perhaps the most

exhaustive investigation of the public relations campaign on behalf of Kuwait was conducted by the Canadian Broadcasting Corporation (CBC), Canada's state media network, which in 1991 produced an Emmy Award–winning television documentary on the campaign entitled "To Sell a War." The head of opinion polling for the Kuwaiti PR campaign is interviewed at length in this documentary. In January 1992, the story was also the subject of a segment by 60 Minutes.

127   "the choice of the Human Rights Caucus to convene the hearings": John R. MacArthur, Second Front: Censorship and Propaganda in the Gulf War (Berkeley and Los Angeles: University of California Press, 1992).

128   "Human Rights Foundation, which occupied free office space": Ibid., p. 60.

128   "I volunteered at the al-Addan Hospital": On the mendacity of the girl's testimony, see Lawrence Freedman and Efraim Karsh, The Gulf Conflict, 1990–1991 (Princeton, NJ: Princeton University Press, 1993), p. 218.

129   "Lantos had known the girl's actual identity": MacArthur, Second Front, cited earlier.

129   "As one observer later commented": Ibid.

129   "So many cars alone were expropriated": For an anecdotal account of the extent of Iraqi looting in Kuwait, see Kenneth M. Pollack, The Threatening Storm: The Case for Invading Iraq (New York: Random House, 2002), p. 60.

129   "It's just unbelievable": George Bush, "The President's News Conference," Public Papers of the President, October 9, 1990.

130   "Bush later admitted that the atrocities": A World Transformed, p. 375.

130   "Hitler revisited": George Bush, "Remarks at a Fundraising Luncheon for Gubernatorial Candidate Clayton Williams in Dallas, Texas," Public Papers of the President, October 15, 1990.

130   "He clearly personalized it": Haass interview.

130   "It worried me that there was a gap": Ibid.

131   "I'm reading a book": George Bush, "Remarks at a Republican Fundraising Breakfast in Burlington, Vermont." Public Papers of the President, October 23, 1990. See also Martin Gilbert, The Second World War: A Complete History, revised (New York: Owl Books, 2004).

131   "Hitler rolled his tanks and troops into Poland": Ibid.

132   "I think in this day and age": Letter, George Bush to Cornelius Ryan, June 15, 1960; cited in George Bush, All the Best, George Bush: My Life in Letters and Other Writings (New York: Scribner/A Lisa Drew Book, 1999), p. 83. See also Cornelius Ryan, The Longest Day: June 6, 1944, reprint edition (New York: Simon & Schuster, 2004).

132   "I hope the guilty receive the treatment": Letter, George Bush to Prescott and Dorothy Bush, August 24, 1944; cited in All the Best, George Bush, p. 49.

135 "We have heard disturbing reports": State Department #282427, "Israeli Reconnaissance Activity," Secretary of State to Embassy Tel Aviv (NODIS), August 23, 1990.

136 "Your settlement policy is a real problem": Interview with a senior Bush administration official.

136 "Bush assumed this to mean": Ibid.

136 "He lied to me!": Ibid.

136 "there was no love lost": Interview with a senior Bush administration official.

137 "You can say the hard things": Ross interview.

137 "He took out all the grace notes": Ibid.

137 "Richard Haass was enlisted": Handwritten Notes on Meeting with Richard Haass and Jewish Representatives on Baker's Speech, Barbara G. Kilberg Files, White House Office of Public Liaison, Bush Presidential Records, George Bush Presidential Library.

137 "Secretary Baker's speech has generated": Memorandum, Bobbie Kilberg to Governor Sununu, "Re: Reaction from the Jewish Community to Secretary Baker's Speech on U.S. Middle East Policy," Kathy Jeavons Files, White House Office of Public Liaison, Bush Presidential Records, George Bush Presidential Library.

138 "This public strategy has undermined": Ibid.

138 "I'll get us together to discuss": Memorandum, Bill Kristol to Cary Lord et al., September 17, 1990, Bill Kristol Files, Quayle Vice Presidential Records, George Bush Presidential Library.

139 "The administration seems to have lost its compass": Thomas Dine, "The Elections, Congress, and Israel," speech before the CJF General Assembly, San Francisco, November 14, 1990.

139 "John, here's the speech I mentioned": Speech with handwritten comments, OA/ID CF00472, John Sununu Files, Persian Gulf War [6], Bush Presidential Records, George Bush Presidential Library.

140 "the Shamir government made known to Washington": Tel Aviv #16825, "The GOI Reaction to a Possible Iraqi Withdrawal," Embassy Tel Aviv to Washington, December 7, 1990. The content of Levy's private message to James Baker earlier that week is referenced in this cable.

140 "Concerned about Iraqi military capabilities": Ibid.

140 "An Iraqi withdrawal that merely": Ibid.

141 "We understand the fears": Memorandum of conversation, "One-on-One Meeting with Prime Minister Shamir of Israel," December 11, 1990, OA/ID CF01508, Richard Haass Files, Working Files—Iraq December 1990 [4 of 6], Bush Presidential Records, George Bush Presidential Library.

141 "If Saddam Hussein does not get out": Ibid.

142 "We have the capability to obliterate his military structure": Ibid.

Chapter 5

143 "On December 18, during a major address": Dan Quayle, "Remarks at the Foreign Policy Research Institute Conference," December 18, 1990.

143 "The idea of a significant reduction of Iraqi military power": Gates interview.

144 "The deputies ultimately agreed on three": Ibid.

144 "We debated a while": Ibid.

144 "There was a rationale": Haass interview.

145 "Ultimately, we unanimously recommended": Gates interview.

145 "Saddam wasn't just going to wait": Ibid.

145 "Our concern was that": Ibid.

146 "Iraq is still actively looking": Baghdad #07062, "Future Moves on the Gulf Crisis," Embassy Baghdad to Washington, December 21, 1990.

146 "Saddam is clearly concerned": Ibid.

146 "if he withdrew from Kuwait, he would not be thumped": John Major, *The Autobiography* (New York: HarperCollins, 1999), p. 223.

147 "The greatest point of vulnerability": Riyadh #11439, "U.S. and Coalition War Aims: Sacked Out on the Same Sand Dunes, Dreaming Different Dreams," Embassy Riyadh to Washington, December 30, 1990.

147 "The Coalition could well fall apart": Ibid.

148 "attacks on military infrastructure units": Ibid.

148 "My mind goes back to history": Cited in *All the Best, George Bush*, p. 498.

148 "I look at today's crisis": Ibid.

149 "Regardless of Saddam Hussein's motivations": "State Paper on Post Crisis Gulf Security Structures," January 11, 1991, OA/ID CF 01584, Richard Haass Files, Working Files—Iraq January 1991 [5 of 12], Bush Presidential Records, George Bush Presidential Library.

149 "The worst-case scenario": Ibid.

150 "By contrast, 'if Iraq is deprived' ": Ibid.

150 "Clarke saw the ideal solution to the problem": Ibid.

151 "On October 30, House speaker Tom Foley": *A World Transformed*, p. 389.

151 "The national security adviser's 1967 PhD thesis": Brent Scowcroft, *Congress and Foreign Policy: An Examination of Congressional Attitudes toward the Foreign Aid Programs to Spain and Yugoslavia* (unpublished PhD dissertation, Columbia University, 1967).

151 "How easy it is": Ibid., p. 199.

152 "It's such a vital problem": Cheney interview.

152 " 'In the end,' Cheney told the president": Ibid.

154 "You know, the president usually likes": Haass interview.

154 "That memo you sent went over like a bomb": Ibid.

155 "if military action is necessary to force Iraq": Defense Intelligence Memorandum 22-91, "Iraq's Armed Forces After the Gulf Crisis: Implications of a Major Crisis," January 1991, OA/ID CF01584, Richard

Haass Files, Working Files—Iraq January 1991 [11 of 12], Bush Presidential Records, George Bush Presidential Library.

156 "A successor government": Ibid.

156 "the successor to Saddam would most likely be": Ibid.

156 "Loyal to the Iraqi dictator to the end": On Izzat's role after the 2003 invasion of Iraq, see Michael Isikoff and Mark Hosenball, "Saddam's New War," *Newsweek*, October 29, 2003.

156 "The most significant Iranian threat": Ibid.

157 "The whole fertile crescent": Jeddah #02964, "An Old Middle East Hand Contemplates the New Order," Consulate Jeddah to Washington, December 5, 1990.

157 "If Iraq sustains massive damage": Paper, "Immediate Post-War Requirements in the Gulf," Case No. 98-0099-F, Richard Haass Files, Working Files—Iraq January 1991 [11of 12], Bush Presidential Records, George Bush Presidential Library.

158 "Realists subscribe to a theory": The foundation work of twentieth-century Realist foreign policy is Hans Morgenthau, *Politics among Nations* (New York: Alfred A Knopf, 1978, rev. ed.).

159 "cut his foreign policy teeth": Scowcroft interview.

159 "The concern was more that": Haass interview.

161 "a battleship *Missouri* ending . . . it goes beyond our domestic writ": Ibid.

161 "There was some concern": Ibid.

161 "the president was in a testy mood that day": Ibid. Haass later recalled wryly about the conversation: "Presidents, like anyone else, want to hear the answer that they prefer. It's never fun giving a president the answer he doesn't want. He clearly was pushing back. . . . I had a lot of good experiences with this president, he's a wonderful guy to work for, as was Brent, but I don't think this was the moment where my star was as high."

162 "Mr. President, I know what you want": Ibid.

163 "Maybe we should just call it a day": Ibid.

163 "Mr. President, we may get lucky": Ibid.

163 "During an August 1990 visit by the king": See Bush's own account of the conversation between the two heads of state in *A World Transformed*, pp. 347–49.

164 "The king had little choice in this situation": Sheikh Ali's remarks are quoted in Jeddah #02964, cited earlier.

164 "On February 2 the king sent Bush a letter": Amman #01361, "King Responds Positively to President's Letter," Embassy Amman to Washington (NODIS), February 2, 1991.

165 "Several years later he would write an op-ed piece": Richard L. Armitage, "Jordan's Potential Role in a Post-Saddam Iraq," *Christian Science Monitor*, March 7, 1994. Some of Armitage's comments at the time seem bizarre in light of later events:

"Post-Saddam, a politically fragmented and economically depressed Iraq will need real leadership and international acceptance to revive its sense of self-respect and to establish itself, for once, in a position of positive regional leadership. Might it be possible for the King of Jordan, drawing upon the goodwill he has accumulated within Iraq, to help the Iraqi people through their recovery process? Might Jordan be able to provide its good offices in encouraging the various Iraqi political factions to cooperate and compete within the context of a parliamentary democracy? . . . Perhaps when Saddam and his clique no longer rule Iraq, the Iraqis themselves—the people, the military, the various factions seeking to take and maintain power—may see it as to their individual and collective advantage to have the King of Jordan help referee their inevitable disputes and midwife Iraq's return to the community of nations."

165 "On February 9 he sent a curt letter": State Department #043327, "Presidential Correspondence: Letter from the President to King Hussein," Secretary of State to Embassy Amman (Immediate), February 9, 1991.

169 "It is all a fantasy": Irving Kristol, "After the War, What?" *Wall Street Journal*, February 22, 1991.

170 "relative stagnation and political impotence": Ibid.

170 "The answer unquestionably has much to do with Islam": Ibid.

174 "A member of his staff at the Pentagon": Fred Iklé, *Every War Must End* (New York: Columbia University Press, 1971). On Powell's interest in the book, see Colin Powell, *My American Journey* (New York: Random House, 1996), p. 519.

174 "treason of the hawks": *Every War Must End*, p. 61.

175 "It's surprising how much I dwell": George Bush personal diary; in *A World Transformed*, p. 484.

176 "Kuwait is liberated": George Bush, "Address to the Nation on the Suspension of Allied Offensive Combat Operations in the Persian Gulf," *Public Papers of the President*, February 27, 1991.

176 "It hasn't been a clean end": George Bush personal diary; in *A World Transformed*, pp. 486–87.

176 "At a televised press conference on March 1": George Bush, "The President's News Conference on the Persian Gulf Conflict," *Public Papers of the President*, March 1, 1991.

177 "On March 1, Clancy sent Gingrich a fax": Cover sheet with attached fax message, Newt Gingrich to John Sununu, March 5, 1991, OA/ID CF00472, John Sununu Files, Persian Gulf War 1991 [2], Bush Presidential Records, George Bush Presidential Library.

178 "Dick Cheney's contribution was the shortest": Cable with attached speech draft, Office of the Secretary of Defense to Bill Sittman, March 5, 1991, OA/ID CF00472, John Sununu Files, Persian Gulf War 1991 [2], Bush Presidential Records, George Bush Presidential Library.

178   "Clayton Yeutter, the Republican Party chairman": Fax message, Clayton Yeutter to John Sununu, March 4, 1991, OA/ID CF00472, John Sununu Files, Persian Gulf War 1991 [2], Bush Presidential Records, George Bush Presidential Library.

178   "I think the Nation wants to celebrate with George Bush": Memorandum, Craig L. Fuller to John Sununu, March 5, 1991, OA/ID CF00472, John Sununu Files, Persian Gulf War 1991 [2], Bush Presidential Records, George Bush Presidential Library.

180   "Six weeks from now the American public": Memorandum, Newt Gingrich to John Sununu, March 4, 1991, OA/ID CF00472, John Sununu Files, Persian Gulf War 1991 [2], Bush Presidential Records, George Bush Presidential Library.

180   "Ten years ago we rejected": Ibid.

181   "A dossier of embarrassing statements made by key Democrats": Memorandum, Bill Kristol to Dan Quayle, March 7, 1990, Bill Kristol Files, Quayle Vice Presidential Records, George Bush Presidential Library.

182   "three different statements before Desert Storm": Ibid.

182   "Even King Hussein sent the president an effusive letter": Memorandum to Robert Gates and Brent Scowcroft, March 1, 1991, NLGB #62, Bush Presidential Records, George Bush Presidential Library.

182   "I am glad the shooting has ceased": Letter, George Bush to King Hassan II of Morocco, February 28, 1991, NLGB #63, Bush Presidential Records, George Bush Presidential Library.

183   "suddenly found themselves in a pitched battle": For an account of the episode from the Gulf theater, see Schwarzkopf, *It Doesn't Take a Hero*, pp. 478–79.

183   "I continue to believe that the crafting": Riyadh #11439, cited earlier.

183   "Achieving the earliest possible surrender": Ibid.

184   "The issue was so important to him": Freeman interview.

184   "All of this would require a lot of intense": Pickering interview.

185   "Bob, what is it that we're doing": Ibid.

186   "There's not going to be any of that": Ibid.

186   "Kimmitt explained that a decision had been made": Ibid.

186   "Pickering thought the plan he and his staff had produced": Pickering interview. See also U.S. Mission UN #02425, "Iraq-Kuwait Settlement Ideas," cited earlier.

186   "We bobbled it badly": Ibid.

187   "We lost sight": Ibid.

187   "Schwarzkopf had beseeched Washington": On the CENTCOM commander's frustration during this period, see *It Doesn't Take a Hero*, pp. 479–80.

187   "For Freeman, it confirmed his worst suspicions": Freeman interview.

188   "total failure of integration between military and political strategy": Ibid.

188 "The first thing Iraq's generals would be expecting": Ibid.
188 "had Saddam been required to sign a surrender document": Multiple interviews. This belief was held not only by Freeman, but by many of the Bush administration's most knowledgeable Middle East hands. For example, Morton Abramowitz, the U.S ambassador to Turkey during the 1991 Gulf War, voiced the same concern almost verbatim.
189 "I thought when the Iraqi generals came out of that tent": Freeman interview.
189 "There were some anxieties right away": Robert Zoellick interview.
189 "It could have been done": Ibid.
189 "I think the cease-fire came too early": Interview with a senior Bush administration official.
189 "I think we were surprised that the regime persisted": David Jeremiah interview.
190 "Robert Kimmitt later coined": Robert Kimmitt interview.

Chapter 6

191 "In your press conference Friday": Letter, Thad Cochran to George Bush, March 4, 1991, Case No. 217851, WHORM: Subject File, Bush Presidential Records, George Bush Presidential Library.
192 "A huge assumption and hope on our part": Gates interview.
192 "Somebody pragmatic, not necessarily pro-America": Charles interview.
192 "Khalilzad had captured these views in a secret planning document": Excerpts from this secret document were first published in Gordon and Trainor, *The Generals' War*, p. 516, n. 14.
193 "On April 12, Brent Scowcroft would finally reply": Letter, Brent Scowcroft to Thad Cochran, April 12, 1991, Case No. 217851, WHORM: Subject File, Bush Presidential Records, George Bush Presidential Library.
194 "I think that what we didn't appreciate": Gates interview.
194 "We didn't want to get into a situation": Haass interview.
194 "Iraq was already a country being convulsed by two separate insurrections": An indispensable account of conditions inside Iraq immediately following Desert Storm is *Civil War in Iraq: A Staff Report of the Committee on Foreign Relations, United States Senate, 1991*, SuDoc Number: Y 4.F 76/2:S.prt.102-27. The report's principal author was Foreign Relations Committee staff director Peter W. Galbraith, who had also played a key role in calling attention to Saddam's use of chemical weapons against the Kurds.
195 "We don't want to be like the Palestinians": Talabani's statement is quoted in Michael M. Gunter, *The Kurds of Iraq* (New York: St. Martin's Press, 1992), p. 49.
195 "For Talabani and the Kurds": Ibid., pp. 50–52.
195 "The Kurdish and Shia uprisings": Gates interview.

196 "We were surprised that they were able to reconstitute": Jeremiah interview.

197 "I think probably all of us had probably underestimated": Kimmitt interview.

198 "Asked whether he saw the possibility": George Bush, "The President's News Conference with Prime Minister John Major of the United Kingdom in Hamilton, Bermuda," *Public Papers of the President*, March 16, 1991.

199 "The Middle East right now requires avoiding symbols": State Department #02047, "Memorandum for the President: Moscow, March 14, 1991," U.S. Delegation with the Secretary in the Soviet Union to Washington (Eyes Only), March 14, 1991.

199 "Clearly, the possibility of being cut into": Ibid.

200 "That was the same argument we encountered throughout the crisis": Ibid.

200 "the Saudi government wished the U.S. State Department to convey an offer": Ibid.

200 "This is a very important development": Ibid.

202 "I think the Saudi move puts us close": Ibid.

202 "At the next small group or Deputies meeting": Memorandum, Nancy Bearg Dyke to Robert Gates, March 15, 1991, OA/ID CF 01076, Nancy Bearg Dyke Files, Persian Gulf—Humanitarian [4 of 11], Bush Presidential Records, George Bush Presidential Library.

202 "That was Wolfowitz predominantly driving that particular train": Interview with a senior Bush administration official.

204 "an unexpected and potentially dangerous public relations debacle": Patrick Tyler, "General's Account of Gulf War's End Disputed by Bush," *New York Times*, March 28, 1991, p. 1.

204 "Obviously, we didn't destroy them to the very last tank": The key excerpts from the Frost interview were reprinted the next day in the *Washington Post*, March 28, 1991, p. 35.

205 "That was a very courageous decision": Ibid.

205 "And the president, you know, made the decision": Ibid.

205 "The decision the president made to stop military action": Ibid.

206 "I understand that—that General—General Cheney": Ibid.

206 "Go ask him, go ask him": Ibid.

207 "Within weeks of arriving at the Pentagon in 1989": For an account of the Welch firing, see Woodward, *The Commanders*, chapter 6, passim.

208 "Woerner 'had been able to find fourteen reasons not to do anything' ": Cheney interview.

210 "There is a general policy we have that Ambassadors don't testify": U.S. Department of State Daily Briefing #45, Wednesday, March 20, 1991.

211 "If, indeed, the Iraqis put out a doctored or inaccurate version": U.S. Department of State Daily Briefing #46, Thursday, March 21, 1991.

213 "I want to urge you to change the course of American policy": Letter,

Al Gore to George Bush, April 3, 1991, Bush Presidential Records, George Bush Presidential Library.

213 "Gore wanted to make clear": Ibid.

214 "Gore ended his missive": Ibid.

215 "I made it clear from the very beginning": George Bush, "The President's News Conference with Prime Minister Toshiki Kaifu of Japan in Newport Beach, California," *Public Papers of the President*, April 4, 1991.

215 "No one was happy with how things were going": Haass interview.

216 "From a humanitarian perspective those images": Kimmitt interview.

216 "The president didn't want to go that far": Haass interview.

216 "Well, it is possible that the United States will have a contribution": George Bush, "The President's News Conference with Secretary of State James A. Baker, III in Houston, Texas," *Public Papers of the President*, April 6, 1991.

217 "In his memoirs, Kissinger would later explain": Henry Kissinger, *Years of Renewal* (New York: Simon & Schuster, 1999), p. 583.

217 "Covert action should not be confused": Ibid. The Pike Commission, convened by Congress to investigate the 1974 abandonment of the Kurds, had a far less charitable assessment: "Even in the context of covert operations, ours was a cynical enterprise."

217 "Is this a one-time thing, or should we foreshadow more to come?": Memorandum, Nancy B. Dyke to Brent Scowcroft, April 3, 1991, WHORM: Subject File—Iraq, CO 072 [2 of 44], Bush Presidential Records, George Bush Presidential Library.

218 "On Sunday morning, April 7, Cheney appeared": Secretary of Defense Richard B. Cheney Interview with David Brinkley on the ABC-TV program *This Week with David Brinkley*, Washington, D.C., April 7, 1991.

218 "Well, just as it's important, I think": Ibid.

219 "Among those with coveted tickets to the game": Kimmitt interview.

221 "There's just something that tells me": Ibid.

221 "The situation is much, much worse than any of us anticipated": Ibid.

222 "Ross was astonished to see that the cool, unsentimental Baker": Ross interview.

222 "We clocked it at twelve minutes": Morton Abramowitz interview.

222 "We've got to use our military to save these guys": Ross and Abramowitz interviews.

223 "It was never a stated objective of the Coalition to intervene": "The President's News Conference with Prime Minister Toshiki Kaifu of Japan in Newport Beach, California," *Public Papers of the President*, April 4, 1991.

223 "Charles, you're off on the wrong track": George Bush, "Exchange with Reporters on Aid to Iraqi Refugees," *Public Papers of the President*, April 11, 1991.

224 "And P.S., the president added": Ibid.

224 "Why let their helicopters continue?": Ibid.

225 "We were reluctant to alter war aims": Haass interview.

225 "There was a combination of the political calculation": Zoellick interview.

225 "this isn't just a question of shooting down helicopters": Secretary of Defense Richard B. Cheney Interview with David Brinkley on the ABC-TV program *This Week with David Brinkley*, Washington, D.C., April 7, 1991.

226 "the two leaders had gotten off to a rocky start": Abramowitz interview.

227 "terrible paroxysms of anger": Ibid.

227 "Cheney got the rudest treatment I've ever seen": Ibid.

227 "That was an episode that changed very much": Ibid.

227 "Among both American observers in Ankara": Ibid.

228 "When James Baker had paid his first visit to Ankara": See Baker's own account of the meeting in *The Politics of Diplomacy*, p. 285.

228 "Saddam is the most dangerous man in the world": Abramowitz interview.

229 "he had launched the notorious Anfal campaign": For a wrenching description of the atrocities committed against civilians by Iraqi troops during Anfal, see David McDowall, *A Modern History of the Kurds* (London: I. B. Tauris, 1996), pp. 357ff.

229 "Ali promptly resorted to the use of chemical weapons": On Iraq's use of chemical weapons against the Kurds, see Michael M. Gunter, *The Kurds of Iraq: Tragedy and Hope* (New York: St. Martin's Press, 1992), pp. 43–45; also David McDowall, *The Kurds: A Nation Denied* (London: Minority Rights Group, 1992), pp. 108–11. On the even American response to the atrocity, see Samantha Power, *"A Problem from Hell": America and the Age of Genocide* (New York: Basic Books, 2002), chapter 8, passim.

229 "the real fallout from Iraq's use of chemical weapons": I am indebted to Morton Abramowitz for sharing this observation with me.

230 "He was very much against it": Abramowitz interview.

230 "It was a big problem for the Turkish government": Ibid.

230 "Dick Cheney was asked about Saddam's offer": Secretary of Defense Richard B. Cheney Interview with Garrick Utley on NBC-TV program *Meet the Press*, Washington, D.C., April 14, 1991.

230 "I don't think I have any way of putting myself in the position": Ibid.

231 "So you have no advice for them whatsoever?": Ibid.

231 "Cheney looked offended at the suggestion": Ibid.

231 "Secretary Cheney, five years from now, ten years from now": Ibid.

233 "You're asking me if I foresaw the size": George Bush, "Remarks on Assistance for Iraqi Refugees and a News Conference," *Public Papers of the President*, April 16, 1991.

233 "The initial assumption in February and early March": Haass interview.

234 "What became obvious was that what we were talking": Ibid.

Chapter 7

235   "Lawrence Eagleburger sent a NODIS cable": State Department #146042, "U.S. Public Posture Towards Iraq," Secretary of State to Embassy London and other embassies (NODIS), May 4, 1991.

237   "A secret May 24 memo": Paper, "Keeping Pressure on Saddam Hussein's Regime: Strategy and Actions," OA/ID CF01585, Richard Haass Files, Iraq Working Files—May 1991 [2 of 2], Bush Presidential Records, George Bush Presidential Library.

237   "Many of our actions, although officially accepted": Ibid.

238   "For him, the Gulf War did not produce the benefits": Abramowitz interview.

238   "Later that year, Abramowitz witnessed a striking display": Ibid.

240   "For the first time in memory, leading Islamic clerics": As Daniel Benjamin and Steven Simon relate in their account of the period, a large number of clerics signed an unprecedented petition against the Saudi royal family, the so-called Letter of Demands, in May 1991. As the two authors note, "the act verged on insurrection." The House of Saud's response was equally unprecedented—hundreds of clerics were arrested; in *The Age of Sacred Terror*, pp. 107–9.

241   "As far as they were concerned, Freeman observed": Freeman interview.

241   "There was an immediate postwar spike in religious militancy": Ibid.

242   "during Secretary of State Baker's 'tin cup tour' ": *Politics of Diplomacy*, pp. 288–90.

243   "The welfare state began to fall apart": Freeman interview.

244   "Containment was a disaster from their standpoint": Ross interview.

244   "There was an understanding that any large U.S. presence was risky": Haass interview.

244   "A permanent U.S. presence will provide a rationale": "Post-War Security Structures in the Gulf," February 8, 1991, OA/ID CF DO839, Richard Haass Files, Working Files—Iraq February 1991 [1 of 7], Bush Presidential Records, George Bush Presidential Library.

245   "It was one of the unfortunate consequences": Haass interview.

245   "That April, Osama bin Laden left Saudi Arabia for the last time": National Commission on Terrorist Attacks, *The 9/11 Commission Report: Final Report of the National Commission on Terrorist Attacks Upon the United States* (New York: W. W. Norton, 2004), p. 56.

246   "In Riyadh, bin Laden was offered a meeting": As Steve Coll relates in a definitive history of al-Qaeda, the Saudi royal family was so dismayed by bin Laden's bombastic rhetoric about waging jihad against Saddam Hussein that they first dispatched several emissaries to meet with him at his home in Jeddah, several hundred miles from the capital. The subsequent meeting with Prince Sultan in Riyadh was a failed attempt to placate bin Laden and dissuade him from doing anything rash. As Coll notes, at this point bin Laden was still being treated "with warmth and

respect" by Sultan and other members of the royal family. See Steve Coll, *Ghost Wars: The Secret History of the CIA, Afghanistan, and Bin Laden, from the Soviet Invasion to September 10, 2001* (New York: The Penguin Press, 2004), pp. 221–23.

247 "The prospect of American troops on Saudi soil": Bin Laden's fury at the American deployment has been extensively chronicled. Virtually every major account sees the deployment of U.S. troops as the precipitating event that drove him to break with Saudi Arabia once and for all and embark on his subsequent campaign of terror against the House of Saud and its American ally. See for instance *The Age of Sacred Terror*, pp. 106ff. Curiously, bin Laden appears to have been especially outraged about President Bush's use of the phrase "New World Order" during the Gulf crisis, interpreting it not as Bush intended, in international legal terms, but as a heretical assault on Islam (ibid., p. 106).

248 "In addition to mingling with jihadists": Quoted in Peter L. Bergen, *The Osama bin Laden I Know: An Oral History of al-Qaeda's Leader* (New York: The Free Press, 2006), pp. 112–33.

248 "Bin Laden harbored a deep, almost personal attachment": See *The Age of Sacred Terror*, p. 96.

249 "The main strategic problem identified by Wolfowitz and Ross": Dennis Ross and Paul Wolfowitz, "Capabilities for Limited Contingencies in the Persian Gulf" (1979); for excerpts from the memorandum, see Gordon and Trainor, *The Generals' War*, p. 480, n. 2.

249 "Wolfowitz believed that the Saudis, the United States": Wolfowitz interview.

250 "The MPS ships were not sent into the Gulf": *The Generals' War*, p. 29.

251 "In order to establish prepositioned equipment here": Interview with a senior Bush administration official.

251 "The Saudis would not be permitted to use the equipment": Ibid.

252 "You'd better discuss that with Crown Prince Abdullah": Ibid.

252 "The idea that somehow the Saudis would buy all": Ibid.

252 "Iraq made its first WMD declaration": Reuters Newswire, April 19, 1991.

253 "In June, UN weapons inspectors were shocked": See Pollack, *The Threatening Storm*, p. 62.

254 "I am sorry to say that I am disappointed in the UN's slowness": Memorandum with Attached Talking Points, "Telephone Call to UN Secretary General Pérez de Cuéllar," Brent Scowcroft to George Bush, April 24, 1991, Case No. 98-0099-F/4, Bush Presidential Records, George Bush Presidential Library.

254 "Is there any timetable you can give me?": Ibid.

255 "The Iraqi leadership appears to believe it can outlast": State Department #187430, "Consulting Key Allies on Keeping Pressure on Saddam Hussein," Washington to Embassy London and other embassies, June 7, 1991.

256 "There was a division of views about this": Gates interview.

256 "Given Saddam Hussein's assault on the Shi'ites and the Kurds": George
Bush, "Interview with Foreign Journalists," *Public Papers of the President*,
July 8, 1991.

257 "Because what I foresee would have been marching into Baghdad": Ibid.

257 "the Wise Men, the legendary Eastern Establishment notables": For the
eponymous work on this group, see Walter Isaacson and Evan Thomas,
The Wise Men: Six Friends and the World They Made (New York: Simon &
Schuster, 1986).

258 "In time, I hope to move more into the policy end of things": George
Bush Personal Papers—UN File, Notes 3/20/71 to 4/19/71, George Bush
Presidential Library.

258 "He is too soft and not sophisticated enough": Telephone conversation,
Richard Nixon and Henry Kissinger, April 27, 1971; in *The Kissinger
Telcons*, National Security Archive Electronic Briefing Book 123, eds.
Thomas Blanton and William Burr, 2004.

260 "I can also provide you with a boat": Letter, Sadruddin Khan to George
Bush, June 1, 1972, George Bush Personal Papers—United Nations Files,
folder "Ambassador Bush Trip"—Geneva, 1972, George Bush Presidential
Library.

261 "The prince was nobody's fool and soon realized": U.S. Mission UN
#02481, "Perm-3 Warn Iraqis to Exercise Restraint to Limit Violence in
North and to Allow the UN Access to the Southern Marshes," U.S.
Mission UN to Washington, July 23, 1991.

261 "At UN Headquarters, Tom Pickering and his counterparts": Ibid.

262 "The NSC staff at the White House": Memorandum, "Rethinking the Use
of Force Against Iraq," Richard Haass to Brent Scowcroft, July 12, 1991.
This memo is still classified.

Chapter 8

264 "the rebirth of history": Balkan historian Misha Glenny's classic
description of the period.

264 "The United States should support a combination": Warren Zimmermann,
Origins of a Catastrophe (New York: Times Books, 1996), p. 42.

264 "The president dispatched James Baker to Belgrade": Ibid., pp. 133–35.

265 "Yugoslavia is poised on the brink of civil war": George Bush Personal
Diary, July 2, 1991; cited in *All the Best, George Bush*, pp. 527–28.

265 "Going back to that 'victory fatigue' ": Kimmitt interview.

266 "There was in Europe, much more than here": Eagleburger interview.

267 "I believe we both agree that Iraq's interference": Memorandum of
telephone conversation with President Mitterrand of France, September
25, 1991, Case No. 98-0099-F/4, Richard Haass Files, Working Files—Iraq
September 1991 [1 of 2], Bush Presidential Records, George Bush
Presidential Library.

267 "We believe that the appropriate response": Ibid.

268 "I agree with this way of handling things": Ibid.

268 "We simply cannot let this crazy man thumb his nose at the world": Memorandum of telephone conversation with Prime Minister Major of Great Britain, September 25, 1991, Case No. 98-0099-F/4, Richard Haass Files, Working Files—Iraq September 1991 [1 of 2], Bush Presidential Records, George Bush Presidential Library.

268 "I don't have any difficulty at all": Ibid.

268 "The other point is, it is time to teach him a lesson": Ibid.

270 "We should take a page from our Iraq experience": Kimmitt interview.

270 "I wish NATO had put a no-fly zone over then-Yugoslavia": Ibid.

271 "I think we began to get distracted a little bit": Interview with a senior Bush administration official.

272 "the king leaned forward and urgently asked the visiting legislators": Murtha would allude to this meeting nearly fifteen years later, and under very different circumstances. At a December 7, 2005, press conference calling for an "immediate redeployment" (i.e., withdrawal) of U.S. troops from Iraq, Murtha recalled his conversation with the king: "When I was in Iraq in 1991, King Fahd said to me—this was an early morning meeting, like two or three o'clock in the morning, when he normally met with people during the air war. And he said: Get your troops out of Saudi Arabia the minute this war's over. You're on sacred ground. You're destabilizing the whole region. I reported that back to the State Department and, as you know, we didn't get our troops out of there. We left our troops there." In "Rep. Murtha Holds a News Conference to Respond to President Bush's Speech," *Washington Post* (online edition), December 7, 2005.

272 "Murtha raised this issue in an October 31 letter": For Scowcroft's reply, see Letter, Brent Scowcroft to John P. Murtha, November 14, 1991, CO 072, WHORM: Subject File, Bush Presidential Records, George Bush Presidential Library.

273 "In our judgment, the current policy towards Iraq": Letter, House Intelligence Committee to George Bush," November 5, 1991, OA/ID CF01585, Richard Haass Files, Working Files—Iraq November 1991, Bush Presidential Records, George Bush Presidential Library.

273 "If we cannot destroy his regime": Letter with attached Reply, Al Gore to George Bush, November 25, 1991, CO 072, WHORM: Subject File, Bush Presidential Records, George Bush Presidential Library.

274 "I have been told that discussions are under way with Harvard": In fact, the documents never ended up at Harvard. Instead, largely through the efforts of Senate staffer (later Ambassador) Peter Galbraith, they were deposited in the National Archives and became the basis for a major investigation of Iraqi atrocities by the human rights organization Human Rights Watch. See Peter W. Galbraith, *Saddam's Documents: A Report to the Committee on Foreign Relations, United States Senate, 1992*, SuDoc Number: Y 4.F

76/2:S.prt. 102-111; also Power, "A *Problem from Hell*," pp. 241–45. I am indebted to Peter Galbraith for relating some of this history to me.

274 "Saddam Hussein is attempting to strangle the Kurds": Ibid.

274 "We are deeply interested in this issue": Ibid.

276 "an announcement widely seen as a stunning repudiation": Indeed, Boutros-Ghali himself later attributed his unexpected accession to Washington's dissatisfaction with Prince Aga Khan's activities in post–Desert Storm Iraq; though Boutros-Ghali assumed that it was Secretary of State Baker who had worked behind the scenes to derail the prince's candidacy. See Boutros Boutros-Ghali, *Unvanquished: A U.S.-UN Saga* (New York: Random House, 1999), chapter 1, passim.

277 "Saddam has used a siege mentality since the ceasefire": U.S. Mission UN #04641, "USUN Meets with International (Ex-Harvard) Study Group on Iraq," U.S. Mission UN to Washington, December 5, 1991.

278 "A tragedy of immense proportions is unfolding": Ankara #16579, "Talabani Letter," Embassy Ankara to Washington, December 11, 1991.

279 "Talabani's letter made two specific requests": Ibid.

280 "the Israeli Defense Ministry and its amen corner in the United States": Unabashed, Buchanan would repeat this charge almost verbatim twelve years later, during the run-up to a second Iraq war. On September 11, 2002, Buchanan would write in his nationally syndicated column: "No wonder Ariel Sharon and his Amen Corner are exhilarated. They see America's war on Iraq as killing off one enemy and giving Israel freedom to deal summarily with two more, Hezbollah and the Palestinians." In Micah L. Sifry and Christopher Cerf, eds., *The Iraq War Reader: History, Documents, and Opinions* (New York: Touchstone, 2003), pp. 308–09.

282 "The series makes no pretense of journalistic balance": John Lancaster, " 'Gulf Crisis': Perle's Wisdom," *Washington Post*, January 18, 1992, p. G-1.

283 "his many admirers considered him the real architect behind the resurgence": For a reverential treatment of Perle's role during the Reagan years, see Jay Winik, *On the Brink: The Dramatic Behind-the-Scenes Saga of the Reagan Era and the Men and Women Who Won the Cold War* (New York: Simon & Schuster, 1996).

283 "One of the things I had promised the king": Secretary of Defense Richard B. Cheney interview with Richard Perle for a PBS series on the Gulf War, with Press Report, January 17, 1992 (interview on December 4, 1991).

284 "If we had gone on to Baghdad": Ibid.

285 "The photographs of American Marines and GIs": Ibid.

285 "UN ambassador Tom Pickering spelled out some of the details": U.S. Mission UN #00634, "Demarche on Iraqi Embargo of Northern Iraq: Perm-Five Talking Points," U.S. Mission UN to Washington, February 14, 1991.

288 "He is a difficult fellow to figure out": George Bush Personal Diary, March 28, 1971, George Bush Personal Papers—UN File, Notes 3/20/71 to 4/19/71, George Bush Presidential Library.

288 "On March 25, Bush sent a memo to his aide Phil Brady": Memorandum with Attached Sheet, George Bush to Phil Brady, March 25, 1992, NLGB #6375–6377, Bush Presidential Records, George Bush Presidential Library.

290 "You're too far ahead of the power curve": George Bush, "The President's News Conference with Prime Minister Ruud Lubbers of The Netherlands and President Jacques Delors of the Commission of the European Community in The Hague," *Public Papers of the President*, November 9, 1991.

292 "The U.S., who had opposed recognition of Croatia": David Owen, *Balkan Odyssey* (San Diego and New York: Harcourt, 1996), p. 344.

292 "The newly recognized Bosnian government": Embassy Belgrade #04390 and #04391, April 9, 1992.

293 "In April 1992, al-Qaeda opened its first European field office": *The 9/11 Commission Report*, p. 58.

295 "Incensed, he sent a memo to Scowcroft": Memorandum with Attachment, George Bush to Brent Scowcroft, June 2, 1992, NLGB #5877, Bush Presidential Records, George Bush Presidential Library. See also Mark Hosenball, "The Odd Couple," *The New Republic*, June 1, 1992.

296 "on June 4 the president was asked about the contrast": George Bush, "The President's News Conference," *Public Papers of the President*, June 4, 1992.

297 "The original letter from the king": Letter, King Fahd of Saudi Arabia to President Bush, June 7, 1992, Case No. 98-0102-F, Nancy B. Dyke Files, Yugoslavia Humanitarian May–June 1992, Bush Presidential Records, George Bush Presidential Library.

300 "Freeman sent a cable to Secretary Baker conveying": Cable, "King Fahd's Concern over Iraqi Use of Fixed Wing Aircraft," Embassy Riyadh to Secretary of State, June 8, 1992. This cable is still classified.

301 "I knew both Powell and Cheney": *The Politics of Diplomacy*, pp. 649–50.

301 "Under our system, the president of the United States": George Bush, "The President's News Conference with Foreign Journalists," *Public Papers of the President*, July 2, 1992.

303 "Some of the headlines alone from Gutman's dispatches": See Roy Gutman, *A Witness to Genocide: The 1993 Pulitzer Prize–Winning Dispatches on the "Ethnic Cleansing" of Bosnia* (New York: Lisa Drew Books, 1993), passim.

304 "I am not interested in seeing one single United States soldier": George Bush, "The President's News Conference with Foreign Journalists," *Public Papers of the President*, July 2, 1992.

Chapter 9

306 "At 9:30 A.M. on the morning of Sunday, July 5": Perhaps the best source of documentary evidence on White House decision-making during the confrontation that would take place at the Agriculture Ministry throughout

the ensuing three weeks is the National Security Council's own "Agricultural Ministry UNSCOM Standoff Chronology" of events. Originally classified Top Secret/Sensitive (one of the most restrictive security classifications), large portions of the NSC Chronology have since been declassified. See Richard Haass Files, Working Files—Iraq August 1992 [1 of 3], Bush Presidential Records, George Bush Presidential Library. The account here is based primarily on this chronology, as it relates events on the ground in Iraq in the same sequence that the senior policymakers in Washington learned about them.

309 "On July 14, al-Anbari told the president of the Security Council": U.S. Mission UN #02977, "Iraq Challenges the Security Council across the Board," U.S. Mission UN to Washington, July 14, 1992.

310 "Continued Iraqi defiance is unacceptable": State Department #224412, "UNSCOM Standoff—Next Steps," Washington to Perm Five Embassies, July 14, 1992.

311 "Due to the most recent avalanche of refugees from Bosnia": Zagreb #01170, "Letter to President Bush from President Tudjman," July 14, 1992, OA/ID CF01424, Nancy B. Dyke Files, Yugoslavia [2], Bush Presidential Records, George Bush Presidential Library.

311 "We're terribly troubled by all of this": Letter, George Bush to William P. Clark, July 21, 1992; cited in *All the Best, George Bush*, p. 565.

312 "Iraq was the topic of a rare Saturday morning NSC meeting": See "Themes on Iraq for July 26 Sunday Talk Shows," OA/ID CF01585, Richard Haass Files, Working File—Iraq July 1992 [2 of 2], Bush Presidential Records, George Bush Presidential Library.

313 "Hasn't he won, in a sense?": Secretary of Defense Richard B. Cheney Interview with Tim Russert on NBC-TV *Meet the Press*, Washington, D.C., July 26, 1992.

313 "I think it would be a mistake to focus": Ibid.

313 "I'm asked that question repeatedly": Ibid.

314 "No, there really isn't, because of course we haven't determined": Secretary of Defense Richard B. Cheney Interview with Charles Bierbauer and Wolf Blitzer on CNN program *Newsmaker Saturday*, Washington, D.C., August 1, 1992.

314 "I think the situation in Yugoslavia is radically different": Ibid.

315 "Charles, the problem—the thing to keep in mind": Ibid.

316 "I want to share with you my assessment of the serious situation": Letter, George Bush to François Mitterrand, July 25, 1992, NLGB #249, Bush Presidential Records, George Bush Presidential Library.

316 "We believe Iraq is still concealing dozens of Scud missiles": Ibid.

317 "the main points of his presentation to the visiting diplomats": Talking Points, "Consultations with Coalition re: Iraq," August 4, 1992, OA/ID CF01585, Richard Haass Files, Working Files—Iraq August 1992, Bush Presidential Records, George Bush Presidential Library.

317 "Saddam Hussein is winning the peace": Ibid.

317 "Saddam is thinking big": Ibid.

318 "We won't let you down": The inconclusive meeting with INC representatives was the subject of a highly critical essay by neoconservative author Laurie Mylroie, who would later attract notoriety for her attempts to prove a connection between Saddam Hussein and the 9/11 hijackers. Writing in *Policywatch*, the newsletter of the Washington Institute for Near East Policy, a prominent foreign policy think tank, Mylroie lambasted the Bush White House for its "old, failed policy—conciliating the Sunni 'elite' in the hope of fostering a coup" and called for the immediate overthrow of Saddam. See Laurie Mylroie, "Iraq Policy Shifts," in *Policywatch*, number 47, August 6, 1992. Scowcroft's comment to Barzani was initially reported by longtime *Washington Post* foreign affairs columnist Jim Hoagland, and is quoted by Mylroie.

It is worth noting that the Mylroie essay caught the attention of at least one key Bush White House official. William Kristol, chief of staff to Vice President Dan Quayle, forwarded a copy to the vice president, calling it "an interesting piece on policy toward Iraq."

319 "One of the Sunni opposition figures in the room": Ibid., p. 2.

320 "the *New York Times* called Richard Haass": Haass interview.

320 "I've got someone in the Pentagon saying he's politically motivated": Ibid.

321 "Anyone who had access to the president": Ibid.

321 "That evening, the president asked Dick Cheney": Secretary of Defense Richard B. Cheney Interview with Judy Woodruff on the PBS-TV program *The MacNeil/Lehrer Newshour*, Pentagon, August 17, 1992.

321 "The fact that things got ratcheted up a bit in July": Ibid.

322 "The thing I find most galling of all": Ibid.

323 "Where in the hell is the cavalry on this one?": Steve Bousquet, Bill Adair, and Chase Squires, "Unlike Andrew, Aid's Right on Charley's Heels," *St. Petersburg Times*, August 17, 2004.

324 "Now, let's get straight what was at stake": George Bush, "Remarks to the American Legion National Convention in Chicago, Illinois," *Public Papers of the President*, August 25, 1992.

324 "Now, some who were faint-hearted and stood in the way": Ibid.

324 "But to double-check, Colin Powell": Ibid.

328 "President Bush, more than any other recent President": Colin L. Powell, "Why Generals Get Nervous," *New York Times*, October 8, 1992.

328 "The Gulf War was a limited-objective war": Colin L. Powell, "U.S. Forces: Challenges Ahead," *Foreign Affairs*, Winter 1992/93.

330 "I think the American people should be the judge": George Bush, "Presidential Debate in St. Louis," *Public Papers of the President*, October 11, 1992.

330 "They get on me, Bill's gotten on me": Ibid.

331 "I've got to respond directly to Mr. Bush": Ibid.

331 "The other night, Governor Clinton raised": George Bush, "Presidential Debate in Richmond, VA," *Public Papers of the President*, October 15, 1992.

332 "For the rest of my minute, I want to make a very brief comment": George Bush, "Presidential Debate in East Lansing, MI," *Public Papers of the President*, October 19, 1992.

333 "I'd like to reply on that, Bush snapped": Ibid.

333 "If you have time, Perot interrupted": Ibid.

334 "Now, let's go back to Saddam Hussein": Ibid.

335 "Let's take Mr. Bush for the moment at his word": Ibid.

335 "It's awful easy when you're dealing with 90/90 hindsight": Ibid.

Chapter 10

340 "He just exuded a sense of presidential and American leadership": Haass interview.

340 "The invitation was exactly the restorative that Bush needed": For a detailed account of the assassination plot, see James Bamford, *A Pretext for War: 9/11, Iraq, and the Abuse of America's Intelligence Agencies* (New York: Doubleday, 2004), pp. 255–61.

342 "They also agreed that given the unusually serious threat": Anthony Lake interview.

342 "With President Clinton's approval, Lake contacted Scowcroft": Ibid.

345 "What are the consequences of this history for the present?": Richard N. Haass, "The U.S. Military Can't Create a New Iraq," *Washington Post*, October 12, 1994, p. A23.

345 "Haass suggested an alternative strategy": Ibid.

347 "Lake was concerned enough that he raised the issue": Lake interview.

347 "Gingrich was not only open to the suggestion; he was enthusiastic": Ibid.

348 "The foreign policy issue that dominated the 1992 Clinton campaign": Lake interview. See also David Halberstam, *War in a Time of Peace: Bush, Clinton, and the Generals* (New York: Touchstone, 2001). See chapter 2, passim, and especially p. 23.

348 "As the historian David Halberstam memorably phrased it": Ibid.

349 "Serbs began laying siege to the safe haven in the town of Srebrenica": For an account of the siege and the killings that followed, see *"A Problem from Hell,"* chapter 11, passim.

350 "For Saddam, it was a serious blow": *The Threatening Storm*, pp. 75–77.

352 "The two authors were not looking to offer an alternative": William Kristol and Robert Kagan, "Towards a Neo-Reaganite Foreign Policy," *Foreign Affairs*, March–April 1996.

352 "where self-proclaimed pragmatists like James Baker": Ibid.

353 "Instead of relying on traditional Realist concepts": Ibid.

354 "In November 1995, five U.S. members": *The 9/11 Commission Report*, p. 77.

354 "That summer, the long-awaited coup attempt": *The Threatening Storm*, pp. 79ff.

355 "Unfortunately, as former Iraqi air force chief Arif Abd-al-Raqazz": see pp. 398–400 above.

355 "The Iraqi dictator was as good as his word": *The Threatening Storm*, pp. 80–82.

357 "President George Bush's judgment to end the war": James A. Baker III, "On to Baghdad Would Have Been U.S. Disaster," *New York Times*, September 10, 1996.

357 "This represents a defeat for U.S. policy": *Testimony by James A. Baker, III before the Senate Armed Services Committee*, Washington, D.C.: September 12, 1996.

358 "The amazing Coalition that President Bush": *Testimony of Paul Wolfowitz before the U.S. Senate Committee on Foreign Relations, Near East and South Asia Subcommittee, Hearing on "The Current Situation in Iraq,"* Washington, D.C.: September 19, 1996.

358 "Deriding the Tomahawk strikes as 'pinprick bombing attacks' ": Ibid.

358 "They pretend that no promises were made to the people": Ibid.

359 "Saddam Hussein is a convicted killer still in possession": Paul Wolfowitz, "Clinton's Bay of Pigs," *Wall Street Journal*, September 27, 1996, p. A18.

359 "We have been listening to the same sad refrain for five years": Brent Scowcroft, "Why We Stopped the Gulf War," *Newsweek*, September 23, 1996, p. 37.

359 "If we had pressed on to Baghdad in 1991": Ibid.

Chapter 11

364 "We seem to have forgotten the essential elements": The complete PNAC Statement of Principles is available at the Project for a New American Century Web site, http://www.newamericancentury.org/statementofprinciples.htm

364 "The only sure way to take Saddam out": William Kristol and Robert Kagan, "Saddam Must Go," *Weekly Standard*, November 17, 1997.

365 "It has become increasingly clear ever since the Gulf War ended": Ibid.

366 "Having follow-up [policies] that constrained and limited Iraq": Zoellick interview.

366 "I remember talking about it, he recalls": Haass interview.

367 "There is nothing wrong with containment": James A. Baker III, "Getting Ready for the 'Next Time' in Iraq," *New York Times*, February 27, 1998, p. A25.

368 "These critics argued that since a war": Brent Scowcroft, "The Power of Containment," *Washington Post*, March 1, 1998.

368 "a recipe for throwing the region into chaos": Ibid.

368   "On August 7, truck bombs were used to attack": *The 9/11 Commission Report*, pp. 68ff.

368   "There was absolutely no doubt in Washington": Ibid.

369   "the U.S. Government had its one and only direct contact": State Department #154712, "Afghanistan: Taliban's Mullah Omar's 8/22 Contact with the State Department," State Department to Embassy Islamabad, August 23, 1998.

369   "Omar said he had no specific message to convey": Ibid.

371   "Ironically, that same day, former secretary of state Baker": James A. Baker III, "On Target: Timing May Raise Questions, but Clinton Took Right Course," *Dallas Morning News*, December 19, 1998, p. A33.

374   "Dubbed the Vulcans, this group": For a fascinating group biography of these individuals, see James Mann, *Rise of the Vulcans: The History of Bush's War Cabinet* (New York: Viking, 2004).

376   "At a private dinner with a few close friends to celebrate his victory": Later reported in the *Wall Street Journal*, June 14, 2002.

Chapter 12

379   "These regimes are living on borrowed time": Condoleezza Rice, "Promoting the National Interest," in *Foreign Affairs*, January–February 2000, p. 61.

380   "Indeed, the new defense secretary had unwittingly latched on": Michael R. Gordon and Bernard E. Trainor, *Cobra II: The Inside Story of the Invasion and Occupation of Iraq* (New York: Pantheon, 2006), p. 15.

380   "His interest in this issue was shared by Richard Haass": Haass interview. See also Richard N. Haass, "Sanctioning Madness," *Foreign Affairs*, November–December 1997.

380   "Iraq was the subject of the Bush administration's first full NSC": See Ron Suskind, *The Price of Loyalty: George W. Bush, the White House, and the Education of Paul O'Neill* (New York: Simon & Schuster, 2004), pp. 70ff.

381   "Rice thinks we cannot afford four more years": Kagan's comment is quoted in Barbara Slavin, "Rice Called a Good Fit for Foreign Policy Post," *USA Today*, December 18, 2000.

382   "A number of Republican lawmakers accused Powell": See, for example, *Testimony of Colin L. Powell before the U.S. Senate Committee on Foreign Relations*, Washington, D.C.: March 8, 2001.

383   "From the spring of 1996, the Clinton administration's Iraq policy": Reuel Marc Gerecht, "A Cowering Superpower," *Weekly Standard*, July 30, 2001.

383   "In a comparison that surely rankled the Bush White House": Ibid.

383   "The Butcher of Baghdad has checked, if not checkmated": Ibid.

385   "My instinct is to hit Saddam at the same time, not just bin Laden": *The 9/11 Commission Report*, pp. 334–35.

385   "On September 12 a sharp discussion had taken place": As reported in

Richard A. Clarke, *Against All Enemies: Inside America's War on Terror* (New York: Free Press, 2004), pp. 30–31.

385 "See if Saddam did this": Ibid, p. 32.

385 "Paul was always of the view that Iraq was a problem": *The 9/11 Commission Report*, p. 335.

387 "If we don't use this as the moment to replace Saddam": Quoted in Elaine Sciolino and Patrick E. Tyler, "Some Pentagon Officials and Advisers Seek to Oust Iraq's Leader in War's Next Phase," *New York Times*, October 12, 2001.

387 "If Saddam Hussein escapes the full wrath of the U.S.": Rich Lowry, "Saddam Must Go," *New York Post*, September 28, 2001, p. 40.

387 "Powell did his best to persuade President Bush": *Washington Post*, September 25, 2001.

388 "It's interesting to speculate": Brent Scowcroft, "Build a Coalition," *Washington Post*, October 16, 2001.

390 "Richard Perle had convened a panel of heavy hitters": A full transcript of the event is available online at http://www.aei.org/events/filter.all.eventID.364. Ledeen's remarks are quoted from a reporter's notes of the event.

392 "But the Iraqi opposition figure with the greatest credibility": Kanan Makiya, *Republic of Fear: The Politics of Modern Iraq* (Berkeley and Los Angeles: University of California Press, 1998, updated ed.).

392 "First reminding his American audience of the U.S. 'abandonments' ": Kanan Makiya, "Help the Iraqis Take Their Country Back," *New York Times*, November 21, 2001.

393 "The biggest tragedy was Afghanistan": Interview with a senior Bush administration official.

395 "Cheney is the real enigma in all of this": Ibid.

398 "The apparently imminent use of American armed forces": Kennan is quoted in *The New Yorker*, October 14, 2002.

403 "I read eight headlines that talked about chaos": DoD News Briefing, Secretary Rumsfeld and General Myers, April 11, 2003. The complete text of the briefing is available online at http:/www.defenselink.mil/transcripts/2003/tr20030411–secdef0090.html

405 "This nation acted to a threat from the dictator of Iraq": David E. Sanger, "In Speech, Bush Reiterates Threat Hussein Posed, but Makes No Mention of Weapons Search," *New York Times*, June 17, 2003.

Epilogue

406 "Indeed, so prevalent was this belief within the president's inner circle": David Frum, *The Right Man: An Inside Account of the Bush White House* (New York: Random House Trade Paperbacks, 2003).

BIBLIOGRAPHY

Works Cited

Baker, James A. *The Politics of Diplomacy: Revolution, War, and Peace, 1989–1992*. New York: G. P. Putnam's Sons, 1995.

Bamford, James. *A Pretext for War: 9/11, Iraq, and the Abuse of America's Intelligence Agencies*. New York: Doubleday, 2004.

Benjamin, Daniel, and Steven Simon. *The Age of Sacred Terror: Radical Islam's War Against America*. New York: Random House, 2002.

Bergen, Peter L. *The Osama bin Laden I Know: An Oral History of al Qaeda's Leader*. New York: Free Press, 2006.

Boutros-Ghali, Boutros. *Unvanquished: A U.S.-UN Saga*. New York: Random House, 1999.

Briody, Dan. *The Iron Triangle: Inside the Secret World of the Carlyle Group*. New York: John Wiley & Sons, 2004.

Bush, George. *All the Best, George Bush: My Life in Letters and Other Writings*. New York: Scribner/A Lisa Drew Book, 1999.

Bush, George, and Brent Scowcroft. *A World Transformed*. New York: Alfred A. Knopf, 1998.

Clarke, Richard A. *Against All Enemies: Inside America's War on Terror*. New York: Free Press, 2004.

Coll, Steve. *Ghost Wars: The Secret History of the CIA, Afghanistan, and Bin Laden, from the Soviet Invasion to September 10, 2001*. New York: The Penguin Press, 2004.

Freedman, Lawrence, and Efraim Karsh. *The Gulf Conflict: 1990–1991*. Princeton, NJ: Princeton University Press, 1993.

Frum, David. *The Right Man: An Inside Account of the Bush White House*. New York: Random House Trade Paperbacks, 2003.

George, Alexander L., and Juliette L. George. *Woodrow Wilson and Colonel House: A Personality Study*. Dover Publications, 1964.

Gilbert, Martin. *The Second World War: A Complete History* (revised). New York: Owl Books, 2004.

Gordon, Michael R., and Bernard E. Trainor. *The Generals' War: The Inside Story of the Conflict in the Gulf*. Boston: Little, Brown, 1994.

————. *Cobra II: The Inside Story of the Invasion and Occupation of Iraq*. New York: Pantheon, 2006.

Gunter, Michael M. *The Kurds of Iraq*. New York: St. Martin's Press, 1992.

Gutman, Roy. *A Witness to Genocide: The 1993 Pulitzer Prize–Winning Dispatches on the "Ethnic Cleansing" of Bosnia*. New York: Lisa Drew Books, 1993.

Halberstam, David. *The Best and the Brightest*. New York: Random House, 1972.

————. *War in a Time of Peace: Bush, Clinton, and the Generals*. New York: Scribner, 2001.

Iklé, Fred. *Every War Must End*. New York: Columbia University Press, 1971.

Isaacson, Walter, and Evan Thomas. *The Wise Men: Six Friends and the World They Made*. New York: Simon & Schuster, 1986.

Kissinger, Henry. *White House Years*. Boston: Little, Brown, 1999.

————. *Years of Renewal*. New York: Simon & Schuster, 1999.

MacArthur, John A. *Second Front: Censorship and Propaganda in the Gulf War*. Berkeley and Los Angeles: University of California Press, 1992.

McDowall, David. *A Modern History of the Kurds*. London: I. B. Tauris, 1996.

————. *The Kurds: A Nation Denied*. London: Minority Rights Group, 1992.

Macmillan, Harold. *Pointing the Way 1959–1961*. London: Macmillan London, 1972.

Major, John. *The Autobiography*. New York: HarperCollins, 1999.

Makiya, Kanan. *Republic of Fear: The Politics of Modern Iraq*. Berkeley and Los Angeles: University of California Press, 1998, updated edition.

Mann, James. *Rise of the Vulcans: The History of Bush's War Cabinet*. New York: Penguin Books, 2004.

Morgenthau, Hans. *Politics among Nations*. New York: Alfred A. Knopf, 1978, revised edition.

National Commission on Terrorist Attacks. *The 9/11 Commission Report: Final Report of the National Commission on Terrorist Attacks Upon the United States*. New York: W. W. Norton, 2004.

Owen, David. *Balkan Odyssey*. San Diego and New York: Harcourt, 1996.

Pollack, Kenneth M. *The Threatening Storm: The Case for Invading Iraq*. New York: Random House, 2002.

Powell, Colin. *My American Journey*. New York: Random House, 1996.

Power, Samantha. *"A Problem from Hell": America and the Age of Genocide*. New York: Basic Books, 2002.

Richardson, Louise M. *When Allies Differ: Anglo-American Relations in the Suez and Falkland Crises*. New York: St. Martin's Press, 1996.

Ryan, Cornelius. *The Longest Day: June 6, 1944* (reprint edition). New York: Simon & Schuster, 2004.

Schwarzkopf, H. Norman. *It Doesn't Take a Hero*. New York: Bantam Books/Linda Grey, 1992.

Scowcroft, Brent. *Congress and Foreign Policy: An Examination of Congressional Attitudes Toward the Foreign Aid Programs to Spain and Yugoslavia*. Unpublished PhD dissertation, Columbia University, 1967.

Sifry, Micah L., and Christopher Cerf, eds. *The Iraq War Reader: History, Documents, and Opinions*. New York: Touchstone, 2003.

Suskind, Ron. *The Price of Loyalty: George W. Bush, the White House, and the Education of Paul O'Neill*. New York: Simon & Schuster, 2004.

Walt, Stephen. *The Origins of Alliances*. Ithaca: Cornell University Press, 1987.

Winik, Jay. *On the Brink: The Dramatic Behind-the-Scenes Saga of the Reagan Era and the Men and Women Who Won the Cold War*. New York: Simon & Schuster, 1996.

Woodward, Bob. *The Commanders*. New York: Simon & Schuster, 1991.

Yergin, Daniel. *The Prize: The Epic Quest for Oil, Money, and Power*. New York: Simon & Schuster, 1991.

Zimmermann, Warren. *Origins of a Catastrophe*. New York: Times Books, 1996.

Further Reading

Freeman, Charles W. *Arts of Power: Statecraft and Diplomacy*. Washington, DC: United States Institute of Peace Press, 1997.

Gates, Robert M. *From the Shadows: The Ultimate Insider's Story of Five Presidents and How They Won the Cold War*. New York: Touchstone, 1996.

Hersh, Seymour M. *Chain of Command: The Road from 9/11 to Abu Ghraib*. New York: HarperCollins, 2004.

Hoffmann, Stanley (with Frederic Bono). *Gulliver Unbound: America's Imperial Temptation and the War in Iraq*. Lanham, MD: Rowman and Littlefield Publishers, 2004.

May, Ernest R. *"Lessons" of the Past: The Use and Misuse of History in American Foreign Policy*. New York: Oxford University Press, 1975.

Packer, George. *The Assassin's Gate: America in Iraq*. New York: Farrar, Straus & Giroux, 2005.

Purdum, Todd S., and the staff of the *New York Times*. *A Time of Our Choosing: America's War in Iraq*. New York: Times Books, 2003.

Richardson, Louise. *What Terrorists Want: Understanding the Enemy, Containing the Threat*. New York: Random House, 2006.

Ross, Dennis. *The Missing Peace: The Inside Story of the Fight for Middle East Peace*. New York: Farrar, Straus & Giroux, 2004.

Sciolino, Elaine. *The Outlaw State: Saddam Hussein's Quest for Power and the Gulf Crisis*. New York: John Wiley & Sons, 1991.

Woodward, Bob. *Bush at War*. New York: Simon & Schuster, 2002.

_____. *Plan of Attack*. New York: Simon & Schuster, 2004.

INDEX

ABOUT THE AUTHOR

Christian Alfonsi received his Ph.D. in political science from Harvard University. *Circle in the Sand* represents the culmination of over a decade of in-depth research into the use of military force in Iraq by both Bush administrations. Prior to this, Alfonsi was a vice president of strategic planning at Young & Rubicam Brands in New York, where he currently resides.